SANDAKAN

UNDER NIPPON

THE LAST MARCH

Glenn Carter

Chris Ward
Jason Tyers
Shayne Northover
GUARD COMD.

Jason Beach
R.A.N BAND.

37 Sqn C130 Crew
John Oddie CAPT
[illegible] Ball FLT ENG
[illegible] (NAV)
David Howard "Hoke"
Walter Neil WOFF LOADMASTER
Bob Foreman LOADMASTER
Wayne Charles Santo 8/12 MDM. REGT. AFD. BTY.
[illegible] 3rd battalion
[illegible] 104 SIGNAL SQN
[illegible] RAN BAND
[illegible] SUBMARINERS
[illegible] RAAF FLT STWD.

33 SQN 707 CREW
Matt Granger CAPT
[illegible] FLT ENG
[illegible] LOADM
[illegible] FLT COPILOT

COLIN BRUCE WOFF.
Colin Bruce FLT. ENG.
M SUMMERS COPILOT.

GG Cowell VIP CAPT
[illegible] FLT STWD.
[illegible] FLT STWD

486 SQN MAINT
Wayne Lacey SGT
DARRIN TIMMS CPL
PETER McSHERRY CPL.
[illegible] SQNLDR

1995 PILGRIMAGE TO SANDAKAN EDITION

SANDAKAN

UNDER NIPPON

THE LAST MARCH

By **DON WALL**

Cover by Clem Seale

All inquiries should be addressed to D. Wall Publications,
98 Darley Street West, Mona Vale, NSW 2103 Australia.

By the Same Author
Singapore and Beyond 1985
Abandoned? 1990
Heroes at Sea 1991
Heroes of F Force 1993
Kill the Prisoners! 1996

First Published August 1988
Revised Second Edition 1989
Revised Third Edition 1992
Revised Fourth Edition 1995
Revised Fifth Edition 1997
Reprinted Fifth Edition 2003
Reprinted Fifth Edition 2007
Published by D. Wall
98 Darley Street West, Mona Vale, NSW 2103 Australia.

ISBN 0646 329 073

Typeset by PS Graphics, Chippendale, N.S.W.

Printed by Success Print, Bayswater
Western Australia.

Introduction

I was honoured to be invited by Dr. Alan Hawke, Department of Veterans' Affairs, to take part in the Borneo Pilgrimage in 1995 celebrating the 50th Anniversary of the Allied victory against Japan, as proclaimed by U.S. President Truman, "V.J. Day".

The Tour's first stop was at Jakarta for a Service held at the Jakarta War Cemetery, followed by Memorial Services at Balikpapan, Tarakan, Sandakan, Ranau, Labuan War Cemetery, Kranji and finally a visit to Changi Gaol where 8 Division members visited a cell in 'C' Block.

It was en-route from Balikpapan to Sandakan in the Hercules aircraft that I decided this Edition would be published together with the autographs of all those who participated on the tour.

During the Service at Sandakan I was reminded by the young members of the Australian Defence Forces present that many of the victims of Sandakan were about the same age; I was also reminded that the same species of birds that followed the men on the death march were also present in the canopy above the Memorial while the smaller birds were singing below.

The Memorial at Sandakan was first erected on the initiative of Bruce Ruxton, A.M., O.B.E. Apart from the official Pilgrimage group, about one hundred people who also attended were from other independent groups organised by the R.S.L. Many of the Service personnel present were not aware of the immense nature of the tragedy.

Next day, the bus tour continued to Ranau and it was not until we reached Paginatan that I realised a stop should have been made to inspect the site of the Paginatan Cemetery where a large number of the victims were recovered – it was between Paginatan and Ranau most of the victims who reached Ranau died on rice carrying parties.

This Edition exposes the false information given by the Japanese, and some of the native people, on the fate of some 290 men who remained back in the Sandakan Camp. Previously the Japanese had claimed the last prisoner of war died on 19 August 1945. We now have proof that the last two prisoners died on 21 June 1945; both Australians – one was beheaded and the other, Pte. S.A. Osborne, was buried alongside him. These two graves are identified as Lot 20 C.12.13. in Labuan War Cemetery.

Sandakan – a name now synonymous with cruelty and brutality inflicted on sick and defenceless people – represents the worst tragedy suffered by Australians during World War II.

Remember them when you visit Labuan War Cemetery.

Don Wall
August 1997

Labuan War Cemetery

Pic: Veterans' Affairs

Sandakan Memorial Park

Pic: Veterans' Affairs

Dedicated to the memory of all those who lost their lives in British North Borneo 1942-1945 under the Japanese.

They are not dead; not even broken;
Only their dust has gone back home to the earth;
For they, the essential they, shall have rebirth
Whenever a word of them is spoken.

— Dame Mary Gilmore

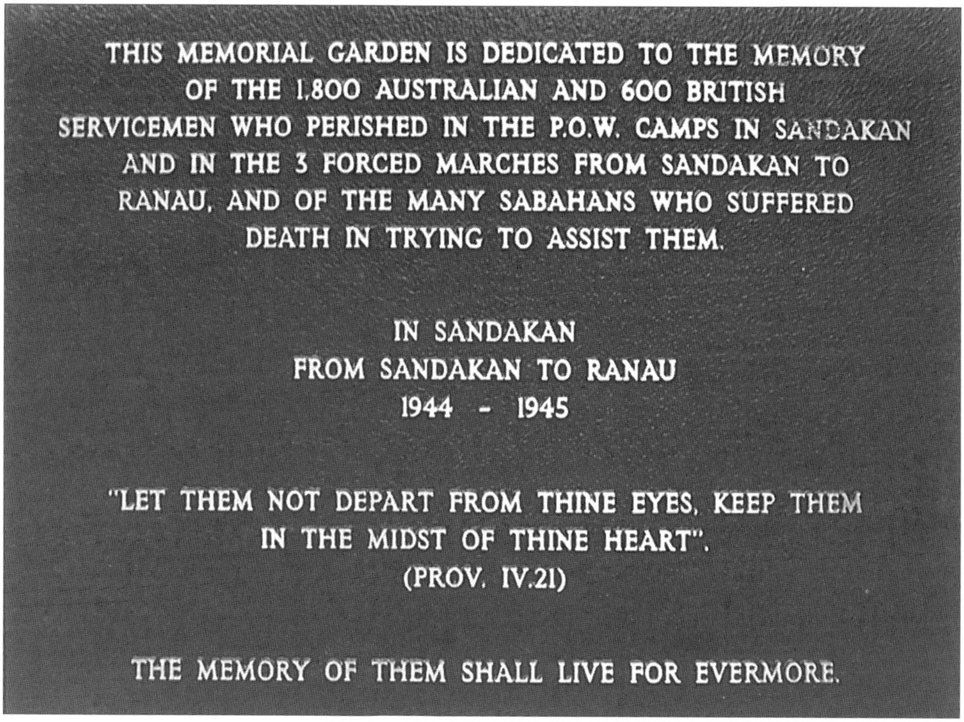

THIS MEMORIAL GARDEN IS DEDICATED TO THE MEMORY
OF THE 1,800 AUSTRALIAN AND 600 BRITISH
SERVICEMEN WHO PERISHED IN THE P.O.W. CAMPS IN SANDAKAN
AND IN THE 3 FORCED MARCHES FROM SANDAKAN TO
RANAU, AND OF THE MANY SABAHANS WHO SUFFERED
DEATH IN TRYING TO ASSIST THEM.

IN SANDAKAN
FROM SANDAKAN TO RANAU
1944 - 1945

"LET THEM NOT DEPART FROM THINE EYES, KEEP THEM
IN THE MIDST OF THINE HEART".
(PROV. IV.21)

THE MEMORY OF THEM SHALL LIVE FOR EVERMORE.

Kundasan Memorial

Pic: Veterans' Affairs

Acknowledgements

I acknowledge with thanks the kind permission to use the private records of Lt.Col. H.W.S. Jackson, MBE (Ret.), particularly in relation to his first-hand knowledge of the people of Borneo, those who witnessed the prisoners on the marches and those who saved the lives of the six survivors.

I acknowledge the assistance given by the Australian War Memorial, particularly Bill Fogarty, Ron Gilchrist and Bronwyn Self; the Staff of the Australian Archives in Canberra and in Melbourne.

After substantially completing my research I was fortunate in having the cooperation of Keith Botterill, Owen Campbell and Nelson Short, covering in-depth discussions on all aspects of the events of prisoner of war life in Sandakan. I gratefully acknowledge their assistance.

My thanks to Tim Bowden of the Social History Department of the A.B.C. for access to the transcriptions of the Prisoner of War Survival Series.

To the many former Officers who assisted, most of whom spent some months in Sandakan in 1942-1943 - K.G. Mosher, J.G. Fairley, C.A. Pickford, R. Ewin, the late Frank Washington, D, Scrivener, D. Garland, Dr. E. Esler - my thanks.

Also the Director of Lands and Survey for Sabah, Mr. Kuleong C. Mopilin.

J.A. Hodges of 'Z' Special who first found Keith Botterill.

Alex Dandie, E.F. Davis, R. Kent, P. Gorrick, R. Newton, Peter Bentley, Hank Nelson, Reg Dixon and the many relatives of those honoured who so kindly provided photographs - my thanks.

To Angus and Robertson I acknowledge permission to use the Dedication verse from 'The Passionate Heart' by Dame Mary Gilmore.

My thanks to Bruce Ruxton, A.M., O.B.E., State President, R.S.L. Victoria, and to the Secretaries of the R.S.L. Sub Branches of Maitland, Tenterfield, Lismore and Wagga Wagga.

My thanks to Harold McManus of Iowa, U.S.A., George Blaikie and Murray Ewen.

For my basic sources I have referred to 'Imperial Conspiracy' by David Bergamini; 'The Final Campaign' by Gavin Long; 'Japanese Thrust' by Lionel Wigmore; 'When The Blossom Fell' and 'Three Came Home' by Agnes Newton Keith; and my 'Singapore and Beyond'.

Special acknowledgements to: Mr. Con Sciacca, Minister for Veterans' Affairs 1995; Dr. Allan Hawke, James Rogers, Heather Jackson, Justin O'Shannassy who organised and participated in the 1995 Borneo Pilgrimage.

Don Wall
August 1997

Contents

Chapter		Page
	Introduction	v
	Acknowledgements	viii
1	You are the Prisoners of the Japanese	1
2	January 1943	23
3	We'll be out by Christmas	43
4	Work on the Aerodrome was Abandoned	57
5	Of 195 PWs, 160 Arrived at Paginatan	73
6	Back at Sandakan	82
7	Takakuwa and Watanabe Visit the Camp	88
8	Escape of Five Men	97
9	Botterill's Party	111
10/11	Sandakan after the Last March	118
12	The Principal PW Compound	132
13	Surrender	137
14	A Time for Thanks	146
15	Honour Roll	148
16	Sandakan Recovery Details	182
17	Labuan Party under Captain Nagai	201
	Index	212

Pilgrimage Party at Kranji War Cemetery, Singapore *Photo: Veterans' Affairs*

Chapter 1

"You are prisoners of the Imperial Japanese Army — I am your Commanding Officer and you will obey my orders and the orders of my men guarding you! You may have been good soldiers for Australia but now you are slaves for Japan and you will carry out my orders! You have been brought here to construct an aerodrome — you will be diligent in your work and will not attempt to escape, if you do the jungle will consume you or you will be shot! You will work for the Japanese Co-Prosperity Sphere and I am prepared to die for Japan in carrying out my assignment!"

Lt. Hoshijima was addressing the 1494 Australian prisoners of war of the 8 Division who had arrived at Sandakan from Singapore. Those present were impressed by his physical bearing — tall, thick-set, soldierly. Educated at Osaka Imperial University Hoshijima graduated in Inorganic Chemical Engineering and later served in China. He spoke fairly good English. In China he was appointed to command an Engineering Unit to be posted to Borneo. On the way his ship was torpedoed by a U.S. submarine. Hoshijima distinguished himself with his men and was impressed by the fact that the US submarine did not machine-gun the survivors in the water.

By June 1943 there were just over two thousand Australian and 750 British prisoners of war under Hoshijima's command. Japan knew the war was lost but they would fight on. On superior orders Hoshijima set in motion a program of starvation and brutality to ensure the PWs would be ineffective soldiers to assist the anticipated Allied invasion. By August 1945 the last PWs were massacred — there were only six survivors.

Singapore capitulated to the Japanese on February 15, 1942 — the troops had become prisoners of war by order of Malaya Command. The Japanese Commander, General Yamashita, generously isolated the PWs in the eastern end of Singapore, Changi, an area which provided barrack accommodation, spacious living, hospital and a gaol.

The Japanese were embarrassed because of the large number of prisoners of war to feed. In Tokyo Hirohito's Imperial General HQ decreed a Bureau of Information be established to administer all aspects and policies of Prisoners of War. The Bureau would account for the deceased PWs. The first decree was 'No Work No Food' promulgated in March 1942. As a result working parties were despatched from Changi to Singapore city and other localities around the Island. The fortunate work parties were located close to the wharves where large storage facilities were located. These were crammed with food, liquor and luxury goods. The guards had no idea of much of the contents. Some of these groups, such as those at the Great World Amusement Park, lived extremely well.

Scrounging continued and trading in other commodities including ammunition commenced. Chinese traders waited outside the Great World for an opportunity to barter food for .303 cartridges and any item which could be used against the Japanese. A young

Chinese girl was caught trading, she was stripped of her clothing by the guards from the Imperial Guards Division and while she was held one guard lit cigarettes and tortured her by burning her nipples with the lighted cigarettes. They were to see the first signs of brutality.

Another large group was sent to the nearby River Valley camp — a camp noted for its large population of hungry bedbugs. The men of this group did not have the access to tobacco and food the Great World parties enjoyed; they were mainly hardware merchants. Some of them became expert at merchandising large consignments of commodities from gramaphone needles to light bulbs. Others became wealthy and were able to purchase the luxury items from the Great World men. One such group was led by Arthur Cooper, ace of scroungers, and carried out well executed assignments. During that period there was no food shortage.

It was here the men learned of the bombing of Darwin on 19 February. The general feeling was not one of sadness despite the tragic civilian losses; they felt the event would bring home to the citizens of Australia the seriousness of the war situation. However the public were never told the extent of losses — 238 killed, 300 wounded — four U.S. Transports, four Australian freighters, one British tanker and a U.S. Destroyer.

The camps were guarded by troops of the Imperial Guards Division, many of them spoke English and always wanted to know where particular troops were in battle. The guards respected them as good fighters, having had experience of them at first hand and often gave cigarettes. There were only a few instances of brutality during this period.

As they left their work each day they would march away from the wharves whistling 'Colonel Bogey'. The Japanese could never understand why they whistled and looked contented. In all the camps in Singapore there was little to complain about — morale was high — radio reports of the war were circulated and many thought when the Americans overcame the initial shock they would be out in eighteen months. The sight of Chinese heads being displayed on sticks in the Chinese quarters disturbed the men — many would say "if the bastards can do it to them they'll do it to us, if they get to Australia they'll do it there too!"

At Lornie Road and Adam Park — two adjacent camps — there were about 3000 PWs located. Captain Claude Pickford recalls "In March 1942 I was sent down there in command of a composite Battalion, about 800 of us, and one of the perks of being Bn. Commander with the rank of Captain was that you didn't have to go out on a working party, you only had to organise the numbers for the following day. So time started to pall after a few days of this. Living was pretty good, food was not bad, we could still get a few odd bits and pieces. A couple of us used to go round the abandoned battlefields and bring in arms and ammunition, recondition it and store it in the roof over the bungalow. We had quite a cache: Bren guns, grenades, 5000 rounds of SAA, gunpowder. Anyway, one afternoon a Jap guard came in and he was humming over 'Auld Lang Syne' and to divert his interest in the place I started to sing the English words to it. His eyes lit up and he said 'You teach me English song!'. So he used to sit down at a low table with me at the other side and I sang the first line to him and he would write them down in Japanese phonetics and away he'd go. Then he would present himself the next day at 2 p.m. and he could sing the first line very well, the second line the same procedure and after a week he could sing 'Auld Lang Syne' very well. I thought I'd had him by this. I wanted to proceed out on the job each day but he came back the following Monday and he said 'You teach me another English song'. So I taught him 'Three Blind Mice', same procedure and after a week he could sing it very well. I had had him by this time, but he came back again and wanted to learn another song so I thought I'll teach him the National Anthem. After a week he would sing 'God Save the King'. At length Lt. Colonel George Ramsay, senior Australian leader in the area, came to me and said 'Pickford you've been teaching this yokel to sing and its got to stop!' I said "That's fine but tell me how? Anyhow", I said, "Why has it got to stop, while he's in here learning singing he's not out there bashing the men'. 'Ummm', he said, "You've got a point but its got to stop'. And I said 'But why, Sir?', and he said 'Well he was down at the Guard House this afternoon, full of sake, and he insisted on all the Senior Officers standing to attention and singing 'Three Blind Mice' while he conducted them! Colonel Ramsay said I didn't mind so much but poor old Colonel Madden who was a real 'Kitchener' type, Gunner, standing up singing 'Three Blind Mice' trying to look dignified while a Japanese Third Class private conducted him — it was just too much, its got to stop!'

In April 1942 the U.S. staged a morale booster for the Nation by sending the US Aircraft Carrier 'Hornet' to the Northern Pacific to bomb Tokyo. This Task Force was under the command of General James Doolittle with his force of specially trained pilots flying B25 Mitchells.

Launched from the carrier the planes flew over Tokyo bombing strategic targets and flying on to China. Many of the aircraft ran out of fuel and were forced down in Japanese Occupied Territory. Eight pilots were captured. Hirohito personally suggested to the Chief of General Staff the eight flyers be executed for crimes against the civilian population of Tokyo. Later, Prime Minister Tojo succeeded in persuading Hirohito to commute the sentence of five and execute three. Hirohito was so incensed that the Chinese in Japanese-occupied territory had assisted many pilots to escape that he deviously and surreptitiously arranged with the Commander of the Japanese Expeditionary Force to take reprisals against the population. 250,000 civilians were killed and their villages destroyed. It was later established Hirohito used Staff Officers close to the Throne to carry out his personal instructions.

Orders were issued for the dispersement of large groups of working parties from Singapore. The first to leave was 'A' Force, comprised of about 3000 Australians under Brigadier Varley of Inverell. The composition of the party was a balanced Brigade group of Infantry — Artillery — Anti-Tank, Engineers and a General Hospital under Captain Tom Hamilton; so if the occasion arose they could rejoin our Forces as a composite fighting group. The men from the Great World camp watched them leave the dock area in May

QX.16680 Gnr. Frederick George Wehl. 2/ 10 Fd.R.A.A. Died Sandakan 2 August, 1945. Aged 39. Roma, Qld. *Pic: Jenny Dey.*

QX.16684 Fred Wehl's younger brother, Roy. They were separated early in 1942, Roy went on 'F' Force in 1943 where he died at Kanburi. *Pic: Jenny Dey.*

1942 — their destination was Burma where they were to be used on the construction of airfields in southern Burma for the Japanese Navy and later were involved in the construction of the Burma-Thailand Railway.

Two months later another party was recruited, 'B' Force. These men were destined for Borneo. The Japanese told Changi Command the men would be sent to an area where food was plentiful and those wounded in action would convalesce. Acting on that information many of those wounded in action who had recovered and the older men chose to place themselves on the draft, hoping to see the war out in comfort. Some of the older men like W.O. Blackie, ex-PW of World War I, carried a walking stick. He had no reason to disbelieve the Japanese that they were going to a better locality where food was plentiful. The medical units were told 'Don't worry about medical supplies, there will be plenty at our destination.'

The group was to be led by Brigadier Taylor, however the Japanese at this time decided to send all Officers above the rank of Colonel overseas. They obviously sensed some danger in allowing senior Infantry Officers access to substantial numbers of men.

Lt. Col. A.W. Walsh was then delegated to lead the Force. He was not a popular choice. Formerly a Staff Officer he was appointed to command the Queensland 2/10 Fd. Artillery in November 1941. The Gunners were not to meet him until they held a parade at Changi in 1942. Short in stature, the Gunners called him 'Gum Drops'.

The group comprised 145 officers, 312 NCO's and 1037 Privates — never did a group have such a high percentage of officers. Many reinforcements arrived in January, only to be allocated to Units as prisoners.

The men of the Force were allocated from Infantry, Artillery, Transport, Engineers, Medical Services so in the event of meeting friendly forces it could be moulded into a composite force. One appointment of interest was that of Lt. Cdr. Sligo, RANVR, as Intelligence Officer. He was formerly of Malaya Command.

The concentrations of all Australians at Changi gave the men the opportunity to catch up with their mates and where possible transfer to Units so they could remain together. Now 'B' Force was being assembled many were prepared to go anywhere. There was Francis Burchnall of Bendigo, Victoria, a Digger from World War I, enlisted in 1941. His only son, named after him, soon followed him to be claimed by his father — they were both destined for Borneo. In all districts those who enlisted together, seemed to have found a new bond and stayed together.

From the Grafton area there were three young men as different as any three could be. They shared a common interest in dairy farming and belonging to a small community. E.J. O'Donohue, later to be known as 'Punchy', whose family owned a dairy farm where John Jackson lived, the son of Kathleen of Moree, an Aborigine/Islander, 'Jacko' as he was known in the Army, possessed a good singing voice, and young John Barnier whose father owned a dairy farm just down the road and at the time of enlistment was a student at the Teachers College, Armidale. These three young men were to meet up on their Final Leave when they were given a send-off by their local community in the tiny, unlined weather-board Hall at Alumny Creek, near Grafton, N.S.W.

During the evening 'Jacko' Jackson sang 'One Day When We Were Young' and in his farewell speech John Barnier concluded by quoting a verse by M.L. Haskins —

> 'And I said to the Man who stood at the Gate of the Year
> Give me a Light that I may tread safely into the Unknown
> And He replied Go out into the Darkness and
> Put your hand in the Hand of God.
> That shall be to you better than Light and safer
> Than a known way.'

The three returned by the North Coast Mail back to camp and sailed for Singapore. Later, Jackson joined O'Donohue in the 2/20 Battalion.

Two brothers, Herbert and Joseph Connor, both married, Herbert with a young family, decided to enlist with their cousin. The two brothers were sent to Malaya and now were in the same Unit with another two brothers, Tom and Syd Bexton.

There were many more who were to claim one another, in normal circumstances they could share so much — news from home — discuss family matters — it was often comforting for the family to know they had one another. Some welcomed the idea of going to an overseas camp where they believed there would be adequate food and imagined they would be treated in accordance with the Geneva Convention; regular supplies of Red Cross parcels and letters from home. News of the death march of the 'Battling Bastards from Corregidor' which suffered about 10,000 deaths had not reached the outside world so the Japanese were able to convince the PWs they were going to a locality where food would be more plentiful and those who had recovered in hospital would be able to convalesce.

Bruce Stewart of Maitland was attending a Wool Classing course at the Technical College when the teacher made a derogatory remark about men enlisting in the A.I.F. He was so incensed he left the class and went straight to the Recruitment Officer. The teacher phoned to advise that Bruce was aged 16 — under age — he was rejected. However, next day he returned and enlisted under the name of McNab. He was also on the draft.

Gnr. Tom Coughlan, of Morundah, who never sought promotion because of private means and didn't want his leisure time restricted, enlisted because of his love of the country. He was content to be going on the force because it might take him closer to Australia and possibly would be the first to be released.

One would wonder why Sgt. Fred Staggs would want to leave Changi — he served at Lone Pine — Gallipoli. His only son, Fred, enlisted in the 2/4 Bn. and before he sailed he put a question to his father — 'You're not going to enlist while I'm away?' 'It depends' he said 'just how serious things get'. He could have sweated it out at Changi at the age of 50 but chose to go with his mates on 'B' Force.

NX.65700 Pte. John Nicholson Barnier, Grafton, N.S.W.

Photo: M. Devereaux.

NX.43479 Pte. Edward John O'Donohue, Grafton, N.S.W.

Photo: M. Devereaux.

NX.7347 Gnr. Tom Coughlan, Morundah, N.S.W. *Photo: F. Coughlan.*

NX.5655 Gnr. Bruce Pendleton Stewart (served as MacNab), Maitland, N.S.W. *Photo: J. Lowenthal.*

James Michael Bowe served as Anderson — enlisted in August 1941 and two months later sailed for Singapore. He enlisted at 16 years of age after being tossed out of a school at Hunters Hill for conducting an SP bookmaking business with the aid of a crystal set under his bed. His father got wind of the fact he was in the Army and he was promptly discharged. Within months he was back in the Army as Anderson, where he gave his age as 21 and his occupation 'Publican'. His Mother, "Mrs. Anderson", address as next of kin was the local radio station. Now he was destined for Sandakan.

There was even prevailing optimism that those wounded in action and unfit for further military service would be repatriated home. Japanese medical officers examined many of the wounded and accordingly classified them. Nothing was to come of the proposal.

Lt. Frank Washington said he put his name down for the force because he was bored with Changi and any other place would have to be better. The troops were moved by truck to Singapore. Most had not seen Singapore since the fighting stopped and were shocked at the appearance of the Chinese heads displayed on sticks. The working parties in Singapore were accustomed to such sights. As heads became unrecognisable fresh ones replaced them. It was during the first few months the Japanese rounded up Chinese of military age, took them to Changi Headland where they were executed by firing squad. When the men arrived at the wharves they became excited as there was a Hospital Ship in the harbour. Rumours were rife they were being repatriated but their high hopes collapsed when they were lined up to board a tramp ship, the 'Ubi Maru'.

Eric 'Mo' Davis remembers: 'They loaded us on trucks headed for Singapore. As we approached Anderson Bridge I was with my mates 'Lofty' John Rankin and Gordon Storey who dug me in the ribs and said 'Get a load of that 'Mo'! pointing to tables on both sides of the bridge displaying heads of Indians, Chinese and other locals who had been beheaded. Above was a large sign "Greater East Asia Co-Prosperity Sphere". Gordon Storey said 'I hope where we are going we are not going to cop that 'Mo'!'. The scene had a sobering

NX.54971 L/Sgt. B.C. Whitehead, Croydon, N.S.W.
Photo: Mrs. Gwen Whitehead.

NX.65285 Cpl. Ernest Fredrich Copp, Rockdale, N.S.W.
Photo: Arthur Copp.

NX.14900 Sgt. Fred Staggs, Inverell, N.S.W.
Photo: Fred Staggs, Jnr.

NX.43983 James Michael Bowe (served as Anderson), Wagga Wagga, N.S.W.
Photo: J. Bowe.

NX.52685 Syd Bexton, Willoughby, N.S.W.
Photo: Mrs. P.M. Mason.

NX.69495 Tom Bexton, Willoughby, N.S.W.
Photo: Mrs. P.M. Mason.

V.X.25598 "Mic" Joseph C. Connor, Swan Hill, Vic.
Photo: Mrs. B. Lynn

V.X.25521 Herbert Francis Connor, Swan Hill, Vic.
Photo: Mrs. B. Lynn

effect on the men. Soon after we arrived at Keppell Harbour. After the usual search we were put aboard a ship we soon recognised as the 'Ubi Maru' — half the group went forward and half aft and soon after loading the ship moved out into the Strait where we remained. We were all cramped up, just sitting up, no room to stretch out, everybody had their knees up on their chins. The toilet arrangements were wooden planks suspended fore and aft on both sides. One could not miss the huge cauldrons on deck for cooking rice and that's all we got for 10 days and 10 nights. We didn't know where we were going or where we were. We bunked on planks and could see a light below. We decided to remove the planks and investigate the cargo. We were lowered down on to a cargo of captured meat and vegetables and we recovered as much as possible. After that we arrived at Miri in British North Borneo and when we were allowed on deck, the ship was at a standstill and it was night time. We opened up the meat and vegetables and you could SMELL it all along the ship. It smelled like a cookhouse! After gulping down the M&V the tins were thrown overboard which gave us a bit of concern as the tins reflected the light as they floated away. It was the last feed we had without rice.

"We left Miri and there was a lot of talk amongst the men that they should take over the ship. There were not many Japanese crew or guards on board and we didn't seem to have an escort but, after discussion with the officers, it was agreed it would be foolish to take any premature action.

"The next morning I was sitting on one of the toilet planks when I saw a submarine surface. We had seen the conning tower but weren't sure. I decided to stay put until the sub surfaced in case I had to take a dive. Anyway it surfaced and immediately sent a message to the 'Ubi Maru' by semaphore. We realised it was probably our escort and if we had made any attempt to take over the ship we wouldn't have got very far".

Between decks in the forward hold there were 340 men — 760 men shared No. 2 hold with rations, baggage and six inches of coal dust, 400 men were bunked on top of cargo in the aft hold. It was the hottest time of the year and the men were travelling under appalling conditions. Bashings, beatings and kickings by the Japs were frequent and the men were developing a feeling of apprehension as to what lay ahead for them. Tea was served three times a day and the meals were of limed rice and cucumbers. Water storage on board consisted of a small tank forward and one aft. The aft tank ran dry after three days at sea making water very scarce and the men had to steal water from the Jap stocks or the winches. The hot, foul air in the holds made it difficult to breathe and the physical condition of the men worsened each day. They were held under these conditions for eleven days and on 18 July 1942 the 'Ubi Maru' sailed around Berhala Island, within sight of the civilian internees who had been held since January 1942, and into the Sandakan Harbour.

Sandakan, on the East Coast of Borneo, was the pre-war capital of British North Borneo. The sight of it now to the tired and dirty men, after ten days of hell on board the 'Ubi Maru', must have been a relief. Most men were disembarked and taken to a padang, while some remained on the ship overnight. Just as they were assembled a tropical shower occurred and, not having had a shower for days, they stripped off and washed themselves in the rain. The locals had never seen white men naked before and they seemed amused and rather astounded. Later the men were taken to the Roman Catholic Church where they spent the night.

The civilians, waving Japanese flags, seemed very interested in the presence of the Australians and wondered how their presence could be advantageous.

The sound of marching men could be heard through the still morning — this sound was to become very familiar to the local people. Not even the constant worrying and harrassing of the Jap guard could stop the men from enjoying the beautiful scenery — the thick plantations and jungle growing close to the road, the chatter and cries of the children — to all intents at first a beautiful, peaceful scene.

Near the 8 Mile peg was the Government Experimental Farm. Here the men turned off to the right on a road which led to the camp where they would spend three long dreadful years and where some would finally be buried. The camp consisted of barbed wire barricades enclosing numerous huts and smaller buildings. On top of a knoll at the Sandakan end of the camp was a huge tree which many of the men were to look at with foreboding over the next few years. Originally built to contain 200 Japanese prisoners of war, now the 1496 men would be crammed into the huts.

It was not surprising when the Australians arrived at Sandakan the hopes of the Chinese Resistance Movement rose in anticipation of being able to take control of Sandakan. Chinese merchants made funds available to assist the Organisation.

The Japanese agreed that a Canteen could be established and the obvious choice as Canteen Officer was Lt. Sligo, the force Intelligence Officer, which gave him the chance to make contact with the natives not only to purchase supplies but to gather Intelligence.

At this time Lt. Okahara, who brought the PWs from Singapore, was ordered to hand over command to Lt. Hoshijima. Written confirmation of this did not arrive until August. It was not long however before the PWs were paraded by him. Lt. Hoshijima, a tall impressive figure, introduced himself and said he was a graduate of Osaka University. He spoke fairly good English: 'You are prisoners of the Japanese and Japan will be victorious even if it take a century. You are here to build an aerodrome' and within a week the men were put to constructing roads to the aerodrome site.

Captain Rowell recorded "At first we were permitted to take charge of the troops; we worked under our own administrations as far as the actual parties were concerned. The Japs would demand 900 odd men and we would supply them in batches of 50 with an officer in charge of each party".

Nine days after their arrival Herb Trackson and his mate Matt Carr, two Queenslanders, decided to make a break. They planned to head south and try and obtain a boat and sail to Australia. After six weeks they were reported 50 miles south of Sandakan in a very weakened state. A Japanese party surrounded them and took them back to Sandakan Gaol where they were well treated. Later they were placed on a boat for Kuching. During the voyage at one stop-over a Japanese doctor was called in to look at them as their health seemed to be deteriorating. Eventually they were handed over to the Kempe Tai where they were treated harshly.

About the same time four other members of the A.A.S.C. also left camp-Allen, Jacka, Harrington and Shelley. They did not leave the Sandakan area. W.O. Sticpewich provided this party with a quantity of food, anti-malarial supplies and a compass and told them he would cover for them as long as possible on the Roll Call.

It was not surprising the escape parties left soon after their arrival. The camp was not secured by adequate fencing, there were guards only at the gate giving the PWs opportunities to leave the Camp area. Walsh took no action to warn the PWs on security matters, he had had no previous experience working with the Japanese on working parties in Singapore.

Cpl. Fairey and his four mates from 2/29 Bn. escaped away from the Sandakan area and hid in the area near the 15 mile peg. Three Chinese, Foo Seng Chow and two brothers, Goh Teck Seng and Goh Teck Chai, were growing tobacco nearby and the five escapees hid in the jungle close by their land. The PWs contacted them, asking for food. They were given ten days supply with a further ten days promised plus materials to build a hut and to furnish it roughly. The PWs stayed there for several months when they decided to try and get a boat and sail to Australia. When they told the Chinese of their plans to sail to Australia in January 1943 they said January was a bad month because of monsoons, also they warned the PWs of the dangers of bad winds and currents between Borneo and Australia but the PWs told them they were good navigators.

So the Chinese began negotiations with a native at Sungei Batang for a boat he had in the river. But this boat was old and leaking and Foo Seng Chow advised the PWs to steal another boat which was in better condition. This they did and, with two months rations and a map, they left in February 1943, after being free for seven months. Foo's son took them out to sea then returned home in his own canoe.

The five PWs had not gone very far when they were caught by the Japs at a headland close to Sandakan Harbour and taken to Sandakan Civil Prison. The Chinese had warned the men if they were caught they were not to divulge any information of the assistance they had received and when they heard of the men's capture they were very apprehensive as to what the Japs may find out.

Dr. Stookes had to visit the gaol as part of his medical duties and as the PWs were ill when arrested it was not long before the doctor visited them. He was able to send food to them through the services of an Indian, Mohamed Zaman, Warder No. 15, who had shown kindnesses to Europeans imprisoned there. The PWs told Dr. Stookes the Chinese had assisted them. This information was passed on by Stookes to Ernesto Lagan and he, in turn, visited the Chinese asking details of their assistance. They were frightened and did not say anything. The Chinese had another fright when the food contractor to the gaol brought a note from the PWs asking them for a loan of twenty-five dollars. They did not take any action but were again very apprehensive that the PWs would be further indiscreet and involve them. The Chinese knew that the Japanese Kempe Tai did not pull punches.

The camp came to life in the morning when Paddy Maguire sounded the bugle. Tired and hungry men stirred, cursed the bugler, cursed the Japs and cursed themselves for not taking notice of their mates when they were queued up for Enlistment, 'You'll be sorry!' they warned them — and then told Paddy what to do with the bugle.

They lined up for breakfast, a sloppy rice called many things like sludge and pap. They ate it, looking forward to the midday meal. The cooks had been up all night to cook the rice as the facilities were inadequate to cook the rice in one batch to give the men a hot meal.

The men were then counted for the three mile hike to the drome site where fresh guards were waiting to put them to work on the fourteen skip lines running from the high ground to the low swampy ground of Sandakan. The Japs brought the skips and line from Burma where the British had used them for the construction of the Burma road. The Japanese were delighted to be able to use the Europeans as coolie labour. Officers from the 37 Army visited the aerodrome and must have expressed concern about the fitness of the men. It was not long before Major Suga, Commander of all PWs and Internees in Borneo and located at Kuching, visited the camp and the drome site, usually addressing the men. Also after each visit there would be a cut in rations — the Army group believed the men constituted a security risk.

If the men were well dispersed they could work at their own speed however they had to be careful of the high bamboo watch towers overlooking the work area. At midday they were given a large serving of rice, each group had their own cookhouse and they were allowed 45 minutes for lunch break. The days were long and the sun hot, the glare took its toll — despite the beltings, the hard work, they marched back to camp singing and looking like soldiers, the guards could not understand why they sang their songs.

One of the big problems for the men working was the lack of footwear — the Japanese issued clogs and rubber plates but that did not protect the feet and soon scratches turned into ulcers and the men became part of the sick community of the camp.

In preparing the drome site the access roads were constructed, the land cleared just as the first settlers had cleared the land in Australia — by axe and crosscut saw. The PWs were always on the watch for any edible reptiles, but most of these moved out when the activity commenced.

The working parties were well dispersed making it difficult for the overseeing guards

NX.40758 Pte. H.J. "Paddy" Maguire. His engraved cigarette lighter found in the ashes at Sandakan.

NX.49915 Pte. Edward Colin Slip, Dubbo, N.S.W.
Photo: Frank Slip.

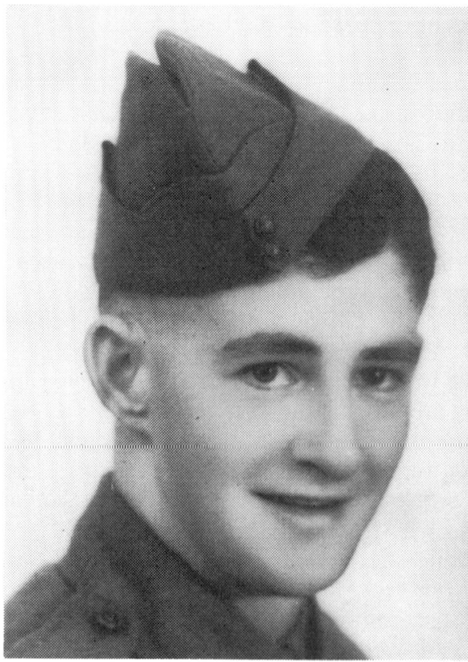

NX. 36657 Pte. Noel Beer, Wagga Wagga, N.S.W.
Photo: Mrs. J. Bateman.

NX.29073 Ray Herbert Bagust, St. Mary's, N.S.W.
Photo: S. Bagust.

to supervise everyone — and everyone was up to every caper to ease the burden of the work. For example, when Denny Garland and his fellow officers were sawing through a long log they would saw half way and then turn the saw over on its back with slow motion until the Jap came close by. Of course the Jap guards also got bored. Hoshijima must have realised progress was not going as well as it could have been when he introduced the 'basher gangs', still, the men continued and when digging drains one man would be 'cockatoo' on top while the others had a rest in the drain. The most common method of holding up work was to distract the guard's attention or to show them some photos — sometimes they would become engrossed in the subject then suddenly become aware they had been 'conned' and would become violent.

The officers in charge of the working parties were responsible for accounting for the tools issued. The men on the other hand were anxious to sabotage the work as much as possible. At the count after each working day if tools were found to be missing the officer in charge was usually bashed. On one occasion during a lunch break an officer withheld food until the tools were accounted for. The men were suffering hunger pains and became irate. One of them struck the officer — the food was served — the officer in charge of the party was in a 'no-win' situation. This action saved the offender's life for he was removed to Kuching.

About this time a goat walked through the Main Gate and down into the camp — it suddenly disappeared from its owner's view and he then asked the guards if they had seen the animal. Someone had seen it go into the camp but there was no sign of it ever being there. While some 'cockie' was milking it another was cutting its throat. In minutes the goat had been killed, skinned, cut up and distributed without any sign or evidence of the slaughter. The guards made enquiries but the PWs just shook their heads and said they had never seen a goat.

Not far from the camp there was a plantation owned by a Mr. Wong who was interned. His wife was Japanese and she and her son and daughter occupied a large weatherboard house. Often on the way back from the aerodrome the Jap guards would take the last four men from the column to do household work there, cutting firewood and any heavy work required. The mother was very kind and the daughter, aged about 25 years, was beautiful. She used to give the prisoners food.

After the fall of Singapore an anti-officer feeling existed throughout the Division. The performance of officers and other ranks was never assessed for retraining and transfer. Later at Changi, General Heath, who served with the British forces in the Abyssinian Campaign, talked to the officers and informed them that 50% of all ranks were transferred to other units after action for lack of performance under fire. During the fighting in Malaya there were failures from General Percival down through the ranks. In one Infantry unit one officer and about 40 ORs had left Singapore during the fighting. Another officer and a large number of ORs left on the 'Empire Star' without permission.

Many resented the large number of officer promotions dated 14 February, the day before Singapore fell. Most of these were justified but there were no NCOs promoted. Later in April 1942 more promotions were Gazetted. One lieutenant was promoted to Captain. He had deserted his Company after the Japanese assault and had arrived back at the R.A.P. wounded in the toe and carrying his boot. There were many ORs who, under normal circumstances, would have been sent home — their services no longer required. However, the 'anti-officer' feeling was strongest in the few months after Capitulation. Some who had not performed well in action turned out to be excellent in handling the Japanese on working parties. This situation mainly applied to Infantry units who confronted the enemy.

However the feeling was still evident in Borneo. The ORs were at first delighted in seeing the officers being bashed about, then, after seeing them on working parties, they began to respect them a lot more. In fact there were occasions when men would have broken ranks to defend officers from punishment. It was good for the officers to be working too as they later learned at Kuching boredom doubled the hours in a day.

During this period the internees were still on Berhala Island including Governor Smith and chief of Police, Major Rice-Oxley. Capt. Matthews was able to establish a line of communication through intermediaries to the former Chief of Police who in turn identified who could be trusted in the Constabulary. There were many natives living close by the drome and as time went on many of them became involved in the Underground organisation.

Work was now being stepped up. The men were often heard singing as they marched to and from work. A tune often heard always relates to a locality or event — when the volunteers left Australia it was the 'Maori Farewell', in Malaya it was 'Terang Bulan', a love song later to become known as 'Malayan Moon'. In Singapore it was 'Colonel Bogey' — to become more famous as the 'River Kwai March', and in Borneo it was 'They'll Be Comin' Round the Mountain When They Come'. There were many verses and civilians remember the time the Australians sang on the road to the drome 'Dropping Hundred Pounders When They Come' — which they did.

For those who contracted malaria in Malaya they were soon suffering from relapses. Many were inflicted with the dreaded disease for the first time, however, the most common complaint was tropical ulcers. Even the slightest scratch, which under normal conditions in Australia would heal up, in a few days here turned into a festering sore which rapidly expanded and became ulcerated.

W.O. Sticpewich, from A.A.S.C. — a 'Jack of All Trades' from First Aid to watch repairs — was put in charge of camp maintenance. (They had brought an assortment of tools from Singapore.) His Section developed a reputation with the Japs. They could repair everything from a watch to large equipment and, as such, were in great demand by the Japanese. Guards would purchase watches from the prisoners and take them to Sticpewich and Co. for repairs. Their woodworking skills soon became known to the Japs and in no time they were turning out wooden buckets for rice. Many Japs sought favours from Sticpewich and in turn he leaned on them for favours. His friendship with many Japs appeared obvious and was resented by many — perhaps some were jealous that 'Stippy' as he was called was getting extra rations for services rendered. As time went on his general condition was good while the other prisoners deteriorated.

The wet season was now approaching and working conditions on the drome, where much of the area was swampy and muddy, were taking a heavy toll on the already fragile footwear. Some of the PWs wanted to preserve their boots and became accustomed to wooden clogs. Some couldn't be bothered with clogs and they conditioned their bare feet on the hard gravelly surface.

About this time Yamamoto, known as 'Doctor', (no one was sure if he was a fully qualified medical practitioner or a first year medical student) visited Sandakan. It was not long before he had a confrontation with Major Rayson, S.M.O. Yamamoto punched him, cutting his face badly and blackening his eyes. He then beat Major Rayson about the head with the victim's wooden clogs which were then lying on the ground. While being beaten Major Rayson was forced backwards several times onto a barbed wire fence, causing severe lacerations to his back and shoulders. This bashing by Yamamoto of senior medical officers seems to confirm his immaturity.

Despite the bashings and the hard work, the morale remained high. Concerts were held occasionally on Saturday nights and those able entered boxing contests. One such match was between popular Jimmy Darlington and Clarry Grinter who, up to that time, thought he could fight. Those who travelled to Malaya on the 'Queen Mary' knew Darlington's ability with the gloves; he took on all comers and won his title.

John Hutchinson, in better times a Pay Sergeant, had ready currency to set up business below one of the huts, to purchase gold, rings, watches, diamonds and other valuables. There was always a dealer of some standing in PW Camps. The money in the camp would ultimately end up in the hands of a few — but in Borneo the Japanese made sure that money in any form could not be transferred and converted to food. The Jap guards were afraid to be caught with gold, preferring to have better quality Parker pens and Omega watches. To meet this market there was always some clever operator who could convert any watch to an Omega or a pen to a Parker — like the operator in Thailand who 'handled' watches, the springs of which were reduced to five minutes running time in order that the timepiece operated during the negotiating stages. It is understood Hutchinson thrived during the early period of 1942-1943 however when circumstances changed and he was unable to trade, despite his wealth he too suffered and lived on the minimum ration. Some of the guards must have kept a close watch on him later to retrieve valuables.

On August 31 Lt. Sligo, Intelligence Officer, died. His place was taken by Capt. Matthews who wasted no time in hatching up excuses for getting outside the camp to gather Intelligence. Capt. Picone of the A.A.M.C. obtained permission for a party to gather nuts which were to be used for the extraction of oil for medicinal purposes, and of course this party included Matthews and Lt. Rus Ewin. While outside Matthews, through an intermediary, made contact with Dr. Taylor, the Australian in charge of the Sandakan Hospital, and with Mr. Mavor of the Sandakan Electricity Supply. Governor Smith on Berhala Island was also informed Capt. Matthews was now in charge of Intelligence operations. In no time Dr. Taylor was able to supply supplementary essential medical supplies to the camp through the Underground.

The Boiler House was situated outside the camp perimeter. It was built by the British to generate power for the camp. When the Australians first arrived it was serviced by civilians, Chan Ping being the principal attendant. It was not long before Capt. Matthews suggested there were competent Australians in the camp who could assist in its operation and Sgt. Alf Stevens was appointed Engineman with several assistants. Chan Ping was pleased to have the company of the eight Australian PWs and they in turn did everything possible to cement a firm friendship between themselves and the friendly Chan Ping, or Ah Ping as he was sometimes called. After all they were beyond the careful scrutiny of the temperamental guards and their kindly attitude towards Chan Ping was being rewarded by gifts of food on his part.

Stevens eventually suggested to Chan Ping that there was need for the PWs to work longer hours at the power plant than they were doing at present. "Why not ask the Japs if we can work for you at night", said Stevens. But the careful Chan Ping answered that he dare not do that in case the Japs would be annoyed. "Never mind". said Stevens, "I will ask my superior officer", and he did. Capt. Matthews was his superior officer and by some means or another he managed to persuade the Japs to allow a permanent party to live and work with Chan Ping. Sgt. Stevens and three assistants moved in and began their new life at the Boiler House.

To service the boiler a Wood Party, under Lt. Wells, was formed which comprised about forty men plus a number of guards and a Jap driver and truck to transport the wood back to the boiler. Both these operations gave Matthews the contacts he wanted.

Back on the drome site work was proceeding with road construction and quarry development to supply fill for what was to be known as No. 1 Strip which ran approximately east/west. At this stage Lt. Okahara, the officer who brought the PWs from Singapore, was supervising work there. To assist him speed up the work the 'basher gangs' went to work on the PWs. First their shirts were removed and they were slashed with lawyer canes.

Late August the Trackson escape party were re-captured and during their interrogation they stated it was the duty of every Australian prisoner of war to escape. The Jap interrogator asked who told them it was their duty and they replied 'their officers'. The Japs then detained the senior A.A.S.C. officers, Major G.N. Campbell and Captain J.D.H. Scrivener. They were taken to Sandakan Gaol on August 27 and interrogated by the Kempe Tai. They remained there until they were placed on board the 'Burong', a small coastal steamer, on August 30 and taken to Kuching for a Japanese Court Martial. At Labuan they were dragged through the streets of Victoria tied together with the six Other Ranks. The Japs seemed to enjoy displaying the white men in this manner. They were then placed on board the 'Margaret' — their shipmates being Japanese prostitutes. The party eventually arrived at Kuching on September 6 and were taken to the local gaol. Here they went through further interrogation, the Japs wanting the officers to admit they ordered the A.A.S.C. men to escape.

On October 13 the officers were released and taken to the PW Compound where they met the newly arrived British PWs from Batavia. Capt. Doug Scrivener recorded 'No wash for 10 days — No shave for 25 days and No shoes for 35 days'.

Colonel Walsh was also paraded and the same questions put to him. He explained it was Australian Army Regulations which required soldiers, if captured, to escape. Under the circumstances he had no power to prevent the men from escaping. Okahara was annoyed, however the decision was one for Hoshijima as written confirmation of his appointment had just arrived on August 15.

The Kempe Tai were now becoming involved in interrogating the escapees. Word soon arrived at Army HQ that there was trouble with the PWs. Security was tightened up and a security fence was placed around the camp and guards strengthened. Previously there were only guards on the main gate.

It was not long before Hoshijima received instructions from 37 Army HQ to make the prisoners sign a NO ESCAPE declaration and to confiscate all writing material. Accordingly, he ordered all PWs to parade on September 2 when he demanded Col. Walsh to instruct the men to sign the declaration. Walsh endeavoured to explain to Hoshijima that their request was against the Geneva Convention but Hoshijima wasn't concerned about the Geneva Convention and became very threatening, which created quite a stir within the ranks. Walsh said 'I for one will not sign' and threw the paper on the ground. Hoshijima then barked orders for the guards to arrest Walsh who was then tied up and dragged away. Major Workman immediately took over and the PWs, almost as one, shouted

NX.53898 Pte. Albert (Bert) G. Doyle 27 Bde. A.A.S.C. Died Ranau 9 August 1945 (Japanese date of death) Age 27. Bexley, N.S.W.

NX .66892 Sgt. Leonard H. Doyle 27 Bde. A.A.S.C. Japanese date of death Ranau 2 August 1945. Age 37. Identity disc found 110½ mile peg. Yoogali, N.S.W. *Pics: Mrs. G. (Tot) Doyle.*

'Sign!'

Hoshijima later gave his version of the event. He had been ordered to order the PWs to sign a declaration to the effect they would not escape "so I wrote the following declaration:

1. We will endeavour to carry out orders of the Japanese Army.
2. We shall not attempt to escape.
3. If we should attempt to escape we would have no objection to be shot.

"Colonel Walsh read this declaration out to the other PWs and said that he could not sign so I took Col. Walsh outside the compound and ordered a soldier to tie him up and then I asked Major Workman why they did not sign. Then Major Workman said the following: 'Europeans did not use 'we' in making such declarations' so I said that is our mistake so we will correct it so instead of putting 'we' I inserted after 'we' 'herewith individually', and after this everybody agreed to sign."

However, from the parade ground the men could see the Japanese preparing to fire, it was at that stage they shouted 'Sign it!'

Capt. Claude Pickford was standing next to Lt. Col. Sheppard and remarked 'What a thing to happen on our wedding anniversaries!' — they both had reason to remember the date.

The PWs remained on parade for some time, during which the Japanese searched and rifled their gear. On release from the parade discussions carried on into the night as to what the consequences would have been if the Japs had opened fire.

Soon after the confrontation the Japanese decided senior officers would be removed as soon as practicable, a move which was not long in coming. Lt. Col. Walsh and the senior medical officer, Lt. Col. E.M. Sheppard, with five other officers, Mr. Wilson, the Red Cross representative, and a number of other ranks including Anderson (Bowe), Crome and Ford, who were being removed for disciplinary reasons, were all placed on board a vessel on October 27 and sailed for Kuching. Eric Davis remembers being told to prepare to leave with Col. Walsh's party. He objected and requested he be allowed to remain but Capt. Cook said 'Your name is on the list there is nothing I can do about it'. Davis remembers 'We were lined up to depart in front of the officers remaining when Capt. Mosher broke ranks and shook hands with one of the men. We were taken by truck to Hoshijima's house where we were given a watermelon each and from there we were taken and put on an inter-island ferry, the 'Treasure'. Everyone was put on the open deck where we remained. No food was provided for the first day. The officer asked if any of the men could cook. Of course I volunteered; the facilities were restricted but we cooked some rice for everybody. When we arrived at Labuan we requested the guard's permission to go ashore and purchase some food and the party were able to purchase a few chooks and vegetables. Wally Ford and Joey Crome soon plucked the chooks and in no time a good meal was under way. All cooks have the privilege of tasting the dish — anyway one of the officers acused us of stealing, so we went on strike. It was a short strike! and when Major Fraser ordered us back to work we said we wouldn't go back until we got an apology. We waited — after a while when their guts got the better of them we got an apology! We arrived at Kuching on November 4. Major Fraser insisted we were not allowed to remain in the officers' camp so we were placed in the British Other Ranks camp where we stayed together. They gave us the end of one hut so all the Australian ORs remained together. Others in the British ORs Camp worked in the Officers' camp on camp duties.

About this time Major Campbell and Capt. Doug Scrivener were paraded before Col. Suga — Campbell wearing his World War I ribbons, Suga also wearing the same ribbons. They asked Suga about his decoration and he explained in World War I he served in the Imperial Japanese Navy and he was on a warship which escorted the ANZACs to the Middle East.

Major Fleming took over as Acting Force Commander on 27 October. His appreciation

Major F.A. Fleming.
Photo: Mrs. Rosemary Davies.

VX.45178 Capt. J.D.H. Scrivener, E.D.

of the Sandakan situation was more attuned with the other senior officers in the camp. He soon formed some semblance of a command structure to be prepared for one of the events and hostilities which the Australians could be involved in. Uppermost in his mind was the strong possibility of a native uprising — with no outside contact what, if any, function were the PWs to play? the possibility of a commando raid? and the most likely — an Allied invasion. In any event a plan was made to be prepared.

A committee was formed which included Capt. Heaslop, Quartermaster, Capt. Alex Bathgate, Finance, Capt. Matthews, Chief of Police, and Capt. Rod Jeffrey as Chief Medical Officer. Capt. Ken Mosher was appointed to command a company of four platoons of the most able men to cope with any eventuality.

Some civilians were permitted in a specified area on the drome where they could sell small cakes etc. The principal English speaking contact was Heng Joo Ming. Frank Martin soon became friendly with Heng who indicated he would help in any way possible with food. Martin discussed with him the possibility of obtaining radio parts. Later Heng Joo was able to supply some items. After getting them back into camp Capt. Matthews took possession of them. He again brought up the subject of escape. Heng said he could get a party away on a Chinese fishing boat going to the Philippines. He insisted it would take some months to arrange but the chances of success were good.

About the end of September 1942 the Japs demanded an officers' working party. The officers refused but when the Japs threatened to cut the ration of the entire camp the officers' work party was formed there being no alternative. They left camp at 0740 hours, marched 2½ miles to the drome site and when they finished work at 1800 hours marched 2½ miles back to camp. They had ten minutes off each hour, a quarter hour for morning cup of tea, 50 minutes for lunch, quarter hour for afternoon tea. Discipline varied. Sometimes it was comparatively lax and at other times was extremely fierce. Bashings were frequent — with hands and sticks. After the officers had been there for some time the Japs put on a crew of 'bashers' whose job it was to keep things moving. The officers called some of these men 'Black Mick', 'The Bull' a lance corporal, and if they were not satisfied with the amount of work being done or the pace they would stand up any individual in the party, with shirt and hat off, facing the sun, with arms outstretched. Capt. Rowell recalls seeing them stand up a very sick man for three or four hours, all the time bashing him with lawyer canes.

The party was under the command of Captain Britz and after a period where the leader of the party received more than his share of bashings it was decided they should rotate the command to share the punishment. The Japs seemed to delight in bashing the officers when there were ORs and coolies close by.

The Japs confiscated all the Public Works plant from Sandakan for use on the aerodrome. This included a steam-roller. The operator was an Australian who had previously worked on road construction at home. The PWs were covering up soft material so the surface would not stand heavy aircraft, and this made it hard for the steam-roller as it was constantly bogged. The driver would be pulled down, bashed by a guard and then there would be cries of 'All Men!' on the end of a rope pulling the roller out. Eventually they abandoned it and used manpower — they would march the men up and down to compact the surface.

Armistice Day was not forgotten — the Japanese gave permission for a Ceremony to be held to commemorate the occasion. Each Unit's representative placed a small wreath of jungle leaves by the Cross and a service was held by the camp's padres. It was a solemn occasion; a hymn was sung and, to the surprise of many present, there was Sgt. Ichikawa Takagoroh, the Quartermaster, wearing Allied medals of World War I. He was just as solemn as everyone else. Ichikawa was a humane sort of person who was never involved in camp conflicts.

A wireless set began operation on November 4. It was constructed by Cpl. Richards, Small and Mills under Lt. Weynton's supervision. In order the set could be used with the camp power an ingenious chemical rectifier, using test-tube wire supplied by Sgt. McDonagh of the Hospital, was used to convert the AC to DC. Primary coils provided the low tension. What a sense of joy it must have been to the men when they secured the first news from outside. The thrill of hearing 'THIS IS LONDON CALLING' would produce indescribable emotions. The BBC, Radio Australia, San Francisco, were all beamed to this area. The BBC News Service was at the most convenient time. It takes a tremendous lot of team work to get a radio into operation under these circumstances as great risks have to be taken. Scouts have to be placed in sensitive areas and apart from the watching of guards there are always indiscreet people who talk too much on the mess parade and have to be watched. Capt. Matthews was well aware of all these problems and had chosen his own officers who were later to fail him.

There seemed to be a lack of appreciation of the security required for the dissemination of the news. The very thought of keeping a wireless above ground was risky as in the event of a raid a hot wireless could be smelled for some time, in any false container it would quickly be located.

As time went on many prisoners became extremely careless and it was only luck that prevented the Japanese from discovering the secret in the early days of the receiving set. The men in the British camp in Kuching were able to operate a wireless for the duration with maximum security and without detection.

It was not long before the job of maintaining the night vigil on the radio set fell on the shoulders of Cpl. Richards. The set was kept in a false drawer in the carpenter's shop. Radio Australia and the BBC News provided most of the material for the news sheet. The

Pte. Walter "Bub" Madden, Narrandera, N.S.W. His watch engraved "To Bub From Mum" was found on a dead Japanese officer in August 1945.

SX.11479 Cpl.R.H. Coker. 4 Res. M.T. A.A.S.C. Died Sandakan 7 May 1945. Age 45. Rose Park, S.A.
Photo: John Coker

Pte. Claude Anthony Gilligan, Coonamble.
Photo: Beryl Petch.

NX.58711 L/Cpl. Raymond Francis Juchau, Randwick, N.S.W.
Photo: Reg Juchau.

three main channels through which the news was passed to Sandakan town were the Power Plant, the Mile 8 Police Post and the Agricultural Farm. It was always wise to disseminate some of the news with interesting 'furphies' to confuse the Japs should they be listening.

Chan Ping, the kindly Chinese in charge of the Boiler House, took communications down to Sandakan and through his friend Ng Ho Kong they reached Mr. Mavor, Manager of Sandakan Light & Power Co. Chan Ping at first did not realise he was taking news summaries to town; he did not read English and thought the letters he was taking were only camp news.

Even while the radio watch was being kept throughout the night other PWs were still receiving punishment from the Japs and Lt. Wells, who assisted in the wireless watch, often walked back to his quarters at 2 a.m. and saw PWs standing to attention as punishment while guards watched from a nearby hut.

As Christmas approached so did the rains. The Japanese gave permission for a camp concert. Captain Claude Pickford recalls "December 1942 — it was an interesting night, it was the first concert we had there called 'Radio Rubbish' and the idea was that to save any elaborate scenes we would have the main scene as a radio studio so we could present each item as though it was a radio program. Being the first program, the whole of the Japanese guards were there including Capt. Hoshijima. About fifty Australian hospital patients were carried out on stretchers to watch the show. The character who appealed to me most during the night was the Japanese Governor of North Borneo, Kumabe Tanuki, who arrived resplendent in uniform with shorts, long underpants under the shorts and worn with short socks. Complete with sword, medals and decorations he looked like a character out of Gilbert and Sullivan.

"But the Finale was something that will remain with me and all those who were there for the rest of our lives. We had pre-arranged that for the Finale we'd have everybody on stage and we'd sing 'There'll Always be an England' followed by the National Anthem, which we did. The enthusiasm was so much that all of the troops themselves took up 'There'll Always be an England' and joined in. Then the climax came and we went immediately into the National Anthem. It caught everybody so much that all the Jap guards stood up, even Hoshijima stood up to attention while the National Anthem was being sung — all except the Governor and he sat down — but it was rather an interesting occasion to me, the whole atmosphere was electric".

Later on Major Fleming spoke — "I think it appropriate on this Christmas evening, as acting Force Commander, I should say just a few words to you and put before you just one or two ideas which may be of some help in the future.

"Before doing so, however, I wish to thank Lieut. Hoshijima (Hoshijima's presence did not make things easy) for allowing us to meet together this evening.

"I have been very happy today to see and to feel the splendid spirit of comradeship, helpfulness and quiet enjoyment of the good food we have been so fortunate as to obtain. I feel that our morale has been steadily rising since the beginning of this Christmas Season and tonight will long remain in our memories as a high water mark.

"On February 15 last we surrendered at Singapore and became PW. To most of us it seemed unbelievable. Our faculties were numbed and we were unable to think clearly. We moved as sleep-walkers, as men in a dream. It seemed the end of all things.

"Then gradually we realised that we were still soldiers and still members of the A.I.F., still wore the uniform our fathers had made famous and still had a duty to ourselves and our Country. Let us resolve tonight, to go on with our heads up and our eyes straight to meet whatever may be our lot in the same spirit as the old AIF fought and won an undying tradition. Let us resolve that no act of ours shall dishonour the uniform we wear of the Country to which we belong.

"Under these conditions we tend to become irritable, over critical and selfish. We see faults and conceits where none are intended and we become shorttempered and quarrelsome.

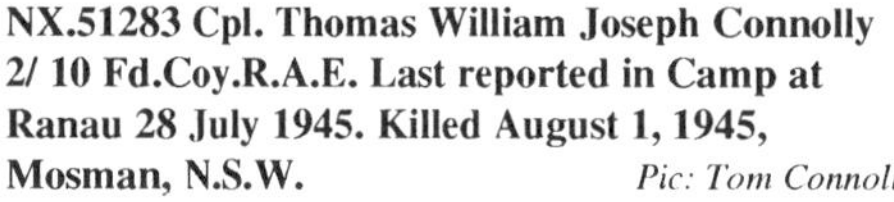

NX.51283 Cpl. Thomas William Joseph Connolly 2/ 10 Fd.Coy.R.A.E. Last reported in Camp at Ranau 28 July 1945. Killed August 1, 1945, Mosman, N.S.W. *Pic: Tom Connolly*

NX .40425 Pte. Thomas Henry Lane. 2/18 Bn. Died 18 April 1945. Aged 40. Tamworth, N.S.W. *Pic: T.H. Lane.*

"I want, tonight, to appeal to you to be more helpful, less critical and more ready to see the best rather than the worst side of his fellows. Let us be ever ready to help the weaker amongst us, to assail those not whose footsteps may stumble and whose will may falter as the road becomes rougher, let us serve this force and each other with good spirit and all our ability.

"Tonight I dedicate myself anew to this force. I pledge myself to continue to serve you to the end, to the limit of my powers and in the interests of you all. That is the pledge I give to you and it is the pledge I ask of you in return.

"Finally, on this Christmas night our thoughts naturally turn towards our homes, to those who love, whose thoughts and prayers will be with us and who wait lovingly for us. We owe it to them to see that we return to them as good men as we were when we left them and that we do nothing that would disgrace them or the names we and they bear.

"And finally, gentlemen, when the going is tough and the way is rough, if conditions become more difficult as indeed they may, when the burden seems well nigh unbearable let us hear a voice saying 'Even these things shall pass'.

"Yes, gentlemen — 'Even these things shall pass' and in the Almighty's own good time we shall return again to Australia — to our homes, to those whose thoughts are always with us and who wait for us.

"We shall be tired, older, not so ready with our laughter but please God not cynical and soured, not broken but more tolerant, more sympathetic even more loveable, ready and able to bear our part with our folk at home in building a new Nation when the war shall have ceased and peace shall truly reign in the hearts of men.

"I wish you all a good Christmas and the best for the coming Year."

Heavy rain fell from Christmas 1942 and continued for some time, turning the camp into a quagmire and taking a heavy toll on the already fragile footwear of the men.

The PWs worked long hours and stress took effect among some of the men — one man wanted to throw himself on the barbed wire so the Japs would shoot him.

Late December 1942, later to be known as 'Humiliation Day' to the officers, Hoshijima paraded the officers.

He commenced by telling them they were a disgrace to be prisoners of war — such a situation would never have occurred in the Imperial Japanese Army — "This is why — even if it takes Japan one hundred years — we will be your masters. You may be educated and many of you have Degrees, but I too have a Degree in Engineering" —

1942 — was a good year —

Chapter 2

JANUARY 1943

The New Year commenced with optimism — 'We'll be out of here before the end of this year' people predicted, not knowing events were just shaping up for another difficult year. Lt. Alan Loxton had taken a party of part-fit and unfit men to the drome site. The Japs ordered the unfit men to work in a special area so he placed the fit men with another party and started to move the unfit men to an area indicated for light duty men when he was prevented by 'Mad Mick' from doing so. Loxton endeavoured to explain but 'Mad Mick' would not listen. He knew the party were unfit so he ordered all to remove their shirts then to stand to attention with arms outstretched and parallel to the ground. Some were allowed to lower their arms after 5 minutes, others were kept in that position for 15 minutes; they were then beaten with a thin rod. Loxton was the last released. 'Mad Mick' and his guards showed obvious sadistic enjoyment at their predicament according to Loxton. The men were then ordered to the light duty area to begin work.

Despite the unpredictable conduct on the drome site many of the men preferred to work there and get a good serve of rice for the midday meal rather than be back in the camp on starvation rations.

The early months of 1943 found the PWs being worked harder on the construction of the Sandakan aerodrome. The footwear position worsened each day and the incidence of tropical ulcers was reaching high proportions. The greater the difficulties of keeping the work parties up to strength the more cruel the Japanese became in forcing men classified as 'light duties' to go out to the aerodrome.

Jimmy Darlington vowed if ever a Jap attacked him for no reason he would flatten him. The opportunity came when a Jap guard, Kata, walked into the cookhouse where Darlington was working at the drome. The cook refused Kata permission to wash his loin cloth in one of the serving containers, Kata kicked Darlington who was nearest to him and the kick was aimed at the crutch. Darlington in defence hit Kata splitting his lip. Kata then attacked Darlington with a 5 ft. length of 2x1. Then, with reinforcements, he made Darlington kneel upon an angular piece of wood for an hour. Another piece of wood was placed behind his knees to prevent him relaxing by resting the buttocks on the heels. Darlington fainted during this torture. Finally his arms were bound and he was placed in the cage until the following night. When his arms were unbound one arm was broken. During the night his cries of pain could be heard in the camp. Eventually Capt. Picone was able to give him some relief. Protests to Hoshijima were ignored. Darlington was sentenced to gaol, which he served at Outram Road, Singapore and later in Changi Hospital where the surgeons re-set his arm. Kata was later to pay for the consequences of his conduct.

The Japs were casual in the use of explosives on the quarry sites, as long as the Japs were warned they would give the order to blast, often causing injuries to the PWs. After this occurred PWs kept clear when the Japs were preparing to blast holes — protests by the officers in charge were completely ignored.

The first time Hoshijima appeared on a small white stallion, he was dressed in white shirt and breeches and it was obvious to the experienced Australian horsemen — like Capt. Gordon Maxwell — that Hoshi was no horseman. Maxwell commented to one of his fellow officers that he would like to have the opportunity of training the horse so when Hoshi touched it with the whip the horse would bolt for the scrub. The animal was to lead a life similar to the prisoners — tied up all the time and fed occasionally on cut grass it normally would not have eaten. Its condition deteriorated at the same rate as the PWs.

However, Hoshijima preferred to have an Australian chauffeur — not everyone wanted the job but there were benefits in the way of better rations which were provided from Hoshijima's kitchen. The disadvantage however was the driver was required to address Hoshijima as 'Master' and as a result he received 'flak' from the other PWs.

It was about this time Eric Davis, while working at the Boiler House, was ordered to accompany Hoshijima to obtain a globe valve for the boiler room. They were driven to Hoshijima's house, previously the home occupied by Mrs. Agnes Newton Keith, the author, located in a superb position overlooking Sandakan Harbour. Davis commented on the beautiful view — Hoshijima replied: "Perhaps not as good as Sydney Harbour, but one day I will have a beautiful home overlooking Sydney Harbour." The hangman was later to deny Hoshijima of his hope but several hundred of his countrymen have achieved his wish without a shot being fired and without opposition from our Governments despite public disquiet.

The interpreter, Osawa San, a civilian better known to the PWs as 'Jimmy Pike' because he was small, bow-legged and claimed he was a jockey and had ridden in South Australia, (in the English camp he was known as 'The Jockey') often became furious when the required number of men was not available for the work parties because of the increasing illnesses. He would call all those looking after the sick to march off to the drome site to do pick and shovel work. Both Capt. Picone and Capt. George Cook endeavoured to protest to Osawa about the 200 sick men being left unattended in the hospital but Osawa refused to give them an audience.

On other occasions if a work quota was not filled a Japanese private would make a medical inspection to select men he considered fit enough to work on the drome. They kept weighing the PWs to ensure their policy of slow starvation was working. As time progressed they stopped this program and did not bother as the results were obvious.

By March the No. 1 airstrip was sufficiently advanced to enable a light plane to land and Suga thought it would be an occasion to celebrate. A senior officer from 37 Army Command at Jesselton was invited to officiate. Hoshijima arranged for all PWs to line the edge of the strip and when the plane came into sight they were to salute and hold it until the plane came to a stop. Many recall the humourous sight of the light plane bouncing along the rough surface with the officer endeavouring to hold his salute. Afterwards the official party were served tropical fruit as they sat in the shade of a nearby lean-to.

During Suga's visit Bugler Paddy Maguire played an unusual call. Suga asked Maguire what it was and he explained it was the General's Call reserved only for very senior officers. Suga was impressed so he gave Maguire some biscuits. His hungry mates told Paddy it was a confidence act.

Hoshijima was pleased with himself and permitted the PWs to have a Sports Afternoon on a nearby cleared area. Prizes were awarded in the form of fruit or a side of dried fish, better known as 'Molly Wong'.

Up to this time Major Fleming supervised the working parties on the drome.

Sgt. Wallace had been canvassing for some months for men to escape with him. He was not liked and generally not regarded as a reliable leader. For a while Frank Martin was prepared to go with him however he decided not to on the advice of Major Fleming. Wallace was able to convince Sig. Harvey and McKay (served as McKenzie) to go with him but they did not get far before they fell out with Wallace going his way. In the meantime the two were reported near a kampong not far from the drome. Word reached L/Cpl. Naguri Takeshi, a Kempe Tai man who was planted in the camp to watch over Hoshijima's management of the PWs. He soon arrived on the scene, surrounded the two escapees but made no attempt to arrest them and take them back to camp. They were shot! Naguri was later to pay for the murders with his own life.

Wallace showed up on 11 May at Joo Ming's house, rather shocked to learn his two mates had been shot and buried at the drome (Hoshijima regarded them as 'criminals' and would not allow them to be buried in the cemetery). Wallace put out 'feelers' to Captain Matthews to see if he could get back into camp but Matthews rejected the idea and said the camp had already suffered enough on quarter rations for some time. Matthews promised however he would endeavour to get him away. In the meantime Wallace relied on Joo Ming for assistance. Ming passed word through the other contacts eventually reaching to Dr. Taylor.

L/Cpl. Koram, No. 142, was out in a prahau fishing when a submarine surfaced nearby. An American officer hailed Koram and gave him a letter and told him to give it to any white man that he saw, he also told him if any white men wanted to escape this was their chance. Koram took the letter to Dr. Taylor, who in turn gave Koram a letter for Capt. Matthews.

Plans were well advanced to speed up airfield construction. The Japs were being pressed in New Guinea and the South West Pacific. Borneo was a vital link to Singapore and their Southern Command located at Saigon. An aerodrome was under construction at Kuching and now they decided to construct a further strip at Sandakan. PW labour was now being moved from Java and Singapore. One party which originally comprised 840 PWs arrived at Jesselton and now received orders to prepare to move to Sandakan. This group was made up of R.A.F. and Royal Artillery; the Japanese officer in charge was Captain Nagai.

The leader of the group was Sqdn. Leader G. Hardie of the R.A.F., most of the party were airforce personnel and included an Australian Flt. Lt. Charles Johnstone who tells his story:-

"We were told on the night of 5 April 1943 we would be shipped to Sandakan. Leaving next day we were loaded on to a rusty tramp steamer. During the day we were allowed on deck and at night we were shoved into the holds. After about 24 hours the ship's engines broke down and we were towed into Kudat by a Jap destroyer. After some delay we arrived in Sandakan on the afternoon of 8 April. We were immediately marched to a padang (open park) in the middle of the business area and put on public display. As it got dark we were then marched about a mile to an Anglican Church to camp for the night. At the back of the church were limited toilet facilities and water taps to get a washdown. We had nothing to eat for about 36 hours, which was not unusual.

"Next morning three motor trucks, driven by Australian Army drivers with Jap guards aboard, picked up our luggage and about 20 of our worst sick cases and without breakfast we started on the 10 mile march to the aerodrome and our camp. One of the Australian truck drivers told us 1500 Australians had been sent from Changi, Singapore and arrived at Sandakan in July 1942. They were building the aerodrome and access roads. Their camp was about 2 miles from ours. He hinted that they had a radio receiver and gave our war news before he was chased away by the guards. The guard Sergeant told us we were not to talk to the Australians. If caught, we would be severely punished. The Japs had laid out buckets of drinking water every 3 or 4 miles. About 2 miles from our camp as we rounded a bend on the road, about 50 Australian P.O.W. wearing hats, shorts and boots were lined up standing at attention. I was proud of them. We pulled ourselves together and returned their salute, marching as smartly as we could.

"On arrival at our camp we had to spread all our kit out on the ground for inspection.

As usual they stole some of our gear but it was a muddled up search and easy to trick the guards. I had an old pair of shorts which I wore and had two large patches on the back where my diary and papers were hidden. Unfortunately we had no radio parts to hide and would have to rely on the Australian camp for news. The camp was the usual attap huts sited in a dry, arid, open patch of ground which was both hot and dusty. The aerodrome about a mile away was clearly visible with no tree growth in between. The jungle was well back on the other sides. We had no electric power but the Jap guard house just outside our barbed wire fence had electric lights.

"I was in charge of a working party digging a drain near a shed in which four Australians were operating a blacksmith shop sharpening picks, chunkels (native hoe) repairing shovels etc. I walked over for a drink of water from a bucket up against a wall, but outside the shed. The Sergeant blacksmith said he'd been told to very discreetly approach an Officer from the British camp and pass on radio news in brief and quickly. He asked to approach the blacksmith shop once per week for news. On returning to camp I went to Squadron Leader Hardie, told him the story and gave him the news. He said to keep the weekly appointment but not to tell anyone. He would pass on the news about a fortnight after receipt as a security precaution.

"Captain Hoshijima caught me on about my fourth trip to the blacksmith's water bucket. Fortunately I was drinking water from a mug and no conversation had taken place when Hoshijima jumped round the corner and let out a yell. He then slapped me hard on the face four times, knocking my cap off. He then stood me to attention facing the sun with my arms extended and called over a Korean guard who watched me. About an hour after, during which my arms had sagged a couple of times and been bashed by the guard, Hoshijima returned, slapped me a couple of times and said in fairly good English 'No contact with Australians'. I hadn't spoken to the Australians for he was on the scene too quickly. He realised I hadn't been talking and sent me back to my working party. On return to camp I told Sqdn. Ldr. Hardie what had happened and it was decided another officer would try and get the news".

The general condition of the British PWs was poor, the ORs had little in the way of personal gear and many of them had inadequate clothing and mess gear — the half coconut shell was the common eating utensil, bedding was scarce and only a few men had mosquito nets.

Nagai, without delay set about making his presence felt, he ordered extra working parties and did not consider they should be depleted because of sickness. He was a good match for Moritake, always letting the guards be more strict and cruel with the PWs.

Nagai became second in command to Hoshijima. For some time he gave no indication he could speak English, the PWs were suspicious when someone said they had seen him with a golf bag and suspected be probably had spent some time in a western country. It was a common Japanese trick to pretend they did not understand what the PWs were talking about. However, Nagai let his guard down when one morning he approached an Australian officer 'Good morning Captain Mosher — how are your men this morning?' 'Not very well' replied Mosher. 'Well you should get your doctor to look at them', Nagai replied. 'That won't do any good he will only say the same thing', said Mosher. So the word was passed around the men to be careful of what they said in Nagai's presence.

On 8 June the Japanese decided to remove another party of senior officers. Major Fleming, 16 other officers and four ORs, sailed for Kuching. Captain St. John was appointed Acting Force Commander. The Japs soon called him the 'Two metre Tai' because of his height. (The rice ration at this time was 17 ozs. per man per day).

The men were now being moved from road construction to work on the aerodrome, an officer in charge of a party of 50 men. Conditions were harsh, there was no shade and the condition of the men began to deteriorate. It was at this stage Hoshijima reaffirmed his statement that anyone attempting to escape would be shot — furthermore, the men

Flt./Lt. C. Johnstone, Mackay, Qld.

Major J.G. Fairley, Collaroy, N.S.W.

occupying adjacent bunks would be shot. This was an effective deterrent.

Availability of canteen food was reasonably good up until the time of the arrests. There was a variety of fruit and vegetables available, rates of pay for officers was 80 cents a day; Other Ranks were 10 cents a day. Bananas were one cent, pineapple up to five cents, a 'Molly Wong' (dried fish) a few cents. Some of the men made pickles of which a spoonful could be purchased for one cent. On the aerodrome the local people were permitted to sell a variety of food — battered fish, battered snake, fried sweet potatoes, fried banana fritters, dim sims and what appeared to be curried dog. The men were receiving a 485 gram tin of rice for the midday meal and were able to exchange it for a variety of food from the natives.

Capt. Nagai was supervising the construction of barracks in the aerodrome locality. One such hut was being adorned with a Rising Sun on the front gable, there were a couple of Australians finishing the job off and one was heard to say "These bastards won't see the sun rise when our blokes have finished with them". Unbeknown to them Capt. Nagai overheard the remark, pulled the men off the job and in an uncontrollable frenzy began bashing them. When the barracks were completed Hoshijima was seen waving flowers as he walked through — this was to rid any evil spirits who may have been lurking in the new huts.

Back in Singapore the Japanese were preparing to move 'D' Force overland to Thailand, the group was to comprise all the fit men who were in prime condition after spending most of their time working close to the wharves in Singapore. This force was composed of various battalions and a minimum of officers to each group. While the men for 'D' Force were being allocated the Japanese called for a further 1000 men — 500 Australian and 500 British — to assemble in a few weeks to go overseas. Major John Fairley of 2/20 Bn. was chosen as leader of the Australians and Colonel Whimpster was Force Commander.

Lt. Col. Galleghan informed Fairley he would have 480 ORs, 16 competent officers,

2 medical officers and two padres. Both Major Howard Eddy and Capt. Oakeshott requested to be included on the force. Fairley was generally satisfied with the officers chosen.

Word soon leaked out the force was destined for Borneo. Some liked the idea and others did not. The feelings were mixed, some said to them 'Come on, be in it — it's close to home, we'll probably be released first'. John Brinkman asked me to swap with someone, suffering from malaria at the time I declined and said I would prefer to go overland. I remember talking to many of my friends, Cpl. Ron Spurway, better known as 'Juicy', cheerful as usual, big 'Bluey' Myers from the Northern Rivers who never knew what fear was, Walter Madden from Narrandera, little Sammy Burns from the Band, he had just attained the age of 18 years, Ray Tinning who in better times was an SP bookmaker from Newcastle. Claude Gilligan didn't like the thought of an overseas trip. He said to his mate Stan Slater: 'if anything happens to me I have a daughter back home.' Pte. Howard Hewitt, VX.19059, 2/8 Bn. 6th Div. Middle East, was being sent back to Australia when Japan declared war and was left at Singapore. He was known as 'The Turk'. When in Changi he organised a small group and paid them for going out through the wire and soon he had a flourishing black market operation. He was able to 'employ' his own 'batman' until he was placed in detention in Changi and kept for export. He was placed in 'E' Force. He carried with him a water-bottle containing his 'bank' comprising diamonds and other valuables plus escape items including a compass.

Major Fairley recalls: "The force left early morning on 28 March 1943. The Jap lieutenant who I met early appeared to be a fairly reasonable type. One problem was to distribute the radio set parts among the officers. Each officer had his own bit. Howard Eddy reckoned he would take all he could get out of Changi and I was given money and certain powers of Court Martial against everyone who went away with the force.

"We arrived at Keppell Harbour and boarded the 'DeKlerk' which was a battered steamer. Formerly an old coal burner she had suffered damage during the fighting and

NX. 29443 L/Cpl. Kenneth Reginald Caterson, Guildford, N.S.W.

Photo: Mrs. Skowe.

Pte. S.G. Davis, one of those arrested and sent to Outtram Road Gaol, Singapore.

had been patched with concrete. The men were confined to the holds most of the time, latrine facilities were primitive — just a plank over the side of the ship."

"Our men went aboard with all their gear but the British left all the medical supplies on the wharf. As usual the Japs were screaming out 'All men aboard! All men aboard!' and the English had gone on board including Lt.Col. Whimster. I got some of our men to go back and take the English gear on board and in the meantime I looked in one of our trucks and there was one of our radio valves sitting on the seat, it had fallen out of a lieutenant's pocket so I picked it up — I'm not sure whether the Jap driver saw it but nothing came of it.

"The trip did not start till next day, a typical Jap action, and bad for the men in the holds. We had a smooth journey, the men were limited to come on deck except to the R.A.P. on the stern of the deck or to the latrines, and I encouraged the blokes when they came up to take as long as they could and if they had a headache or something to come to the R.A.P. and we'd keep them as long as we could, with the result that on the whole the men got out of the holds more than the Japs ever intended".

On this ship there was a group who for some time were planning to escape. They were waiting for the chance to get a ride as far as Borneo. One was Pte. McLaren who had escaped from Changi Gaol early in 1942 with his mate Burnett (Pte. Edgar Robert Burnett, QX.12664, 2/10 Ordnance Workshop. Died 30 March 1945 aged 25)* They were joined with the Chinese Guerillas for a time and later were betrayed by the Malays and taken to Puda Gaol at Kuala Lumpur and later returned to Changi. McLaren vowed the next time he had a 'go' he would succeed.

There was Sgt. Smyth of 10 A.G.H. who had also prepared to escape when the opportunity was right. He had carried to Sandakan charts of the area together with an oil compass and other assorted escape items. There were others who carried closely guarded items essential for escape. If all these were pooled there would have been surprisingly sufficient arms, charts, medical supplies for an organised escape bid.

Major Fairley continues: "We were watching the ticker going over the stern of the ship measuring the distance we were travelling when Ray Steele and Charlie Wagner raised the point of seizing the ship and going somewhere. It was a splendid idea. We discussed it. We had a map so we knew approximately where we were. With a limited amount of oil, we didn't know where we could get any more and with a thousand bodies on board it would be an impossible thing and could be a disaster. But Ray Steele stood firm on his idea to seize the ship — but what would we do when we had seized it? The proposal was put to Colonel Whimpster, the senior officer, who would not consider the matter and went below, not prepared to discuss it any further.

"There was a cargo of baked beans and cigarettes on board for the Japs and our fellows got into the baked beans, in the middle of the moonlit night you would hear 'plonk!' and it was an empty case going over — and us wondering when the crackers were going to go off!

"Next morning the Jap Commander summoned Lt. Col. Whimster, his Adjutant and me, lined us up on the deck – adjutant behind us and out came his sword! I don't know how long we were flicked around our ears, caps, bellies and things and he spent his rage –

"Soon after we arrived at Kuching and disembarked. Squashing the 500 men into the three huts in the camp was a bit difficult. The electricity for the camp came through one of the strands of barbed wire surrounding the camp and next evening unfortunately one of our boys, Pte. Picken, grabbed the wire, screeched and was dead — that was a very sad start.

"We were put to work — Capt. Gaven and Lt. Wagner and parties unloading drums of cement off barges on to the docks and as many as possible went into the river, between them doing as much damage as they could and following the principle we had had at Havelock Road, and in most camps, we did everything we could to interfere with the

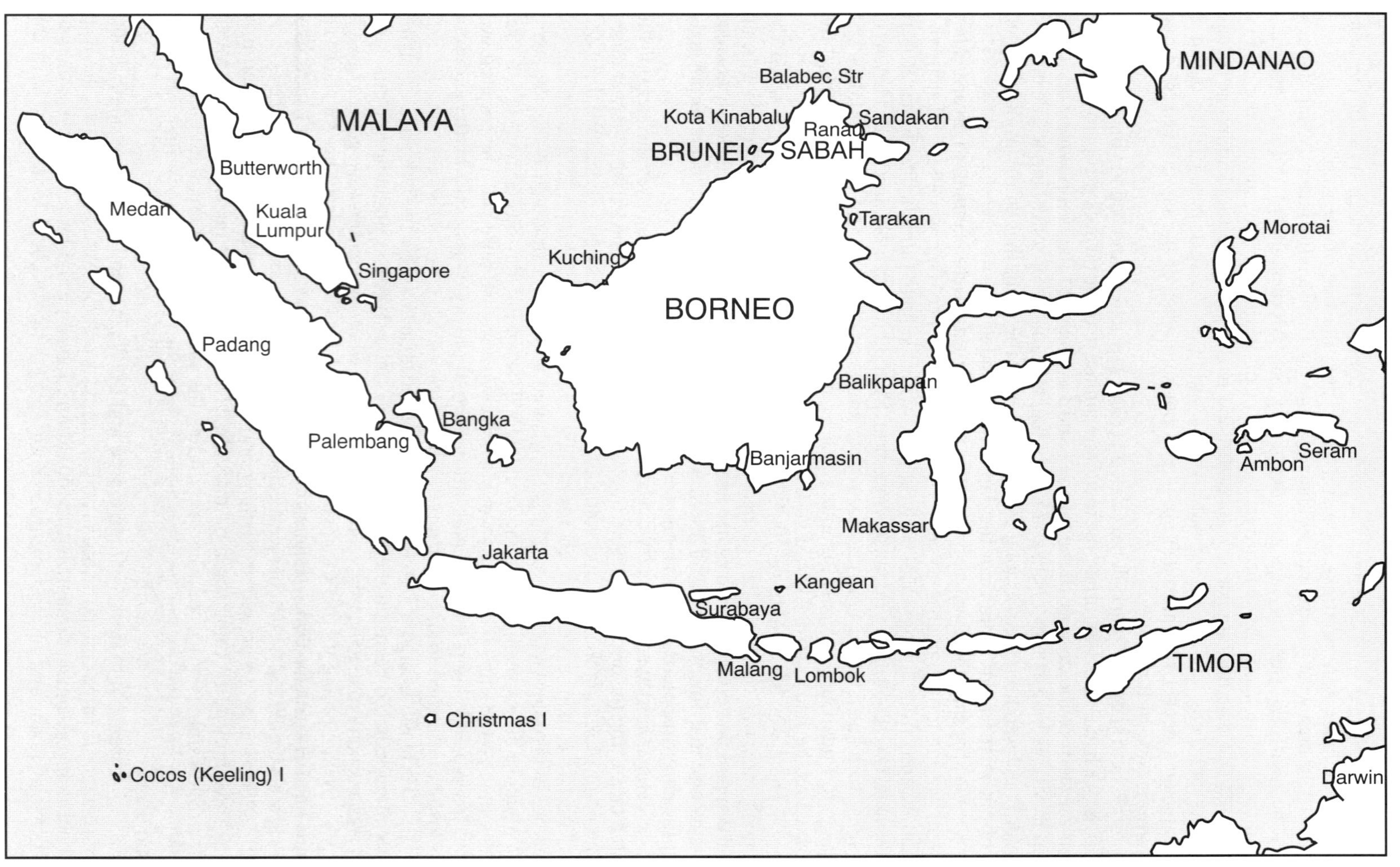

MALAYA
Balabec Str
MINDANAO
Kota Kinabalu
Ranau
Sandakan
BRUNEI
SABAH
Butterworth
Medan
Kuala Lumpur
Tarakan
Morotai
Kuching
Singapore
BORNEO
Padang
Balikpapan
Bangka
Palembang
Banjarmasin
Seram
Ambon
Makassar
Jakarta
Kangean
Surabaya
Malang
Lombok
TIMOR
Christmas I
Cocos (Keeling) I
Darwin

NX.65767 Pte. James Picken, Greta, N.S.W.
Photo: Bill Picken.

Capt. R.J.D. Richardson

Japanese war effort."

Agnes Newton Keith mentioned in her book 'Three Came Home' that Australians had called out to the women in the compound and one of them said he would leave them some lipstick. It is now known that this was thrown into the compound by 'The Turk' — the black market operator.

Major Fairley continues: "On the second day we were summoned to Jap HQ by Major Suga. He told me it was an Imperial Army HQ order that no field officer could go beyond Kuching. He had already taken the field officers from Sandakan and brought them to Kuching so I would stay in Kuching when the troops moved the following day.

"The same day we were ordered to sign this 'Non Escape Declaration'. Having been through that in Changi and found there was no point in making the troops' lives more miserable, I lined the parade up and told them I was going to sign and authorised them to sign which we would do under duress anyhow and all the troops signed the document. I think it was all a farce but at the time it may not have been. Anyhow that was British Command and Galleghan's opinion after the Changi Square incident. They took it as far as they could therefore I felt justified in taking the action I did". This protest at Changi cost several lives.

Major Fairley appointed Captain R.J.D. Richardson in his place on 6 April 1943, with Capt. Ray Steele as his 2 i/c. The balance of the force embarked on the 300 ton 'Taka Maru', leaving behind 15 ORs, who were replaced with 17 Australians who came to Kuching with the British from Java via Singapore, a few 'B' Force men and two sailors from the HMAS Perth.

When the 'E' Force men marched out of the camp Nelson Short remembers the women singing 'Old Lang Syne' — their singing has remained with him through the years and when the song is played now it takes him back to that day.

The ship was steel hulled and completely unlined, making conditions on board uncomfortable. The worst part was everything was covered with raw cement and cement burns were common. Food was scarce and only two meals a day were allowed; drinking water was also rationed.

Capt. Richardson said: "The men were crammed into the hold of the 'Taku Maru' in such a manner that it was impossible for all to lie down at the one time. In one section the ceiling was only 4 ft. so it was impossible to stand upright and to make matters worse many had been seasick, some had dysentery and, as access to the deck was prohibited, the stench was soon beyond description.

"Latrine and general hygiene facilities were of the most primitive nature and totally inadequate. The decks were of steel and the hold uninsulated from the sun in any way. After seven days it was like a furnace. The rations issued were only sufficient for two small meals of rice and vegetables while drinking water was not available, half a mug of weak tea being issued twice a day."

During the voyage the troublesome men Col. Galleghan was holding in gaol at Changi for 'export' soon emerged as the troublemakers on board, endeavouring to take charge of the troops. They gave notice that those in charge would have to refer to them as self-appointed delegates. Sgt. Major Cummings, the 'no-nonsense' Senior Warrant Officer of the force, suggested to Capt. Richardson that these troublemakers be fed to the sharks. Richardson sympathised with Cummings' suggestion but rejected it, saying it was his duty to get all the men home. 'Nutsy' Roberts and his mates were soon pulled into line.

Captain Steele, still keen to take over the ship, approached Capt. Richardson but Richardson would have no part of the suggestion, which he thought was premature.

The ship called at Labuan to coal and during the stay there the troops were permitted to swim off the end of the pier. Eventually, on April 15 they arrived off Berhala Island which lay adjacent to Sandakan Harbour.

Capt. Frank Gaven recalls: "We landed on the jetty at Berhala Island and marched to an area the size of a football field. Nearby was the Quarantine Station which consisted of several huts surrounded by a barbed wire fence. We were ordered to line up and lay our gear on the ground — the search was on. My main concern was the radio transformer in my possession, also a parang. The Japs had told us we were to hand in all pens, pencils and writing materials.

"In front of the troops was Hoshijima, mounted on a platform with a row of guards in front of him each about 6ft. away. Next to me was Rex Blow. I'm wondering what to do with the transformer when Blow said 'Hold this ground sheet up' and while I'm fiddling he put a pistol and ammunition underneath it. So I thought if he could do that I could conceal the transformer so I wrapped it in my mosquito net. When the guard came by I held it up and shook the bottom of it in front of him, he was more interested in a roll of paper I had. I explained by demonstration it was 'benjo' (toilet) and he allowed me to keep it.

"The search turned up all sorts of things including a Bofors shell. Some of the more astute guards would note the men who had fountain pens and that night they would be along to make a deal. Pens, watches, scissors and any item of substance was the currency of the time. At this parade Hoshijima threatened us that if we attempted to communicate with the other camp we would be shot to death".

Captain Richardson said: "Berhala was an old Quarantine Station previously used by the British and its only permanent inhabitants were a colony of lepers. Our guards were a few Japs and a dozen native police, 'boys' who were supposed to have changed sides. However almost immediately I was contacted by their leader, Corporal Koram, who said they were still loyal and would help in any way possible. Through him we were able to establish contact with the Underground on the mainland. The huts at Berhala were inadequate for the numbers and the rations basically maize instead of rice. This had to be crushed before cooking and even then it was almost indigestible."

'E' Force remained on Berhala until June 5, 1943. During this period Capt. Ray Steele, through Corporal Koram, was making final arrangements for their escape. Steele's party comprised Lt. Blow, Wagner, Gillon while Pte. McLaren had planned to depart in a small canoe with Kennedy and Butler. To Steele's embarrassment they were requested by the Underground to take Sgt. Wallace who had escaped outside Sandakan camp and remained there causing some concern to the Underground who insisted that Steele should take him along. Wallace had run out of steam and it is most probable his escape would not have been successful without him joining Steele's party. Furthermore it was decided both parties would hide out on Berhala Island after the initial escape, Steele's party were to proceed to Tawi Tawi by prohau captained by a member of the Filipino Guerillas, while McLaren was going to paddle his own canoe with Kennedy and Butler.

The men were allowed to swim at the beach and Blow and Wagner took advantage of the opportunity — every chance they had they were swimming up and down the beach. When they left one of the Japs said 'Ah so — the men who escaped were the men swimming all the time!"

At Berhala the men of 'E' Force first met Captain Hoshijima, Commander of the PWs in the Sandakan area. He told the camp they would be put to work cutting timber to be used for camp construction. He warned anyone attempting to escape would be shot like the others who had attempted to escape. They would then be put to work on the construction of an air-strip on the mainland.

On June 4 the Japanese brought a large barge to Berhala Island which meant the men were being moved to Sandakan. That night both parties left the camp and eventually escaped in their separate boats — McLaren, Kennedy and Butler rowed all the way to Tawi Tawi in their dug-out canoe where they met the guerilla leader, Colonel Saurez, on 14 June, ten days after their escape. On June 30 Steele's party of five (Steele, Blow. Wagner, Gillon and Wallace) arrived, together with the others, the only eight Australians ever to escape from a Japanese prison camp in this area.

On June 6 all 'E' Force personnel were transferred to 8 Mile Camp. The Japanese had said that transport would be provided for the movement of stores. The 'transport' turned out to be a party from 'B' Force. The new arrivals were separated from 'B' Force and not permitted to contact one another, however, there was great excitement yelling across a valley with various messages enquiring about their mates and brothers from their respective units. They were placed in a separate camp and in order they could be quickly identified their heads were shaven. This camp was about half a mile from 'B' Force Compound. Here they learned there were about 700 British troops in another compound.

Later, the PWs were marched to the aerodrome where the Japanese officer in charge said they would be permitted to greet their fellow Australians from 'B' Force. The two parties were lined up facing each other fifty metres apart. To his delight Captain Frank Gaven of 'E' Force found himself facing his brother, Staff Sgt. Jack Gaven of 'B' Force, whom he had last seen over a year ago in Changi. The two parties were kept apart and the 'greeting' was confined to a silent salute.

The Force were shocked to learn there were about 300 in the camp hospital from a total of 1496 who had arrived earlier. Initially these were allocated a medical staff of 156, however, it was not long before this number was reduced to 24, forcing the others to work on the airfield construction. Major Fleming protested to Hoshijima that it was against International practice as they carried International Red Cross bands. Hoshijima replied that they made NO difference and Japan would only observe the Geneva Convention when it suited....

Jack Lo, employed by the Japanese, hated the PWs or anybody who had dealings with them. He was well known, always anxious to please his Jap masters. Captain Matthews had a narrow escape from the clutches of the Kempe Tai and first experienced the spite of Jack Lo when Matusup bin Gungau, who was in charge of the cow shed at the Mile

QX.11283 Gnr. Clarence Watson, 2/10 Fld.Regt. R.A.A. Died Sandakan 14 March 1945. Age 30. *Photo: R.L. Watson*

NX.41097 Dvr. W.O. Anderson. 3 M.T. Coy. A.A.S.C. Died Sandakan 25 December 1944. Age 23. Bingara, N.S.W. *Photo: Mrs. E. Harding*

8 Experimental Farm and where Capt. Matthews worked occasionally looking after the cows, had gone to Sandakan town in order to purchase some food and had sent this food to his wife, Halima binte Binting, by an Indian. Capt. Matthews was talking to Halima and had asked her where her husband was when Jack Lo approached and asked what they were talking about. When Halima answered 'Nothing in particular' Lo told them to accompany him to the Japanese camp. Capt. Matthews and Halima refused to go with him but after Lo returned with a Japanese guard they were forced to go. Hoshijima asked Halima again what she was doing talking to the Australian PW and on giving the same reply she was struck with a stick around the head. Halima and Matthews were then taken to opposite sides of the house, tied to a post and left there in the sun for an hour. When Matusup returned from Sandakan he tried to approach his wife but was threatened by the guards and told to keep his distance. He sat on the ground nearby and waited until his wife was untied. After further questioning by Hoshijima, without results, both Halima and Capt. Matthews were released with a warning that if they were caught talking together again they would both be severely punished. No doubt Hoshijima remembered this incident at a later date when the names of Capt. Matthews and Matusup were again linked.

Lt. Weynton had written a news summary for forwarding to the British camp. The method of delivery was for the Australian driver to throw it as close as possible to the British working party. On this occasion the guard intercepted the paper before the British could pick it up. It was signed by Weynton — he was punished by a severe and brutal beating by Lt. Hoshijima and sentenced to 14 days in the cage which was partly in the open. At the time of his arrest he was a patient in the hospital suffering from gastric trouble and was removed from his bed to undergo the sentence.

Captain Crozier had seen Hoshijima knock Weynton's glasses off and mark his face. He struck him a second time and forced him to stand to attention without a hat while facing the sun.

Some of the local population were also anxious to keep in with Jack Lo to ensure their popularity with the Japanese and there were many who were willing to come to him with information. One of these, and Indian, Bah Chik, worked with the PWs on the drome. He had another friend, Dominic Koh, who in turn was a friend of Heng Joo Ming.

Rice and other food supplies were becoming scarce in Sandakan. Joo Ming and Dominic took advantage of this and at weekends they would go to the small islands nearby where they could purchase rice etc. Besides supplementing their own stores they were often able to make a little on the side by dealing with others. Unfortunately, on one of their food buying forays, Joo Ming and Dominic had an argument which left Dominic resentful. He knew that Joo Ming had sheltered Wallace at his home and was mixed up with some organisation who were giving help to the PWs. Dominic thought he could put this information to value and he approached Bah Chik with a proposition. The pair of them came to an arrangement whereby Bah Chik would approach Joo Ming, tell him he knew what was going on and unless Joo Ming paid up the information would be given to the Japanese. Heng Joo Ming was not aware that Dominic was behind all this and he refused flatly to have any dealings with Bah Chik. After a quick consultation the two traitors decided that the best thing for their own protection was to tell all to Jack Lo — and what a tragedy unfolded from such a small beginning.

About twenty Japanese together with Lo and Bah Chik arrested Heng Joo Ming on 17 July 1943. He was immediately taken to the HQ of the Kempe Tai on Tannahmerah Road where they commenced to interrogate him. He was bashed and thrown around the room ju-jitsu style then spread-eagled on the ground. A cloth was placed over his face, one Jap poured water into his mouth until Joo was waterlogged then another Japanese jumped from a chair on to his distended stomach — so the 'water-torture' was brought to Sandakan. Joo Ming's father-in-law, Jakariah, was brought in and tortured. The Japs began to hear names — Chin Chee Kong, Apostol, Cpl. Abin, L/Cpl. Koram, Wong Mu Sing, Dr. Taylor, Captain Matthews, Paddy Funk and Ernesto Lagan. In the early morning of 18 July Chin and his friend En Wei were arrested together with Siti binte Jakariah, Henry Chang, Ting Kiang, Lamberto Apostol and Siti's mother, Mrs. Jakariah.

On 18 July all these people were taken to Kempe Tai HQ and their questioning began. Chin was only eighteen years old and the Japs probably considered he would be an easy source of information. The little 'Sini' was subjected to five different forms of torture — after the 'water cure' he was strung up by his wrists and severely beaten with wooden sword sticks. He was then thrown round a room ju-jitsu fashion by experts working in relays. These fiends were experts in the art of kicking a man savagely in the spots where it hurt most. Chin was then forced to kneel on a plank with rough points sticking up from it; another plank was placed behind his knees. Two Japs then sat on each end of the plank and played see-saw, grinding the knees further on to the points and causing painful lacerations. But despite the severity of his treatment Chin did not divulge anything. He was thrown into another room and told the torture would continue unless he made a full statement to them.

Also in this room were Capt. Matthews, Joo Ming, Abin and Wong Mu Sing — they were not permitted to speak to each other and were forced to sit on crossed legs, Japanese style. They did however 'talk' to each other by writing letters on their thighs with their fingers. Their message to 'Sini' was "don't confess to anything, tell the Japs that they alone were responsible, put the blame on them and then Sini's sentence would be lighter. They wanted someone to remain alive and eventually tell the story." When Chin was interrogated again he admitted that he had had some dealings with Joo Ming and Dr. Taylor in connection with the escape of Sgt. Wallace.

At 7 a.m. on 18 July a car stopped outside the home of Ernesto Lagan just as he was about to leave for work. The car took him to the Sandakan Civil Hospital where the Japanese asked him to arrest Drs. Taylor and Wands. Lagan refused but after being threatened with violence he was forced to obey. Lagan was a Detective in the Sandakan Police Force but he was then arrested and taken to the Kempe Tai HQ. Constabulary members who had been found to have assisted the Allies were particularly brutally treated by the Japanese and Lagan was no exception, the Japs going out of their way to inflict terrible torture on him. Dr. Taylor was also subjected to extreme cruelty and the sound of bashing, kicking, cries of pain and screams became part of the daily sounds. The gallant Dr. Taylor did not yield one inch, he refused to divulge or admit anything despite unbearable torture. The Japanese would slash a wooden sandal previously rubbed in wet sand across his face which rapidly became like a piece of raw meat. Dr. Taylor was a middle-aged man of small stature and it seems impossible that he could have survived the terrific floggings which were meted out to him. Unfortunately Lagan was not able to keep his silence for long and the Japanese were able to extract considerable information from him together with a signed statement which implicated many.

Mrs. Lagan was continually harrassed and interrogated by the Japanese who maintained because she was his wife she must know all the details of his activities. They would call and interrogate her and her children at any hour of the day or night but never did any of them break down. Ernesto Lagan had told his wife to destroy his diary if he was arrested and this she had done so when the Japs persisted in their search for it she would be able to say it did not exist. When Katherine was allowed to visit her husband she found him thin, pale and devoid of strength and they were only allowed to speak of home affairs and the children.

A fortnight after Ernesto's arrest Katherine Lagan begged of the Japanese to be able to see him. They gave their consent but warned her they must only speak of home affairs. She brought him a change of clothes and went into the bathroom with him while he put them on. As he was changing she noticed a large blue bruise running down the left side of his body and a large cut on his back which had been stitched up. Katherine started

NX.57758 S/Sgt. Jack Gaven, Collaroy, N.S.W.
Photo: Jaqueline Tolnay.

L/Cpl. Jack Harpley, Parkes, N.S.W.

to weep and asked him how he had received the injuries but he tried to pass the matter off by saying he had fallen down. He mentioned nothing about torture or the treatment he had received from the Japanese. She took this opportunity of whispering to him "Is there anything you want to tell me?". The spirit of the man is reflected in his answer "Yes, please send me extra food as I want to give some to the five Australians who are imprisoned here with me". When Katherine told him it was difficult to get money to buy the food even that she was bringing him Lagan said "You sell my clothes and shoes and buy more food with the money". After all he had done and suffered for the Australians even in his darkest hour Ernesto Lagan still wanted to do more for them.

The Japanese tortured L/Cpl. Koram but the tough little Murut divulged nothing. He was given a severe form of the water torture. He managed to escape from the Japanese and set out for the West Coast and twenty days later he reached Jesselton, then went on to Kota Belud in the North. Koram then did the long trek to Keningau and eventually arrived at Pensiangan, not far from the border of Sarawak where his father lived. Koram's grandfather had also set out from this region with his Murut compatriots to carry out their intermittent forays on the Dyaks.

On July 22, with most of the important members in Japanese custody, Hoshijima, feeling frustrated he was not able to extract information from Matthews, surrounded the camp with guards, removed all personnel there — most of the PWs were working on the drome — and conducted a thorough search, rifling through everything, personal gear, and searching under the huts. The search revealed a variety of firearms, maps, compasses and aids to escape. After the search a large number of men were stripped naked and ordered to carry many articles the Japanese wished removed from the camp to Camp HQ, 200 yards from this camp.

One of the first to learn of the consequences was Cpl. T. Graham, he was told when he returned from the drome the Japs had found his pistol and some ammunition. He went to his officer, Lt. Frank Washington, and sought advice. Graham's first reaction was to 'shoot' through — Washington urged him not to, he said 'You don't stand a ghost of a chance'. The pistol had belonged to Major Beale who was murdered by the Japs at Alexandria Hospital Massacre on February 14, 1942. "You go straight to the Japs and front up, tell them the pistol belonged to Major Beale who was killed in honourable battle and you were with him and you are taking it home to give to his family, just as Japanese officers' swords are returned to their families" Washington told him. Graham took his advice and served 18 months in Outram Road finally returning to Australia.

Other finds implicated a group which hoped to catch the next prahau to Tawi Tawi — this party comprised Sgt. Holly, Sgt. Lander, L/Sgt. A. Weston, Ptes. S.G. Davis and T.H. Rumble. They were arrested. Later at Kuching Sgts. A.W. Weston and Lander were released.

But the find for the day was Lt. Wells' diary which disclosed incriminating information, despite the fact that some of it was in code. In a short time Lt. Wells, who was on the Wood Party, was arrested.

Hoshijima later gave his account when being questioned about the beating he gave Wells. "I found Lt. Wells' diary. In it it said there was a wireless set in the compound. So after the wood cutting party had finished their work I lined them up and took Lt. Wells to a spot 30 metres from the wood party and I accused him through the translator of having a wireless set in the compound. He denied this so I repeated the question and asked whether he was absolutely sure of this and he said there was definitely not a wireless set, then I told him if he was lying I would hit him and he answered 'that will be alright'. At that time I had Lt. Wells' diary in my pocket. I took it out with my left hand and showed it to Wells, and with my right hand I hit him. I only hit him once. I did not hit him repeatedly." Despite Hoshijima's statement, Lt. Wells received severe punishment.

Hoshijima continued "I told him to take me to the spot where the wireless was. He took me into the carpentering room and we look for the set in this room and could not find it, after this he took me to the office, this was the technical section office of the PWs and Wells opened a hidden compartment under a desk and even there there wasn't a wireless. At last after further investigations two Captains told me the following: On a previous night they saw Captain Matthews coming back from the latrines with a shovel. This was about 11 o'clock at night. I went there and near the latrine saw some overturned earth and digging at this position I found the wireless."

Hoshijima had previously arrested the officers in Matthews' cubicle. Two were taken and were seen standing to attention outside Jap HQ and Captains Rowell and Waddle were placed in the cage. Pte. Reither was already there for another offence. Later, when Captain Filmer returned from the working party and found his colleagues were arrested he asked Capt. Cook what he should do. He was taken to Lt. Moritake by Osawa the interpreter and later placed in the cage with Capt. Rowell and the others. More arrests followed.

Pickering and Sgt. Stevens of the power plant were taken to the Jap office for interrogation. Apparently Stevens admitted to a small part in the general plot and he was immediately struck and kicked by Lt Moritake. Pickering did not make any statement and was told to remain. Sticpewich and Davidson were then brought to the office for interrogation. Sticpewich was told that everything was known about the wireless set and also that he had assisted. Sticpewich refused to admit any guilt. He was then bound. Together with Davidson and Pickering they were forced to stand out in the middle of a thunderstorm and they were left in the rain for eight hours. At odd times they would be brought in for further questioning. Pickering and Davidson were without shirts all this time. At 1.30 a.m. on the morning of 26th they were taken to the cage and, still bound, were put inside. The rain had tightened the ropes around the men's arms and as a result of that they lost all use of their arms for a time. Reither undid their bonds.

On the 22nd of July Lt. Weynton was arrested and placed in gaol. There he was subject to intensive questioning and torture. Soon after, Corporals Richards, Small and Mills were also arrested.

The cage was on stilts and was two feet off the ground, it measured 6' x 5' x 4' and was made of wood with wooden bars and had barely enough head room for a sitting man. While they were in the cage their rations alternated between normal camp rations and salt and water. They were only allowed out of the cage twice a day for sanitary purposes and often were forced to urinate through the bars of the cage. The three officers together with Reither, Sticpewich, Pickering and Davidson were released. Sgt. Stevens was bound and taken to Sandakan.

Alex Funk, who was arrested at Kemansi on 8 August, was taken to Sandala Estate where his wife Maggie and his other relatives were 'grilled' regarding the conversion of Australian currency and the whereabouts of a .303 rifle that was thought to be hidden close to the Mile 8 camp.

The forceful Wong Yun Siow, or 'Pop' as he was known to the Australians, found thirteen a very unlucky number because it was at 10 a.m. on 13 August 1943 that Ehara, alias 'The Bully', an infamous member of the Kempe Tai, together with a compatriot and Lamberto Apostol, came to a rice field near Mile 8 and called out 'Pop's' name. He was then taken away to the Tannahmerah Road interrogation centre. On arrival he was slapped twice on the face and asked where the radio valves were. Apostol then addressed the Japs in his presence and said that he had given Wong two valves. Wong denied this but the Japs immediately gave him the log torture. Ehara followed this up by giving him the water torture and continued to slap him across the face with a Japanese wooden slipper. This continued for half an hour. The Japs kept asking him throughout the treatment what he had done with the valves. Wong repeatedly answered that he had thrown them away and that they had been broken. Ehara then unsheathed his sword and threatened to decaptiate 'Pop' who immediately responded by appearing to be very frightened. Wong was then scratched for fifteen minutes and severely lacerated with a sword scabbard. He was perspiring freely from the water torture at this stage but he still told the Japs that he had broken the valves and had not given them to anybody. He was then tied on a table in the form of a cross and again severely beaten. After being kept in this position for an hour he was taken into another room nearby.

Amongst his fellow inmates in this room were Dr. Taylor, Mr. Phillips, Mr. Mavor, Apostol, Chan Ping, Abin, Capt. Matthews, Sgt. Stevens, Alex Funk, Paddy Funk, Felix Adzcona and Heng Joo Ming. Conversation was not permitted and Wong could see Capt. Matthews and Dr. Taylor conversing with each other by spelling out letters on their thighs with their fingers. Wong had heard that the Japanese had a 'soft spot' for mentally afflicted people and decided on a plan of action. He developed a wild look and roughly opening the door he tried to jump down the stairs. The Japanese immediately grabbed him and transferred him to the Sandakan Gaol. He was released from the Gaol on 18 November and fined the sum of fifty dollars. When he paid this amount the Japs gave it back to him and told him to buy medicine with it. 'Pop' Wong's acting ability probably saved him a lot of misery and pain.

The corpulent Goh brothers and Foo Seng Chow were arrested as the result of information given by Lagan. The Goh brothers reasoned that they could not stand up to much in the way of torture and so they admitted to only having given the escaped PWs of the 2/29 Bn. small quanitities of food on a couple of occasions. Damodaran, the gaol clerk and Gurlaman of the NBAC, were also arrested in August. Damodaran was severely thrashed with a malacca cane around the face and head. He was also kicked and eventually forced to sign a confession.

And still the arrests went on, the list of people grew as more Asiatics and Australian PWs were gathered in by the sadistic Japanese. Johnny Funk was arrested early in September 1943. During his interrogation he received five forms of torture, firstly the log torture, then

Capt. James Edward Heaslop. QX.6413. 2/10 Fd.Regt.R.A.A. Cremorne, NSW. Died Ranau 19 July 1945. Age 30. Capt. Heaslop was in charge of Canteen until 1944 when supplies were denied by Japanese. *Pic: L. Heaslop*

Capt. George Robin Cook. NX.76185. H.Q. A.I.F. Mittagong, NSW. Appointed Chief Administrator Sandakan POW Camp. Handed over all Records to Capt. Watanabe for despatch to Allied Forces. Watanabe stated he destroyed the documents at Ranau. Capt. Cook was shot by Japanese August 1, 1945. Age 38. *Pic: Mrs.P. Balderston*

the ju-jitsu course, the bashing across the spine with the wooden swords, the striking across the forehead with the small whip and also the slipper slapping. After Johnny's interrogation he was placed in the same room as Capt. Matthews. Captain Matthews, who had undergone terrible torture, gave Johnny the full story of the organisation by tapping it out in morse code with his foot. He told Johnny that he had not divulged anything and advised him not to say anything either. His last message to Johnny was "If anything happens to me Johnny, and if you ever happen to meet my wife, or any Australians, tell them that I have died for my country."

One of the members of 'E' Force, Spr. Keating (with Marshall, Jenson and Davis) when staging through Kuching made contact with Mr. Harry Keith, a Forestry official from Sandakan, seeking his help and advice on escape. It appears prior to this Harry Keith gave him a note to Lamberto Apostal as one of his Sandakan employees who could be trusted. Keating and one of his mates were probably the men who crawled up to the wire and spoke to Mrs. Agnes Keith — two Australians told her they were going to escape (ref: Three Came Home by Agnes Newton Keith). (It also appears Harry Keith's letter implicated him at a later date when he was tortured in Kuching and Suga probably intervened to save him from further punishment.)

When Keating eventually arrived in Sandakan he was able to make enquiries as to where he could make contact with Apostal. This was later made through Moo Sing. Apostal sent money and advised them to be patient. When the Underground collapsed Keating's contact, Apostal, was arrested with the note from Keating, possibly implicating Keith.

Hoshijima was in a foul mood, annoyed he had the security problem on his hands, he feared there would be some sort of uprising. The thought of submarines picking up and dropping intelligence operatives concerned him greatly. He could not piece the jig-saw together, he was getting all sorts of stories — some of them matched, others had him confused. He was not getting any satisfaction from Matthews, neither were the Kempe Tai, so he took his temper out on the men on the drome; the 'basher gangs' stepped up their presence.

Cpl. Fitzgerald was punished by Hoshijima for burning rice on a shovel to make colouring for a stew — if circumstances had been normal Hoshijima would have had his work cut out containing Fitzgerald as he was a professional fighter accustomed to roughing it with the best of Jimmy Sharman's Troupe.

Lt. Okahara, the officer who brought 'B' Force to Borneo, was now supervising work there. Lt. Moritake, officer in charge of the guards and a nasty operator, was taking every opportunity of belting someone over the ears and the guards were given a free hand. The spite was also taken out on the civilians trying to sell food to the camp. The only Japanese who did not get involved with aggressive conduct was Sgt. Major Ichikawa — an old hand who had served 15 years in China — and the fellow who turned up on Armistice Day 1942 proudly wearing the Allied medals of World War I. He did his best in bartering, bargaining, with the natives, trying to get the best deal on food supplies. Often he warned PWs not to talk so much about war news. He could understand and speak a fair bit of English. Yet there is no evidence he pulled anyone into line.

Despite all the pressures in the camp a gambling house was established under one of the huts where PWs could play any game of chance. In order that they could operate at night they hooked into the main supply of electricity which was uncovered power lines running through the huts. This operation attracted elements of 'con men' who thought 'B' Force was going to be a holiday home.

Lt. Moritake, was an unpleasant character at any time, to be avoided if possible, but when there was no alternative the result of any approach could be quite unpredictable. Capt. Picone, the camp medical officer, requested Moritake return an electric light bulb which had been taken from the camp hospital operating theatre. Moritake became abusive and forced Capt. Picone to stand to attention. At the conclusion of this tirade Moritake started hitting Picone with his closed fist, knocking his glasses off and finally knocking him off his feet. When he regained his feet the beating continued until Picone's face was bruised and marked. He was then made to face the sun, standing to attention, outside the guard room for a period of 2 to 3 hours before he was allowed to return to camp.

Hoshijima, at this stage, addressed the officers and confidently told them 'Your lives are in my hands — you will finish the drome'. With all his problems emerging he became more aggressive.

During the period of arrests the rice ration was again cut, bashing increased on the working parties and the guards became more aggressive, picking on PWs for the least trivial matter.

Tobacco was in great demand. It came in the form of evil smelling substance called 'Java Weed' which seemed to have been artificially coloured. The PWs washed it a couple of times and dried it in the sun. Paper of course was scarce, even the edges of the sacred letter from home were smoked and when there was nothing else they were able to use the young bamboo leaf in its curled form as a cigarette paper. Some addicts, desperate for a smoke, bartered some of their food for a cigarette. The lucky PWs who carried a Bible were able to exchanges pages for food. The smart operators could split the pages of the Bible and double their sales. Smoking Bible paper was referred to as a 'Holy Smoke'.

Paper was never available for toilet requirements so leaves were carefully selected in size and texture. It was not uncommon for some of the men to get a good supply carefully put away in a coconut shell.

Although Dr. Taylor and Capt. Matthews were closely connected as far as the Organisation was concerned they did not meet until the arrests had taken place. What a contrast they made, the tall, thin, bearded Matthews and the short, studious, inoffensive looking Dr. Taylor. Despite the contrast in their appearances both of them will always be remembered as the heroes of the Sandakan saga.

The Japanese finally settled on fifty-two civilians and twenty PWs as the total required for the trial of those concerned in the 'Sandakan Incident'. They left Sandakan for Kuching on October 19 and within a week the officers on the drome were ordered back to camp, given little notice to collect their belongings and assemble for transportation to the wharf where the coastal steamer 'Tiesen' was lying. No time was given to them to farewell their men — and the men didn't know they had gone until they arrived back from work that night.

The Japs kept Capt. George Cook as Administrator, Capt. Heaslop, Canteen Officer, Lt. Gordon Good, Quartermaster, the three medicos, Capt. Oakeshott, Capt. Jeffrey and Capt. Picone. Despite representations they took two Roman Catholic padres and left the two Protestant chaplains, also Acting Padre Garland.

Captain Cook formed an Administrative Committee with the remaining officers and senior WO's. His assistants were W.O. Lawrie Maddock and Sgt. Harry Hewitt, who in better times had worked for the Manly Daily and when he enlisted became 2/20 Bn. Orderly Room Sergeant.

The senior NCO's or 'hanchos' as the Japs preferred to call them, would report incidents on the working parties and there in turn the matter would be taken up with the Japs by Captain Cook. What a thankless job to be on the end of the line for a bashing, depending on the mood of a Jap.

There was no immediate change in the daily life of the PWs at Sandakan after the departure of the officers. Work continued at the aerodrome and the PWs always had the company of Japanese 'kitchi' guards (Malay for 'small' and used by the Austrlians to signify young Japanese soldiers). By the end of 1943 there were very few of the men with leather footwear and tropical ulcers were increasing daily.

In November 1943 Captain Hoshijima was not satisfied with the amount of information they were able to 'extract' from Ernesto Lagan and his family so he called at the Lagan home. He informed Katherine her husband would soon be free again and this

VX.40573 W.O.II Norman Lawrie Maddock, Toorak, Vic.
Photo: Cliff Moss.

NX.26818 L/Cpl. John Joseph Prendergast. At age 16.
Photo: G.M. Prendergast.

NX .33361 Pte. Richard Murray 22 Bde. H.Q. Died Ranau 20 May 1945. Aged 30. Hurstville, N.S.W.
Pic: Frank Murray.

QX.11137 Pte. Victor Clyde Rummell. 2/26 Bn. Died 18 March 1945. Aged 38. Thalton, Qld.
Pic: Rhonda Brighton

was her last chance to talk. Every day for a week she had to report to him at 9 a.m. but her answer was always the same 'There is nothing I can say'. Hoshijima then told Katherine Lagan that he was very lonely and would she mind if her eldest son went to his office each day and played with him. She reluctantly gave her consent and for the next ten days the boy went to the Kempe Tai HQ. Despite the fact that Hoshijima loaded the boy with sweets, toys, Lux soap, the little boy gave him no information and each night was carried home at 2 a.m. sound asleep in the arms of a Jap. Japanese attention to Mrs. Lagan and her children ceased after this.

Chapter 3

The year 1944 commenced with the usual optimism — 'We'll be out by Christmas' — others thought earlier — some didn't believe they would ever survive. Malaria, with the combination of beri beri, was making many feel depressed, the odd Concert gathering helped the morale. Some were fed up with the old acts and laughed only because they had seen them before. However they never got bored listening to those who could sing and many remembered 'Happy Harry' Smith at Changi and how he would stand on the stage in silence and say 'You'll never get off the Island!' and everyone would laugh.

While rice was cut further conditions were reasonable but treatment unpredictable. For example, Hoshijima would invite Capt. Cook and Capt. Mills (British Army) to his house for a meal. Cook could not decline and he would endeavour to cajole Hoshijima into improving some aspect of treatment or conditions. Later in the year Cook was always embarrassed going to Hoshijima's house as he was compelled to walk past the cage knowing there would be many eyes watching him, their owners making derogatory remarks about their C.O. dining with the enemy. Some would say 'you can't blame him, at least he'll get a feed'.

The sick were growing in number — the hut which was a hospital was now too small to hold the number of patients.

The Japanese had made up their mind to make a big thing of the 'Sandakan Incident' and had arranged for five special judges to be brought from Singapore to conduct the trials. The prisoners in the meantime had been confined to what was called 'the fowl pens'. These were cages which contained about twenty men who were forced to sit, Japanese style, look straight to their front and not speak. They were often taken out for further interrogation which of course included the attendant tortures.

The trial was held in three groups. Dr. Taylor, Mr. Mavor and some of the Australian PWs had their trial on 3 February 1944. A bigger batch was tried on 29 February 1944 and Capt. Matthews, Lt. Wells and three other ranks were tried on 2 March 1944. As he passed the cages the gallant Captain Matthews signified to his fellow prisoners that he was to be executed. He calmly divided his food and possessions with his fellow prisoners before being taken out for execution and comforted their grief for him by saying that the Japanese would never beat the Allies and it was their duty to maintain their morale.

When the prisoners came up before the judges for sentence they were tied, or chained, in groups of eight. The front group of eight were Ojaga Singh, Wong Mu Sing, Abin, Alex Funk, Heng Joo Ming, Ernesto Lagan, Felix Adzcona and Matusup. When the judge announced that they were to be executed, a pitiful scene ensued. Some of the sentenced men, weakened by their months of imprisonment and torture, began to weep loudly and beg for mercy. The group was dragged out of the court by a length of rope, still wailing.

Then a further group of eight were advised of their sentence. The Kempe Tai had probably been conferred with before the show; Hoshijima sent Osawa over to represent his interest and to make sure those detained did not stand a chance.

There were some surprises before the trials, indicating discussions must have taken place earlier with the prosecutors. Sgt. Col Landers was advised he was being released — he was given his boots and joined the officers camp. Sgt. A.W.. 'Joe' Weston was also set free; his name was confused with a Pte. A. Weston.

Sapper Keating died at Kuching before he stood trial, on 11 February 1944, from beri beri, malnutrition and amoebic dystentery. Had the Japanese allowed him to receive medical attention it is quite likely he would have survived. Mr. Mavor died from beri beri at Singapore on 5 May 1945.

Capt. Matthews retained his valiant bearing to the end. He faced the firing squad unflinchingly, without an eye bandage, side by side with the eight loyal Asiatics on 2 March 1944. He was buried in a grave by himself while the other eight were buried in a common grave.

Colonel Walsh was informed of Capt. Matthews' execution on 2 March and was told a number of officers could attend his burial. The Service was conducted by Padre Henthorne, a civilian from the POW area. Col. Walsh, Major Johnstone, Lieuts. Esler and Ewen, two of his Sig. officers and Capt. Rowell attended. There were also Maj. Suga and other Japanese representatives. There were several guards present with fixed bayonets. Earlier, Australians from the British camp were called upon to dig the grave and act as bearers.

The helpers of the organisation who were sentenced to imprisonment at Kuching continued to be given a bad time. Some were put to work with the road gangs, others with timber cutting parties. On a number of occasions the prisoners were tied together to buffalo carts and were forced to act as beasts of burden. Some were on carrying parties taking supplies across the border of Sarawak into Dutch Borneo. When the re-occcupation of

Captain L.C. Matthews, G.C., M.C.

Captain Matthews was posthumously awarded the George Cross for gallant and distinguished services whilst a prisoner of war of the Japanese at Sandakan, British North Borneo between August, 1942 and March, 1944. During this period he directed an underground intelligence organisation and arranged delivery of sorely needed medical supplies, food and money to the prisoners of war. He was instrumental in arranging a radio link with the outside world and was also responsible for organising the British North Borneo Constabulary and the loyal natives in Sandakan into readiness for an armed uprising against the Japanese. He also successfully organised escape parties. Arrested by the Kempe Tai, he was subjected to brutal treatment and starvation, but steadfastly refused to implicate his associates. He was tried by a military court and executed by the Japanese, at Kuching, on 2nd March, 1944, and even at the time of his execution he defied the Japanese. The Military Cross was awarded for outstanding conduct during operations in Malaya.

Australian War Memorial.

NX.57905 Spr. W.H.W. Hinchcliff. Died 10 April 1945, Age 27, (see page 52). Corrimal, N.S.W. *Photo: Mrs. D. Dal Santo.*

WX.7999 Pte. R.P. Ferguson. 2/4 M.G. BN, Died 23 March 1945 on first march with the Dorizzi brothers. Toodyay, W.A. *Photo: W.G. Chitty*

Kuching took place in 1945 by the Australian troops, the surviving Asiatic prisoners who had helped the PWs in the Sandakan camp were taken to the 9 Aust. Div. Reception Camp at Labuan where they received medical treatment before being repatriated to their homes. Dr. Taylor, who was transferred to Singapore in March 1944, was also reunited with his wife at Labuan when the war ended.

The majority of the Australian PWs survived their imprisonment at Singapore after being transferred from Kuching. A number of the natives of Sandakan suffered still further as a result of their imprisonment. Their families were left without means of support, many of their homes were destroyed or ransacked after their arrest. In two cases young wives were forced to subject themselves to Japanese immorality to prevent starvation.

Sgt. Yusup was attending a Japanese school of instruction at Kuching at the time of his arrest in September 1944. When the Japs searched his house they found a pencil drawing of Capt. Matthews, pictures of the King and Queen and of Winston Churchill. The Japanese then began to beat Yusup's wife until she started to vomit blood. She returned to her kampong in 1944 still suffering from the treatment she had received from the Kempe Tai. Unable to get medicine or help for her injuries she died before the release of her husband from prison.

Guriaman's wife died of a broken heart one week after his arrest; also his twelve year old daughter died in 1944. Chan Ping's wife died while he was in prison. When Ng Ho Kong was arrested his wife and three children went to his parents' home to live. His mother and father died of worry soon afterwards, leaving his wife and children without support and as a result two of his children died from malnutrition.

Plan of 8m Camp – Late 1943-45

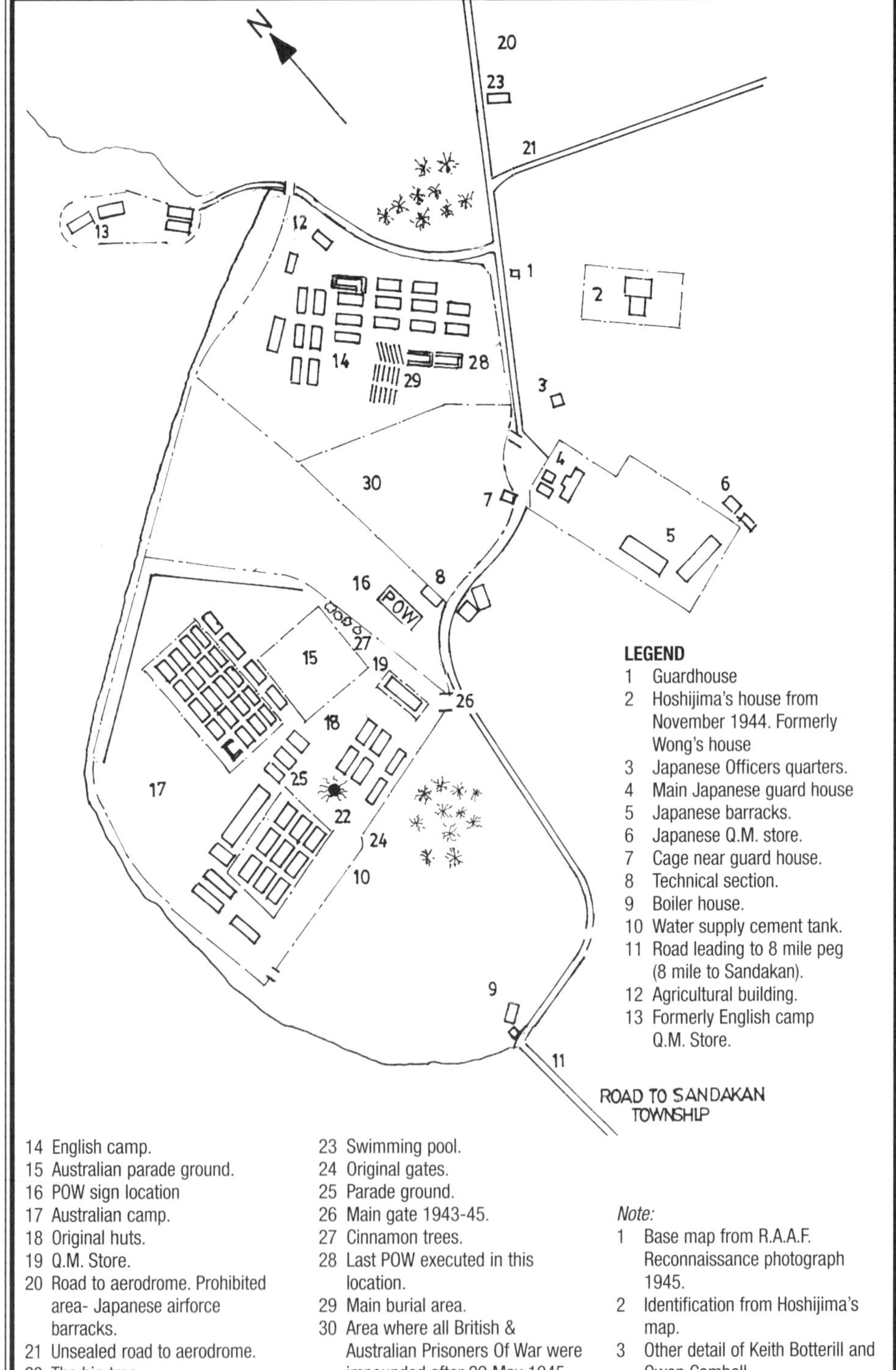

The complete list of sentences were:

DEATH

	Capt. L.C. Matthews, MC., 8 Div., Sigs. AIF *Jemadur Ojaga Singh, NBAC* *Sgt. Abin, NBAC* *Detective Ernesto Lagan* *Heng Joo Ming* *Wong Mu Sing* *Alex Funk* *Felix Adzcona* *Matusup bin Sungau*

IMPRISONMENT

15 Years	*Dr. J.P. Taylor* *Mr. G. Mavor* *Sgt. Yusup, NBAC* *Sgt.Maj. Yangsalan, NBAC* *Damodaran of the Sandakan Civil Prison*
12 Years	*Lt. R.G. Wells, 8 Div. Sigs., AIF* *Peter Raymond Dal Kiu Fook of Sandakan Civil Hospital* *Mehamet Salleh of Berhala Island Quarantine Station*
10 Years	*Lt. A.G. Weynton, 8 Div. Sigs., AIF* *Ng Ho Kong of Sandakan Light & Power Company* *Lamberto Apostol of Sandakan Forestry Department*
8 Years	*Inspector Guriaman, NBAC* *Chin Piang Syn (alias Chin Chee Kong)* *Amigaw and Soh King Seng — these two died in prison serving their sentence*
7 Years	*Peter Leong of Liberty Theatre, Sandakan* *Dick Majinal of Department of Agriculture*
6 Years	*WX.227 Sgt. A. Stevens, 2/4 Machine Gun Bn., AIF* *NX.68389 Cpl. J. Richards, 2/3 Motor Ambulance Convoy, AIF* *Henry Chang Ting Kiang* *Paddy Funk* *PC. Kassiou, NBAC* *Chan Tian Joo*
5 Years	*Foo Seng Chow* *Jakariah* *Si Dik — died in prison while serving his term*
4 Years	*WX.10932 Spr. D.G. Marshall, 2/6 Fd. Park Royal Australian Engineers, AIF. Died in Outram Road Military Prison, Singapore, in 1944, while serving his sentence* *Johnny Funk* *Felix Tang*

	Chan Ping *PC. Gorokon, NBAC* *PC. Lumatep, NBAC*
3 Years	*NX.73282 Sig. F.J. Martin, 8 Div. Sigs., AIF* *Mr. Phillips* *Samuel Aruliah of Sandakan Customs Department* *PC. Mohammed Tahir, NBAC*
2½ Years	*Lau Bui Ching* *Ngui Ah Kui*
2 Years	*TX.4197 Cpl. C.C. Mills, 2/3 M.A.C., AIF* *WX.9682 Spr. C.E. Jensen, 2/6 Fd. Park R.A.E., AIF* *NX.38818 Pte. S.G. Davis, 2/10 Ordnance Workshops, AIF* *Surat Min* *Mandor Kassim — died in prison while serving sentence at Kuching*
1½ Years	*NX.1685 Cpl. T.G. Graham, 22 Bde. HQ AIF* *Cpl. Roffely, 84 L.A.D.* *NX.26960 Cpl. A.L. Small, A.A.S.C.* *NX.27101 Spr. R. Davis, 2/12 Fd. Coy.* *NX.52132 Sgt. R.B. Holly, 2/18 Bn.* *NX.10567 S/Sgt. J.H. James, 27 Dental Unit* *NX.56669 Sgt. A.M. Blain, 2/12 Fd. Coy* *(Cpl. Small and Spr. Davis died at Outram Road Military Prison, Singapore, in 1944, while serving this sentence.)*
1 Year	*Goh Teck Seng* *Goh Teck Chai* *Dahlan* *Major Rice-Oxley* *PC. Kai of NBAC* *Dr. Laband*
6 Months	*QX.7940 Sgt. W.J. McDonough, 10 A.G.H.* *VX.64660 Pte. E.H. Rumble, 27 Ord. Bde. Wk. AIF*

In June 1944 the food ration was again cut, the rice ration was reduced to 8 ounces per man per day. The PWs were really on a starvation diet now. They were still able to get green vegetables but the variety was reduced to swamp water cabbage and tapioca root. Sweet potato was also available in small quantities. The issue of meat and fish virtually ceased after this date. The PWs raised a few pigs but could only kill them when the Japanese gave their approval, which seemed only to be given on the occasion of a Japanese holiday or festival. Dugong was the only real meat that the Japanese still issued, but it was seldom seen. The only other meat that the PWs were getting was the entrails of butchered beasts; the heart and liver were always taken by the Japs. Sometimes but rarely the men were lucky enough to get the feet or the head — less the tongue. (The meals were reduced to two per day in September when the rice ration was reduced to 6 ounces per man per day).

Charlie Forrester was one of the first to start a garden. Later every vacant patch of ground was cultivated with kang-kong which in turn attracted a bonus in the form of slugs.

It was frowned upon for anyone to steal the slugs from another's garden. The slugs were gutted, speared on to a wire, and slowly cooked over a fire.

Japanese brutality seemed to increase as the PWs got weaker. Sick men were subjected to all types of indignities for reporting sick and were often bashed and forced to take their place in the work party. Padre Greenwood on several occasions secreted himself as a member of a work party in order to prevent a sick man from being sent out. Eventually he was caught and paid for his unselfish actions by being imprisoned in the cage for a day and a half.

The men were being beaten for nothing at all. If one man stood up to wipe the sweat from his forehead the guard would come over and line the squad up then hit everyone across the back with long thin canes. Some of the prisoners who were bashed were in a very weak condition and sick. The sick men were actually beaten more than the others because the Japanese hated them and considered them to be a nuisance. Men were belted with sticks and rifle butts, if they fell down on the ground they were kicked by the Korean guards who sometimes used to kick them in the testicles. On occasions men were made to stand to attention and then the Korean guards brought up their knees into their testicles. If they collapsed water was thrown over them until they came to again, then the bashings would continue.

Japan had failed in Peace approaches through their delegation in Europe. In the field of battle she had not won any victories since 1942. Her armies in New Guinea were isolated and starving. They had set out optimistically and foolishly believing they could live from the land and by capturing supplies from the Australians. Isolated and lacking in supplies they were disorganised in New Guinea and in desperation they cut flesh from Australian dead.

Borneo was now isolated as the rest of the South West Pacific was but had not been ravaged by earlier fighting. If Japan had any chance of holding the southern region the airfields in Borneo would have to play a vital role as the sea lanes from Japan to the south were now severed by U.S. submarines. Only a few ships from each convoy from Singapore carrying essential oil from the Dutch Indies arrived in Japan after hugging the China Coast all the way to their homeland. Privately, Hirohito's Imperial HQ conceded the war was lost; they would have to return all captured territory since they moved on to the Mainland of Asia in the 1930's. They had hoped to be able to retain countries for colonising as the British had for centuries. Confidently, before declaring War on the United States and Great Britain, they had placed Peace Missions in Europe hoping to strike a deal — that was the best they could hope for. They were ignored.

Guards openly told the PWs they would have to die in battle — with that in mind they were determined to take it out on the PWs while they had a chance.

In Changi a Korean guard had observed Padre Sexton conducting Mass; at the completion of the Service the guard approached the Chaplain and said he was a Christian and explained that at home in Korea he had a family who were also Christians and he wanted to take Confession. Sexton told him he would have to lay his rifle and bayonet down before he entered the Chapel. The man told Sexton his officer had told him he was to be transferred to the New Guinea area where he was expected to die for the Emperor — obviously he was very depressed.

Soon after the Normandy landing in Europe Admiral Nimitz, with a force of 26 Carriers supported by one hundred other warships, attacked the Mariannas. By July 6 all organised resistance had ceased.

Saipan, with a large Japanese civilian population, was taken and of the 25,000 civilians 10,000 were now prisoners. Hirohito found the capture of them disturbing. Previously he had urged his commanders to promise those who died there an equal spiritual status in after life with that of the soldiers fighting and dying in battle. To make matters worse for the Emperor it was not long before the U.S. State Department, through the Swiss Government, offered to exchange the 10,000 civilians from Saipan with sick or wounded

Sandakan Camp Site after 29 May 1945. Note area cleared by wood party.

American prisoners of war. Of course nothing came of this proposal. Japan could not afford to let loose 10,000 civilians on the population with knowledge of what was in store for them in Japan. Instead, the Japanese again reassessed the value of Allied prisoners of war held by them in the hope they would be able to negotiate a more favourable deal in any peace talks.

Orders went out to Southern Command to move the healthiest PWs in Thailand (where there was the greatest concentration of them at that time including those who had worked on the Burma-Thailand Railway) to Japan as ships became available. The convoys were to assemble at Singapore and wait for an escort as U.S. submarines were causing heavy losses to Japanese shipping en route to Japan. The 'Rakuyu Maru' was carrying a total of 1300 Australian and British PWs including Brigadier Arthur Varley of Inverell, NSW. They first left Singapore in mid-1942 for Burma, having completed this task they were being transferred and the fittest of them were to go to Japan to work for the enemy war effort.

On September three ships were sunk by U.S. submarines. One was the 'Kachidoki Maru' with 900 British PWs, another was the 'Rakuyu Maru', with several hundred. Many were massacred as they hailed a Japanese frigate to pick them up, while others were rescued by other Japanese ships including Gnr. Tom Moxham who was in the same lifeboat as the Japanese ship's Captain. They cut away from Varley's group of 14 boats tied together and were picked up by a Japanese destroyer. Tom's brother, Harry, died on September 16 just hours before his group was rescued by an American submarine. The third Moxham brother, William, with the 8 Division was to become one of the six survivors of the Sandakan tragedy. It seemed to confirm Japanese officers had discretionary powers as other PWs were just left drifting. A total of 159 British and Australians were picked up by U.S. submarines and taken to Saipan. These men had been in the water for several days and were in a shocking condition. One of those picked up was Arthur Bancroft (known as 'Blood' to his comrades) — he was a sailor from HMAS Perth which was sunk off Java together with the USS Houston in 1942 — became a prisoner of war and was later taken to Burma to work on the Burma-Thailand Railway. Chosen as one of the fit he joined Varley's party for Japan. He was in charge of one of the rafts and had seen others picked up by the Americans and had watched as the submarine, fully loaded, sailed away leaving his lot behind. His turn came days later when the 'Barb' and 'Queenfish' were ordered into the area to search for survivors. The 'Queenfish' located Bancroft's raft. The prisoners were covered in oil, sunburned and in a pitiful condition. A crewman was surprised when one stood up, saluted him saying 'HMAS Perth!' Some of the men died on the way but all survivors were taken to Saipan where news of the rescue, together with full details of the Japanese atrocities and conditions on the Burma-Thailand Railway, together with the disposition of PW forces, became known to the world.

As a result of these embarrassing disclosures, Hirohito's HQ issued a further directive to all Commands that measures were to be taken to prevent PWs falling into Allied hands. The Emperor was personally implicated in this order.

From October on conditions deteriorated. Borneo was now isolated by sea. Up to this time, despite the brutality and illness, conditions were more or less bearable.

There were still some ships going to the oil ports of Tarakan and Balikpapan. Allied bombers from Morotai raided Sandakan, this was a great morale booster for the men and, despite casualities, they cheered as the aircraft rained bombs on the Japanese.

In October the U.S. forces, in an armada of 840 ships, assaulted Leyte and the size of the assault force gave the Japanese notice of American power in the Pacific.

In November the PWs had their morale boosted by the sight of the first large scale appearance of 75 B29's over Singapore. This sight sent shudders throughout the Japanese Southern Command. Even the guards in Borneo talked of 'America boom boom Singapore'.

As the Japanese position deteriorated so did the condition of the prisoners. Earlier, Sgt. Bill Hearl remembers a Japanese officer arriving in Thailand from Borneo at this time together with his batman, who was later to disclose to our men "In Borneo many men die, very bad". This was probably Colonel Otsaka, C.O. of the Sandakan Garrison, who spent several months there.

The Allies were close to Sandakan, the Japs were getting apprehensive and the PWs hopeful. It was at this stage that a large POW sign was made at the camp and put in place. It was not always visible from the air. The proximity of the Allies seemed to spur the Japs on to greater efforts in an endeavour to reduce the number of PWs, either by starvation, hard work or a combination of both. The PWs were supposed to maintain a working party strength of 800 a day in September 1944. These men were used on the aerodrome, wood cutting, wood carrying, road gangs, gardening party, water carrying party. No. 1 Compound, which held the Australian PWs, had a strength or just under 1600 at this time and the figure of 800 men for work parties was extremely difficult to maintain due to the fact that in September there were 400 hospitals patients, 200 men classified 'No Duty' because of illness etc. and nearly 150 'Permanent Duty', men who were engaged as hospital orderlies, cooks, camp administrative staff etc. There were few men to spare if some were to be allowed to rest to conserve strength. The Gardening Party consisted of all sick men; towards the end of 1944 there were very few PWs who did not have at least one leg or foot ulcer. The rapid spread of dysentery can be attributed partly to their work and most cases of secondary infection of ulcers came from PWs who had been on the Party detail. Their main work was spreading human excreta mixed with water; it was ladled out of buckets with small tins and the barefooted PWs were soon carrying the infection around on their feet.

Sapper Hinchcliffe was discovered by the Japanese to be away from his work party at the aerodrome. He was later found to be in possession of pieces of coconuts. The Japs forced him to kneel on a piece of rough firewood and a log was placed behind his knees. Then followed the usual 'see-saw' act by two Japs one on each end of the log to complete the 'log' torture with the exception it was added to by a Jap jumping on the log as well. His appeals for relaxation of the treatment went unheeded. Pte. White and Pte. Young also received the treatment. They were forced to face the sun with their arms at their side while this took place. Several other guards came up at odd intervals and added to the torture by beating the men harshly with a stick. Hinchcliffe was forced to stand to attention outside the guardhouse after this. As soon as he started to relax through fatigue the guards would come out and bash him. He was then placed in the cage; he was not given food and could only get water when he was allowed to visit the latrine twice a day. Early morning and late afternoon he would be taken out and beaten; for the remainder of the time he was forced to sit at attention.

A guard, Kitamura, who had previously earned the loathing of the men by his habit of tripping them up and displaying feats of judo on them, went out of his way to tantalise the pitiful inmates of the cage. He would walk up and down in front of the cage, eating food and throwing tasty scraps away while the starving men gazed at him. He would add to their misery by throwing things at them or spilling half their meagre issue of food in front of them. To obtain the little food they eventually did get they were forced to humble themselves on the ground in front of Kitamura and thank him profusely for it. Failure to do this resulted in further bashings. The Japs would not let the confined men wash so they became infested with lice and covered with scabies and other skin complaints. The Japs would hold their noses and spit on the PWs when they passed them.

Earlier, soon after their arrival, Kitamura had seen Cpl. Ron Spurway wrestling with one of his mates so he approached him where he was working in the kitchen. The ashes had just been raked out from under the cauldron to let the rice steam out when Kitamura said 'Okay — we wrestle!' Spurway tossed him into the hot ashes and, to everyone's amazement, Kitamura just got up, wiped off the ashes and left. 'Juicy' Spurway (as he was affectionately known) was expecting him back in any moment with reinforcements, but nothing happened — Kitamura preferred to stand over the weak.

The first bombs fell on 14 October 1944. The Japanese had introduced a black-out prior to this and had laid down strict rules regarding smoking and the showing of lights. The reaction of the PWs to the raids was naturally a very favourable one and a comfort to know that the possibility of relief was more than just a chance. A force of ten P38 Fighter planes strafed the aerodrome on 22 October and damaged sixty Jap aircraft on the ground. Due to the fact that the POW sign was badly placed the PW camp itself was strafed by two planes during the raid and three PWs in No. 1 Compound were killed. The PWs appealed to the Japanese after this incident to have the sign moved and placed on high ground between Nos. 1 and 2 Compounds and this was done.

The introduction of the blackout, together with the fact that the PWs were hungrier than at any previous time, was responsible for the after dark foraging parties. The men would sneak out through the double apron wired fences and seek or steal food. They became very daring, and a party of eight broke into the Jap QM Storeroom which was only a few yards from the Guardhouse and continually under the eyes of the ten guards. The QM Store incident occurred in November but it was not until December that the culprits were caught while eating some of their loot. The Jap search after this revealed many private caches of food and a quantity of stolen goods.

The eight men concerned in the QM Store raid were severely bashed and placed in the cage. Each morning they were taken out and given the Japanese form of PT which meant a severe beating interspersed with kicks to various parts of the body. Some men were carried back into the cage crying, others were barely conscious but a bucket of water thrown by a Jap brought them back to the painful reality they were still alive. Sgt. Bancroft and Ptes. Annear, Anderson (Bowe) were sentenced to be imprisoned for the duration. After three months of the sentence all had died. Their reason for breaking into the QM Store was to obtain food for the sick men.

One of the men involved in the QM Store raid was Pte. Keith Botterill. This party

NX.31849 Pte. Percy R. Addison, Inverell, N.S.W.
Photo: Mrs. Jean Campbell

NX.17793 Pte. John Cooney, Bass Hill, N.S.W.
Photo: M. Devereaux.

did not receive any water for the first three days in the cage; the Japs then gave them water and stood over them, forcing them to drink and drink until they were sick. After the seventh day they were given just enough food to keep them alive.

One night in December, Ptes. Barber, Clement, and Weeks were caught outside the wire by the Japs, as they were stealing food from the PW garden. They were put in the small cage on the hill and Hoshijima took advantage of the occasion by addressing the camp. He told them that the three Australian PWs were caught stealing food outside their camp and that he took a very serious view of it; any acts of a similar nature would result in the culprits being shot on sight. He told the camp that Barber, Clement and Weeks were going to be severely punished, he also punished the camp by stopping their rice ration for that day despite the fact it had already been cooked.

The three men were brought from the small cage after seven days and placed in the large cage near the Jap guardhouse. The altered appearance of the men came as a shock to the others; they had obviously been ill-treated and without food for the previous seven days. The change in Barber and Clement was particularly noticeable. Barber's weight when he was put in the small cage would have been about twelve stone, while Clement, a provost, was also a heavily built man. Ten days after their transfer to the large cage Barber died; when his body was placed in the morgue it weighed only six stone. This loss of weight, in a man who was free from illness and disease when he was placed in the small cage, was due only to the treatment he had received at the hands of the Japs following the sentence meted out by Hoshijima. Shortly after Barber's death, Pte. Weeks was carried from the cage on a stretcher. He was suffering from paralysis and internal injuries caused by his treatment and he died three days later; Pte. Clement was very ill when he was released and died five weeks later.

A Chinese youth, Wong Hiong, who came to the camp at this time to work for the Japs in their cookhouse, was shocked and horrified at the appearance of the white men whom he had always known as immaculate, well-groomed and nourished. What a shock it was to see the pitiful specimens that the Japs were lording it over at the camp. Painfully thin men with their ribs and facial bones showing, clad only in a 'G' string, legs that were little more than skin wrapped around bone and knees swollen to nearly the size of a football due to beri beri. The sight of white men without buttocks amazed him, also their yellow, wrinkled skin, swollen sagging stomachs and their painful, shuffling gait. Some of them looked like Indian fakirs or blinded oriental beggars with their tattered clothing and sticks used to assist them in walking. Some of the guards were from Formosa (Taiwan) and spoke Chinese. Sometimes they would speak with Wong Hiong, especially after they had been drinking. During one discussion he heard a Jap say, when referring to the PWs, 'Don't give them clothes, clothing keeps them healthy'. The Japs were also getting weaker at this time.

Many cartons and packages marked 'U.S. RED CROSS' were seen in the camp by various PWs and WO. Sticpewich actually saw some of them being unpacked in the Japanese RAP for the use of their own personnel. The drugs and bandages were badly needed at the time. There is no doubt that the Japanese policy was to systematically murder the PWs, either by starvation, ill-treatment and neglect or all three.

It was early in December that the food collecting parties came into operation. They consisted of about twenty PWs who went out under the guard of two Japs to dig up sweet potatoes and tapioca from the native gardens. Half of the food they collected was given to the PWs, but the Japs stopped issuing rice later and the vegetables collected had to take its place.

The PWs received a great Christmas box on Christmas Day 1944 in the form of a heavy bombing raid by Liberators at 1100 hours, putting the aerodrome out of action and ending Japanese air activities in the Sandakan area. The raid also uncovered some of the sabotage which the PWs had carried out over a long period. Newly made bomb craters revealed Japanese shovels, chunkels, picks, metal bars, trucks and many other useful appliances; all had been buried while the PWs were working on filling in and levelling off for the aerodrome. The day after the big raid found a party working filling in craters as the Japs endeavoured to make one strip serviceable again. The Jap guards at the time were about 110 in number, but the rapid deterioration of the PWs health and the increasing number of deaths did not require any guard reinforcement.

After they were no longer required to work on the aerodrome their usefulness to the Japanese ceased. While malaria was taking its deadly toll in the camp no less that 160,000 quinine tablets were lying unused in the Japanese RAP at the camp together with many other medical stores which were worth more than gold at this particular time.

The Allied air domination of the area around Borneo virtually cut that country off from the rest of the Japanese controlled areas and Japanese shipping was rapidly approaching the point where it would have to be referred to in the past tense.

The Japanese forces in North Borneo at this time came under the 37 Japanese (Southern) Army Corps, commanded by Lt. Gen. Baba, and in December 1944 they commenced to take steps to secure their forces in the British North Borneo area. Their appreciation was that an Allied landing would take place on the west coast and they desired to transfer their main forces to that area in order to meet the threat.

It was Japanese policy not to let Allied PWs fall back into Allied hands, and in all areas rather elaborate plans were drawn up and precautions taken to ensure that no such thing happened. They were determined to adhere to this policy even though it would probably mean mass murder. They had managed to get the PWs in the Sandakan area to such a physical state by starvation and ill-treatment that any immediate threat by them in the form of physical action could be quickly dealt with. Although the Jap appreciation was that the west coast was the danger spot they knew it was still a little early to take this appreciation as a water-tight conclusion. Should the threat by the Allies switch to the east coast the Japs knew that they had a method of evacuating the Sandakan PWs away from the coast and that this method would probably be the means of disposing of the PWs as well.

The roads in British North Borneo are confined to several of the larger towns situated on the coast. There was no way of travelling from east to west prior to the war except by sea or air. There was no road across Borneo and, apart from native trails, there was no other method available for the interior peoples when visiting adjacent villages. There were several British tracks or 'rentis' running from the east coast to nearby districts such as Beluran in the Labuk area etc. Prior to the war very few white men could claim to have been across this hazardous country by foot. After the Japanese occupation of British North Borneo they realised it was a necessity to have a method whereby troops and gear could be moved by land from one coast to another, so they made plans to make this possible. By using Javanese labour they were able to cut a rentis through jungle from the 15 mile peg where the road finished from Sandakan to Ranau, approximately 165 miles to the west of Sandakan and 76 miles east of Jesselton. At Ranau this rentis linked up with a British surveyed and built track from Tuaran near the 23 mile peg on the road which runs north from Jesselton.

When the Japanese started work on the rentis from Sandakan they employed a native, Kulang, who was Headman of the Dusan people in the area. He was an outstanding hunter, deadly with blowpipe and rifle, well skilled in the use of his 'parang', and like most of the people of Borneo he hated the Japanese. At every opportunity he made sure he did something to hamper them. He alone holds the secret of many a Jap death in Borneo. His job as pathfinder and surveyor was to cut the rentis from Sandakan end to the Maunad River (Sungei Munyed) as it was considered he knew the area best. He used his knowledge to take the rentis through the most difficult path he could find; unfortunately he was not to know then that the hundreds of British and Australian PWs would suffer as a result of his endeavours to sabotage the Japanese war effort. Many a time he deliberately arranged to cut the track up the side of a steep hill to make conditions difficult for the Japanese.

Hoshijima and his officers now felt it safer to be close to the PW camp and get the benefit of the POW sign displayed between the No. 1 and No. 2 Compounds so he vacated the home he boasted of as previously belonging to Agnes Keith, evicted Mrs. Wong and family and moved into their spacious weatherboard cottage. Built well above ground level he used the space beneath the house to store the rice he was withholding from the PWs. About this time Sticpewich was assisting moving the rice and was able to lift two bags; he was regarded as the fittest in the camp and resentment of his position was building up.

By late 1944 the Australian Government were well informed of the situation at Sandakan. Captain Steele had been evacuated to Australia by U.S. submarine with Wallace carrying Sgt. Blain's letter to the Minister for the Army, Mr. Ford. (Sgt. Blain was the member for the Northern Territory in the House of Representatives.)

The Australians had an up-to-date briefing also from the survivors from the 'Rakuyu Maru' and other intelligence sources.

The PWs left at Sandakan derived no benefit from the efforts of the escape party. Many had dreamed of their A.I.F. mates crashing through the camp and everyone able had planned what course they would take.

"It was Christmas 1944, 'Ramona' was on guard outside the fence at 6.30 a.m., one of our men was there smoking which was at an authorised time and 'Ramona' called him over to the fence several times. The PW took no notice of him and after a while answered him back, telling him to 'Go and get f......!' The PW could not be identified in the half light except for a bandage on his leg, so when 'Ramona' came off duty at 8 a.m. everyone with a bandage on his leg was pulled out of the work parties and put in a separate squad. A few other guards stood around while 'Ramona' walked through the squad bashing every man and concentrating his thrashings on every wound which was bandaged" said Sticpewich.

Top left: QX.11174 Sgt. H.T. Taylor. 2 Coy. A.A.S.C. Died Sandakan 5 June 1945. *Photo: V. Grayson*

Top right: QX.14844, Gnr. C.G. Johnson 2/10 Fd.Regt. R.A.A. Died on first march 11 February 1945. Age 32. Toowoomba, QLD. *Photo: E. Jane Oliver*

Bottom left: NX.58549 Sgt. W.R. Mann. 2/10 Fld.Amb. A.A.M.C. Died Ranau 6 July 1945. Arncliff, N.S.W. Photo taken at brother Robert's wedding. *Photo: J. & G. Mann*

Bottom right: QX.17462 Pte. E.H. Gower. 2 Coy. A.A.S.C. Died Sandakan 15 September 1942. Age 41. *Photo: R.M. Gower*

Chapter 4

The work on the aerodrome was abandoned on 10 January 1945 and there was no official issue of rice by the Japs after that date; they were able to use their own reserves which amounted to 4 oz. rice per day. The outside leaves of the swamp water cabbage were the main item of diet; the Japs kept the heart of the vegetable for their own use. Sometimes the PWs would come in for a grand treat when they would be given fly-blown meat condemned by the Japs, or sun dried fish which had gone bad. The PWs cooked them without oil and ate them ravenously. Their drinking water came from a buffalo wallow, now being used as a dam.

Then all knives, shaving gear and any other item which could be used as a weapon were taken. Unable to cut their hair it became long and matted and unless you were close to the particular man it was not possible to readily identify him. Some of the survivors remembered many as they used to be, but could not recall them on the march. Again they were broken up into small parties.

Hoshijima's horse, which was, like the PWs, tied up for the duration, was now in the same condition as the men. It was generously given to the PWs for food. At this time about 650 had died and there were about 700 men able to work from the original total of 2,700 men.

When Lt. Gordon Good made representations to Sgt. Maj. Ichikawa to purchase food from the natives, he replied he had approached Hoshijima who rejected the proposal and warned him on NO account were the prisoners to obtain additional food. He seemed sympathetic but was unable to help.

The ration squeeze was further tightened. Hoshijima must have been pleased with himself carrying out the Imperial orders to the letter — he still had several hundred bags of rice hoarded under his house and knew the several hundred PWs in hospital had no hope of surviving on the present ration of 4 oz. of rice.

Rex Blow and Jock McLaren, who escaped from Berhala Island soon after 'E' Force arrived from Singapore, remained in the Philippines fighting the Japs and seemed to be enjoying it. They probably were the most experienced guerilla fighters in Australian forces at the time; they were now ordered to proceed to Morotai where they were to meet General Blamey who requested their transfer. This seems to confirm Blamey never considered up to this time any move for the relief of PWs in Sandakan. In April the two men arrived at Land H.Q. where they were outfitted in new Australian hats in preparation for their meeting. Blamey was well briefed on their exploits and fighting the Japanese in their own territory. They talked for some time then Blamey explained the forthcoming activities against the Japanese and the part they were expected to play. They raised the subject the two had often talked about since their escape. McLaren broached it "What about the blokes behind the barbed wire in Sandakan — can we help them?" "I think we can", Blamey said. "They had reports on the condition of the prisoners"... "and we know where they are", he said. "Look General" said McLaren "we know the Jap Garrison; it is at Lahat Dutu and that's nowhere near the camp at Sandakan. Why can't we go in with parachute troops and get them out on to barges on the coast? I know a spot where we could beach not three miles from the camp, there's a road there too". Blamey looked at McLaren "You think it could be done?" "Of course it could be done!" said McLaren.

They talked it over and finally General Blamey said "If it could be fitted in with other operations we'll do it — and you two will be in it". As they parted, Blamey said "By the way, you're both confirmed a rank and you'll be able to go on leave to Australia". Private Jock McLaren was now Captain and Lieut. Blow was now Major.

McLaren and Blow probably had a better appreciation than anyone of the situation in Sandakan camp and strength and condition of Japanese forces in the area. Their proposal was studied, code named 'Kingfisher' but over-planned as a major amphibious operation so when it reached MacArthur's H.Q. it was thrown out.

Despite all the information available to Blamey's staff and to the Government there were no military or political initiatives to give the PWs any relief. It may be claimed had any large scale attempt been made to rescue the prisoners at Sandakan the repercussion elsewhere may have been disastrous. However, no repercussion took place after General MacArthur sent in a tank column in Manilla to rescue the PWs and Internees at Santo Tomas — for this action he received a good press in the United States. Other under-cover measures could have been taken to give the prisoners some relief from malaria and dysentery — that was not to be.

It was not until March 3 that the first S.R.D. members were landed into North Borneo to gather intelligence — parties too small and too far away to give escaped prisoners any assistance. Furthermore they were told not to be seen by the PWs.

The stage was set for the first use of the rentis by the Japanese against the expected Allied invasion. A signal was sent by 37 Jap Army Corps to the 25 Mixed Regt. in the Sandakan area. Instructions were given to Captain Yamamoto Shoichi to take delivery of 500 PWs from Captain Hoshijima at Sandakan camp and to march them across country from Mile 15, the end of the bitumen, to Tuaran, a distance of approximately 250 miles. The PWs were to carry ammunition and equipment required at Jesselton.

The track from Ranau first joins a vehicular road at Tamparuli, near Tuaran, but Tuaran with its police barracks etc. was the more favoured by the Japanese as a terminal point for overland parties coming from the interior bringing supplies for Jesselton. The Japanese plan was that when the PWs reached Tuaran they would be further used as coolies in carrying parties. The transfer of 500 PWs from the East to the West coast also suited the Japanese plan; it meant that if it was necessary to evacuate the remainder of the PWs from Sandakan it would not be so difficult.

Capt. Yamamoto had not been in the Borneo area long; he arrived at Labuan Island from Manchuria on 9 September 1944 and went to the Muara Islands where he stayed until middle October and then moved via Labuan, Jesselton and Kudat to Sandakan. On arrival at Sandakan he was put in charge of an Infantry unit numbering about 360 men who were camped in the 9 Mile region and were engaged in the construction of defence works etc. in the area. Yamamoto had barely been in the Sandakan area for three months when his orders came to march his unit overland and take the 500 PWs with him. The 44 year old, monkey-faced, bespectaled Yamamoto considered his new assignment a little peculiar for a man such as he, who had gone to Manchuria at the age of 21, held the appointment of Sgt. Major and been given a commission in the Emperor's Army during the lean years of 1938. Nevertheless he went ahead making arrangements to ensure that no time was wasted to get to the west coast. The proposed move was discussed with members of his unit and contact was also made with Capt. Hoshijima, the Commandant of the

Sandakan camp. The latter agreed with Yamamoto that the PWs chosen to make the journey with him would need to be the fittest men in the compounds. This did not mean that the men were actually fit because in January 1945 the average PW was three stone lighter than when he first came to Sandakan.

This was Yamamoto's first assignment since the outbreak of the Pacific War in which he was to have dealings with the white man. Up until now he had not been given an opportunity to vent his spleen on them and it gave him a certain amount of satisfaction to know that very shortly about 500 of their lives would be in his hands. An itinerary was received by him from 37 Army HQ laying down that the time for the march from Sandakan to Tuaran would be 21 days. Yamamoto wanted to improve on that time and it was his intention that Ranau should be reached in twelve days, an almost impossible task even with fit men. The march from Ranau to Tuaran represented the most difficult and strenuous portion of the whole track, even if the men did reach Ranau in twelve days they certainly wouldn't be fit to attempt the mountainous journey to Tamparuli and Tuaran. There can be no doubt that Hoshijima gave the sadistic Yamamoto much advice on how the PWs should be treated. The final arrangements made by these two were that Hoshijima was to deliver the PWs to Mile 9 where they would be taken over by group commanders. The men were to be marched out of the camp in groups of fifty, ten groups in all, and commencing from 28 February, one group to leave each day. Track rations were to be issued at the commencement of the march and supply depots along the route set up by the Japanese were to issue supplementary rations. The ration points were to be at Maunad (49 M.), Sapi (60 M.), Boto (103 M.), Pacan (120 M.) and Paginatan (138 M.).

On 24 January 1945 a further communication from 37 Army HQ intimated that they wanted the march to commence as soon as possible. Yamomoto had a conference with the officers who were to take charge of the various parties and gave them some instructions. Lt. Abe was not present at the conference due to the fact that his unit, the one to march with the PWs to Tuaran, was a few miles from where Yamamoto Butai were stationed. His instructions generally were that the march was to be completed as soon as possible and he expected the parties to reach Tuaran in 20 days; the order of the march was detailed, as also were administrative details connected with it. There was no doubt left in their minds when Yamamoto had completed his instructions that PWs who could not carry on or keep up with their party were to be disposed of.

The fact that the wet season was in progress did not seem to worry the Japs as a factor to be considered when finalising their plans. Yamamoto was to find that the streams to be crossed and the swamps to be traversed would have a slowing down effect on his programme. Hoshijima's only action, to overcome the absences of leather footwear among the PWs, was to issue them with the inferior cloth and rubber Japanese boots. Some badly worn shirts and shorts were given to PWs who had nothing else to wear.

Rumours were buzzing around the camp on 25 January 1945. Work on the aerodrome had already ceased two weeks previously and the PWs had received news that some of them were to be transferred to another part of Borneo where there was plenty of food and which was a veritable garden of Eden. To men who had been starved and beaten for three years there could be no doubt that this fantasy was true. Why should the Japs tell lies now, they know that they cannot hold out much longer, they want to fatten us up before the end comes, they realise how wrong they may have been and they are going to make amends at last! This was the reasoning of the men. Nothing could be worse than Sandakan so they accepted the news that there was to be a transfer as something to look forward to. The men to go on the march were picked out according to their physical fitness and most of the men who were not chosen were very disappointed. It was on 27 January 1945 that the personnel for the various parties were assembled. The men were given extra food to eat and Hoshijima gave approval for some of their small pigs to be killed. There were many touching farewells when the first party went, men who had enlisted together, or came from the same town, even brothers, were parted by virtue of their selection to make this journey. They had endured the same treatment during the past three years and now that the time had come to part it wasn't very easy. They wondered if they were to see each other again, they even wondered where they were going. Although they had been in Borneo for two years, and some for two and a half years, most of them had no idea of the geographical location of their camp nor did they know what lay to the west. Names like Jesselton and Kuching meant little to them except they had heard them mentioned, and knew that there were other PWs in those areas.

For some reason or other Hoshijima never made available the full number of 500 men that he was supposed to pass on to Yamamoto. Although he gave as a reason that there were not enough fit men he could have easily found another 45 men as fit as some of the others that he had selected; the original plan that Yamamoto was to follow made provision for ten parties each of 50 men, but owing to the fact that Hoshijima only provided 470 men the number of parties were reduced to nine. The 470 PWs included 370 Australians and 100 British.

Capt. Yamamoto Shoichi decided that he would move on the first day with the first party which would be in charge of his Adjutant, Capt. Iino Shiguro while Lt. Sato Tatsuo, his QM., was also to move with this party.

At 6 a.m. on 28 January 1945 a party of fifty Australian PWs were marched to the guardhouse at the camp. Included in this first party were Capt. Jeffrey of 2/20 Bn., WO. Watson, A.A.S.C., and Sgt. Smyth, 2/10 A.G.H. They were marched from the camp by several Formosan guards and then headed up the bitumen road away from Sandakan and were eventually taken to the rendezvous with the older soldiers that Yamamoto was taking to Tuaran. The thin, sick looking PWs with their tattered clothing and ugly ulcers did not impress Yamamoto as possible sources of danger. His main interest in them was to consider whether they could carry a load of fifty or sixty pounds weight. This load was made up of ammunition, rice, Japanese officers' gear and anything else that could be found to lessen their chances of reaching their destination in a fit condition. Hessian sacks contained the load. The ammunition was slung in front of the chest in the form of a hessian pack and the bag of rice etc. was carried on the back. About ten per cent of the PWs were in possession of leather footwear and the remainder, who wore the Japanese rubber boots, realised after the march of one mile from the camp to the rendezvous that their footwear was not going to stand up to any heavy wear. There had been some heavy rain prior to the commencement of the march and the rain was still in the vicinity. The usefulness of these boots in sticky mud was a debatable point, especially when the feet inside them were without socks.

The bitumen road continues for four miles past the camp, it then becomes a macadamised road for another three miles and then the track proper commences. The entrance to the 'green cage' is a track about ten feet wide which had been cut through the dense growth. Once you leave the road and commence to walk on this track you feel as if you have left the last shred of civilisation behind you; it feels as if you are starting a journey into another world. Tall timber and the brilliant green secondary jungle growth flourish in this area, also wild life. Elephant tracks often help to make the rentis uncomfortable in the wet season while cobras and many other varieties of reptiles are plentiful. Other forms of animal life in this area are orang-utan, monkey, mouse deer, barking deer, wild pig, wild cattle, crocodiles, iguana and several varieties of the cat family. In the Kinebalu area there are rhinoceros. Although the jungle is teaming with this wild life, with the exception of the reptile family, it keeps out of one's way.

When the first party and their Japanese escorts reached the end of the road at the 15 mile peg, they were a little puzzled as to what was to happen next. Certain additions were made to their load here and they were told that the food they had been issued with was to last them four days. They had not gone far on the rentis when it narrowed down to a width of about four feet and the mud became evident. The going became strenuous but the Japanese were not allowing for the fact that the PWs were weak after their treatment of the last three years. Although the country was flat generally speaking there were many short sharp rises which made it difficult for the men to negotiate with their heavy loads. The rubber boots were dragged off their feet by a combination of mud and their feet becoming slippery through perspiration. The leeches were particularly bad in this swampy region and the bare feet attracted many of these tenacious creatures which sucked greedily at the not too nutritious Australian and British blood. The brown leech of Borneo is an eager and aggressive customer. He can be seen on a blade of grass, rotting logs or stones, gently waving to and fro waiting for an opportunity to cling to anything that passes within reach, from a caribou to a headhunter. It does not alway confine its activities to the leg and foot and often enters the body by the frontal or rear passage, many fatalities have been caused by this happening.

It wasn't long before most of the men were without footwear and dark red lines on the legs indicated that the hungry leeches were already at work. The unpleasant factor about being bitten by a leech is that once it starts to bleed it is difficult to stop owing to the clotting qualities of the blood being affected. Violent thumping within the ears and short painful breaths told the men that their weakened state would not permit of their continued journey at the present pace, but the Japanese were not permitting any slowing down. Beating the back of the neck with a stick, or prodding with a bayonet or rifle butt were the rewards for a reduction of speed and thus the men were forced ahead like cattle. If Yamamoto wanted to complete the 164 mile journey to Ranau in twelve days he would have to average 13½ miles per day, an impossible feat for men in such a weakened state and carrying a load. A mile an hour in this type of country is very good going.

Many of the creeks were running high and a considerable amount of difficulty was experienced in crossing some of them. The undulating nature of the rentis, with the help of the rain, provided many slippery slopes and some of the barefooted men slipped and slithered down them causing many cuts and abrasions. Often the men were up to their knees in mud. The party soon began to stretch out despite the Japanese shouts and blows. The PWs who were at the end of the column did not profit by the rest periods because by the time they reached the rest point it was time for the column to begin moving again.

At the end of the first day No. 1 party had penetrated six miles into the 'green cage'. It had rained all the afternoon and it was still raining when that night they stretched themselves as best they could on the side of the rentis. If you were lucky enough to get hold of a few leaves from a banana palm you could make a 'sulap' (lean-to) or at least some form of cover which would keep the rain off. The stillness of the night was disturbed by the heavy breathing of the exhausted men or the racking coughs. Three years of malnutrition and the treatment they had received had caused many of the PWs to contract tuberculosis. The sound of the rain on the secondary growth drowned any insect noises that may have been in existence. Any thoughts that exhaustion permitted a PW to have must have been divided between home and whether he had been fortunate in being chosen to make the present trip. The Japanese had no need to worry about their prisoners escaping, the PWs did not have enough strength left to make a break for it.

The following morning brought no relief for the harrassed men. They were wakened stiff, hungry and cold and driven forward like beasts of burden. The mud began to get worse on the second day and the Sungei Tindok Kechil (Little Tindok River) began to cross the track quite frequently. At the time that No. 1 party were struggling along the rentis in the vicinity of the 21 Mile, No. 2 party were leaving the camp. The latter party consisted of 55 Australians and were under command of Lt. Hirano Yukihiko assisted by Warrant Officer Takeda Kazuhiro, the 26 year old Hirano also had 49 Japanese soldiers in this party. No. 2 party left Sandakan on 29 January and followed in the steps of their comrades who had left the previous day. No. 3 party commanded by Lt. Toyohara and assisted by Warrant Officer Gotanda Kiroku departed 30 January 1945. Included in the 55 PWs who made up this party was Pte. Keith Botterill of Katoomba, one of the six Australians destined to survive the tragedy of British North Borneo.

On the day No. 3 party departed from the camp the No. 1 party were having a difficult time of it as they headed towards Kolapis, the 42 Mile from Sandakan. The previous day they had reached the very swampy portion which commenced at the 27 Mile. This portion of the journey was still on the old Sandakan-Baluran rentis built by the British before the war; it was close to the estuary of the large and muddy Labuk river and at this point drained by the Samawang river. The area was thickly studded with the Nipa palm and the mud on the track was deep and treacherous. The PWs had very little left in the way of rations and were horrified when they were told that the rations which had been given to them at the commencement of the journey and which were only supposed to last them for four days were now required to last them for eight days. Half of the rations had been eaten by the second day and permitted only of two meals a day each meal consisting of about a pint of watery rice garnished with whatever greens they could get — usually edible foliage from the jungle and nearly always fern tips.

No. 4 party consisting of 50 PWs departed Sandakan on 31 January and was led by Capt. Mizuto assisted by Sgt. Major Ito Takeo.

Captain Mizuto Ryoichi later stated: "Although our Unit had been sent from Japan three months before and of it two-thirds were suffering from malaria, it was thought to be one of the well-conditioned troops amongst the Japanese forces in Sandakan. It could not be imagined that the PWs, who had been interned for three years, would be in the same condition as us.

"When I received PWs on 1st February 1945, I thought their conditions fairly endurable to make a journey, but it became clear on the afternoon of the first day that the bad condition of the road and the difficulty to overcome it was far beyond my expectation.

"Since then we have lost 4 Japanese and 10 PWs during the march of 165 miles in 18 days. The rest houses on the route were provided with neither medical personnel and medicine nor sufficient food to restore the party from fatigue. Several times we carried sick PWs by stretchers. To leave them on the way meant their death.

"The utmost difficulties on the way made us reach our destination four days later than the expected term of the march. In spite of our best efforts to carry them safely, 4 Japanese and 10 PWs died on the way.

"It was the order of the Army Headquarters that compelled us to venture such a painful and disastrous march.

"I think that our efforts were appreciated by the PWs who thanked us and regretted very much when we started from Ranau to Tuaran."

The No. 5 party consisted of 55 PWs led by Lt. Sato Tatsuo and Sgt. Maj. Sato Hideo, and departed Sandakan on 1 February 1945. The senior PW in this party was Warrant Office A. E. Johns of the Royal Army Medical Corps who impressed the Japanese immensely by the manner in which he attempted to protect the other PW members of his party.

No. 6 party left the camp on 2 February in the charge of Lt. Tanaka, a 48 year old officer of the old school. His assistant was Sgt. Yamaguchi and the strength of this party was 40 Australian PWs.

No. 7 party, which left on 4 February under the command of Lt. Sugimura, consisted of 50 mixed British and Australian PWs. Included in this party was Bdr. William Moxham of Toongabbie, NSW, another of the six survivors from Borneo. The senior PW was Warrant Officer Kinder of the Royal Australian Air Force.

No. 8 party consisted of 50 British PWs under the command of Lt. Morikawa assisted by Warrant Officer Toyo, and the last party —

No. 9 party commanded by Lt. Abe — consisted of 55 PWs from the United Kingdom. This party left on 6 February 1945.

NX.45310 Pte. S.A.N. "Sammy" Burns, age 16 at embarkation.

NX.27779 Cpl. Arthur Chapman.

NX.56325 Pte. Jack Stanley, Glebe Point. N.S.W.

NX.34301 Sgt. Arthur S. Lawrence, Nowra, N.S.W.

The Japanese rentis part from the old British Sandakan-Beluran rentis near the Kolapis and Labuk rivers. The PWs were told that they would reach the staging camp at Maunad (49½ Mile) on the fifth day. It was only this thought that enabled some of the men to hold on to their strength and not fall out before reaching Maunad.

No. 1 party arrived there on 1 February but several of the members had to be assisted over the last stretch between the Kolapis and Munyed rivers.

The Japanese staging camp was situated at Tangkual crossing and was not completed at the time of the arrival of the No. 1 party. The rest hut was still being built by the people of Maunad kampong. The Headman of this kampong was assisting his people to complete the attap work on the roof. His name was Kulang and his lively eyes took in as much as they could of the PWs without creating suspicion with the Japanese that he was over-interested. Kulang was small, light brown, lithe — he looked very inoffensive and rarely ever spoke but when he did his people took notice of him. He could hit an apple with his blowpipe from a distance of 200 yards people said and was extraordinarily skilful with a rifle. The 'parang' in its scabbard at his side was razor sharp and he wielded it in a manner which could only have come from long experience. This man had helped the Japanese to cut the rentis in the Maunad area and they had found nothing wrong with his work. He was also one of the best hunters in the whole of Borneo.

Kulang had an opportunity to speak to a member of No. 5 party which arrived at Maunad on 6 February. Sgt. Major A.E. Johns was in charge and Kulang was impressed with this tall fair man and his cheerfulness. Opposite the main Rest Hut on the other side of the stream was a smaller hut. On one occasion when WO. Johns called to the eleven PWs in the smaller hut to come over for their meal he told Kulang that there was one man in the hut who was ill and could not walk. When Kulang told Johns that if he hid the man in the bushes he (Kulang) would arrange to have him picked up and cared for, Johns approached Lt. Sato and made the same suggestion. Sato informed Johns that he

(The person described as W.O. Johns/Johnny Land is most likely W.O. Ron Laing who was in charge of No.5 Party.)

Top left: QX.9488
Sgt. E.D. Bancroft. 2/26 Bn. Died Sandakan 10 June 1945. Age 25. (Pic taken at Light Horse ball, Kyogle). Rapville, N.S.W. (Near Casino).
Photo: Keith Bancroft

Top right: 818029
Sgt. J.H. Rooker. 12 Bty. 6 H.A.A., Royal Arty. Died 4 August 1945. One of the 10 N.C.O.s shot at Ranau on 1 August 1945. Portsmouth, U.K.
Photo: N. Rooker, U.K.

Bottom left: NX.56694 Sigmn. S.V.J. Reay. 8 Div.Sigs. Died 8 February 1943 on first march, Japanese stated at Muluhatu, listed as Ranau. Age 23. Eastlakes, N.S.W.
Photo: J. McConchie

Bottom right: WX.7007
Pte. E.G. Burton. 2/4 M.G. Bn. Died 21 February 1945. Age 24. Midland Junction, W.A.
Photo: Beatrice Sullivan

could not agree to it as a senior officer was likely to come along and check up on it. When this party left Maunad two sick men remained in this hut. One of the PW could not walk. The fitter of the two men commenced to boil some water soon after the party had departed and Kulang, who had resumed work on the attap roof, could see the PW blowing through a piece of bamboo tube in order to coax the fire to burn. Two Japs then entered the hut and told the man tending the fire to continue with the journey and catch up with the remainder of the party. They also obtained two soldiers from the nearby Japanese unit and ordered them to carry the sick PW on a stretcher and take him up the track for about 100 yards. Kulang saw them taking the stretcher past the barracks hut where the Jap soldiers lived and shortly afterwards he heard two pistol shots. Kulang helped an Australian War Graves Unit to recover the body approximately twelve months later.

No. 3 party had its first loss on 3 February 1945 when they were about five miles on the Sandakan side of Tangkual crossing. It was at this stage that an Australian sergeant who had been lagging behind was told by WO. Gotanda Kiroku that there were only four or five miles to go before the Rest House was reached. The PW seemed to lose his mind and began to taunt and abuse the Japanese NCO. He then asked Gotanda to shoot him. The officer in charge of the party, Lt. Toyohara, hearing the commotion approached the PW and was also asked by the Australian to shoot him. Toyohara agreed to the shooting providing the Australian officer was also agreeable. In the meantime Gotanda made ready to carry out the shooting but finally said that he would not do it. He handed the revolver to the Australian officer who then agreed to carry out the shooting. Toyohara, Gotanda and two PWs who were attempting to pacify the sergeant then moved along the track and left the Australian officer and sergeant together. The officer later caught up with the remainder of the party and told them that he had to shoot the sergeant.

Most of the shootings did not take place until after Maunad was reached, it was here that Kulang witnessed the shooting of Spr. Haye, WX.7247. Somehow he obtained his identity and later wrote it on a photograph belonging to another prisoner on the same party. (Later the Recovery Team found his dixie with his name engraved on it — some bodies were also found).

That portion of the track between the 30 mile and 42 mile (Kolapis) exhausted the men a great deal as it was knee-deep in mud for most of the twelve mile stretch. After leaving Maunad it did not take the PWs long to realise that if they fell out they were going to be disposed of. It was usually of a morning the men would realise they could go no further and they would tell the senior PW of this fact. The Japanese would then amend the roll and the remainder of the party would continue their journey. Shortly afterwards the marching men would hear a shot or shots. Sometimes the man who was going to fall out would give away all his personal belongings to his comrades and give them messages to pass on to his mother, wife or family when they returned home. A number of PWs were proud possessors of battered leather boots when they fell out and these were always given to one of their mates. As they passed along the track members of the later parties often caught sight of the remains of those who had fallen out of earlier parties.

When No. 7 party reached the 23 mile from Sandakan, VX. 50155 Pte. G. C. Carter of the 4th Reserve M.T. Coy., together with a British PW and two Japanese guards, were told by the Japanese OC (Lt. Sugimura) to return to Sandakan for treatment and join a later party. Carter was suffering from malaria and beri beri; the others were also malarial cases. This party had left the camp on 4 February and had reached the 23 mile on 6 February. The four sick men did not hurry themselves on their journey back to Sandakan and did not reach there until 12 February. Carter died about a month later, the other PWs died ten days later. The PWs who had been left behind at the camp were able to glean their first information about the march from these two men. They did not of course receive very much in the way of information but at least they got some idea of the type of country over which their comrades were passing.

Top left: QX.10822 Pte. R.E.C. Hodges. 2 Coy. A.A.S.C. (Centre back row) Died 9 June 1945 on second march with Dick Braithwaite. Age 26. Blackbutt, QLD.
Photo: Max Hodges

Top right: QX.23326 Pte. R.J. Boese. A.I.F. R.A.A. Died on first march from Sandakan 29 March 1945. Age 26.
Photo: Greta Allen

Bottom left: QX.21956 Gnr. R.B. Collins. 2/10 Fd. Regt. R.A.A. Died 26 April 1945. Age 26. Kyogle, N.S.W.
Photo: Mrs. M.J. Thompson

Bottom right: QX.10433 Bdr. C.G.H. Jukes. 2/10 Fd.Regt. R.A.A. Died Ranau 23 July 1945. Age 39. Annerley, QLD.
Photo: Joyce Richardson

On the day Carter returned to Sandakan, No. 1 party, under the leadership of Capt. Iino and accompanied by the leader of the march, Capt. Yamamoto, were completing the final stage of the march to Ranau which they reached on 12 February. The original 55 PWs were reduced to 42 by this day. As the PWs slipped and slithered down the track about three miles from Ranau they caught sight of the rich green river flat on which the kampong is located. It was not until they actually reached it did they realise how big this river flat was with tall lalang grass on the other side and through which the track continued. As they dragged their weary feet through the mud they thought little of the beauty surrounding them. With Mt. Kinebalu dominating this sheltered spot, the rest of the world seemed far away. Thirteen members of No. 1 party had died since leaving Sandakan and an additional two were to die that day, leaving forty men out of the original fifty-five.

Later, Keith Botterill gave his account of the march —

"On commencing the journey we were given 3 pounds of rice, ¼ pound of dried fish and an ounce of salt and there was about 1 lb. of sugar given to the officer in charge of the party. We moved out the gate and down to the road and we were given about 120 pounds of rice. That rice was packed in Army packs. The party of PWs carried that rice. On average the POWs carried 40 to 60 pounds, whatever they were assigned to carry. The loads of the PWs consisted of ammunition, rice, and Japanese officers' gear. The load was split up among each man. The rice was sewn up in a hessian bag and the ammunition was in a bag which made into a sort of pack and worn on the chest. There were about 10 bags of ammunition. Before we left we were issued with a pair of 2nd hand shorts and a shirt or a giggle jacket and we were issued with rubber shoes which were no good as they slipped straight off our feet. About 6 or 7 had boots and they were the boots they had had all along. During the whole march it rained about 3 days and it was very boggy being in the rainy season and the bog was above our knees a lot of the way. We had difficult crossings over creeks and going along jungle tracks our feet were cut. The country we went through was swamp and hills and no flat country at all. I would know my track shown on the map. We passed through Boto, Paginatan and that is all I can remember of the names of the towns. I had no idea of the direction we were travelling. Our officer in charge of the party (Japanese) used to find us camps along the road about every 10 mile and we used to try to make them each day so we could sleep in them. We slept in about 5 camps during the march and the rest we couldn't make by dark and so we couldn't sleep in them. Most of us only had a ground-sheet because we couldn't carry the blanket. We came across 5 ration points and at one stage we got 6 cucumbers between 40 men for 3 days, and a bundle of tapioca leaves. At some supply depots we got rice issued to us to do us for 3 days until we reached the next supply place and it would work out at about 150 grams of rice per day. At some outposts we got no rice, we got tapioca and corn instead. The last 3 days of our march we got about 1 lb. of rice per day and our officer let us trade 2 blankets for a small pig at Paginatan. We gave the Japanese half and we had half of that pig the second day out of Ranau. The Japanese had at least 3 times the amount of the rations we had, bar the first five days when we had as much as them. During the period when we had the 6 cucumbers they did not have very much at that period but although I do not know how much they got, they got sufficient. Their ration was of rice. At the commencement the condition of the PWs was very bad. There were men about one or two left behind every second or third day. Of a morning those who were too sick to move would tell our Australian officer in charge that they could not move with the party and the Japanese Sgt. or officer would count us and move us off and we would get along the road about a ¼ mile and we would hear shots. The Japanese officer would tell our officers that they had to shoot the men who were left behind. At times when we were marching along the road and the men were too weak to keep up and they dropped behind the Japanese would shoot them. The way I know the Japanese shot those men was that the Japanese officer told us at night. I do not know the name of the Japanese officer in charge of us. I can remember going up a big mountain at Boto when we lost 5 men. They were shot and I myself I saw a Japanese Cpl. shoot 2 of them. Sgt. Gotanda went ahead of the party to Paginatan. That night we crossed the mountain and camped at the bottom and the next day we moved off towards Paginatan and there was one Australian soldier whose name I forget who was crawling up this mountain on his hands and knees and we went past him and got through to Paginatan. As we were going in we met the Japanese Sgt. Gotanda coming out and he said 'Why have you got those mosquito nets'. We were carrying the mosquito nets for the Japanese and we said 'The Cpl. made us carry them' and he told us to leave them behind at Boto. The Sgt. told us to leave them at Boto as we could never get over the hill with them and he told us to just carry what we had. When we told him the Cpl. made us carry the nets he said 'why' and he asked us if we were all there, we said that there were 2 men about 3 miles back, and one was very sick and the other was helping him along, so the Sgt. went back to them and came in with the Aust. soldier who was helping the sick man. He came into Paginatan and after he arrived we asked this Aust. soldier what happened to his mate and he said 'The Sgt. had to shoot him, he could not come any further'. The journey took us 17 days altogether. The total distance was about 150 miles. From Paginatan to Ranau was 26 miles. I have been that distance 5 times and I knew where the mile stones were and I counted them. When I got to Ranau there were between 150 and 200 PWs."

Yamamoto's soldiers were well organised, they were prepared for the hazards of the rentis. Each night the regular Jap soldiers would wash themselves and their clothes in the creek then dry them around the fire and prepare for the next day. The boot repair team would produce a last, someone else would carry the repair material, another soldier would have pliers and hammer. Everyone would have their footwear repaired.

In comparison the prisoners, with little clothing would walk into the creek with whatever clothing they had on and then find a place to stretch out in the open, so tired they would collapse and sleep anywhere. All the shaving and cutting aids were confiscated early in January so the PWs were extremely untidy in their appearance.

The river flat on which Ranau was situated had an elevation from sea level of 2,500 feet; the kampong was on the western portion of the padang with the Japanese air strip half a mile to the east of the kampong. The river flowed past the northern edge of the small village and the southern tip of the airstrip, a swift flowing stream, no more than twenty feet wide. The surrounding mountains are heavily wooded and show no sign of habitation.

The kampong of Ranau proper consisted of a small group of 'kedals' or shops and when the PWs arrived these were devoid of most things apart from a few vegetables and fruits.

Capt. Yamamoto did not waste any time at Ranau, he knew by the condition of the men that it would be futile to attempt to take them any further until they had rested. He did not have to make up his mind what to do with them because a change of plans by the Japanese had now made the terminal point of the march Ranau, and not Tuaran. Major Watanabe Yoshio took over from Yamamoto and the latter departed for Jesselton on 14 February 1945.

The Japanese rentis was cut through an area devoid of any habitation and natives were warned by the Japanese that they would be killed if they did not keep away from the rentis. The only people the PWs saw apart from other Japanese were natives who had been conscripted by the Japs as carriers and who passed along the rentis with their loads and natives at Puginaten.

The 53 mile journey from Maunad to Boto proved very dismal and trying to the various parties, rain dogged them all the way and the slippery mud proved very tiring. Every day more troops fell out and every day they were murdered by their Japanese masters. The PWs who died near the rest houses were usually buried but in view of the fact that rest

VX.15674 Pte. John Newton Ollis, Hamilton, N.S.W.

Photo: Ron Ollis.

NX.34442 Pte. Patrick James Clyne, Drummoyne, N.S.W.

Photo: A. Dandie.

houses were only reached every two or three days many of them were simply taken a little way off the track and then disposed of. The rentis comes close to the source of the Sapi river (Sungei Sapi) near the 80 mile and skirts the kampong of Boto on the Labuk river. About ten miles from Boto the rentis crosses a stream near the kampong of Telupid and then rises as it starts its traverse of the Maitland Ranges. For the next sixty miles until it reaches Ranau the rentis winds around the side of mountains. Many streams are crossed and many deep gorges and valleys flank the route of the track. The rises are invariably sharp, most of them are short but many of them represent a full day's march. Once the high country was reached the condition of the PWs took a decided turn for the worse. Whereas at the beginning of the march the PWs carried on some type of conversation they now became completely silent, their bent heads seemed glued to the track over which they were passing and they looked neither to the right nor left. They were beginning to throw away some of their articles to lessen the load. Where a man was in possession of a blanket he would cut it in half and throw the unwanted piece away. Even identity discs appeared to be a burden to some.

The commanding officer of No. 6 party, Lt. Tanaka Shojiro, was an old soldier. He was 48 at the time of the first death march and had been in the Army since 1926. He had only been on war service since the previous year and had not learnt the secret of travelling light. It took about half a dozen thin and weakened Australian PWs to carry his personal gear, some of which had been packed in boxes and slung to carrying poles as used by Chinese coolies. The Australians were not used to this method of carrying and found it an effort to support the weight on their shoulder while trying to negotiate the muddy track and sharp rises with their bare feet. The tempers of the PWs in No. 6 party were not improved by the sight of the high ground that lay before them after they left Boto. The Japanese guards began to use their sticks and rifle butts with gusto at this stage in order to coax some of the tiring PWs up the greasy, twisting slopes. A PW named Richards

NX .68380 Pte. Michael Keating. 2/3 M.A.C. Died February 1945. Aged 49. East Sydney, N.S.W.

Pic: Joseph P. Henderson, Fair Lawn, NJ. U.S.A.

NX.69389 Cpl. Donald Arthur Murray 2/3 M.A.C. Died March 1945 at Ranau. Aged 40. Roseville, N.S.W.

Pic: J. & B. Murray

took exception to a Jap guard who was prodding him in the back with his rifle, with the result the Jap tied him up and, after beating him badly, threw him down one of the slopes into a gully where he was left for dead. The following morning some members of the following party heard moans coming from a gully and they found Richards in great agony and partly paralysed from his treatment. He was taken along the track by the other PWs but was eventually forced to fall out again and was never seen again.

For the first few days of the death march the Japanese ate the same amount of food as the PWs but after that the Japs had at least three times as much food as them. It was not uncommon for the Japs to take some of the PWs scanty food when they were cooking it. The Japs with No. 6 party were the worst offenders in this regard. The members of No. 7 party were also feeling the stress of the climbing and many of them were beginning to stagger and slip in the mud which was adding strain to the already strenuous journey.

On 13 February 1945 when they were in the Boto area near the kampong of Telupid, Pte. Dawson and Gnr. Fuller fell out to await their fate with two British PWs named Gnr. Roberts and LAC Beardshaw who were also in a similar position. Roberts was a member of the Royal Artillery and Beardshaw of the Royal Air Force. The four men knew it would not be long before the Japanese completed the job of their disposal and finally decided that they would split into two groups and make a break for it. The two Australians decided to move to the east and the British decided they would make for the river and hide for a day or two. Some guards saw the PWs when they made their break and opened fire on the Australians, a bullet tore through Dawson's left elbow but he kept going and they managed to shake off their pursuers.

Hussin was grey-headed, moustached, tall for a Dyak and he lived at Telupid near the rentis. He was well aware of the fact that the Japs had warned all village people to stay away from the rentis and that they would severely punish anybody found there. Although Hussin was not now living in a Dyak kampong he still retained a Dyak's curiosity and often went on a personal reconnaissance of the rentis area.

On the morning of 17 February while moving through the jungle about half a mile from the Telupid kampong he saw two white men; they were hiding near the river and beckoned to Hussin when they saw him. When he came close to them he noticed their poor physical condition and knew they were prisoners who had escaped from the Japanese. They indicated to Hussin they wanted him to let them know when the Japs had gone and they would then go into the jungle proper. About 4 p.m. Hussin returned and took the PWs to his house. Dawson spoke a little Malay which made things easier for the whole party. Each of the men in a signed statement offered Hussin $400 if they could get to the Allied lines with his help. (This note was later handed in to the S.R.D. patrol.) Hussin was apprehensive about the PWs remaining at his house so he decided he would take them to the kampong of Kemansi, about a mile away as he considered their chances of remaining undetected from the Japanese would be better there than in the larger kampong of Telupid.

After the PWs had eaten a meal cooked by Hussin's wife and had washed themselves with hot water they felt better. Dawson's elbow was attended as best they could and a parcel of food was given to each man for the journey to Kemansi. It was about 10 p.m. when they set out for the house of Orang Tua (Headman) Onsi. The people of Kemansi went out of their way to do all they could to look after the white men. Orang Tua Onsi told them to build a 'sulap' or lean-to for them and each of the twenty-one houses in the kampong shared in keeping the PWs alive with food and comforts. All the PWs had dysentery and beri beri and were in a weakened state when they arrived at Kemansi. Three of the men had to be carried to the sulap. The village did not have any medicines apart from local herbs etc. and the PWs did not face a very bright future.

Early in March the first PW died, an Englishman, Gunner B. Roberts, 842317, R.A., Pte. Dawson died towards the end of March and the other Australian, Gnr. Fuller, died five days later. LAC Beardshaw, R.A.F., was the last man to die in May 1945. The loyal

NX.34384 Gnr. Eric Fuller, Branxton, N.S.W.
Photo: George Sprod.

VX.42544 Dvr. James Harold Nixon.
Photo: Wilga Nixon.

people of Kemansi who had risked so much in harboring and trying to help the four men laid them to rest close to their jungle village and there they remained until their bodies were recovered by 31 Aust. War Graves Unit. They were re-interred in the War Cemetery in 1946.

In the early stages of the march the members of No. 7 party were told that No. 6 party was the worst party in the march. They had evidence of the brutality of Lt. Tanaka in the Boto area. As No. 7 party struggled along they noticed an Australian PW sprawled dead across the tracks with a shovel in his hand. When some of the members of No. 7 party tried to investigate they were warned off by the Japs. They were only able to establish the fact he was a member of No. 6 party by the markings on his hat.

The No. 2 party arrived at Ranau on 15 February, three days after the No. 1 party, No. 3 arrived on 16th, No. 4 on 18th and No. 5 on 19 February. The natives could see the new arrivals from the other side of the river where the main area of the kampong was situated. They knew that to venture too close to the white men would result in physical harm to themselves.

The No. 1 camp at Ranau, close to the air strip, was built under the supervision of Capt. Nagai Hirawa, ('The Snake' as he was called) the same Capt. Nagai who had left the Sandakan camp in 1944 and taken the British PW party to Labuan Island; he had not been seen since he left with this party. He recognised some of the men and said 'How is my friend Mr. Sticpewich?' — they replied he wasn't on the march with them and had remained at Sandakan.

Nagai was to supervise the rice carrying parties. Although he kept away from the prisoners he was under orders from Major Watanabe Yoshio, Area Commandant, to ensure the rice reached its destination. The orders were clear — if they were too ill to carry rice the prisoners were killed. About the sixth trip WO. Kinder informed Capt. Nagai the prisoners were refusing to carry rice as they were unfit. Nagai replied 'Well if you don't carry rice I'll march you back to Sandakan'.

At that time there were about 100 left, said Botterill. There was no evidence Nagai personally supervised any beatings at that time. He returned to Ranau on 23 February 1945. Major Watanabe took over the parties as they arrived but was disappointed to notice their poor state. Capt. Yamamoto told Watanabe that many of the PWs had died en route from sickness. When he learnt of their condition Watanabe decided that the PWs should be given a rest and an opportunity to regain some of their strength for the many duties he had in store for them. The cruel and sadistic Capt. Nagai was to be in charge of the rice carrying parties. This scheme provided for the carrying of rice and other commodities between Paginatan and Ranau, Nos. 1, 2, 3, 4 and 5 parties remained at Ranau for a rest of about fourteen days before their work began in earnest.

W.O. W. Sticpewich. Picture taken December 1945. *Pic: AWM.12275*

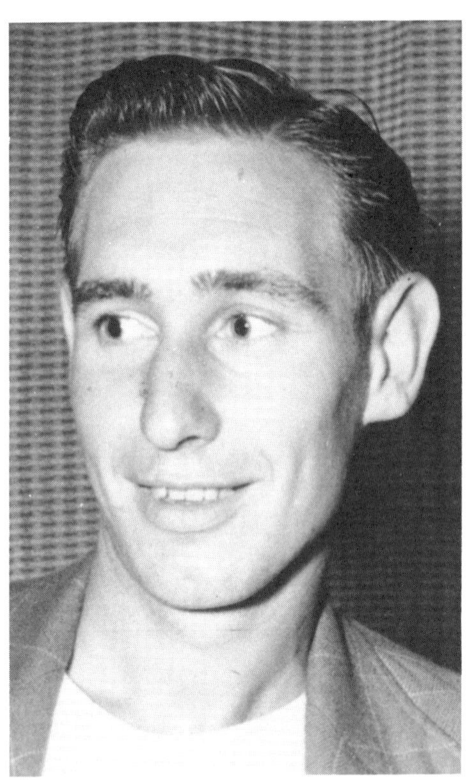

Keith Botterill on his return from hospital 1946. *Pic: AWM.41485*

Chapter 5

Of the 195 PWs who comprised the original Nos.6,7,8 and 9 party personnel, 160 of them arrived at Paginatan about 20 February 1945. This kampong is close to the river on a flat stretch of the rentis; the jungle appears to descend on it from all sides. The rentis runs through the kampong's main eight dwellings situated on the track itself, and a number of other huts built in the jungle or close to the river. The river, during the months of January and February, often runs as a muddy stream about 200 yards wide but despite its fearsome appearance the water is no more than knee depth. On the southern side of the rentis on the same side of the river is an impressive looking bamboo fence which protects the river flat gardens from the kampong's pigs. The huts are built of attap, the largest belonging to the Headman. At the western end of the kampong on the northern side of the rentis is a rest hut overlooking the river 100 yards to the south and it dominates a slight dip which meets a creek eight yards to the west. When you cross this creek you start on the five mile undulating journey to Segindai.

The 160 men left at Paginatan remained there for about a month, during which time about 100 of them died. When at the end of March the Japanese mustered the remaining sixty men, only thirty were fit to be moved to Ranau.

Bill Moxham said: ". . .Out of my party of 50, about 44 reached Paginatan, but at Paginatan we lost a lot. We stayed there for about a month. The six who died there included a chap from the 2/10 Aust. Field Regiment. He just died from exhaustion and exposure; he could not go on any further. He stopped about 2 miles from where we camped. Four of us went back that night, after getting permission from the Japs, and brought him to camp but he was dead next morning. We buried him there. The next chap who dropped out was from the 2/15 Field Regiment. The Japs would not permit us to return for him however the Japanese themselves went back for him. It was a good way back, I supposed they shot him — they wouldn't let us go back for him.

"The guards kept us going at full pace all the time and along the track we smelt and saw bodies. They were Australian soldiers' bodies, from the previous marches, we could recognise them, some we knew personally. One was in the middle of the track with a shovel in his hands; we were not allowed to stop and investigate. A chap from the 2/10 Field Regiment was on a log beside the road — dead. I saw his colour patch, which was the same as mine. Just as I got over to the body and saw by his hat who it was that was lying there the guards were on to me. I could not see whether he had been shot or not.

"On the way I suppose I saw or smelt between 20 and 30 Australian bodies; there could have been a lot more —

"Men from my own party could not go on. Boto was the first place where we had to actually leave anyone; we had to leave four there as they could not proceed. At the next place, at the bottom of a big hill, we left two more men and later heard shots. In all of my dealings with the Japanese I have never seen any of our chaps after they have left with the Japs. Once you stopped — you stopped for good. The Japs had no time for the sick, they would not even feed them.

"I was at Paginatan for a month; No.6 party of Australians and all of the rest of the Englishmen — 6 to 10 — were there. They remained there. The previous parties 1 to 5 had gone on to Ranau. We were told the reason for our being retained there was that the Ranau barracks were not finished; but that was a joke because they were never built. Of those parties, 6 to 9, there were originally 200 men — less than that, there were three parties of 50 and one small party of 20, a total of 170. Of this 170 about 38 men marched out, fit to march, from Paginatan to Ranau. There were still 20 to 30 who could not march, they were very sick. The rest had died. We have been burying four to five a day every day for the month we remained at Paginatan. The men died from malnutrition, reaction, dysentery, malaria. On the march the men used to get some ferns and even snails and frogs, to eat, and one party caught some pythons. They got anything at all to make up for the food they should have got from the Japs. We marched up and down big hills, up to our knees in water and mud and over and through rivers. Acting Padre Garland died soon after we arrived at Paginatan. There was a doctor who went with the first party in February, Capt. Jeffrey, he had gone to Ranau. We had no medical officer at Paginatan. There were some Jap medical officers there but they did nothing at all for us. The Japs had plenty of medical supplies but we got none from them. We set off with a party from Sandakan numbering 50 and after a month at Paginatan only about 6 or 8 of us were able to march on to Ranau.

"There were a lot of beatings there, sick and all. We had to carry and get our own wood, and clean up the barracks. A Warrant Officer Kinder took charge of us, eventually taking charge of the whole of the parties at Paginatan. He went up to some of the Japs and was able to get some food from some of them. Some of the Japs however would come down and beat the men, and Kinder himself was beaten when he took somebody else's part. He was belted with sticks. The guards at Paginatan were new men, I believe they had come from Kuching.

"Under Kinder 36 men started out on the march to Ranau from Paginatan. I was one of these 36. We did the march in four to five days; we could have done it more easily but we were only able to do 6 or 7 miles a day. One day we only did 5 miles. We would start off at 7 o'clock in the morning and we would be beaten along to get to our destination — a set mileage. We might arrive at 10 o'clock and we would be knocked up completely. You could not then have a rest because we were split into small parties to go out looking for food for the Japanese. We were not given any rest. We went to the native places and the Japs would get stuff from them.

'The Japs would take our blankets and any clothing or anything else we had and trade with the natives. The Japs thus obtained some sweet potatoes and pigs. We got only a few sweet potatoes. On the march from Paginatan to Ranau, I think 24 of our 36 died. One was puffed up with beri beri in the legs and face and was getting along all right on his own and could have made it but the Japs would not leave him alone; they tried to force him along and eventually he collapsed. They kicked him on the ground, Kinder and I in front saw it. The Jap turned and saw the man had gone down and he struck him over the head with his rifle butt. The soldier was left there and the party marched on.

"When this happened, Kinder told me that in several instances when he was at the rear of our party on this section to Ranau from Paginatan, wicked things happened. The Japs used to make him stay behind while a man was shot to death or kicked to death. They made Kinder watch it.

"On the scrounging parties on which we were forced to go, the Japs scrounged, in exchange for our own clothes, food and some pigs and boots. I was on one of these parties

NX.10554 Gnr. Andrew M. Miller, West Ryde, N.S.W.
Photo: Mrs. E. Brennen.

VX.35140 Gnr. Keith Tyres, Numurkah, Vic.
Photo: Cliff Moss

and we got very little of whatever food was obtained. All we were given were a few small sweet potatoes. Once we got the skin of a pig. Out of our party of 38 that left Paginatan about 12 died on the trip to Ranau.

"Out of the original 470 men, including the 100 Englishmen, who set out from Sandakan, we had been reduced to about 120. Sergeant Stacy, the Quartermaster, told me his biggest crowd for a meal was once 140. That would be about the end of March 1945."

Around Ranau grew a small red chilli — very hot. The prisoners started eating a few with their meagre rice and as they became accustomed to them then the quantity was increased. Leaves of all varieties supplemented the bulk. Botterill's party stripped the leaves from a paw-paw tree and boiled them up for a meal, then ate the branches and finally grated the trunk and ate that too. They tried other plants including banana but it proved unpalatable.

The sick would dread being allocated to the rice parties to Paginatan — they knew if they became worse they would have to fall out and be killed. However Botterill didn't mind; he saw them as an opportunity to pick up a few scraps of food. On one trip he noticed some green orange peel, picked it up and ate it; on a later trip the tree was located and when the opportunity came they raided the tree. It was unusual for citrus to be found in the area.

Botterill recalls: "After we had reached Ranau I was one of a party of Australians sent back 28 miles towards Paginatan to carry rice for the troops coming on, and for the Japanese. The journey would take us five days — three days out and two days back. Three parties who were making the journey to Ranau stayed at this place and it was for them that we carried out the rice and also for the Japanese guards. Each of us had to carry a 48 pound bag of rice on his back over hills and swampy ground. As a result of the hard conditions, several men died while thus carrying rice. We used to help those who were weak and practically carried many of them back to camp. While carrying rice on one occasion a soldier was shot nine miles from Ranau and two others were bayonetted by the Japanese 20 miles from Ranau. They were too weak to carry on and fell out. I saw the bayonetting myself; the men were on the ground at the time. The corporal and myself used to go into the gardens for tapioca which we could cook up and make a decent meal of, so I was one of the fittest men in the camp. On this occasion of the bayonetting and shooting one soldier was on the ground calling out 'Don't shoot me' and put his hands up, but nevertheless he was shot and left lying on the ground. I made this trip five times.

"When I first got to Ranau about 75 had arrived before us. I discussed with other men of other groups the conditions of their trip. We worked out that No.6 party was the worst party of the lot. The Japanese officer in command of that party had about eight Australians carrying his gear besides the ammunition and rice. His gear consisted of large boxes and two Australians had to carry each box which was lashed to a pole and the pole on each shoulder. The Jap guards of No.6 party used to take the Australians' rice issue after it was cooked. There was a soldier in No.6 party who was wearing a gold ring and the Jap soldier killed him and took his ring. Of the 50 who started out from Sandakan in my party, 37 reached Ranau. The trip took us 17 days as we went straight through marching every day. The Japanese who came with us were in very good physical condition and they had more rations than we did on the march. A couple had malaria but they were left behind at the outposts and came along later when they felt fit enough. I saw these men coming through about six weeks later."

The 130 PWs who represented the remaining PWs of Nos.1,2,3,4 and 5 parties and who reached Ranau died just as rapidly as their Paginatan comrades. The strain of the march seemed to cause a rapid deterioration in their condition. The people of Ranau often had opportunities to study the white men at close range when the Japanese took them to the gardens to collect vegetables for the camp. There were many cases of swift assistance by men, women and children of the market place; small packages of rice and other food

NX.34761 Capt. Roderick Lionel Jeffrey. **NX.57251 Pte. Ralph Shields. Died 21/11/44.**

were often passed and quickly hidden inside the shirt of a PW, providing he was fortunate enough to own a shirt.

In normal times it was the usual thing for some of the men from outlying kampongs to come to Ranau on market days and stay the night, get drunk and sleep it off on the verandah of the Police Post. In 1945 this practice had changed but the market day gave some of the outlying villagers an opportunity to see the pitiful state of the white PWs. Some of the reports taken back by these natives found their way to other natives who were employed by the S.R.D. commandos. A number of the natives who came to Ranau on market day often brought small parcels of food with them in case they passed any of the PW parties and could secretly pass food to them. The PWs tried to tell the natives of their needs by making signs to them, fingers to mouth, indicating they were hungry. Food was also a problem for the natives and this fact, coupled with the realisation the PWs had no way of hiding anything large, forced the gifts of food to be small. As only a few of the PWs were taken to the gardens there was no chance of any large scale smuggling of food into the No.1 jungle camp.

Whereas the PWs invariably shared what they had or obtained prior to the movement from Sandakan, when they arrived at Ranau most of them developed the habit of keeping all they could get for themselves. Jealousy and suspicion were rife, maltreatment and starvation had affected some of their minds to such a state they acted like primitive people and animals when they were quarrelling over food.

Some of the PWs would criticise Capt. Jeffrey, the medical officer, for treating the guards. Jeffrey ignored their complaints and replied: 'I'm doing the best for you and the best for myself.' The guard would reward the medical officer with perhaps a piece of fruit; it was a matter of survival. Jeffrey died in the hut at Ranau. The prisoners shared his belongings and used his scalpels to operate on those suffering from carbuncles.

The reason why the Japanese left some of the PWs at Paginatan was that they would have a centre for replacements in the rice carrying parties at each end of the 25 mile route between the two kampongs. Capt. Nagai, officer in charge of these parties, was accompanied by 2/Lt. Suzuki, Sgts. Beppu and Okada, together with a Formosan guard, Ishii Fujio.

The rice parties began in earnest in March 1945. The men were forced to carry bags of rice weighing 40 to 50 pounds between these two villages. Included in these parties were also local natives who had been conscripted by the Japs as coolies plus a few Javanese laborers who had been brought to British North Borneo by the Japanese. From Paginatan the rentis rises and falls for a distance of five miles before it reaches Segindai, where a small rest hut is sited on the northern side 30 ft. from the rentis.

After leaving the creek at Segindai a severe four mile climb twists around the mountainside through beautiful jungle country. It was this portion of the track that proved the most disastrous to the rice parties. As they fell out they were disposed of and Capt. Nagai informed accordingly. When the PWs reached the top of the climb they knew that the mile posts would be reached more easily during the next three miles of rentis before reaching Nelapak. Some of the fitter PWs who made the journey with the rice parties on a number of occasions learned to know this portion of the track and the location of the various mile posts which the Japanese had installed. The rentis continues for a further six miles from Nelapak before Muruk is reached. Muruk was often used as an overnight stopping place, the Kenanapan river crosses the track here and forms a natural swimming pool at its southern junction with the track, many a sick PW rested here and wondered if he could survive the eight mile walk between Muruku and Ranau.

From Muruku the rentis climbs three miles through beautiful timbered country abounding with birds, then it descends winding down through the mountains until reaching the Liwugu river three miles below. Once this is crossed it is only a matter of crossing the two mile river flat before the No.1 Ranau camp is reached. The PWs were losing condition rapidly and every time they did the Ranau-Paginatan-Ranau trip it seemed more difficult and longer.

Including the 30 PWs who were brought from Paginatan to Ranau the total number still alive at Ranau by 27 April 1945 was sixty-five. About this time the Allied air raids on the Ranau airstrip began and considerable damage was done to it. Major Watanabe had been considering an alternate PW camp site for some time and had ordered Capt. Nagai to make the necessary arrangements. A new camp had been prepared about a mile away from the Ranau camp, this camp was near a kampong to the northwest of its predecessor and was called the No.2 Jungle Camp.

The move to No.2 Jungle Camp was completed on 27 April. The following day half the prisoners were taken to the other side of the river to a point near the 110 mile peg on the Tambunan road. Nagai, Beppu, Okada, Takahara and Ishii were in charge of this party who were taken to the new location for the purpose of constructing the new camp.

The Japanese knew that there was to be another batch of PWs brought from Sandakan and this was to be their camp. Nagai was relieved here on 10 May by 2/Lt. Suzuki when he received orders to proceed to Tuaran. The rice carrying parties which originally consisted of 50 PWs were eventually reduced to about 12 men. When the Japs realised that their condition was too poor to do the trip they utilised them in wood gathering and vegetable carrying parties around the Ranau area.

Meanwhile the death roll mounted and it often took several PWs all their strength to drag the emaciated body of their comrade to the cemetery. Those able to would carry the dead to the cemetery on the hill. This required considerable energy; thin arms and legs would be tied together with a haversack strap and a bamboo pole would be placed through the straps. The weaker would lead so the stronger could push as well as carry. On one such task when a prisoner finished burying a dead man he saw that his mate who had helped him carry the body had just died in a sitting position.

Allied air raids continued in the area as the Jesselton and Ranau areas were subjected

NX.15554 Pte. William Noonan, Kyogle, N.S.W.
Photo: John Hayes.

NX.46184 Pte. George Noonan, Kyogle, N.S.W.
Photo: John Hayes.

to heavy bombardments. By 10 June 1945 only eighteen PWs were alive at the No.1 Jungle Camp. Ten of these were able to walk but the other eight were lying cases awaiting death due to beri beri, malaria, dysentery, starvation and maltreatment. It was on this day that the ten walking PWs were escorted by Haneda and Toyada to the No.2 Jungle Camp near the 110¼ peg. The Japanese who stayed at the No.1 Jungle Camp with the eight sick men were 2/Lt. Suzuki, Sgt. Iwabe and six guards. 2/Lt. Suzuki and Sgt. Iwabe ordered the guards to bring the sick men from the camp to the small hospital which was in the jungle behind the camp. A guard, Takata, was sent ahead by Suzuki to keep natives away from the area while the remaining guards with two stretchers brought the PWs out of the camp two at a time. When the guards had carried the first two PWs 300 yards Suzuki told them to leave them where they were and go back for another two. As soon as they started back 2/Lt. Suzuki shot the PWs. When the next two were brought up Sgt. Iwabe and Suzuki were ordered to dispose of them and take the bodies to the hole where the first two had been placed. When the third pair of PWs was brought up guards Kawakami and Ishii shot them. The PWs were too ill to move and were shot where they lay on the ground. The last two PWs were also brought up and were killed by the guards Yanai, Suzuki, Saburo and Takata. The last two PWs were not killed by the first volley and begged the Japanese to finish them off before they put them in the hole with the others. The following morning the Japanese left the No.1 Jungle Camp and transferred to the new camp at the 110¼ peg.

During the early part of June 1945 PWs were often seen with Jap guards near the market place and when gathering firewood. Their numbers were steadily reduced until 25 June only six remained alive. Two incidents which took place while 2/Lt. Suzuki was in command will always be remembered by the two men who are the only ones alive who can tell the story. The first concerns the unselfishness of an Australian, Private Richard Murray. A raid had been made on a Jap store by some PWs and some biscuits and rice stolen. The Japs discovered a number of PWs eating the food and Private Murray told them he was solely to blame as he was the one who took the food and gave it to the other men without them knowing where it came from. As a result of this confession Suzuki ordered his immediate execution without trial. The other incident concerned the escape of two PWs who were betrayed to the Japs.

At this time Gnr. Albert Cleary and Gnr. Wally Crease escaped and were recaptured by some natives and handed over to the Japanese for a reward.

Some two days after their recapture both men, who had been tortured and beaten, were untied. Crease was seen stretching himself then he stumbled up a nearby gully. The Jap guards, who were busy counting the rice party, realising he was gone, left and chased him, shooting him on the run.

They then tied Cleary up and after taking his clothes from him, put a chain around his neck and chained him to a stake. The guards would continually kick him, spit and sometimes urinate on him but never touched him with their hands because they feared they would catch dysentery — he was putrid and starving. Occasionally they would throw him some scraps. He starved to death and died of a broken heart said Botterill. He had been tied up for 11 or 12 days and when the Japs realised he was dying they allowed the PWs to untie him. Botterill helped untie him and carry him down to the creek where he was washed thoroughly then carried to the hut, where he died. Capt. Jeffrey told those present 'If any of us get out of here this atrocity must be reported!' That day was March 20, 1945.

The six PWs from the first death march who were alive on 25 June 1945 were — Sgt. Stacy, Sapper Bird, Bombardier Moxham, Pte. Botterill and Pte. Grist of the A.I.F., and a British PW named Frost.

Moxham and Botterill had already made tentative plans to escape and intended to go to Jesselton where they thought the Allies had already landed. They were about to carry out their plans when on 26 June the leading men of the second death march arrived and

NX.67306 Spr. Arthur W. Bird, Stanmore, N.S.W.
Photo: Norman Bird and Pat Ross, (children), pictured.

NX.26451 Sgt. Richard Lucas Stacy, Singleton, N.S.W.

NX.36660 Pte. Norman Grist, Wagga Wagga, N.S.W.
Photo: Mrs. Coe.

NX.49425 Pte. Charles Douglas Pepper, Petersham, N.S.W.
Photo: N. Short.

they were anxious to find any news of what had happened to the other PWs who had been at Sandakan over the past four months. They discovered that Capt. Picone, A.A.M.C. was among the new arrivals and immediately made plans to contact him. When they were able to talk to one another Picone asked where the rest of the men were. Botterill told him they were the only ones left — the rest of them had died.

NX.25611 Pte. Herbert Robinson 22 Bde.Coy.A.A.S.C. Died 4 June 1945. Aged 27. Mosman, N.S.W. *Pic: Mrs. Shirley Sinclair.*

NX.67279 Pte. Harold David Matchett 27 Bde.Coy. A.A.S.C. Died Ranau 22 July 1945. Aged 43. Kogarah, N.S.W. *Pic: J. McConochie*

1st MARCH

No.1 PARTY — 55 — Capt. Jeffrey, W.O.1 Watson, Sgt. Smyth
No.2 PARTY — 55 — 29 Jan.
No.3 PARTY — 55 Aust. — 30 Jan.

No.4 PARTY — 50
No.5 PARTY — 55 — W.O. Ronald Laing

No.6 PARTY — 40 Aust.
No.7 PARTY — Brit. & Aust. — W.O. Kinder
No.8 PARTY — 50 British
No.9 PARTY — 55 British

Japanese Officers I/C

Capt. Iino,
Capt. Yamamoto
Lt. Hirano, 59 Jap. Soldiers
Lt. Toyohara,
Ass. W.O. Gotanda
Capt. Mizuto, Sgt./Maj. Ito
Lt. Sato Tatsuo
S/Maj. Sato Hideo
Lt. Tanaka, Sgt. Yamaguchi
Lt. Sugimura
Lt. Morikawa, W.O. Toyo
Lt. Abe

2nd MARCH

No.1 PARTY — Capt. Heaslop
No.2 PARTY — W.O. Sticpewich
No.3 PARTY — Padre Greenwood
No.4 PARTY — Capt. Oakeshott
No.5 PARTY — Capt. Picone
No.6 PARTY — W.O. Dixon
No.7 PARTY — Capt. Cook
No.8 PARTY — Lt. Good
No.9 PARTY — Flt./Lt. Burgess, RAF
No.10 PARTY — Capt. Daniels — Brit. Army
No.11 PARTY — Lt. Chopping, Brit. Army

Lt. Suzuki
Lt. Watanabe
Sgt. Tsuji
Together with the remainder of the camp guards

Chapter 6

Back at Sandakan air raids were almost daily — the men could set the time on their arrival. Lightnings — P38's would shoot up the Sandakan area and, despite the sign, the camp would be attacked by low level strafing. The PWs had our own planes to contend with as well as the Japs.

When the raids were on the sick could not be moved. There was no protection for them so they just prayed. It was during one of these raids that Acting Chaplain Cpl. Garland raced out into the open and waved an Australian flag; none knew where he got it from — he never considered his own safety in endeavouring to protect others.

Working at the Pump Station near the Boiler Room gave some the opportunity to scrounge. The Japs often searched and when they found something prohibited they would be contented and would not search the rest. On this occasion Pte. Cull was caught with a chook. He was severely beaten and placed in the cage — he never recovered. Others were able to get their stolen food into the camp; it was a risk that all were prepared to take.

WO. Maddock, one of the senior 'hanchos', had the unpleasant duty to allocate work parties. He was outstanding in his endeavours to protect the sick. Speaking with a little Malay-Japanese-English-French he was able to get his point over, often to pay the price with a bashing.

The concert stage was still permitted to be used and an occasional concert was permitted. Norman Chenhall, also known as 'Snowy', put on a one man football match which always amused the men. Nelson Short and his mate Jack Stanley specialised in the old vaudeville act with a banjo-ukelele made from a coconut shell and a few strands of old signal wire, walking onto the makeshift stage singing 'Walking My Baby Back Home'. Always remembered was 'Jacko' Jackson singing 'Beautiful Dreamer' and 'Galway Bay'. Cpl. John Bastin assisted and wrote songs including —

Australia far over the sea
There's a girl daily waiting for me
For fear in her heart My only sweetheart
Longs for the time I'll be free —
She knows one day I'll return
To the land of the gumtrees and fern
Oh dear God heal her tears and comfort her fears
Of my loved one far over the sea.

Early one night in March 1945 the stillness of the Sandakan camp was broken by a rifle shot. A babble of Jap voices indicated that somebody was dead. Hoshijima gave an order 'Remove the body!'. He then told Lt. Moritake to take a tally of the PWs to check who was missing. The hut 'hanchos' reported to Moritake all men were present. Moritake informed them they were wrong and to make another check. It was then reported to him that Pte. John Orr was missing.

The following morning, the camp leader, Capt. G. Cook, was sent for and asked to identify the body of Pte. Orr. When Capt. Cook returned he informed some of the PWs that Pte. Orr had been shot in the back and had a large wound in the chest. When a party of four PWs went to collect the body for burial they noticed it had been moved from where it fell. They could tell by the blood where he had been shot; this was very close to the wire and he had been shot from a very short range, powder marks were visible on the body. The PW had been trying to steal out of the compound garden to find some food. Orr was shot by Hinata Genzo.

By the beginning of April there were 400 hospital patients at Sandakan camp. The sick men had to contend with the swamp rats coming into the huts at night and attacking the seriously ill — they were too sick to fend them off. Although the PWs were not getting an issue of rice Hoshijima had 90 tons stored under his house. The PWs had saved a total of 100 bags up to January 1945 and were owed an additional 70 bags by the Japanese. Since January 1945 the only rice they received was what they had saved themselves or part of what the Japs owed them. The initial reason for storing food from their meagre supply was to cope with a situation such as existed after the end of 1944. Because the Japs had not supplied them with rice since January they were only allowed three ounces per man per day from their own reserve. The amount of nourishment from three ounces of rice was not sufficient to prevent further wasting of body. At this time the rice being issued to Hoshijima on behalf of the PWs was in fact being used by the Japs themselves who had sufficient to last them until the end of 1945. Some of the Japs would leave what rice they could not eat in their meal bowls and would never give any to the PWs despite the fact that in March ten or twelve a day were dying from starvation. The Japs would not allow any trading or bartering for food with sympathetic natives and flogged and kicked

Twins Bdr. Cecil Ross Glover and Gnr. Fred Macara Glover of Mosman, NSW, were well known. They were the only two in the camp who got diphtheria; Cec became very ill and was in hospital in 1945 and Dick Braithwaite had taken some fruit down to their hut; Geoff Brownlee and a few others were there too; they were sitting talking when one of the raids started. Dick Braithwaite heard the bomb coming and flattened himself in the corner of the hut and out of the corner of his eye he saw something fly across the room when the bomb hit; when it was all over the hut was wrecked, he was alright but Cec was dead; it was his leg Dick had seen flying across the room. Braithwaite had the job of telling Fred his brother was killed and Fred cried for a week, they had been so close to each other. But everyone was affected by it, if they hadn't been twins it would have been just another death. Fred was heartbroken and was to go on the second march and die at Miru on 2nd March 1945.

Photo: A. Glover

PWs for trying to.

The Japs were now accepting the large number of deaths daily and were not checking and confirming the deaths. Some men took the opportunity of feigning death and got their mates to carry them out of the camp to the cemetery, later to escape. Unfortunately they did not leave the area and were arrested and shot.

The Wood Party were having a rest. They were told 'All men sit in circle' — while they were there an Allied aircraft went over, circled, and dropped one bomb in the centre of the circle, killing about 20 PWs and several Japanese. Owen Campbell and his mate were fortunately away from the party at this time. They witnessed the bombing and later took one of the wounded Jap guards back to camp where they were rewarded. They were concerned the Japs may have accused them of somehow being implicated. Raids became more frequent when the POW sign was removed in April.

In May 1945 Germany surrendered to the Allies — PWs in Japan were told by their guards 'Germany finish, Nippon fight alone!'. Hirohito also knew Japan was a beaten nation. The 20th Air Force, operating their B29's from the Mariannas, were pounding Japan and one by one were burning their cities by fire-bombing. Japan had hoped her Peace Envoys, which they had planted in Europe prior to entering the war, would be able to negotiate an early peace thus giving them a big slice of Asia. No one would listen to their approaches — Pearl Harbour was too fresh in Allied minds and they were determined when Europe was finished the Japanese would be defeated like no other nation had been defeated in history.

In the battle for the Philippines Hirohito felt Japan could never surrender while so many seafaring ships were afloat. Following their defeat in the battle of Philippines Sea they could have surrendered early 1945 and again in May.

The 26 Brigade of the Australian 9 Division assaulted Tarakan, an important oil port just a couple of hundred miles south of Sandakan, on 1 May 1945. Prior to this assault a feint attack was carried out in the Sandakan area — this boosted the hopes of the 824 PWs remaining — dreaming their AIF mates would come fighting their way into the camp to rescue them. The Sandakan area was only lightly defended with no more than 2000 of Col. Otsuka's troops extended along the coast.

Despite their pitiful condition the PWs remained optimistic; each day when the Allied planes went over they believed their release was imminent.

In Australia the Public subscribed over 3 million pounds to the Red Cross Relief Fund for Prisoners of War; the Japanese Government refused permission for the food to be delivered. They were not to know the War Ministry in Japan had sent a further telegram to all Commands confirming previous directives:

> "Prisoners of War must be prevented by all means available from falling into enemy hands.
>
> They should either be relocated away from the front or collected at suitable points and times with an eye to enemy air raids, shore bombardments etc.
>
> They should be kept alive to the last wherever labour is needed.
>
> In desperate circumstances, when there is no time to move them, they may, as a last resort be set free, then emergency measures should be carried out against those with an antagonistic attitude and utmost precaution should be taken so that no harm is done to the public."

Hoshijima now knew the Allies had announced the setting up of a War Crimes Tribunal in Europe. He was a very intelligent person and must have requested a transfer of duties — the order was to come from Southern Command at Saigon to 37 Army and Col. Suga indicating it may have come from Tokyo because at that time there were other transfers from POW Administration to less sensitive areas. But Hoshijima was trapped and isolated in Borneo. He was to make his way with a couple of natives and guards to Jesselton.

Capt. Takakuwa Takuo was first informed on 26 April 1945 that he was to commence duties with a PW Unit. He was later advised by Col. Suga he was to take over the duties as Camp Commandant at Sandakan Camp from Capt. Hoshijima; this was to take effect on 17 May 1945. He understood Col. Suga received instructions from the Prisoner of War Information Bureau in Tokyo and also from 37 Army Headquarters. He was well aware, when taking command, the prisoners were not receiving any rice ration and were eating only what they were able to grow. He was also briefed on how the PWs should be treated. This instruction came from the PW Information Bureau whose formation and policies were first enunciated on instructions from Hirohito in 1942. Takakuwa claimed he tried to get rice for the PWs then was informed none was available for them — rice was reserved for the Japanese.

Takakuwa was ordered to take all PWs to Ranau irrespective of their condition. After inspecting them he signalled back to Army HQ there were 400 stretcher cases and 200 who could not walk. On 27 May 1945 while Takakuwa was waiting for advice from Army HQ the bombardment of Sandakan by sea and air took place. This event expedited any plans he had made because at this time the Japanese were very apprehensive, so he decided to leave 288 PWs behind and gave orders to the camp leader, Capt. Cook, to prepare the remainder to move.

Up to the day when Capt. Takakuwa arrived the only news the PWs had received about the men on Capt. Yamamoto's first death march group was from the two sick PWs who had returned from the 23 Mile.

Before Capt. Hoshijima handed over to Takakuwa he had been in contact with 37 Army HQ regarding the bombing at Sandakan and had suggested the PWs be moved. 1/Lt. Moritake was sent to Kemansi following receipt of a communication from Army HQ suggesting that this be the place to where the PWs should be evacuated. Moritake found there was insufficient food at Kemansi to cope with the probable demand and informed his commanding officer accordingly. On 20 May 1945 Takakuwa received his instructions from 37 Army HQ to close the Sandakan camp and the PWs be transferred to the existing compound at Ranau which he would take charge of.

The condition of the PWs who were available to Takakuwa was in no way to be compared with the men of the first death march party who had moved to Ranau at the beginning of the year. Those men had represented the fittest men in the camp at that time and the present strength of the PWs at Sandakan included 400 hospital cases out of a total of about 900 men. Takakuwa knew it was unthinkable and useless to try and clear the camp of all the PWs and commence the march because the hospital cases were dying at the rate of ten a day. He knew the march would probably kill all or most of the men. He had heard of a force of 800 Japanese soldiers who had set out from Tawao for Jesselton in January 1945 and only 200 men arrived at Jesselton under their own power. Earlier in May of that year Major General Akashi with 150 cavalry troops had marched from Sandakan to Ranau and only forty survived. Takakuwa was aware that this trip was not going to be easy, in view of the fact that at least 200 of the men would have to be taken over the route by stretcher and PW stretcher parties would not last more that two or three days.

The most favoured Japanese appreciation was that the Allies would land one Division at Sandakan and two Divisions at Kudat on the northern tip. The rentis was a withdrawal route for Colonel Otsuka's garrison of 2000.

When the bombardment by Allied ships commenced the Japanese were certain that Sandakan would be occupied by 30 May. It also made the Japs realise that the PW camp was in an exposed position should such a landing take place and that the PWs were likely to fall into Allied hands at a very early stage of the operation.

The Japanese guards and soldiers who were to march to Ranau knew that they were to go to Ranau for some time prior to the march but did not know the actual date. Most of them were already getting extra rations in order to gain condition to sustain them on the march. The PWs noted that they were receiving meat every alternate day and wished

Top left: NX.69261 Pte. Albert Anderson. 2/3 M.T. Motor Amb.Coy. A.A.S.C. Died Sandakan 11 May 1945. Age 39. Glebe Point, N.S.W. *Photo: Faye Corbett*

Top right: WX.8633 Spr. E.G. Kilminster. 2/6 Fd.Pk. Coy. R.A.E. Died Sandakan 4 December 1944. Age 32. Perth, W.A. *Photo: Trevor Tough*

Bottom left: NX.33835 Cpl. Ronald Sullivan. 22 Bde. Coy.A.A.S.C. Died Ranau 31 March 1945. Age 30. Ulamambri, N.S.W. *Photo: Sister Helen Sullivan*

Bottom right: QX.9260 Gnr. L.G. Barnard. 2/10 Fd. Regt. R.A.A. Died 18 March 1945. Age 24. *Photo: Mrs. F.M. Wilcox*

WX.7054 Spr. S.C. Goldfinch. 2/6 Fd. Park.Coy., R.A.E.Died 13 July 1945. Age 44. Innahoo, W.A. The Japanese date of death is incorrect, more likely 13 June 1945 at Sandakan. (see page 121 pic of plaque). *Photo: S. & P. Goldfinch*

NX.68161 W.O.I. R.E.H. Sadler. Audit Sect., Aust. Army Pay Corps. Died Sandakan 1 June 1945. Age 26. *Photo: Mrs. M. Kinsela*

that they could participate in such luxury. The PWs did not realise what significance it held in relation to their own fate.

On 28 May Takakuwa called a conference of the personnel for the second death march. His instructions were simple and there should have been no doubt as to their full meaning. During the day the whole camp was to be destroyed, also ammunition and store dumps. PWs who were unable to walk were to be taken to the gardens in No.2 Compound and left there in the open. Sgt. Major Morozumi with fifteen guards was to remain with the lying cases and when they had all died he was to march overland and join the remainder of the Japanese at Ranau. Morozumi was to hand over command to Lt. Moritake when the latter returned from Kemansi.

Further details of the plan were that the whole party would move in three groups. It was estimated that about 435 Australians and 100 British PWs out of the 824 remaining PWs would be able to attempt the march. It was proposed that twelve parties, each of 50 PWs, would be split into three groups. Each group would take its turn to lead the remainder and this leap-frogging would continue until Ranau was reached. Lt. Suzuki from a nearby Japanese unit would command the first group, Capt. Watanabe, 2 i/c to Takakuwa, would command the second group and Sgt. Tsuji would command the third group. The guards would change groups each day. Stragglers would be passed to the rear for disposal, which in fact meant they would be murdered. Sgt. Tsuji would always travel at the rear with Suzuki in the lead and Watanabe in the centre. Capt. Takakuwa ordered Sgt. Major Ichikawa to travel two days ahead with his party and establish food dumps. With him was the camp interpreter, Osawa San, better known as "Jimmy Pike", and S/M. Fujita, the medical supervisor.

An issue of rice would be made to the PWs at the end of the bitumen road; the issue would be four pounds and this was to last them for ten days. Five of the camp pigs were to be killed, cooked, and the meat taken on the march by the PWs.

When a start was made on the morning of 29 May in burning down the buildings, Nelson Short helped carry the sick from the huts before they were fired. The sick were just left in the open. Japanese guards with machine guns surrounded the men. "I nearly stayed behind — I had an ulcer between my toes — and an old mate said 'The war's over, don't go, stop where you are, the trucks will come and take us down to the wharf.' I said 'No I'll go with the mob' and when I started on the march the beri beri went down and my ulcer healed up while others became worse," Short recalled.

At the camp, Takakuwa and his men had plenty of opportunity to study the physical condition of their charges; they were veritably an army of cripples. Many of them wore wooden appliances to support the weight of their body which the leg bones, infected by tropical ulcers, could not support. Very few of them had footwear and the majority of them just hobbled around the camp as best as their joints, stiffened by beri beri, would permit. The hospital patients were carried to the open ground in No.2 Compound and left in rows in the open. During the course of this transfer some of the men died and were placed in slit trenches for burial. The bulk of the men left behind were British.

Meanwhile explosions shook the camp as Japs busied and bustled around driving the PWs on the many tasks that were needed. The sudden panic on the part of the Japanese gave the PWs the impression that the Allies had already landed and rumours flew around the camp, most of them to the effect that the war had ended and the Japs were trying to destroy evidence of their bestiality before the Allies took over. Their hopes were raised by the rumours which had the appearance of being genuine. When they were told later in the afternoon they would kill five of the pigs it only helped to support the rumours that the war was over.

Chapter 7

Takakuwa and Watanabe visited the camp at 0900 hrs and soon after they left the huts in No.2 and No.3 Compounds were set alight. The PWs in No.1 Compound were told that their compound was to be clear by 1100 hrs and the sick were to be taken to the gardens in No.2 Compound. It was at 1700 hrs that the PWs were told that all those fit to walk were to be ready to move in an hour. Some of the men were actually commencing their evening meal when the Japs came and started to push them outside the camp gate. A considerable number of them were on crutches and could only walk with the aid of a stick. The huge cavities in their legs which represented dried muscle and sinew from a healed tropical ulcer did not encourage any thought of rapid movement. Even men who were not fit enough to be on their feet attempted to join in with the walking parties because they thought they were being taken down to Sandakan town for handing over to the Allied forces who had landed in the town. The actual march commenced at about 7 pm. The men prayed their mates were not far away.

The senior PW in each party was: No.1 — Capt. Heaslop, AIF. No.2 — W.O.1 Sticpewich, AIF. No.3 — Padre Greenwood. No.4 — Capt. Oakeshott, AIF. No.5 — Capt. Picone, AIF. No.6 — WO. Dixon, AIF. No.7 — Capt. Cook, AIF. No.8 — Lt. Good, AIF. No.9 — F/Lt. Burgess, RAF. No.10 — Capt. Daniels, RAMC, British Army. No.11 — Lt. Chopping, British Army. The total personnel on the march was 536 men: 439 Australians and 97 British.

There had not been sufficient time to cook all the pigs and only about 100 lbs. of pork had been distributed.

"When we asked why we were to be shifted, the Japs told us that we had requested it because of Allied bombing, but that was incorrect. We asked to stay at Sandakan and so be allowed to put up signs showing it was a POW camp or to fly the Geneva Red Cross, but this was refused. We asked about the men being left behind and the Japs said 'Don't worry we will look after them'. On one occasion when the planes came over we waved two Red Cross sheets. We were seen by a Jap guard who immediately levelled his rifle at us. Capt. Cook was brought out, his face was slapped a few times and he was threatened he would be shot if it happened again," stated Sticpewich.

The pitiful column moved off from the camp gate in great hopes and marched as best they could down the road from the camp which joined the bitumen road running from Sandakan to the Sungei Batang region. Any hopes they had of going to Sandakan were dashed to the ground when they received the order to turn right when they reached the bitumen road and they began their journey up the road away from Sandakan. Many of them knew they would probably not see another day out and the disappointment of not turning left towards Sandakan, where some still believed they would be handed over to

NX.53067 Gnr. James Gregory Ryan, Redfern, N.S.W.

NX.1655 Pte. Roy Ruane, Darling Point, N.S.W.

the Allies, sapped any reserve morale they may have had remaining.

The main column of the PWs reached the 12 mile at 11 pm that night. The Japs had a dump of about 50 tons of rice here but only issued twenty three 100 lb. bags of it to the men; this was immediately split up among them, each man getting about 4 lbs.

A nominal roll of each party was also prepared by the senior NCO and these rolls were handed to the Japanese. The only information that the PWs could get out of the Japs was that they were going to a place where there was plenty of food but this place was a long long way away. The same old lie!

By the time the end of the road at the 15 mile was reached some of the men had already dropped out but were forced on by the guards at the rear under Sgt. Tsuji with the aid of rifle butts, sticks and bayonets. Some of the men were actually given Japanese officers' bed rolls to carry when it took all their strength to lift their own feet.

The march continued throughout the night, several men attempted to escape into the jungle and were shot. 'Gunboat' Simpson told his mates he was 'off' and headed straight for the jungle, not to be seen again.

The third group did not halt until the following forenoon before they had a meal. They had not completed the first mile of the rentis when they halted at 11 am on 30 May. They immediately commenced to cook a meal and rest as best they could. It did not last long however for at 1400 hrs four Allied planes flew over the area causing them all to scatter and seek shelter in the surrounding foliage. After this diversion they continued their rest until at 1730 hrs the Japanese intimated that the march would continue. Seven of the men, all of whom were cripples unable to walk without a stick, could not continue and remained when the rest of the party moved off. Two Japanese stayed with the seven men and waited until the main party had moved a little further down the track. Corporal Katayama, the senior Jap guard present, then attempted to force the PWs to walk down the road. He and his men commenced to beat the men with the sticks they had used to march with. They were only successful in moving them another twenty or thirty yards after which they were forced to move into the thicker jungle just off the track.

This spot was just at the rear of a Chinese gardener's house. Chin Min Choi, with his brother and another Chinese, heard shots coming from this point and went out to investigate. They found that six of the men had been shot in the back, four of them were dead and the other two seriously wounded, but the seventh had escaped into the jungle and was now being searched for by the two guards. The Chinese commenced to bury the four men and shortly heard a shot from the jungle. While they were burying the first four the Japs returned and shot the two wounded men in the head. When the six had been buried the Chinese made a search for the man they believed had been shot in the jungle. Eventually they found him dead, doubled up with a wound in the stomach.

Watanabe, the keeper of the killing Roll, recorded at the 11 Mile that four men returned to Sandakan, leaving 532 to be accounted for.

As Katayama and the other guard set off to join the rest of the party they met Sgt. Hosotani who was suffering an attack of malaria and who was living in the 15½ mile region. Katayama told the sergeant if he saw any stragglers it would be advisable to shoot them. When Hosotani was returning to his billet he saw two Australians sitting on the side of the track; they were badly affected with beri beri. He went into his hut which he shared with Yaten, a NBAC police boy, took Yaten's rifle, went outside and shot the two PWs in the head. They were later buried by the Chinese. Hosotani, a member of the dreaded Kempe Tai, was an old hand at killing. He admitted to having killed several Chinese in Sandakan whom he suspected of being spies. Many shootings took place that day and about the same time as Hosotani was carrying out his murders another PW was shot near the 17 Mile by a member of the Kempe Tai, 'Nakao'.

The chances of escape were slim as in many cases the ratio of guard and prisoners was one for one and as deaths increased the chance of escape diminished.

After the first two days some sort of routine was established. The leading group would move off at 0630 hrs, the second group at 0800 hrs and the last group at 0900 hrs.

Parties were beginning to pass and overtake each other, according to the plan, but as the journey progressed the men got weaker and the column stretched out further. Every morning as the march started a number of men would remain behind. Sgt. Tsuji kept his guards busy in the rear disposing of the stragglers. Usually the men were shot but often they were beaten to death with rifle butts and sometimes with the very crutches they had relied on for walking. Tsuji's complement of guards changed every day in order that they all had an opportunity to participate in the killings.

The prisoners knew what their fate was to be when they fell out and calmly shook hands with their mates and gave them messages to pass to their relatives when the war ended. They also knew the Japs would keep any food the PWs may have had and they would distribute their small portions between their mates before they finally fell out.

It was not uncommon to see a PW sitting on a log or a stone on the side of the track and as his fellow PWs passed he would give them messages to pass on to another friend in a leading column of the march. Many of these men went to their deaths shouting curses and insults at the Japs and telling them to 'let me have it'. Nelson Short remembers 'Smiler' Watts saying "Nelson, if you make it tell Mum this is where I fell out".

When the first party commenced it had been raining for a day prior to the march and it rained fairly heavily in the first three days and there was intermittent rain for the next week. While the wet season had finished at the time of the second march there was still plenty of mud about and this they met on the third day out. The PWs averaged about eight miles a day. When they reached the muddy area it was thick and grey, crawling with small crabs which gave the impression of lice. "My only clothing was a pair of shorts a mate made from an old kit-bag and a little mat I used to sleep on," recalls Nelson Short. "It was raining and I slipped and rolled back down the mountain and hit a rock, my mat cushioned the fall and saved me. Above was a Jap watching to see if I was able to proceed, otherwise he would have finished me off."

On 4 June on the Sandakan side of the 42 Mile they began to see signs of the previous march. A skeleton was propped up against a tree while nearby lay a mouldy Australian pattern hat and Rising Sun badge. They began to realise then that this was not the first death march. About this time Osawa, the camp interpreter died. Sgt. Major Fujita, the medical orderly, stayed with him until he decided it was unlikely he would recover then he was shot in accordance with orders. Fujita also carried the records of those who died up to his departure on 29 May, records of deaths up to that date in the Sandakan camp.

Maunad was reached on 6 June; the same place was used as a ration point for the second march. The physical condition of the men was much worse than the men of the first march and it seemed probable that a large number of them would not proceed further than Maunad. They were given a further ten days ration and told that when they reached the Boto region, another ten days march, there would be plenty of food for them. Many of them knew they could not survive another ten days, five of these men decided they would do something about it. They were Gnr. Campbell, Cpl. Emmett, Syd Webber, and Ptes. Austin and E.K. Skinner. The opportunity came on June 7th.

Sticpewich said "When we moved out in the morning there would be some men who simply could not move, who would be crippled by exposure and who were in bad shape before they started. I never ever saw any of these men again as we left them as we marched off. When we had marched a mile or so from our overnight camp we would hear rifle fire and machine gun fire from the direction of the camp. Different guards told us that it was bad to stop because if you did you would be 'marti' meaning dead. I never actually saw any of the stragglers shot but I did see WO. Dixon beaten to insensibility by a guard we called 'Top Hat'. He wanted Dixon's gold ring and he refused to give it to him. I did not see Dixon again but later I saw 'Top Hat' wearing his gold ring."

L to R: NX.31921 Pte. Terence Waller, Walcha, N.S.W., NX.40910 Pte. Francis Carl Dezius, Bundarra, N.S.W., NX.32277 Pte. Ellis Roy "Smiler" Watts, Ashford, N.S.W.

Photo: Mrs. R. Peel

When the marching PWs departed from Maunad 73 men remained behind. They were massacred at Tangkual Crossing with rifle and machine gun fire, and the last party heard the distant shots as they struggled along the track. Gruesome relics of the previous march became more evident after Maunad was passed. Bleached skeletons and decomposed bodies were often seen; at many spots on the track there exuded the stench of death. Items that had been thrown away by the PWs could be portions of footwear, tins used for cooking rice, rotted webbing, belts, paybooks and photographs which had been destroyed by the elements.

On 7 June three Allied aircraft made a sweep over the straggling column causing them to seek cover. It was this diversion that gave the five men the chance they were waiting for. They made a break into the jungle on the northern side but not before they had rifled some Japanese gear and added six pounds of rice, six tins of salmon and some dried fish to their own store of gear which already included a compass and some fishing lines.

They made slow progress through the wild jungle and had only covered about a mile when they decided to stop for the night. They tried their fishing lines but found that the Borneo fish had not been educated to the civilised form of fishing with a line and hook.

On the second day they continued in their efforts to reach the coast and managed to do about two miles. That night Campbell contracted malaria and a halt was called for the 9th June while he endeavoured to shake off some of the fever with quinine tablets.

They continued their travels on 10 June but once more were forced to halt due to an attack of dysentery which caused Pte. Skinner to be unfit to move.

On 13 June they decided to split the party into two, the food was divided and Campbell stayed with Skinner, who was not getting better. Campbell himself was still in bad shape due to beri beri. Skinner was trying to encourage Campbell to leave him and not jeopardise his own chance of survival but Campbell remained.

On the third day they had been on their own — June 16 — Campbell went down to the river to get some water and to inspect his fish lines. When he returned he found Skinner had committed suicide by slashing his throat. Campbell knew that Skinner had done this so he could continue and join up with the rest of the escapees. Campbell was in a very poor condition due to beri beri and lack of food and it took him a considerable time to scratch a hole in which Skinner would be given protection against the jungle life. Campbell was existing mainly on fresh water and any beetles or grubs he could find.

The party had set out in a north easterly direction when they made their break and Campbell headed in this direction with the intention of trying to link up with them. On 18 June he came to the Munyed River and found Pte. Austin sheltering under a blanket and badly affected by dysentery and malaria. Cpl. Emmett and Pte. Webber were about 100 yards away attempting to catch some fish. After a short discussion they decided to appeal to any native craft which came down the river, they being of the opinion that this was the only way in which they could hope to reach friendly hands.

It wasn't long before they heard the sound of somebody speaking Malay, so with Emmett leading followed by Webber and Campbell, they went to the bank to hail the prahu which had an attap cover to protect any passengers from the sun. From under this attap cover a Japanese appeared armed with a repeating rifle when the craft was about 20 yards from the three men. He fired four shots and Emmett and Webber fell dead into the river, Emmett shot through the head and Webber through the chest. Campbell immediately took to cover and the Jap appeared content to let him get away and Campbell returned to Austin and told him of their deaths.

Over the next three days they lived on fish Campbell caught and some jungle tree fungus. Austin was too far gone and passed away on 21 June 1945. Campbell buried him as best he could, then pushed on down river towards the coast.

Campbell saw plenty of jungle life about him. He saw a huge python which would have been a good meal but he was so weak he was afraid to attack the snake in case their roles were reversed. (Austin not known to A.I.F., possibly Hotston.)

When he wanted to cross the river to the east bank he knew the only means available would be to swim or to paddle across on a log. He was too weak to try to swim and finally found a log he could paddle. He was half way across the river when a Jap appeared on the bank and fired at him, the bullet hitting him in the wrist, but he managed to slip off and swim underwater to some mangroves. Several more shots failed to find him and he managed to make the river bank.

He became delirious on 25 June and until 3 July 1945 he roamed the jungle like something wild. After the last attempt on his life he stayed away from the river for a while but despite his mental illness he subconsciously wanted to return to it. He was fortunate to escape another messy fate while he was wandering in the jungle. He was lying practically naked, asleep under a tree, when a wild pig, thinking he was dead, came up to eat him. It was about to bite him on the knee when he managed to get hold of a piece of stick and poke it in its eye and the pig ran off. When dawn came he followed the pig's trail and finally reached the Munyed River. He watched the river traffic for a while and saw that many boats were manned by Japanese. His eye was finally attracted by a small canoe which seemed to be avoiding the river traffic. He had reached such a state that he decided that however slim the chance was he had to take it. He called out 'Abang!' (Malay for 'Older Brother') and noticed that the canoe started to head his way. It was at this very moment that Campbell started to faint . . . .

Lap and Galunting came from kampong Maunad, the same kampong where Kulang was the Orang Tua — Kulang the famous hunter and the same man who helped to build the rentis and the Jap rest hut at Tangkual Crossing. But Kulang wasn't with his kampong any more, he had gone into the jungle on some secret mission and he did not even tell his people where he was going. It was thought that he was engaged in some anti-Japanese work further inland. Actually Kulang was assisting an SRD party who were operating in

NX.41647 Pte. Edward K. Skinner, Tenterfield, N.S.W. A brave and gentle man, he was known to carry his Bible with him.

Photo: R.S.L., Tenterfield

NX.56172 Cpl. Douglas Rupert Meek, Hobby's Yards, N.S.W. Died Renau.

the area. These 'behind the lines Commandos' had been operating in Borneo for some time and had organised local guerilla forces to play havoc with the Japanese lines of communication. Kulang had his own particular method of dealing with the Jap. He would hide beside the track with his rifle and parang; depending on circumstances, the Jap would be despatched with either. Kulang was cunning enough not to take any loot from his victims; if he was ever searched it would be embarrassing for him. He only broke this rule on one occasion and he still bears his trophy, a cheap Japanese made fountain pen engraved with the name NIRO.

Lap was a cripple and his right leg swung helplessly as he struggled along with his stick. Galanting and Lap had installed a number of fish traps along the Maunad River and they both took the precaution of avoiding Jap craft on the river; they did not like the Japs and did not want to be questioned on happenings at their kampong.

The two natives paddled their small canoe up a tributary of the river to allow some Jap craft to pass. When they thought they had passed they entered the main stream again in order to inspect their fish traps. They had not gone very far when they heard someone call out 'Abang!' and they were very surprised to see a naked, thin and hairy individual on the bank, obviously a white man, but they immediately made towards him. Lap could not get out of the boat easily or quickly so Galanting caught hold of Campbell just as he was passing into a faint. They took the sick PW to their acting Orang Tua, a man named Saliam.

Saliam could see the PW was weak and immediately obtained a pair of trousers for him and gave him a bath. His wife also boiled some water for him to drink. He could see Campbell was too weak for solid food so he gave him only broth for the first two days. On the third day he gave him cooked rice and whatever he could get to add to it. Ambiau was living with Saliam at this time and he also proved very helpful, particularly when anybody came to the kampong. It was Ambiau's job to take Campbell into the jungle and hide him, after the visitors had gone Ambiau would bring him out from hiding, give him a wash and cover him with blankets. Sometimes he took him to the river and held him whilst he had a bathe. He used to assist him to and from the river. He was beginning to gain a little strength but Saliam was still a little uncertain what was going to be the next move. Then it was solved for him.

The people of kampong Maunad had deserted their usual kampong and were living further into the jungle about a mile away. They were very nervous because of Jap movements on their river but because they now had a white man with them they were more nervous than ever. On 16 July, the thirteenth day of Campbell's stay, they got a bad fright for they heard men marching close by. Thinking it was the Japanese they were trying to hide Campbell when Kulang came into their clearing.

Ambiau came forward and greeted him, telling him of the white man. Campbell could not speak Malay and was unable to understand what was happening. He was trembling when Kulang approached him. Kulang noticed how thin the white man was, saw his growth of hair and his scabies and thought to himself he looked truly like an orang utan.

Campbell was naturally suspicious and could not understand Kulang's questions in Malay. Kulang gave up and smiled at Campbell who returned the smile, then Kulang showed him a letter from the S.R.D. stating that Kulang was in their employ. Campbell embraced Kulang and said many things in English and that he would follow him anywhere.

Kulang decided because of Campbell's condition he would wait for three days before attempting the return to Bongaya where he was working with the S.R.D. cutting a rentis from Bongaya to Ulu Tungud (in the Klagan area). During this period he gave Campbell the best attention he could. The escapee seemed to improve a little but was still apprehensive about Kulang and seemed reluctant to let him out of his sight.

On 19 July 1945 at 5.30 pm four large prahus paddled their way down the Munyed River. Altogether 47 people were contained in the craft. The first three acted as a screen

No 1 STRIP UNSERVICEABLE
P/W CAMP
31 MAY 45
100 200 300 400
58

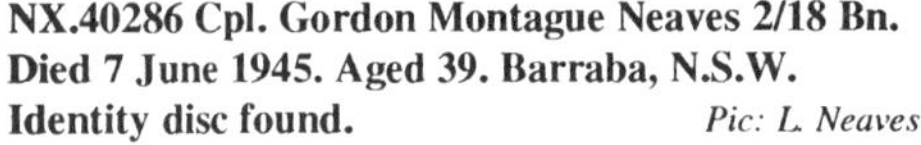

NX.40286 Cpl. Gordon Montague Neaves 2/18 Bn. Died 7 June 1945. Aged 39. Barraba, N.S.W. Identity disc found. *Pic: L. Neaves*

NX.40332 Pte. Thomas Archibald Reading 2/18 Bn. Aged 33. Barraba, N.S.W. *Pic: Kay Steinbeck*

because in the fourth prahu lay Campbell under the protection of Kulang. Campbell clutched an Owen gun, Kulang had an Austen gun and there were four .303 rifles with the rest of the party. They rowed all night and reached the mouth of the Bongaya river at 4 am on 20 July. At 6 am they stopped and prepared food, after which they continued on upstream towards where the S.R.D. camp was situated. In the meantime Kulang had sent a boat ahead to inform the OC he was coming to the camp with a white man. He did not want to invite small arms fire from the S.R.D. by coming upon them unannounced.

Lt. 'Jock' Hollingsworth was the senior member at the camp when Kulang's message came in. Major Sutcliffe and Captain Harlem were in another part of the territory. There was rather an emotional scene as the brawny Hollingsworth and the thin, emaciated Campbell embraced each other; even the frail-looking but tough Kulang shed a tear.

At a discussion held shortly after the reunion, plans were made. It was decided a letter be sent by runner to Harlem from Hollingsworth and at 3 am the runner returned with a signaller and a radio set. At 8 am Major Sutcliffe was contacted by radio and advised of the rescue, he instructed Hollingsworth to contact Morotai and arrange for a flying boat to be sent to rescue Campbell. The reply received from Morotai stated that Campbell was to be at Kandawan Island on 24 July at 8.30 am. At 3.30 pm on 23 July 1945 Lt. Hollingsworth, the radio operator, Kulang, Galanting and other loyal natives set out from the Camp. Campbell was in a very weak state and after they had gone about seven miles he fainted as if dead and remained unconscious for about five minutes, during which time Kulang massaged him with warm coconut oil. When he came to he began to talk deliriously. They reached Kuala Bongaya at 0730 hrs on 24 July and waited there without seeing any aircraft until 0930 hrs when they decided to go out to sea for a distance of seven miles. Eventually they sighted an aircraft circling a long way in the distance and they signalled. As they approached the aircraft they could see the crew were suspicious and stayed at their guns, however they soon opened up the hatches and beckoned to the men to come quickly. Campbell's stay in British North Borneo came to an end as he was lifted by strong hands into the plane. The spray was soon being blown away by the slipstream and Gunner Owen Campbell was heading for the U.S.S. Pocomoke, an aircraft carrier, anchored off the mainland. He was taken on board and given medical treatment and he remained there for some days. During this period some of the Australian members of the S.R.D. endeavoured to talk to him about conditions at the camp. The natives were coming out to the Carrier selling their vegetables. Campbell observed them and called the officer and suggested that there were Japs in the party.

Chapter 8

The escape of the five men from the column was not discovered until some time after it had re-formed and the aircraft had gone. The Japs did not attempt to seriously search for the men and continued with their efforts of forcing the tragic column to greater speed.

About the same time as Campbell's escape, Bombardier Braithwaite in No. 5 party began to realise that his condition was getting worse. Each time a stop was made he found it harder to get going again and often was subjected to a blackout. He had already been bashed by a Jap guard for slithering down one of the steep slopes. The guard had left him for dead after searching him for any food or valuables but Braithwaite managed to get up again and rejoined his own party. As he was making his way up the track he heard the shots from Tangkual Crossing, but did not know of course it was the massacre of the 73 PWs. He thought that the machine gun fire was the result of an Allied landing on the coast to the north and he then made up his mind to escape.

That night in the Sapi river area he had a talk to his friend, Gnr. Blatch, who advised him not to make an attempt but said if he really made up his mind he would come also. Braithwaite knew that he would be a drag on his stronger friend so he decided he would make the break up on his own. The next morning two of his particular friends could not stand up to resume the march. The rest of the party had not gone far when Braithwaite heard the two shots and this incident made him more than ever determined to make a break for it. His chance came shortly after when he was crossing a small creek; the Jap guard at the front and rear were out of sight so he veered off to the southern side of the rentis and hid behind a log. A malarial cough caused a Jap guard who passed a little later on to investigate and although he looked at Braithwaite and unslung his rifle he continued on his way. After a long rest and allowing time for the various parties and Japs to pass by Braithwaite walked back along the track in the direction of Mandoring. While he was making his way slowly along the rentis he saw a lone, unarmed Jap coming towards him. He lay in wait for him and when he came alongside he let him have it with a large piece of branch. He succeeded in battering the Jap to death, spurred on by three years of indignities and the foul murders of his mates.

For five days without food Braithwaite tried to reach the coast. He followed elephant and wild pig tracks, he fell into moss morasses thickly infested with deadly snakes; he thought his time had come one time when a large scorpion fell down by his neck as he sat resting under a tree.

On the sixth day he was nearly driven to surrender. He was on the bank of a river and he could occasionally hear Jap voices. He dare not sleep because of the crocodiles and he was attacked by a large colony of jungle ants and forced to climb a tree for protection. He had made up his mind he would surrender when dawn came. It was a long time coming but when it did he heard someone paddling a canoe. When it came into sight he found it was an old river fisherman so he called out 'Mari Sini!' (Malay for 'Come here') and the canoe made towards him.

The man, Abing bin Luma, was out inspecting his fish traps; he could not understand what the white man wanted so he took him back to his village where his son-in-law, Amit, helped Braithwaite into the house. There were many Japs in the area and they made immediate plans to hide Braithwaite. They already had a false wall in the house in which they hid valuables and rice in case of a Jap search. After some food and a bath Braithwaite began to feel happier, more so when he was told there were white men in the area and Amit and his father-in-law would try to get a boat to take him to them. Meanwhile Braithwaite was to sleep.

When he woke later he found many men of the kampong were discussing what action was to be taken with him. A Filipino who spoke excellent English was one of the principals. He was already a fugitive from the Japs for trying to organise the Filipinos in the Sandakan area against them. Although he was not keen on the idea, because of Japs in the area, volunteers were called for to paddle Braithwaite out to Libaran Island and at 7 pm that night two boats set out. With Braithwaite and Padua were Sagan, Omar, Sapan, Mangulong, Salim and Buang. Abing went too but Amit had to stay as his wife was ill. Braithwaite thanked him when he went, apologising he had no money to pay him for his work but he gave him his two fountain pens as a memento.

The canoes travelled all night and next day reached Libaran Island. Here, U.S. PT Boat 112 under the command of Lt. James, USN, took delivery of Braithwaite. They left him at the Island while they went off to strafe Beluran and when they returned they took him to Tawi Tawi. Later Braithwaite recalled: "That evening there were about twenty people in that Sick Bay, senior officers from everywhere, all wanting to know the story of where the other prisoners were, what had happened to them, how they had been treated, and I was able to give them this information; having been told that the march was going to the foothills of Mt. Kinabalu was a point where they could start a search and they said they would get on to it straight away. Unfortunately, about a week later, an Australian Colonel came to me and said, 'How are you feeling?' I said, 'Well, I'm pretty good', and I was coming good apart from a poisoned leg from the ant bites, I was eating normal food and the doctors were giving me liver injections every hour and vitamin pills, they really filled me up; but the Colonel said, 'We're going in now to look for your friends', and I just rolled on my side in the bunk, faced the wall and cried like a baby and said 'You'll be too late!'" He was the second survivor of the only two successful escapes from the actual Borneo death marches.

Bombardier Braithwaite escaped before the dreaded Boto region was reached; after this region the Japs increased their ill-treatment of the PWs. Men did not have to fall out towards the end of the march to await their end because the Japs took to ordering a man to fall out, especially if this man had any valuables such as rings, watches, etc. Some time later the Jap would return wearing the watch or ring of the victim. Some of the haversacks and blankets were taken by the Japs and sold to the natives as they passed carrying supplies for the Japanese. The track became so bad that the best some men could do at times was to crawl up the sharp slopes and slide down the other side.

Chaplain Harold Wardale-Greenwood was known to all PWs in Sandakan. He worked hard consoling, assisting the men and often replaced them on the work parties so they could have a 'rest day' from the work on the drome. When he was caught he spent time in the cage. It was known he was distressed at having to leave the sick and helpless back at Sandakan when he was placed on the second march. He urged men to pray. As the march progressed he became disillusioned and depressed. As they approached the high country, when so many men were forced to drop out knowing what fate awaited them, he was himself suffering from ulcers on the feet. He had no footwear. Walking in the mud often up to

NX.76223 Capt. John Oakeshott, Lismore, N.S.W.
Photo: Mrs. Secombe.

VX.38675 Chaplain The Reverend Harold Wardale-Greenwood, Stanley, Tasmania.
Photo: Robert Goldsworthy.

his knees, starving, suffering from beri beri, they stopped at a rest area near Ranau. Nelson Short went to gather firewood so they could cook a small amount of rice for the senior members of the group, including Capt. Oakeshott. He heard Chaplain Greenwood say "There cannot be a God, there just cannot be a God for men to suffer and be treated like this". He collapsed and died soon after — broken physically by the cruelty he had endured and witnessed.

They were now moving over what was the Croker Range, some thousands of feet above sea level. Moving in a fog of cloud, coming out on a hill above the cloud was 'like walking in heaven' said one the survivors, with Mt. Kinabulu, the sacred mountain, in the distance.

Nelson Short remembers: "The line was strung out, the guards were belting the men from behind and yelling "Lekas! Lekas!" ('Quickly' in Malay) and above the treetops in the jungle canopy the birds seemed to be imitating the Japs shrieking "Lekas! Lekas! Lekas!"

The march took 26 days. Out of 50 of the PWs only about 8 or 9 reached Ranau, including Captain Oakeshott. "We carried a blanket and eating utensils together with Japanese ammunition. Later I asked an old Jap soldier who arrived late what happened to the sick back at Sandakan. He said they were 'done over'.

"There were ten guards to each party. As most of the party died or were shot it was difficult for the remainder to escape.

"During the march those too weak to stand up were left. They used to shake hands, knowing the fate awaiting them.

"The men were dragged to their feet until they couldn't stand it — they were belted with rifle butts on their backs — "Faster! faster!"

"Those who could not march in the morning would fall out and go to a spot when we moved out — after we would hear shots. As individuals fell out the guard would accompany them and come on later alone. The Corporal told us anyone who fell out would be shot."

River crossings were frequent and on one occasion as they were crossing over on a single log one of the men lost his nerve and could not move. There was a camp of Jap civilians and soldiers on the opposite bank and when the man lost his nerve and was blocking the party a Jap civilian took out a pistol and was going to shoot him. WO. Sticpewich went back and carried the man and his gear across and when they reached the river bank the Jap civilian took all the man's gear, leaving him with nothing but what he stood up in. This PW died when he reached Ranau.

When the second party reached Ranau there were five Australian and one British PWs who were the remnants of the first march. Two of the Australians, Spr. Bird and Sgt. Stacy, told the new arrivals that 183 men of their party had reached Ranau but had since died from starvation and exhaustion after being forced to work on carrying rice from Ranau to Paginatan, 26 miles of mountain track.

There had been no provision made for the men at all in the Ranau Camp. The Japs had three huts built under jungle cover in the creek bed in preparation for an Allied invasion. The men were confined in an area about 50 square yards, which was above the Jap quarters. They had no shelter other than jungle scrub, no cooking facilities, no sanitary arrangements, no medical treatment or supplies available. They were forced to walk half a mile to draw water for all purposes and the Japs limited the number of buckets of water the men were allowed to struggle back with. The PWs were only permitted to get water from below the Jap camp and the Japs would do their laundry, bathe and urinate in the creek before it reached the area where the men were permitted to fill their buckets.

The rice ration was 70-75 grammes per man per day or about a small cup of very

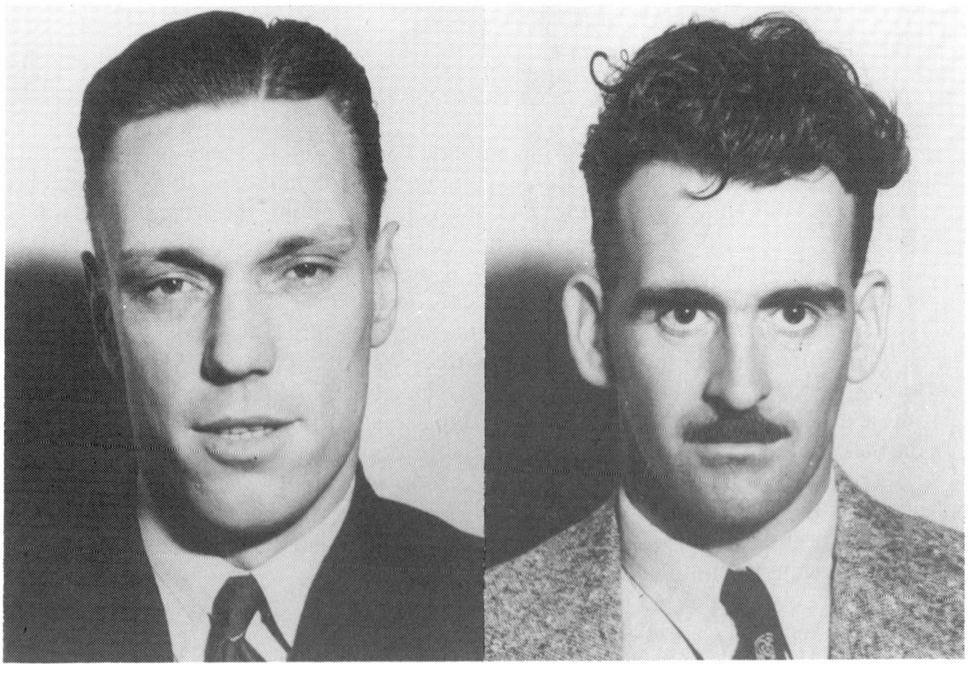

Bdr. Richard Braithwaite. Picture May 1947. AWM 41488.

Gnr. Owen Campbell. Picture May 1947. AWM 41489.

sloppy rice per man per day. Although the men were used on vegetable carrying parties, the only vegetables they had were what they could steal.

PWs had to supply working parties to carry rice in 50 lb. packs from a distance of three miles and had to do this twice a day making a total of 12-13 miles per day. The vegetable party were still doing the 18 mile trip and at this time they were given a very small issue of vegetables.

In the meantime the 9 Division supported by Allied Air and Naval units commenced operations against British North Borneo. The 20 Aust Inf. Brigade under Brigadier Windeyer landed in the Brooketon area while the 24 Bde. under Brigadier Porter landed on Labuan Island. Both of these landings were unopposed. Later it was established that before these operations the PWs in the area were shot.

The Australians occupied large areas without meeting the enemy — nowhere had the Japanese put up extensive resistance. The forces received outstanding co-operation from the native population who had been harshly treated by the Japanese. A surprising number of Japanese prisoners were taken. The natives, now knowing the Japanese were no longer the masters, commenced their own war against them.

As the Australians pushed inland, the Japs retreated further. By the end of July Australians had secured all their objectives including the Island of Labuan guarding the entrance to the strategically important Brunei Bay, which was to be used as a forward fleet base of operations further west (Malaya-Singapore-Thailand) coinciding with Mountbatten's Offensive against Malaya planned for August-September.

On 30 June WO. Sticpewich and four men began to build a bamboo, native type hut for the men. An attap carrying party also went once a day to the old camp at Ranau and returned to the new camp, a trip of six miles each way. The rice, vegetable, attap and bamboo working parties still did their arduous work each day. Conditions worsened and from 30 June to 13 July forty Australian PWs died and a greater percentage of British, due to starvation and the appalling conditions under which they were forced to work and live. The camp was 3300 ft. above sea level, warm by day and cold by night; what clothing and blankets the men had they shared with each other.

When the prisoners moved into the hut they had to carry Sgt. Col Smyth, a big man but now suffering from advanced beri beri. A Formosan guard had given him a beating but Smyth couldn't feel much because of the beri beri. A fluent speaker, he would relate to the men, in a low voice, his experiences working in a mental institution. He was much older and most of the men were interested in listening to him. The morning after one of his talks he was dead.

Sticpewich was the dominant person. His friendship with the Japs had paid off; there was no challenger, the weak were too weak. Capt. Cook had kept reasonable relations with Hoshijima at the top but the top had toppled whereas Sticpewich developed friendships from Capt. Nagai down to the guards which were later to keep him supplied with the vital quinine.

By July discipline had broken down — it was a matter of every man for himself, there was nothing they could share. The strong issued the rations.

The Japs continued their beatings of the sick and starving men for not being able to remove their dead quickly enough, for getting a drink of water from the creek, for relieving themselves. The men were so weak it was impossible for them to lift the bodies of their mates and it would take five men to drag a body along by rattan tied about the arms to a hole which had taken four men three hours to dig. All the time they were trying to do these jobs they were persistently harrassed and beaten by the guards. Botterill asked one man to help. The man said he was too weak and Botterill said "Well you get on the front end and I'll push you along". When they got to the graveside the man sat down by a tree and died.

'Taking' was not regarded as 'stealing' — it meant survival; anything a prisoner got

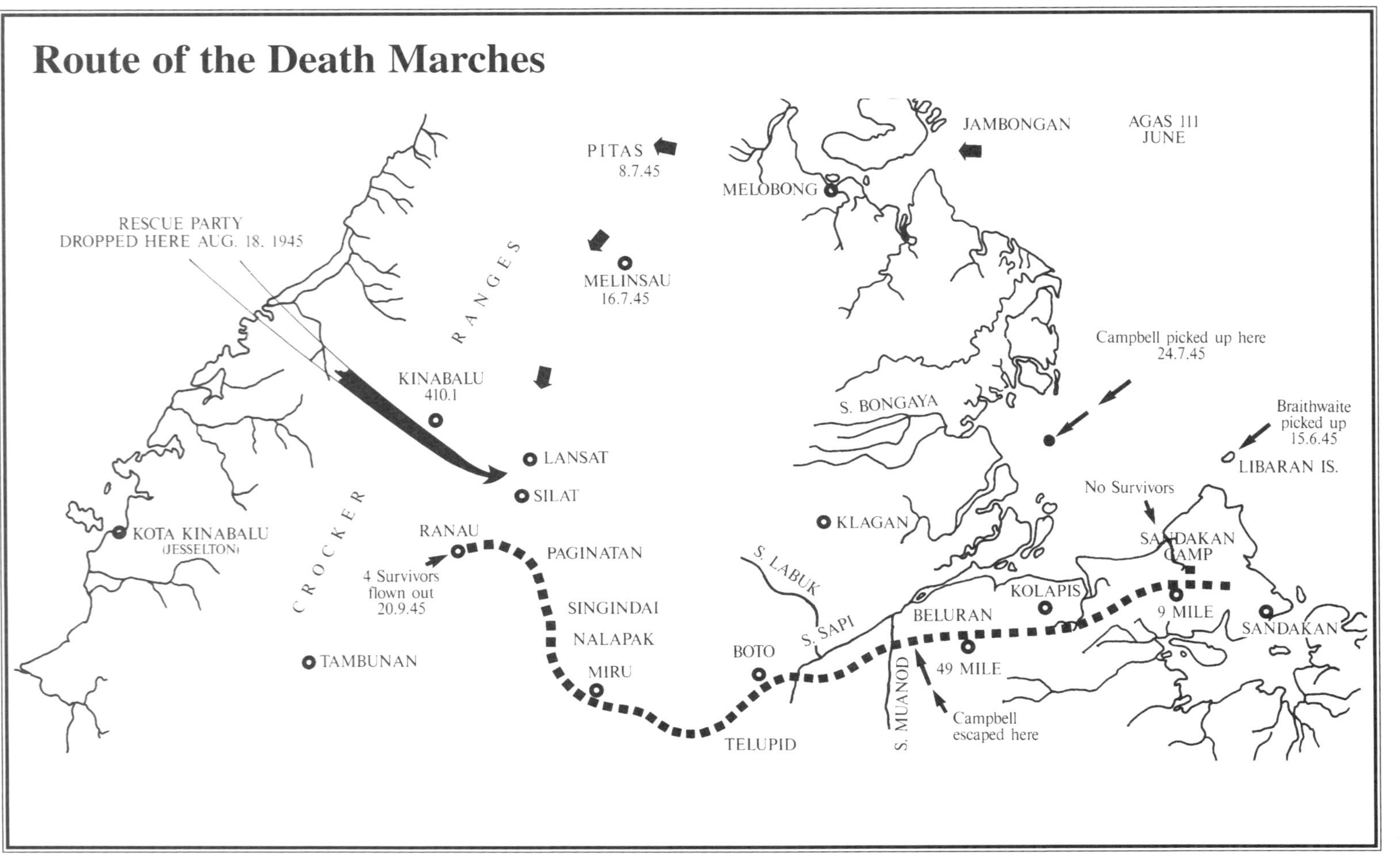
Route of the Death Marches
RESCUE PARTY
DROPPED HERE AUG. 18. 1945
PITAS
8.7.45
MELOBONG
JAMBONGAN
AGAS 111
JUNE
RANGES
MELINSAU
16.7.45
KINABALU
410.1
LANSAT
SILAT
KOTA KINABALU
(JESSELTON)
CROCKER
RANAU
4 Survivors
flown out
20.9.45
PAGINATAN
SINGINDAI
NALAPAK
MIRU
TAMBUNAN
BOTO
TELUPID
S. BONGAYA
KLAGAN
S. LABUK
S. SAPI
S. MUANOD
BELURAN
49 MILE
Campbell
escaped here
KOLAPIS
Campbell picked up here
24.7.45
Braithwaite
picked up
15.6.45
LIBARAN IS.
No Survivors
SANDAKAN
CAMP
9 MILE
SANDAKAN

Top left: NX.72749 Cpl. John Jackson. 8 Div. Provost Corps, later transferred to 2/20 Bn. son of Kathleen. Moree, N.S.W. Died 19 April 1945. Age 29. "Jacko" Jackson was a popular identity and singer. Survivors remember him singing "The Holy City" on board the "Ubi Maru" en-route to Borneo. *Photo: Mrs. Olga McElligott*

Top right: NX.25058 Spr. G.H. Wilkins, M.C. 2/12 Fd.Coy. R.A.E. Died 9 April 1945. Age 54. Potts Point, N.S.W. Served as Lieutenant in World War I and was awarded M.C. *Photo: Mrs. D. Bohnert, U.S.A.*

Captain 'Jock' McLaren, M.C. with Premier of Queensland, Mr Ted Hanlon, after receiving the Military Cross from the Governor.
As Pte. McLaren he escaped from Berhala Island in June 1943 with Ptes. Kennedy and Butler, Capt. Steele, Lieuts. Blow, Gillon, Wagner and Sgt. Wallace while the balance of the officers awaited a craft to be sent from Tawi Tawi. He, with Blow, was among the outstanding commandos of World War II *Photo: Ken McEwen*

NX.36653 Sig. George Daniel Conquit, Wagga Wagga, N.S.W.
Photo: A. Dandie.

NX.70110 Gnr. Fred Jackson, New Lambton, N.S.W.
Photo: Frank Jackson.

NX.60143 Pte. Harry Longley, Yass, N.S.W.
Photo: G. Longley.

SX.8384 L/Cpl. George James Evans, Torrensville, S.A.

he would eat even if it was a spoonful of salt; it would be taken with water — he couldn't hoard it as there would be many starving eyes watching. If you left it in the place it would be gone. Even the Japs would question the prisoner if he was eating away from ration time; if moving his lips he would be asked to open his mouth. You were not supposed to survive — there was always the thought in the guards' minds the prisoners just might outlast them.

On the afternoon of July 7 1945 the last remaining six survivors of the first march were placed with survivors of the second march who had arrived a week before, in the open on the side of a hill. The group included Botterill, Moxham, Short and Anderson who decided they would leave that night. Botterill had located a rice dump. They asked Fitzgerald if he wanted to join them. He declined because of his condition. They asked others also; some wanted to escape but realised they would only be a hindrance, because of ulcers, to the stronger members. It was important the party was strong enough to fight off any unfriendly natives who might be seeking rewards from the Japs for jumping them.

About 10 o'clock that night they left and it was very dark. Moxham walked into the Englishman Frost's camp which was a ground sheet supported by sticks. Frost was startled and he asked what they were up to? Botterill said "Shut up, we'll be back". He regretted he did not invite him to go with them because he was fit enough. There was only one way out. The camp was surrounded by jungle on three sides and on the cleared side there was no barbed wire. They moved out past the guards who were just sitting around, then continued on their way along a track for what seemed to be miles — each man was hanging on to the other in the dark. The track was faintly visible. Botterill could still recognise where the rice dump was located. They moved in quietly and felt around for the bamboo door and found it was locked. Their eyes by this time were fairly well adjusted to the dark and each member fumbled with the door until it opened. Apart from the rice the store contained baskets of native tobacco which they helped themselves to and also gathered what rice they could carry. They froze for a while when one of the Jap guards went to the latrine at the back of the hut. When he settled down again the men went on, heading through what was Ranau — it has been previously bombed out by Allied aircraft — turned left and headed towards Jesselton.

On 18 July the hut, consisting of a roof and a floor 20 ft. by 18 ft. wide and raised off the ground, was finished. The surviving 72 Australian and British PWs moved down to it. Thirty-eight men lived on the raised floor, but the remaining men were so ill with dysentery they could only crawl under the floor. There was a pit latrine 10 yards from the hut but after a few days it became a moving mass of flies and maggots. The PWs still had no medical attention. The men now were too weak to bury their dead and the Japs opened up a new cemetery 30 yards above their new hut.

Up to 20 July a work party of six men did water carrying, cleaning and preparing vegetables, chopping wood for the Jap kitchen, also washing the Japs' clothes. To carry water involved struggling down and back up an incline so steep the men could scarcely stand and 130 buckets of water per day was the requirement of the Jap officers. Plus other kitchen duties, one man did this alone — the other five men were on the other jobs. As the water carrier became too weak for the job and dropped out another took his place but every one of those men died just days after dropping out. Eighteen or nineteen men died on that particular job. (Except Dvr. Evans, and he dropped out because he was badly beaten, injured dreadfully internally and externally, and was unable to move. The reason for his dreadful beating was a Jap claimed he had not stopped another man from thieving vegetables. Later Botterill helped bury him.)

Nelson Short had to carry water for the Japs and light their fires for them in the pouring rain while they watched from the shelter of their tent. One time he was carrying water and because he was so weak could only manage to carry a few inches of water in the bucket at a time and Suzuki took a swipe at him across the head with his rifle butt. Short just managed to move his head in time and the butt caught him across the forehead, opening up a big gash above his eye.

In the camp the Jap guards were going through the men's gear and taking anything they wanted. S/Sgt. Horder caught two guards taking his watch and ring and called them 'mongrels'. He was immediately set upon and so badly and viciously beaten that he died that night.

The only 'meat' the men received was the stomach and intestines of the the occasional cattle killed.

One Jap guard, Takahara, was a Christian and he tried to help the PWs by stealing small amounts of quinine and atebrin from the medical store; sometimes he would leave a small bunch of bananas. But he was watched by the Japs as he had already been removed from Sandakan for being too friendly.

After the PWs had arrived at Ranau, one of the Japanese-conscripted Formosan guards got into trouble for having a dirty rifle and a few days before the four men made their escape he was complaining to WO. Sticpewich that he had been beaten by Takakuwa and Suzuki for having a dirty rifle. Sticpewich told him that no such thing would happen in the Australian Army and that even the Japanese prisoners in Australia were well treated. The guard said he had heard of that and that now the Allies were advancing all the Japs would soon be dead. The guard then told Sticpewich all the PWs were to be killed and that they should attempt to escape as soon as possible in order to avoid being killed. He also told Sticpewich he had seen Takakuwa's papers ordering their disposal. The Formosan guard apparently took the discussion to heart because on 15 July he shot Lt. Suzuki dead, wounded Takakuwa and Fujita, the medical sergeant who stole supplies from the PW's stores, and would have killed many more Japanese if he had remembered to pull the pin out of the grenade he threw into their quarters. He completed his 'hate' by committing suicide. Medical officers Captain Oakeshott and Captain Picone were now called upon to treat Takakuwa. (Earlier at Sandakan, St. Fujita would go into the camp hospital and dispensary and take medical supplies, instruments and anything he wanted. Capt. Picone and other staff protested but the practice did not cease. A couple of days before he was shot he called Capt. Picone down to him and demanded that Picone sell his watch. Picone told him he didn't want to sell his watch. Fujita then promised quinine and a quantity of medical supplies in exchange for the watch. Picone refused and told him he should supply him with the medical supplies without having to buy or trade for them. Fujita then ordered Picone to hand over the watch which he took and said 'I will give you quinine for it' — the quinine of course was never handed over.)

While the last prisoners were awaiting their fate at Ranau the Allied leaders finished their meeting at Potsdam; on July 26 the Potsdam Declaration, signed by Truman, Churchill and Chiang Kai Shek, was released. It called for Japan's surrender.

The Japanese Premier Suzuki told a press conference on July 28 the Potsdam Declaration would be ignored.

President Truman then gave the 'go-ahead' for the first operational atomic weapon to be dropped on Japan. The target chosen was Hiroshima — Colonel Suga's home town which had been spared from the B29 bombing. The date chosen for the drop was August 6. Truman received news of the successful mission when returning to the United States and he issued a statement warning Japan what they were to expect. The B29s from the Mariannas were pounding the cities of Japan and running out of targets for strategic bombers. Many of these aircraft were allocated for laying mines around Japan. Japan's overseas armies were now isolated, food was not arriving from the mainland and Japanese civilians were now showing the effects of starvation.

After the bomb was dropped on Hiroshima the United States waited for a change of mind from Suzuki. Truman then ordered the second bomb to be dropped. The target was Kokura, however, due to weather conditions, it was dropped on Nagasaki on August 9.

The Japanese Cabinet was discussing peace terms when news came through that

Nagasaki was bombed. To make matters worse for Japan the Soviet Union declared war — something the Japanese feared. Hirohito then gave the signal the war must end.

At noon on August 15 the Japanese people first learned of the Surrender. They huddled around wireless sets; prisoners there remember seeing them coming away weeping. They knew the war was over because there was no work and there were no planes overhead.

On 26 July there were only 40 PWs alive and these were reduced to spending the days in their hut. Capt. Cook was the fittest, despite the wound he had received when the guard had committed his 'hate'. The camp leader was endeavouring to conserve his strength as he wanted to keep himself alive for the purpose of retaining the camp records he had so painstakingly kept since they first arrived in Sandakan on 18 July 1942.

WO. Sticpewich's friendship with a number of Japs and Formosans, which had been the subject of discussion amongst some of his comrades, stood him in good stead finally and was eventually responsible for his escape from Ranau. He did all the cooking for the Japs, he was pretty well looked after; he hardly ever was in the camp; he was a 'Jack-of-all-Trades' and they seemed to look after him because of his usefulness.

Sticpewich continues " . . . then when Takahara (the Formosan guard) gave me the warning on the night of 27th I thought it was time I got out and get anybody else who was willing to come and take the risk. I had a consultation with Capt. Cook, Capt. Picone and Capt. Oakeshott, the two doctors, and told them of the situation, the same way as I had kept them posted with all the information I got in the past. I had convinced Capt. Picone that he could attempt to escape, Capt. Oakeshott said he could not do it owing to his having no boots and a big ulcer on his foot. Capt. Cook was too sick to make the attempt, Pte. Reither was sick but was willing to have a shot. The other men were all too sick to make the attempt.

"The next day it was impossible to bury the dead because there was no one fit enough to do it. I laid up for the day with the pretence of being too sick, in preparation for my escape.

"On the night of 28 July I cooked the meal and served it as usual. At 9.30 Reither and I sneaked out of the camp. When we had moved into the new hut the guard on the camp had been doubled; their beat would be less than a quarter mile around where we were camped. The guard house was just above us and it had a good view of us as there were no sides to our hut.

"We got up to the road however and laid low for the next day. We were still in the camp area and could see the general confusion in the camp at our escape. There was plenty of Jap guards' face slapping by the Jap officers and we saw the search party go out looking for us and return about 5 pm that evening. At dusk we made our way out along the road toward Ranau."

The two men moved from the camp area after the initial panic had died down. They were eventually found by a native, Girgaas bin Gangass, and while they were in a hut owned by him a Jap came but the men were hidden under a grass mat. Later they found their way to kampong Samang to the house of Dihil bin Ambilid. It was here Reither became seriously ill with dysentery and he died on August 8. In the meantime they had heard of the S.R.D. forces in the area and a note had been prepared and sent to them. The OC, Capt. Ripley, received the note and Sgt. Galenty came back with the runner, Limbuang, to Dihil's house and took Sticpewich back to the S.R.D. force in the Lansat area on 9 August.

Capt. Takakuwa was informed of Sticpewich and Reither's escape. He immediately ordered Sgt. Awabe to mount a search for he could not afford to have any prisoners to survive to tell the story of what occurred under his command. His movements were restricted because he was still suffering from a wound inflicted by one of his guards.

After the departure of Sticpewich, Capt. Cook must have considered the best action to take regarding the Rolls and Records he had so painstakingly kept since arriving at Sandakan. He previously informed Sticpewich they would be buried at an indicated place but later decided to hand them to Capt. Watanabe for despatch to Allied Command. The

Japanese identified the prisoners by their number. When they first arrived every PW was allocated a number, in the order of 'B' Force, English Party and 'E' Force; these numbers were then added to the cards kept at Kuching and the Prisoner of War Information Bureau, Tokyo, with all details of the prisoner. After the events of the next few days Watanabe burnt the records with his personal gear.

Sticpewich later indicated those who could have been in the camp at the time of his departure. After checking with other survivors, the Japanese account, and other sources, some of these present were:

JAP. DEATH CERT. DATE	*NO.*	
12.8	*NX.76184 Capt. Cook, G.R.*	*Voyage only Officer*
6.8	*QX. 6280 Capt. Picone, D.G.*	*A.A.M.C.*
1.8	*NX.76223 Capt. Oakeshott, J.B.,*	*10 A.G.H.*
9.8	*NX.51283 Cpl. Connolly, T.W.T.*	*R.A.E.*
9.8	*NX.53898 Pte. Doyle, A.G.*	*27 Bde. A.A.S.C.*
2.8	*NX.66892 Sgt. Doyle, L.H.*	*27 Bde. A.A.S.C.*
8.8	*WX.10289 Pte. Thorne, A.S.*	*2/4 M.G.*
6.8	*NX.68401 Sgt. Codlin, J.M.*	*A.A.P.C.*
11.8	*NX.43479 Pte. O'Donoghue, E.J.*	*2/20 Bn.*
9.8	*NX.27883 Cpl. Maskey, L.W.*	*27 Bde. A.A.S.C.*
30.7	*VX.47920 Sgt. Vaughan, W.J.*	*6/L/Sec. Corps. Sigs.*
30.7	*QX.17149 L/Cpl. Kealey, J.V.*	*2 Coy. A.A.S.C.*
13.8	*NX.25571 S/Sgt. McDonald, W.B.*	*2/18 Bn.*
30.7	*VX.43593 Sgt. Ferguson*	*A.A.P.C.*
5.8	*VX.39252 Pte. Koponica*	*A.A.O.C.*
30.7	*VX.39259 Pte. Wiseman*	*A.A.O.C.*

BRITISH ARMY

	Capt. Daniels	*M.O. A.M.C.*
	Flt./Lt. Burgess	*Liaison Officer, R.A.F.*
	Lt. Chopping	*R.A.S.C.*
	S/Sgt. Edwards	*R.A.O.C.*
	S/Sgt. Rooker	

On 1 August 1945 Takakuwa made his final decision regarding the PWs. There were 32 still alive and he decided not to consult the Area Commander, Major Watanabe Yoshio but called a conference of his staff which included his 2 I/C Capt. Watanabe Genzo, S/Maj. Tsuji, Sgt. Okada, Sgt. Beppu, S/M. Fujita and Sgt./M. Ichikawa, Quartermaster.

He commenced by saying that owing to certain regrettable incidents of PWs escaping over the last fortnight it was necessary for the rest of them to be disposed of. After considering the problem of disposal he finally decided on a method and issued the following instructions.

Sgt. Okada was to take all those too ill to walk, which comprised mostly Other Ranks.

S/M. Tsuji took charge of the party of ten, mostly NCO's, and Sgt. Beppu, one of Capt. Nagai's experienced killers, was to take the officers.

Beppu took eight guards and escorted Captains Cook, Oakeshott, Picone, the British Medical Officer, Capt. Daniels and Flt./Lt. Burgess of the R.A.F. Beppu had protested to Takakuwa he was too ill to carry out the task, nevertheless he had no option but to obey orders. One of the guards, Hashimoto Masao, a Formosan, who was with Beppu's party, stated "Beppu himself had gone ahead to the 111 Mile and told them to send the officers into the shade on the side of the track for a rest; the officers sat down. Then Beppu told us and the PWs to smoke. Whilst smoking Beppu told us that Takakuwa had issued

S/Sgt. William Baird McDonald. NX.25571. 2/18 Bn. Age 44. Armidale, NSW. Japanese stated date of death 13 August 1945. Most likely August 1, 1945. Assisted many by making shorts from old kit bags
Pic: Helen Evans

NX.35953 Dvr. Owen Evans, West Wyalong, N.S.W. Dvr. Owen Evans was the seventh man alive from the first march at the end of June according to Keith Botterill who got to know him over the last month of the march. He was caught with food in his possession and was severely bashed by the guards; he died the following day and was buried nearby with three others. Botterill was later to meet General George Wootten and give details of his nephew's death.

NX.68401 Sgt. John Morton Codlin, Coogee, N.S.W. Represented the A.I.F. in cricket against local teams in Malaya. Was Paymaster at Sandakan Camp and received severe beatings from Kitimura.
Photo: Alice Codlin

NX.27883 Cpl. Lance Maskey, 27 Bde.AASC., A.I.F. Camp interpreter, suffered severe punishment in his duties to protect the sick. Was one of the last 33 heroes living from the original total of some 2500 POWs. Was shot by the Japanese on August 1, 1945.
Pic: Enid Maskey

TX.5859 Pte. J.A. Clear. 2/29 Bn. Died 24 May 1945. Launceston, TAS. *Photo: Alex Brookes*

VX.47920 Sgt. W.J. Vaughan. Aust. Corps of Signals. Died Ranau 30 July 1945. Age 26. East St. Kilda, VIC. *Photo:Claire Kelly and Margaret Bradford*

orders that these officers were to be killed here. The five of us then fired at the PWs. Beppu used his pistol. I had to shoot Capt. Daniels. The PWs were unaware of their impending fate and made no attempt to escape. They were buried in two graves." Beppu denied he took direct part in the murders but all the eight guards gave evidence he had fired with his pistol.

S/M. Tsuji took his party of ten PWs 400m. along the Tambunan Road. He selected a location and informed the guards that the PWs were to be killed. He ordered the guards to surround them, then he addressed them and said 'There is no rice so I'm killing the lot of you today. Is there anything you wish to say?' There was no reply. The prisoners probably understood sufficient of the Malay Tsuji was speaking to understand what was about to happen. The guards always claimed they gave them cigarettes and water — a doubtful claim. Tsuji then ordered the guards to bring one prisoner at a time to the killing site. Toyuoka Eijiro was then ordered to shoot one PW. Toyuoka replied "I'm afraid". Tsuji said "I have pain to order you to do it and I order you to fire!" Toyuoka fired and killed the PW. Another guard was ordered to shoot — Nishikawa Moriji — he said: "But I do not want to," and Tsuji replied: "We are sons of the Emporor and must do". After some hesitation he fired and shot the prisoner and was present while they were all shot.

After the killings were completed one of the guards arrived from the camp and provided a meal.

Sgt. Okada Toshimaru was one of Capt. Nagai's experienced NCOs and had come from Labuan where there were no survivors from the party of 300 British PWs.

He was ordered to take all the sick to the cemetery and kill them. He then detailed a party of nine Formosan guards. He posted four guards in the camp area and the others were ordered to get the PWs to the cemetery. Some were carried on stretchers and others were herded from the huts with rifle butts. When they were there they sat around in a circle. Moricka Teickichi, Formosan guard, said: "After we were all at the grave site Sgt. Okada demonstrated the killing — he used a rifle and shot a PW. We were then ordered to line up and shoot the PWs. I was ordered to shoot Maskey but did not. Lieut. Watanabe viewed the proceedings and the results."

On their return to camp Tsuji told Takakuwa that several of the guards had objected to killing the men and Takakuwa dressed the party down for carrying out such a clumsy job.

This day was 1st August 1945.

In the jungle with the escape party Botterill asked Barigah what day it was; Barigah looked up at the sun and said it was August. It was Keith Botterill's twenty-first birthday.

And the last of those three who were farewelled at Alumny Creek in 1941 — John O'Donohue, was now dead.

Chapter 9

Botterill's party were on the edge of a rainforest where they came upon a small hut where they hid out until the afternoon on the following day. After considering their plan further they decided to hide out down in a gully close to water; it took the rest of the day to negotiate the down hill track. Here they found an overhanging ledge, forming a cave. The party soon covered in the front with bushes, settled down and lit a fire using Botterill's magnifying glass to get it going and cooked their rice and stew of wild green leaves. Here they stayed for four or five days.

When they left the cave camp they only had about two pounds of rice between them. Botterill and Moxham had endeavoured to steal a horse which was in the possession of a Japanese. The horse was to provide transport — and possibly rations for several days. The men huddled together for warmth at night — they continued to follow a track which they felt apprehensive about so decided to leave it, finding another small hut. Here Botterill suffered a bout of malaria.

Moxham and Anderson found an abandoned garden in which they found some tapioca and sweet potatoes which they soon boiled up. After a meal they decided to return to the garden to scrounge more supplies. In the meantime Short was sitting out by the hut when a Jap approached and asked for a light, in Malay. Short ran away. Botterill noticed him running and as he did the Jap looked in the hut and seeing pale Botterill suffering from malaria, said something in Malay.

One of the escaped prisoners said they were on a working party and the Jap sergeant in charge was down at the creek. The Jap mumbled something to the effect he was not convinced. Botterill pointed to Moxham, who was yellow with malaria and looked like a Jap. The Jap was not convinced but he went away. The party was called together and decided to move without delay. They tipped their stew out and moved to another location.

Barigah, a Dusan native, was on his way from his kampong Batu Lima when he heard noises from the deserted hut and was surprised to find the four very thin and bearded Australians there. When he asked them where they were going they told him 'Api Api' (Malay for Jesselton) and he told them they had best stay where they were as there were Japs at Jesselton. The PWs said they would stay if Barigah built them a sulap and continued to bring them food which he agreed to do and the men went with him. With the help of his kampong friends and Orang Tua Gunting he built the men a sulap near a small stream called 'Kihanot'. Many people brought food to them, particularly Barigah, Gunting, Ladooma, Magador, Kantong, Sumping. From the pro-Jap kampong of Bunda Tuhau some natives brought food. On one occasion a Japanese came into the dwelling where the men were living but they told him they were part of a Jap working party. After he went away they made for the jungle again. Barigah helped them build two sulaps. Anderson was getting

Group, l.to r.:
WX.7997 Pte. Herbert Dorizzi, Died 11 February 1945. Age 26.
WX.12884 Pte. T.H. Dorizzi, Died 11 March 1945. Age 31.
WX.9274 Pte. Gordon Dorizzi. Died 11 February 1945. Age 28.
The three sons of Thomas John and Mary Ann Dorizzi of Mungarin, W.A. served with 2/4 MG. Bn. **(see page 130)**

Photo: W.G. Chitty

Bottom left: QX.13888. Pte, J.McK. Warren 27 Bde. Coy. A.A.S.C. Died Sandakan 14 June 1945. Age 39. Red Hill, QLD. Former featherweight champion of Queensland.

Photo: Barry Laing

Bottom right: NX.51227 Pte. H.R. Gault 22 Bde. A.A S.C. Died Sandakan 27 April 1945. Age 30. Trundle, N.S.W. Hugh Gault, at age 7, remembers collecting the telegram advising of his uncle's death.

Photo: Hugh Gault

much weaker and he died on 29 July 1945. (Gnr. F.D. Anderson. QX.6866. Kelvin Grove, Qld.)

The men were now in a very weak state; they were rapidly approaching the stage where they would have done physical violence to each other if they had been able. The division of every little piece of food was jealously supervised and they were apt to suspect each other of trying to get more than their share of food. This dreadful position was relieved somewhat when Barigah brought news that there were some Allied soldiers in the Lansat region of the Ranau area.

Flt.Lt. Ripley had landed at Jambogen Island on June 21, 1945, with his party and made their way to Melobong and proceeded on foot to Pitas. On July 8, 1945 they left Pitas and arrived at Milinsau on July 16, 1945. O.T. Andong Ajak joined the party.

As no suitable dropping zone was available the party moved to Kioyid where they received a supply drop on July 25, 1945. On August 2 the party moved to Lansat.

On August 8 Gimbahan brought information that two Australians who had escaped from Ranau were living in the jungle west of there. He produced a note written by Sticpewich. O.T. Gilenki of Lansat agreed to investigate and left immediately with medicine and food. The party then moved closer to Narawang.

On August 10, 1945, Gilenki and Gimbahan returned to Narawang with Sticpewich in a very weak condition. He reported that Pte. Reither, who escaped with him, had died of dysentery on August 8. Sticpewich also reported that Botterill, Moxham, Short and Anderson had escaped earlier but he had no news of them. Agents were immediately sent out to make enquiries.

The three men wrote a pencilled note which was taken to an S.R.D. party commanded by Capt. Ripley. Gunting and Barigah made the trip and were given medicines by an S.R.D. officer, also a police boy to guide the escapees to Silad where the Australian commandos were camped. This was the note they carried —

'To O.C. in charge of English or American Forces.

"We are three Australians, prisoners of war escaped from camp early in July as Nippon was starving all men they were dying six and seven a day. After a few days out this dusan O.T. Baragh found us and has looked after us ever since building a little hut in the jungle.

"We are still in very weak condition but quite O.K. O.T. Baragh is a Tuan Besar around here and you will find all the dusans very friendly and sincere.

"Today they called in wanted me to write this note and one O.T. Baragh and O.T. Gunting are going to contact you.

"Hope it will not be long before I see you as there are to my knowledge about ten or twenty men (prisoners) left out of 3000 or more.

Do all you can for Baragh pronounced Baruga.

Bdr. Moxham

We are 5 mile from Ranau.

W.M.

NX.58617 Pte. Short
NX.42191 Pte. Botterill
NX.19750 Bdr. Moxham

Anxiously waiting to hear from you.

W.M."

On August 13 Barigah came back with food and medicine and a note which said the war was almost over but the Japs are still hostile so stay where you are. Then the collaborators started looking for them so Barigah moved them three or four miles closer to Ranau. They thought of the rest of their comrades at the camp near the 110¼ Mile peg.

Ripley informed Morotai of the situation and called for reinforcements including a doctor. He also sent Gimbahan to the Ranau camp to ascertain the number of prisoners still alive. He was unable to gain access or any authentic information.

Centre of Group: L to R: Short, Sticpewich, Botterill

Labuan 19 September 1945
R.A.A.F. Record States: 16 A.O.P. Flight — Group Captain Fleming, Flt. Lt. Muggleton, Flt. Lt. Cocks, F/O Dowse and P/O Thomas. A11-27 . 13 . 3.5 . 29 31 — forced back by bad weather in an attempt to land at Ranau to evacuate Australian PWs.
Sept. 20 — Same men same aircraft flew to Ranau to evacuate PWs. Flt. Lt. Cocks F.11.35 crashed on take-off, his passenger slightly injured. Medical Officer passenger in A11-13 elected to remain behind and the injured man was flown out.

Two Liberators of Flight 200, the Special Air Transport Unit for S.R.D., were despatched from Moratai on August 18. The aircraft were commanded by Flt.Lt. J. Wallace and F/O Weir. The party comprised a Medical Officer, Major Foster and Capt. Nicolls, 'Z' Special Group — Sgts. McNeale, E.G. Gore (Signaller), Les Gilham (Medic), J.A. Hodges and N.A. Wallace.

As the first aircraft 'A72-195' approached the dropping zone they could see four white smoke signals and a Union Jack. After a dummy run they dropped two operatives, then another one on the next run. A further three runs over the area dropped storpedoes of supplies.

The following Liberator 'A72-192' made five runs over the dropping zone, dropping the rest of the party and supplies. Here they were met by Flt. Lt. Ripley and Sgt. Hywood, his signaller, and a large contingent of natives who assisted in gathering in the stores. Without delay they set off to find the escapees who were known to be heading their way.

Botterill, suffering from malaria and advanced beri beri, was being helped by Barigah and Kalingal. His back was aching, he was hunched and couldn't straighten; they tried to carry him but it hurt too much. His testicles were so swollen they had to be supported. He was struggling to lift his legs when a snake crossed his track — he whacked it with his stick as his aides lifted him to avoid the snake and they caught him before he fell. Short and Moxham were not as badly affected. They had walked all night. Barigah had made the torches — he cut dry bamboo, shredded the ends, lit them and when they died down he would turn them into the middle to keep them glowing — later, when the moon came out they were not required.

Botterill said: 'The next day I was lying down, thinking that I couldn't walk another step, when I looked up and saw an Australian face bending over me. He was a big six-footer, he just sat down beside me and cried, and I cried too'. He was Sgt. J.A. 'Mike' Hodges.

During the march in daylight the leading commando urged Barigah to assist in cutting the path to carry Botterill. Barigah ignored their request — the Jap parties were still looking for the escapees and Barigah was concerned the commandos were cutting the brush and leaving a trail anyone could follow. As an expert jungle operator he was accustomed never to leave the slightest sign of his track; he thought cutting or breaking a twig was unnecessary exposure, so much could be learned from a break in a branch.

Botterill and Moxham were carried into the camp on stretchers but Short managed to keep on his feet. Botterill was in the worst condition, his weight was reduced to 84 pounds and at least a stone of this was fluid caused through beri beri swelling. His scrotum had a diameter of nine inches due to these swellings. Moxham's weight was 66 pounds and Short weighed 63 pounds; they all had matted hair and long beards which helped to boost their weight.

Sgt. J.A. Hodges immediately sent a native runner back to inform the rest of the party including the doctor the escapees had been located. Major Forster didn't think that Botterill would last the night — Mike Hodges said he was as close as being dead as he'd ever seen. However, it wasn't long before the PWs began to respond to the care and attention given them by their own men.

The same day a start was made on an Auster airstrip about one and half miles from Silad with the intention of evacuating the escapees. On the completion of the strip, a fuel drop was made by parachute and later the Auster flew over but did not land. A few days later the strip was declared unsuitable due to the surrounding jungle.

Botterill remembers when P.C. Mentod was brought in suffering from a bullet wound in the wrist, he stated he had been shot by the Japanese. His arm was amputated above the elbow by Major Forster. Next morning he was missing from his bunk when Botterill saw him down at the creek having a wash.

During this period Major Forster endeavoured to keep the escapees on a strict diet of Marmite and limited bread — they were responding quickly. When a food drop was

Rear L to R: Sgt. J.A. Hodges, Cpl. L. Grinham, Sgt. Hywood (Sig.), Cpl. E.G. Gore.
Seated L to R: Sgt. N.A. Wallace, Sgt. J.A. McNeale.

made it included apples, something they hadn't seen for nearly four years. They found it was an effort to eat the apples as their jaws soon became tired. A special air drop of salt was made; this was required as currency to pay the natives for collecting firewood needed for the camp.

It is obvious the S.R.D. resources were strained — the aim of Ripley's party was to set up an R.A.P. in the vicinity of Ranau to assist any escapees. Had there been a large scale breakout it is not known what forces they had to cope with such an eventuality.

The main S.R.D. party left for Ranau on September 14, leaving behind the escapees in the care of Cpl. Grinham. It was now decided the best hope of evacuation was to repair the airstrip at Ranau, however the Japanese were still hostile. Many knew the war was over — leaflets had been dropped in the area on August 18 but many thought it was a propaganda ruse and they had no way of communicating with their H.Q. General Baba, the Commander in Borneo, was prepared to fight on.

So the commandos were forced to work at night to prepare the strip. Firstly it was mapped in the dark, plotting every bomb crater. Filling was collected in preparation for placing in the holes in the strip at night. When the strip was considered serviceable for Austers to use, Cpl. Grinham and the escapees made the trip to Ranau on horse back. During this trek the natives took them to the site of a crashed Kittyhawk. The remains of the pilot were later found to be those of Flt.Lt. Cooper of the R.A.A.F. They buried the remains and marked the grave with a cross.

On September 20, 1945, the escapees were evacuated to Labuan.

FOOT NOTE:

Bill Moxham's minor injuries were soon attended to by Major Forster who remained behind to look after him.

From left: Short, Botterill and Moxham (still showing the effects of beri beri). *Photo: Paul Moxham*

FOOT NOTE:

The Official Report stated:

On 19th September 16 A.O.P. Flight — Group Capt. Fleming, Flt.Lt. Muggleton, Flt.Lt. Cocks, F/Officer Dowse and P/Officer Thomas in Aircraft A.11.27, 13, 35, 29 and 31 were forced back by bad weather in an attempt to land at Ranau to evacuate Australian escaped prisoners of war.

On September 20 the same crews flew to Ranau to evacuate the POW. Flt.Lt. Cocks, A.11.35 crashed on take-off and his passenger was slightly injured. Medical officer in another aircraft A.11.13 elected to remain behind and the injured man was flown out.

Normally this unit was commanded by Flt.Lt. Clancy who participated in the attempt to rescue them at Suad but was transferred on 18 September.

Chapter 10/11

Author's Note

In previous Editions, these chapters have described what happened at the 8 Mile Camp after the departure of the second march on 29 May 1945.

There were no survivors. The only information available was from the Japanese who were placed in a Compound soon after the surrender and here the guards were known to have prepared their alibis in order they all told the same denials of committing atrocities to the War Crimes Investigators.

By April 1946, all the major war criminals' Trials had been completed and a large number of Japanese death sentences were carried out at Morotai and Rabaul. The War Crimes Investigators returned to Australia without leaving representation with the War Graves Recovery Units which were now in the process of recovering the remains.

Many of the guards and senior NCOs who received gaol sentences were detained at Rabaul.

The War Crimes Section was now operating from Melbourne. Any new evidence found by the War Graves Units was referred to Melbourne. The War Graves personnel were not briefed as to the past events.

In January 1947, LANDFORCES Melbourne, on the recommendation of the POW Enquiry Contract Group (who had marked many of the grave sites between Sandakan and Ranau and recommended that the natives who had assisted the POWs be rewarded) sent Major H.W.S. Jackson, together with Colin Simpson (ABC) and Major Dyce (Brit.) to Sandakan and Ranau where the natives were given a Certificate of Appreciation and cash rewards.

During some of these interviews, allegations were made that a victim had been nailed to a cross and later the victim was burnt together with the cross and the ashes were washed away in the rain.

Meanwhile, back at Sandakan Camp after the departure of the second march, Lt. Moritaki, the senior Japanese officer left in command of POWs, returned from Kemansi on 1st June 1945 to the smoldering remains of the huts; he inspected the emaciated prisoners lying on the ground exposed to the elements and he was reminded of the order by his Sgt.Major Murozumi that Captain Takakuwa's instructions were to be carried out: the prisoners were to be disposed of.

There was not one prisoner of the Japanese who had not heard the guards state that "when British American come — all men die!".

The Japanese troops remained on the unoccupied portion of Morotai when the U.S. Forces occupied all they required as a base for the assault on the Philippines in October 1944. The Japanese Command were well informed of the Allied troop movement and they were able to observe the huge concentrations of Allied shipping and aircraft. General Baba, Commander of the Japanese 37 Army, anticipated a Division would land at Sandakan — the Japanese were now anxious to ensure no prisoners would be alive to be rescued and they believed the invasion was imminent.

It seems Moritaki gave instructions for the leader of the English group to be wired to a tree and tortured in retaliation for refusing to leave the sick, the dying, and go on the march. Moritaki then. set out to destroy by fire all camp records which had not already been destroyed: identity discs and other items of identification; and senior personnel remaining in the camp. A few English officers were too ill to go on the march, the senior Australian NCO would have been disposed of quickly — his date of death was recorded as 4 June 1945. At this time all the prisoners were moved to No.2 Compound.

Hoshijima would have known what had happened back at the Camp. At his Trial he described the NCO as an Administrative Assistant to Captain Cook and regretted that "due to an unfortunate incident" the NCO was unable to be present in the Court as a witness to describe the difficulties that he, Hoshijima, had had to face as Commandant of the Camp. The details of this "unfortunate incident" were now beginning to unfold. No members of the Court asked Hoshijima to elaborate on this.

After the Japanese-Government accepted the conditions of the Potsdam Declaration the guards were gathered in a compound at Tuaran and they were there for over two weeks awaiting the arrival of the Occupation Forces. They all had ample time to get their alibis together and were aware, as early as April, that the Allies had created a War Crimes Tribunal to place War Criminals on Trial.

There was no evidence the prisoners were fed, the survivors — Sticpewich, Braithwaite, Campbell and Short — all witnessed the huts being fired and the burning of medical supplies and important Camp records. There was no water supply, the only water available was from the gutters, puddles and a nearby swamp hole.

Having disposed of the leaders and camp records by 9 June, Moritaki then assembled those who could walk and this pathetic assembly of 75 men moved off down the Eight Mile road — without supplies or personal belongings — and turned west along the track to Ranau. They were led by Lieut. Iwashita of the Okayama Unit and did not get very far before men began to die or were killed. Only one Japanese survivor reached Jesselton but he died before he could be interviewed.

Moritaki was known to be ill and he would have been anxious to kill the prisoners as the Japanese Command were aware the Allied invasion fleet was off Labuan (where they landed on 10 June); the Japanese also believed an invasion of Sandakan was imminent.

Moritaki was suffering from malaria. He was usually described as "a nasty bastard" and was responsible for carrying out Hoshijima's brutal orders. He would have been anxious to ensure no POW out-lived him; he is reported to have died on 18 July however it is more likely he died 18 June — he would have been unconscious for several days before his death. Therefore, the orders for the killing of the last of the POWs would have clearly been his responsibility.

Later, War Graves located his grave five yards from the flagpole close to the Japanese H.Q. Cpl. Evans was present when the grave was opened and all the Javanese labourers agreed it was Moritaki.

At this time the Japanese claimed the last PW was killed about 19 August. Medical experts state that, under the conditions and circumstances of the prisoners, it is highly unlikely any of the men would have lived more than two or three weeks.

Moritaki then sought and found a further 23 prisoners who could walk, these would have been the ones able to care for the sick and the dying; Moritaki would have figured that getting rid of these men would speed up the dying process. Whereupon he arranged for trucks, as the guards admitted later, to take them to the rubber plantation where they were shot; there seemed to be some urgency in the use of trucks, it would appear this massacre took place on 13 June — not 13 July.

By June 16, the Australian 9 Division had won Labuan and Brunei and other landings were taking place.

The Japanese were now killing the survivors of the Labuan 300 party which comprised 100 British from Sandakan and 200 from Kuching, including several Australians. Sgt. Sugino acted on orders at Labuan to kill the prisoners in June — most likely Moritaki and Murozumi were acting on the same orders.

Wong Hiong claimed the last PW was beheaded about August 15. Again, it would be a miracle for PWs in an advanced state of illness in June, without food, shelter, medical supplies and subjected to brutality, to live for a further 10 weeks.

Murozumi was again interrogated in July 1947. He admitted the last two prisoners died on the same day in No.2 Compound but denied having beheaded one. At this time he was unaware the remains of these two prisoners had been recovered. Further questioned, he said he saw them the day they died.

Hoshijima, Takakuwa, Watanabe and Yamamoto all received the death penalty and by April 1946 the Prosecutors and War Crimes Investigators left Borneo for Australia.

At this time two War Graves Units were in the area to recover the victims of deliberate brutality carried out by the Japanese on orders from the highest authority. There is no record of Hirohito reprimanding officers for carrying out atrocities, similar atrocities were committed throughout all areas occupied by the Japanese.

The War Graves Units first arrived at Sandakan and Ranau about March 1946. No

This is the site in No.2 Compound where about 170 remains were found of those who were left behind at No.1 Compound after the departure of the second death march. Susan Funk, now Mrs. Wong of Melbourne, is standing as a 'marker' (single figure left) to indicate where the last two Australians were killed and buried. *Photo: A.W.M. Graham Robertson Collection*

WX.7634 Pte. S.A. Osborne. 2/4 M.G. Bn. Died 21 June 1945 Age 31. Swan View, W.A. The Japanese Administration gave Osborne's date of death as January 1943. It was not until the investigation for the last PW seen beheaded, was Osborne's grave found adjoining that of the beheaded Australian. S/M. Murozumi was again questioned, he denied executing the other Australian. He admitted two POWs were seen alive that day.

Photo: Brian Osborne

WX.7627. Pte. J.McL. Goldie. 2/4 M.G. Bn. Died 4 June 1945. Busselton, W.A.

Photo: N. Griffiths

The Australian Cemetery. Inset: The plaque was engraved by Spr. Goldfinch and placed on the cross at the entrance to the No.1 Cemetery. It was at this spot where War Graves Unit Recovered several beheaded remains, believed to be senior personnel who remained in the camp after the departure of the second march. (See Goldfinch photos on page 86). *Main Photo: G. Robertson Collection; photo of Plaque: R. Battram*

Crimes Investigator accompanied them; all sensitive information was dispatched to Melbourne for determination. These Units would rely on the work carried out by 23 War Graves under Captain Houghton, who came ashore with the 9 Division Invasion Force on 10 June 1945 at Brunei Bay, the first time a Graves Unit had done so. This was brought about by the knowledge 'Z' Special Unit was able to convey to Allied H.Q. They knew in advance the vast problem it faced in recovering over 3000 victims of Japanese brutality killed in Borneo. When Captain Houghton opened the first graves on Labuan, he was shocked to find naked victims.

His Unit set off to Ranau to open graves and locate those who perished at Ranau and to place crosses and markers on all graves. He reported to H.Q. the enormity of the task ahead; and Special Units would be formed to carry out this task.

When the PW Enquiry and Contact Group reached Sandakan with Capt. Houghton, a thorough investigation was carried out to locate the cemeteries. Capt. Houghton reported in October 1945; "Within the Compound [Map Ref.: 919508] a mass burial ground was found. On opening the grave and examining the remains it is quite logical to presume death was four to five months previously." Colonel Johnston, 13 Field Ambulance, concurred. An identity disc, VX.643385, was found amongst the number of bodies and it is difficult (or impossible) to pin it on to any particular one. However, one of those bodies was Irving. (The Japanese gave Irving's date of death as 1 June 1945).

During December 1946, War Graves at Sandakan was advised a Reward Mission would visit Sandakan in January 1947 to compensate local people who had assisted the prisoners. Major H.W.S. Jackson was in charge of this group; with him was Major Dyce, an Australian in the British Army, and Colin Simpson, Journalist from the ABC together with his sound technician. The need for this action was first recommended by Sgt. W.A.C. Russell of 'Z' Special Unit who was in the area for three months prior to the Japanese surrender.

Wong Hiong, standing in the grave in No.2 Compound, claimed he witnessed S/M. Murozumi executing a tall, dark-haired Australian. On left of pic is Lt. W. Sticpewich. On bottom left corner of pic was Osborne's grave — it was separated from the other grave by 2 ft. of solid earth. There were no other remains in the trench. (see map of location). *Photo: Aust. Archives*

NX.71546 Pte. Michael James Coffey 2/10 Fd.Amb. Died 18 April 1945. Aged 32. Beni, N.S.W. *Pic: M.M. Coffey.*

NX.45810 Pte. Thomas Cyril Lethbridge 2/10 Fd.Amb. Died 15 July 1945. Aged 38. Maitland, N.S.W. *Pic: Yvonne Sipple.*

VX.45352 Dvr. Francis James Fitzpatrick 4 Res.M.T.Coy. Died 5 August 1945. Aged 45. Pascoe Vale, Vic. *Pic: Alan Bennett*

NX. 13844 Pte. Geoffrey Keith Cox. 2/18 Bn. Died 5 April 1945. Aged 19. On 30 July 1994 a Memorial notice was placed in the Wagga Advertiser: "In Memory of Geoffrey Cox. At fifteen you fought for your country, at nineteen you gave your life at Sandakan. Tomorrow we bring you home in our hearts." *Pic: Ivy Molkentin*

Wong Hiong, a 16-year old Chinese who had worked for the Japanese responded to the notice he had seen in Sandakan offering a reward for information concerning prisoners of war. He described an alleged crucifixion of a Naval Officer and how this man had been nailed to a seven foot cross. (This account has been printed in previous editions of "Sandakan — The Last March" together with a description of the beheading of the last prisoner of war). Recent research of files, which were not previously available, now disclose investigations revealed flaws in Wong's accounts. Wong claimed the remains on the cross were burnt and the ashes washed away in the rain, More interrogations were ordered, each one resulted in further discrepancies. Eventually, War Crimes Office in Melbourne ordered Wong be interrogated again and insisted he point out the locality where the crimes were committed. Wong was probably under pressure by the Japanese and Japanese spies, he was warned by War Graves officers his statement would be made in the form of an Affidavit and would be presented to the Court and he may be questioned again. Whatever effect this statement had on Wong, in August 1947 he took Lieut. Sticpewich to a site in No.1 Camp where the remains of an English officer were found, together with wire and three inch and four inch nails — but no nail mark on the skull — as reported previously, he had claimed observing an eight inch spike being nailed through the victim's head,

This account agrees with the information War Graves Unit personnel were told by various local people — that a PW had been "wired to a tree". This atrocity occurred in the middle of No.1 Camp about the time Moritaki returned to Sandakan. Soon after this event, all prisoners were yarded into a fenced area in No.2 Compound.

Four days later, Wong took Sticpewich to a position in No.2 Camp Compound where he claimed he had witnessed the last prisoner being beheaded. Here a victim was found, his head severed from his body. (See Locality picture in this Chapter). This grave was separated by two feet from another remains which were later identified as Pte. S.A. Osborne, further enquiries were made and War Crimes investigators established Osborne died the same day as the Australian was beheaded. They changed the date of death from 23.01.43 to 21.06.45.

The Japanese had already given a false date of Osborne's death because they had knowingly committed a crime — this procedure was common Japanese practice.

About mid-June, Major Rex Blow, now of 'Z' Special Unit, was put ashore with a couple of frightened natives he collected on Libaran Island and intercepted the track to Ranau — he found no sign of any prisoners. Many enquiries were made, Blow advised H.Q. there were no prisoners alive at Sandakan Camp.

On 22 June 1945 LANDFORCE Melbourne cabled C-in-C India for information War Office. Para.2 of this message read: "At Sandakan 1 June 500 Australian and British PWs moved westwards from PW Camp which was destroyed by Japs. 150 PWs too sick to walk remained. Fate unknown."

Pte. S.A. Osborne is buried in the Labuan War Cemetery in Plot 20 Grave 12; the beheaded Australian is buried in Grave 13. From the information provided by War Graves it is likely this victim may have been identified and his identification withheld.

It is hoped Sandakan Memorial Park Trustees will regard this vacant land as a significant Memorial Site and open it to the Public to enable them to pay homage to all those who perished there.

On August 18 Allied planes had dropped leaflets telling the Japanese the war was over, but they believed these to be propaganda and the leaflets were ignored.

By the end of July Japan indicated she was ready to accept the Potsdam Declaration subject to a condition to clarification as to the future of the Emperor's role should not be prejudiced. While Britain was prepared to accept the Emperor as a figurehead Australia was not.— "We would insist that the Emperor as Head of State and Commander in Chief of the Armed Forces should be held responsible for the Japanese Acts of Aggression and War Crimes and would thus demand his removal".

Britain's reply to Australia was unacceptable — a further cable went off to Washington:

"The Emperor should have no immunity from responsibility for Japan's acts of aggression ... The visible dethronement of the system is a primary means of shaking the faith of the Japanese in the heavenly character of the Emperor in whose name they have committed many atrocities. Unless the system goes, the Japanese will remain unchanged and recrudescence of aggression in the Pacific will only be postponed to a later generation.

"At your request we postponed publication of the report which is now before the War Crimes Commission ... In our view it discloses a deliberate system of terrorism and atrocity which must have been known to the Supreme Authorities in Japan not excluding the Emperor. It would be a very difficult matter to justify discrimination in this respect as between Hitler and his associates on the one hand and Hirohito and his associates on the other.

"For these reasons we are opposed to the acceptance of Surrender on the understanding which the Japanese are attempting to attach to the Potsdam terms .... it should be clearly understood by the Japanese .... that the person of the Emperor is to be regarded as at the disposal of the Allied Governments in the same way as each and every other person of the surrendering Enemy State"

At this point agreement was already reached by the Major Powers. United States then told Australia the Emperor's power to rule would be subject to the Commander-in Chief who will take such steps as he deems proper to effectuate the surrender terms.

The senior advisers continued to smart over the fact their Emperor would be be subject to a foreigner. The debate continued for some time on the imperial rescript; eventually it was agreed to and signed by the Emperor.

The war with China didn't rate a mention, despite the fact that 20,000,000 people were killed in the China incident. There was no mention of Surrender or Capitulation — 'We have decided to effect a settlement' — accordingly they accepted the provisions of the Potsdam Declaration. Hirohito went on to say Japan's declaration of war on America and Britain was out of a sincere desire to ensure Japan's self-preservation and the stabilization of East Asia — it being far from their thoughts either to infringe on the Sovereignty of other Nations or to embark on territorial aggrandizement. Later researches found Hirohito's involvement in supporting the Army of Japan from the early thirties.

He went on to express the deepest sign of regret to all Allied nations of East Asia who consistently co-operated with the Empire towards emancipation of East Asia. One cannot help remembering the evil treatment of the people of Asia by the Japanese and how harshly and cruelly treated they were, the tortures they carried out — putting people of the Philippines in cages below the tide limit — the wholesale beheading of the Chinese, just because they were Chinese. In fact by 1945 the Japanese were hated like no other race —there were many accounts to be settled.

The important message to his people by the Emperor "was to maintain the structure of our imperial State. Let the entire nation continue as one family from generation to generation. and finally keep pace with the progress of the world".

In Japan, many PWs witnessed the Japanese coming away from the radio set after the broadcast weeping — they changed their attitude immediately — not a word was said about Surrender.

In no time they were bowing to the PWs. The Emperor convinced his soldiers they were not prisoners of war. He had simply taken action to terminate the war he was largely responsible for. General MacArthur was later to say he was impressed with the Emperor's authority to stop the war but puzzled why he could not have prevented it. While the Surrender arrangements were being made the Japanese sent signals to all Commands to destroy documents, particularly those communications from the Prisoner of War information Bureau. General Baba indicated to imperial General HQ the Army was prepared to fight on; a special Emissary was sent to Kuching to persuade the General to conform with the Emperor's wishes.

NX.68663 Pte. P.E.J. McCardle. 3 Res.M.T. Coy. A.A.S.C. Died 20 April 1945. Age 43. Mascot, N.S.W. *Photo: Pat West*

NX.68904 Dvr. Leo McCarthy. 2/3 Motor Amb.Corps. A.A.S.C. Died 2 March 1945 at Paginatan. Age 44. A World War I veteran. *Photo: Smithfield R.S.L.*

Reconnaissance aircraft had observed the plane on the ground at Kuching. A few days later a signal from Southern Command indicated they would co-operate with food drops in the PW camp. The first supply drop was made on 30 August over Lintang Barracks. This consisted on 2000 Ibs. of medical stores and 2500 lbs. of rations together with 300 Ibs. of Comforts. These drops were made daily, except for two days, up until September 11.

Colonel Suga addressed the camp and informed the assembly the war was concluded; America had dropped a cruel bomb on Hiroshima. He was emotionally affected and obviously believed his family had been wiped out; he was not to know they had been evacuated by his brother.

On 2 September 1945 — three years to the day when Hoshijima ordered the 'No Escape' document be signed — Japanese representatives of the Emperor's Government signed the instrument of surrender on the U.S.S. Missouri in Tokyo Bay.

The same day a message was laid out on the ground at Kuching stating there were 1740 males, 243 females and 38 children and a total of 410 stretcher cases. This information permitted the Recovery Group to plan for their evacuation after landing there in September. In the meantime, Colonel Wilson, G.1. of the 9 Division, visited Kuching on September 5 and arrangements were made for Colonel Walsh to return to Labuan for discussions. Walsh returned on September 7 in a new set of jungle greens, a glow of whisky and a bottle of Scotch which he failed to share with any of his fellow officers. Later, two medical officers were flown in on September 8 with more medical supplies including blood, sulphur drugs and penicillin. A transmitter was delivered; this was operated by 8 Div.Sigs. Lt. Gettens and Sgt. Joe Weston who transmitted messages to Baba's outlying forces who had been out of contact.

On September 10 General George Wootten, Commander of the 9 Division, accepted the surrender from General Baba. The following day the Relief Force arrived at Kuching. After establishing control of the town they moved to Lintang Barracks, the PW Compound.

On September 12, Capt. L.G. Darling, PW Liaison Officer from the Recovery Forces,

Top: **Late Colonel Suga**
L to R: Harold McManus, C.P.O. Stone, Lt. Reg Dixon.

Photo: R. Dixon.

Bottom: **Centre: Col. Suga's Batman wearing Suga's belt.**
Behind: Sgt. Watts.
Right: Lt. R. Dixon.

interviewed Col. Suga who, at his request, handed over all records of PWs and Internees held at the Lintang Barracks where the PW Compound was located. Suga handed Capt. Darling a memo in which he endeavoured to disassociate himself from the Sandakan-Ranau movements and denied any knowledge of the Labuan-Miri force of the 300. He maintained he was out of communication since early 1945. There is evidence he, accompanied by Lt. Katsuji Yamamoto, the so-called 'doctor' of Kuching, visited Sandakan during February 1945. He would have seen for himself the advanced state of illness and starvation and known what to anticipate; he would have been aware of the ration cuts and the ultimate fate of the PWs. The death certificates of several hundred PWs were certified by him, several hundred kilometres from the scene of massacres and death, as having died from malaria and beri beri.

There was no atrocity committed by Col. Suga at Kuching, however he would have had to explain the 600 graves in the cemetery of English PWs who died from malaria, beri beri and starvation.

Within a short time Colonel Suga was taken to Labuan with his batman. There he was handed over to Lt. Reg Dixon to be placed in a compound. Soon after his arrival he stood in the open for a short while, placed a cigarette in his mouth and beckoned his batman to light it for him. When it was lit the spectators, who comprised many American sailors, cheered and booed. Suga turned to Dixon and asked why should they do that to him. He was later taken to this tent where he was fed and retired for the night.

In the British camp at Kuching there were two surviving sailors from the gallant ship, the U.S.S. Houston, which was sunk during the battle of the Java Sea. An American war correspondent brought them from Kuching so he could obtain a photograph of Suga bowing to the former US prisoners. First opportunity in the morning they approached Lt. Dixon to visit Suga where they found the batman kneeling beside his body. During the night Suga had pierced his throat with a table knife and bled to death. He had asked his batman to burn incense for him but as the man did not have any he lit a mosquito bomb. C.P.O. Stone took Suga's pen and Harold McManus took his spoon as souvenirs. Lt. Dixon said there was no other evidence as to the cause of death. Earlier, when he searched him Suga had resisted parting with a map of Australia he had kept. He told Dixon he was to be Commander of Prisoner of War Camps in Australia.

The death certificates were quickly despatched to the Translation Services at Land H.Q. Morotai. They would have covered known graves, there were many hundreds to follow.

Soon after, Casualty Lists were published in Australia in October and by early November death notices were being inserted in the newspapers by relatives and next-of-kin. Many were still seeking news — the first notification of the status of men after the fall of Singapore was released through Tokyo and the International Red Cross in 1942-43. Telegrams went out in 1943 confirming those which were prisoners of war. The worst was to come — one in three PWs under the Japanese were to die, a total of 7,777 and of these, 1,800 from Borneo. Many of the relatives were first informed in 1944 they were still alive, telegrams went out and advised next-of-kin that some were believed deceased — more waiting — it was not until December that the final advice was received.

The anguish of relatives waiting for news over this period was almost intolerable — the sight of the telegram boy pushing his bike along the street increased the tension of fearing the worst. Some, like Mrs. Core, waited until December to receive final confirmation that her son, Sydney Russell, had died on June 10 at Ranau. He had enlisted at the age of 15 and had arrived with the last contingent of reinforcements — untrained — in time for the final battle on the Island and later to be sent to Borneo.

And up in the rolling hills of Ashford in northern New South Wales the Postmaster received a telegram addressed to 'Smiler' Watts' next-of-kin, his mother, who lived eight miles out at 'Roseneath', an old slab homestead. He decided he would give the telegram to young, 15 year old Ruby Watts at school to give to her mother after riding home. It

Major Hugh Rayson, R.A.M.C., who was Senior Medical Officer at Sandakan after the departure of Lt.Col. Sheppard with Col. Walsh to Kuching in October 1942. (Story page 14). Major Rayson was recovered from Kuching on 11 September 1945, soon after the recorded events in his journal which represent a significant contribution to the history of Sandakan.

Photo: David Rayson

NX. 72848 Spr. Charles Hamilton White 2/12 Fd. Coy. R.A.E. Died 6 April 1945. Age 38. Roseville, N.S.W.

Photo: Peter White

The Labuan War Memorial *Photo: Tony Wilkins*

was not until next morning Ruby remembered the telegram and gave it to her mother who read what she had feared most. Word spread quickly and in no time the minister, friends and relatives arrived to comfort her.

There were many brothers who claimed one another in PW Camps. Irrespective of Units they wanted to stay together and in many cases the older brother would claim the younger one. Sid Bexton and his brother Tom, aged 24 and 25, died in June and July 1945. The shock of the Dorizzi family in Mungarin in Western Australia must have been shattering, Gordon and Herbert, aged 28 and 26, died on the same day 11 February 1945, probably shot on the first march. The elder brother Tom died exactly one month later — three sons... (Lt. Katsugi Yamamoto certified one died at Sandakan and the other on the march.)

The Frost brothers, Edmund and Henry, of Stawell in Victoria, died two weeks before the war ended.

Then there were the very young — Charles Mainstone from Earlwood, must have enlisted at the age of 15 or 16. He was known to his friends as 'Baby' and tried to overcome the nickname by shaving more regularly. He died in March 1945 near Paginatan. His father, a Digger of World War I, was now a PW in Germany. And Spencer Anzac Neville Burns from Wallsend, known as 'Sammy', didn't start shaving until he had been in Malaya for about a year; he died 31 January 1945, aged 20.

The two Connor brothers — Henry and Joseph — both married with children. They came from Windsor and Rosebud in Victoria and would have stayed together to help one another; they died within twenty days of each other.

Joey Crome from Bondi, who thought he had bad eyesight due to surfing at Bondi and not from the vitamin deficiencies he was suffering, volunteered to join a working party from Kuching to Labuan — when the 9 Division landed they found no survivors.

The DeFaye brothers from Victoria died within a month of each other.

Private J. W. Ince who had survived a massacre on Singapore Island when the Japanese tied prisoners up and executed them, leaving them for dead. One of them called out 'Anyone alive?' — he survived then, only to die in June 1945.

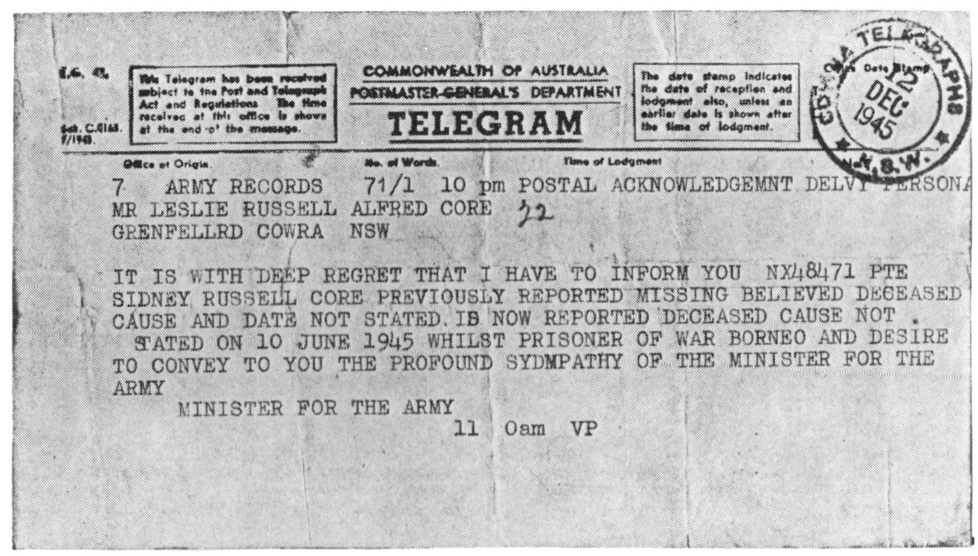

COMMONWEALTH OF AUSTRALIA
POSTMASTER-GENERAL'S DEPARTMENT
TELEGRAM

This Telegram has been received subject to the Post and Telegraph Act and Regulations. The time received at this office is shown at the end of the message.

The date stamp indicates the date of reception and lodgment also, unless an earlier date is shown after the time of lodgment.

TELEGRAPHS 12 DEC 1945 N.S.W.

Office of Origin. No. of Words. Time of Lodgment

7 ARMY RECORDS 71/1 10 pm POSTAL ACKNOWLEDGEMNT DELVY PERSONA
MR LESLIE RUSSELL ALFRED CORE 22
GRENFELLRD COWRA NSW

IT IS WITH DEEP REGRET THAT I HAVE TO INFORM YOU NX48471 PTE SIDNEY RUSSELL CORE PREVIOUSLY REPORTED MISSING BELIEVED DECEASED CAUSE AND DATE NOT STATED. IS NOW REPORTED DECEASED CAUSE NOT STATED ON 10 JUNE 1945 WHILST PRISONER OF WAR BORNEO AND DESIRE TO CONVEY TO YOU THE PROFOUND SYDMPATHY OF THE MINISTER FOR THE ARMY

MINISTER FOR THE ARMY
11 0am VP

NX.48471 Pte. Sydney Russell Core, Cowra, N.S.W.

NX.897 Pte. Charles Douglas Mainstone.
Photo Nell Mainstone

Sandakan 26.10.45. Capt. G.M. Cocks and Lieut. E.K. Robertson both of 3rd. Aust. POW Contact and Inquiry Unit listing identifiable names and numbers of items found at Sandakan.
Photo: AWM 121783

Chapter 12

The principal PW Compound in Borneo was first established at Kuching on August 15, 1942, under the command of Major Suga, English speaking, who had spent some time in the United States as a teacher. In private life it is believed he was in the teaching profession at Hiroshima. Assisting him was a staff of 112. His second in command was Lt. Nekata.

The camp was situated at Lintang Barracks, formerly occupied by 2/15 Punjabi Regt. stationed there in peace time, and just three miles from the town of Kuching, capital of Sarawak.

This compound was subdivided into nine small camps —

1. Australian officers (Commanded by Lt. Col. A.W. Walsh)
2. British officers (Commanded by Lt. Col. T. C. Whimster)
3. Dutch white officers and ORs (Commanded by Lt. Col. A. Mars)
4. British ORs (i/c RSM S.T.G. Sutherland)
5. Indian ORs
6. Indonesian ORs
7. Male internees (i/c W. C. Adams, Esq.)
8. Female internees (i/c Mrs. W. C. Adams)
9. Dutch male internees - priests

The Australian officers' camp commenced when Colonel Walsh was evacuated from Sandakan in October 1942 with Lt. Col. E.M. Sheppard, Major Fraser, Blanksby, Workman, Lawler and Capt. Owen, Mr. R. H. Wilson and four ORs. Later when Major Campbell and Capt. Scrivener were released from Kuching Gaol they joined the others. The next intake was not until June 1943 when 'E' Force arrived at Kuching where Major Fairley and Carter were off-loaded, then Major Fleming's party. Soon after the balance of the 'B' and 'E' Force officers from Sandakan were sent to Kuching.

From the time Col. Walsh arrived he kept to himself, ate alone for three years, and generally was not popular.

Some of these officers had clashed at Staff level during the fighting and now confined in the same small hut in Kuching were still squabbling, some were even ignoring one another. Col. Mac Sheppard, popular medico, did his best to keep the peace. Matters improved as more officers arrived from Sandakan, however it was not until the bulk of the officers arrived in October 1943 did the atmosphere improve. Capt. Claude Pickford, with some of his helpers, wasted no time in getting a concert party under way and this assisted in breaking the boredom. The officers were not permitted to work and effectively confined to their quarters most of the time they introduced various means to further their education.

Collectively, there was considerable talent available, it was decided to share knowledge — 'George' Washington, an expert in shorthand, taught many the skill. The Sig. Officer,

Rus Ewin, and his colleague taught Morse Code. The school teachers enjoyed their chance to lecture a class again.

As in most camps the Medical Officers were outstanding. Most remember Capt. Frank Mills on his knees clearing out a wound and rubbing wood-ash into it. Nothing seemed to be too much trouble for them, they acted as doctors as well as nurses.

Col. Mac Sheppard was able to leave the Officers' camp and tend the small bunch of Australians in the British Other Ranks camp. While they did the same work as the English there were to be no deaths among them. Some of them had a background of misconduct at some stage — usually associated with survival — so they were carrying on black market and other activities which would have made the Mafia look pale — For return for medical services they made sure Col. Sheppard always was able to return to the officers' camp with something extra.

The Japs gave them permission to cultivate 'kan-kong', a fast growing plant like the 'nasturtium', it would grow anywhere with the aid of a daily drink of urine — everyone was compelled to save their urine for the garden. Later the latrine waste with "livestock" was also scraped out and spread on the garden. There were occasions when some officers would take the bucket from their adjoining mates if they were not up early enough and spread it. The Japs permitted some fowls to be kept but these needed supervision — and ground.

Generally, everyone shaved daily no matter how blunt the blade was — until you have used one razor blade for three years you've just no idea what it's like — have a shave with cold water — no soap and blade honed on glass.

The officers were reasonably free of bashings and they were in a position to observe activities in the camp. Often the Nuns and women would regularly go to Jap H.Q. where they would spend hours sifting the weavils from the rice and other chores, like sewing. They often observed Agnes Keith and her young son going to Suga's H.Q. when he demanded her presence to discuss her work.

Unit officers usually kept together and there were many ways to ease the boredom. The Bishops brought in books from outside, everyone took advantage to learn two extra words per day, words they normally did not use. For example, Walsh must have taken advantage of this also, for one day he caught one of the young officers urinating on the kan-kong, he called out 'Don't micturate there!' — the officer had never heard the word used. He raced into the hut and asked one of his school teacher mates what it meant?

Lt. Nekata and his guards kept a strict control over the camp while 'Doctor' Yamamoto acted in an arrogant and hostile manner, particularly towards our Medicos.

Like any other group of men confined in a small area there were problems with everyone conforming to an acceptable code of conduct under crowded and difficult conditions. As the war continued to go against the Japs the food ration was cut accordingly, every available piece of ground in the compound was sown down in some type of vegetable crop.

Lt. Yamamoto showed his hatred in many ways, like most Japanese under those conditions they were unpredictable; he could be kind but was more likely to be nasty. When an officer's spectacles fell off he crunched them under his boot; a similar occurrence was when an officer was ordered to open his mouth, his teeth fell out and they too were trodden on; however, like Colonel Suga, he would tell the officers to look after their 'healths'.

Many men suffered from scabies and were confined to a special hut so as to isolate the problem. Mateship existed particularly amongst men of the same unit — they stuck together and helped one another.

By August 1945 several officers had died; the number would have accelerated but for the sudden termination of hostilities. Food drops saved many lives and by the time relief forces arrived most PWs were in reasonably good shape; Kuching camp was to have one of the lowest death rates in Asia. However it was not until they were evacuated on the

Lt. Garland — 1940.

Lt. Dennis Garland, Collaroy, N.S.W. Photo late September, 1945, Morotai A.G.H.

NX.41648 Pte. J.F. Skinner. A.A.M.C. Tenterfield, N.S.W. The Japanese gave his death as 15 August 1945. Age 31 *Photo: R.S.L. Tenterfield*

NX.58548 Sgt. Kenneth Charles Witt 27 Bde. A.A.S.C. Died Sandakan 20 April 1945. Aged 27. Wollstonecraft, N.S.W. *Pic: Hazel Thomson*

'Wanganella' they were informed orders were found in Col. Suga's office instructing him to evacuate the compound and remove all prisoners and internees to Dahan which would have been the 'cover' to eliminate them all in accordance with superior orders. In every PW camp in Japanese occupied territory provisions were made for the elimination of PWs in the event of Allied invasions. In Japan they were to be taken up to the hills and left in the snow to die; in Thailand moats were constructed around camps with machine gun posts positioned strategically; in Changi the gaol was to be packed to capacity with PWs then the water supply was to be cut; those PWs who had been digging defensive tunnels in Singapore and Johore would have been placed in the tunnels which would have been sealed and fired — just as the Japanese did in Pelawan. The Prisoner of War Information Bureau in Tokyo had plans for notifying the deaths of the prisoners — the documents the organisation which the Emperor Hirohito personally created are still Restricted by Congress.

AWM 1118405
Australian Officers broadcasting messages home.

AWM 118426
Lt. Col. Mac Sheppard (centre) with the Australians from the British Other Ranks camp. Beri beri can be observed on man far right.

AWM 116956
Australian Officers, Kuching Camp. Those in the dark clothing have been refitted with jungle greens.

13th Sept., 1945
L to R: Lt. R.W. McIver, Capt. D.S. Johnston, Capt. J.J. Rowell, Lt. V.M. Nicholson, Lt. E.N. Dengate, Capt. A.C. Arvier.

Chapter 13

On the 7th September, after several messages had been exchanged, Lieut. General Fusataro Teshima, signalled that he had been ordered, from Saigon, to negotiate matters personally with the Australian commander.

The surrender ceremony took place at Morotai on the I Corps sports ground at the sides of which troops were lined up seven ranks deep. At 10.50 a.m. on 9th September the troops and the Japanese party were in position, the Japanese standing about 10 yards from a table. At 10.58 the parade was called to attention. At 11 o'clock General Blamey arrived at the table and a guard gave the general salute. General Blamey then read the terms of surrender. General Teshima moved forward to the table and signed the document of surrender. Then Blamey signed the document and handed Teshima a written instruction — "Second Japanese Army Instruction No. 1". Teshima returned to his former position and Blamey gave an address:

"In receiving your surrender I do not recognise you as an honourable and gallant foe, but you will be treated with due but severe courtesy in all matters. I recall the treacherous attack upon our ally, China, in 1938 (sic). I recall the treacherous attack made upon the British Empire and upon the United States of America in December 1941, at a time when your authorities were making the pretence of ensuring peace. I recall the atrocities inflicted upon the persons of our nationals as prisoners of war and internees, designed to reduce them by punishment and starvation to slavery. In the light of these evils, I will enforce most rigorously all orders issued to you, so let there be no delay or hesitation in their fulfilment at your peril.

"The Jap Navy has been destroyed. The Jap Merchant Fleet has been reduced to a mere fraction. The Jap Armies have been defeated everywhere and all that remained for them was to await their total destruction, Japanese cities lie in waste and Japanese industry has been destroyed. Never before in history has so numerous a nation been so completely defeated.

"To escape the complete destruction of the nation, the Emperor of Japan has yielded to the Allied Forces, an an instrument of total surrender has been signed in his name. He has charged you to obey the orders which I shall give you.

"In carrying out these orders the Japanese Army and Navy organisation will be retained for convenience. Instructions will be issued by the designated Australian commanders to the commanders of the respective Japanese forces, placing upon you and your subordinate commanders the responsibility for carrying out your Emperor's directions to obey all orders given by me to you.

"You will ensure that all Allied personnel, prisoners of war or internees in Japanese hands are safeguarded and nourished and delivered over to Allied commanders. You will

Suspected war criminals. From R.to L.: Captain Hoshijima, Dr. Yamamoto, Captain Nagai Hirowa, Captain Yamamoto and Lieut. Watanabe. All received the death sentence except Capt. Nagai who was responsible officer in charge of the Labuan party of 300 — there were no survivors. He left Labuan early 1945 to take command of the rice carrying parties at Ranau to Paginatan. He was designated War Criminal No.7. When he arrived at Ranau he enquired of Keith Botterill, "where is my good friend Sticpewich?" And they told him he was back at Sandakan. Nagai, like Hoshijima, was removed from POW command in April 1945 when the Allies announced the setting up of a war crimes tribunal. The question remains unanswered: who were the officers responsible for not proceeding with charges against Nagai? Botterill and Sticpewich were in Tokyo together for General Baba's trial and staying at the Empire Hotel, Botterill asked Sticpewich: "when does Nagai's trial come up?" "You leave Nagai to me" he replied, "we might need him — we might be fighting the Russians soon!" *Photo: Reg Dixon*

collect, lay down and safeguard all arms, ammunition and instruments of war until such time as they are taken over by the designated Australian commanders. You will be given adequate time to carry this out.

"An official date will be named and any Japanese found in possession after that date of any arms, ammunition or instrument of war of any kind will be dealt with summarily by the Australian commander on the spot."

And now the Compounds were ready at Labuan and Morotai to take in the suspected war criminals, being all those who had had any dealings with POW Administration. A War Crimes Officer was appointed — interrogation commenced without delay — legal officers were seconded from other Units to assist. Australians who had done a 'crash-course' in Japanese were now acting as Interpreters where lives were at stake. Hoshijima was later to say they were equivalent to Japanese Primary School standard.

Hoshijima was first interrogated by Captain Brereton on September 24 and was tried in an Australian Military Court convened under the War Crimes Act of 1945. He was charged on four counts covering confining Prisoners in inhumane conditions, permitting torture by guards under his command, failing to provide adequate medical care and food, permitted underfed prisoners to be employed on heavy manual work.

He was found Guilty on all charges and sentenced to death by hanging. He later appealed against the sentence which was upheld and he was hanged at Rabaul on 6 April 1946.

During his Appeal he admitted: during the period of his command of the PWs 900 died, that he withheld large quantities of rice and medical supplies, that those attempting to escape were shot, that severe punishments were inflicted for minor misdemeanours, that the majority of PWs were in a weak and dying condition when he handed over command to Takakuwa.

In earlier evidence Hoshijima explained his policy for caring of PWs:— "Impartial administration and severe security. I would like to describe how the general attitude of the Japanese with regard to the administration of the PW. Europeans regarded their people who became PW in the best light but this was not the Japanese attitude. For instance in the Russian-Japanese war the Kamimura fleet saved all the Russian seamen whose ships had been sunk, gave them treatment and interned them in one of the hot springs in Japan, but in the Nonohoman incident Japanese officers who had been taken prisoner by the Russians and returned to Japan later on were ordered to commit suicide. For that reason the Japanese did not fully recognise the significance of PW camps. For this reason it was very difficult for myself the administration of the camp was difficult for myself and other Japanese personnel.

"Even the Japanese higher officials found it hard to understand and recognise the customs with regard to the treatment of PW. In the Japanese Army beating is not permitted but in actual fact soldiers are daily beaten. There is not one Japanese soldier who has never been beaten, even I have been beaten even as an officer. By beating I mean slapping by the hand. Beating is only done as a warning and to correct their conduct. This is an old Japanese and Chinese custom. If you read Japanese and Chinese history you will see that this is true. There is one word 'bentatsu' which means to inspire and instruct with cane. Whenever you ask any guidance from your superior the Japanese and Chinese use this word which means to inspire and instruct with cane, that is why in Japanese schools, monasteries and apprentices they constantly beat the pupils.

"Next it was my duty as the commander of the PW camp to protect the PWs and keep a severe watch on them. Also it was my duty as Commander to let the PWs observe the regulations and keep their morale high. And as a Commander I demanded that both PWs and Japanese soldiers observed my regulations, and I treated them equally according to the regulations. And as I said a number of times already I did not order any ill-treatment or hard work, nor did I permit others to do so. Next, regarding the large number of deaths among the PWs in my opinion the war situation was the main cause of this. Everyone can understand the difficulties at Sandakan when they take into consideration the coming of the operations in Sandakan and the geographical situation of Sandakan. Also Sandakan was the most forward PW camp in the southern area during this war. I request the court to understand the difficulties of the situation in which we were placed and to understand we did our best within the limit of our capabilities despite the lack of understanding in others. I believe that if the War had not approached Sandakan that the conditions there would have been just as good as they were in 1942 and 1943, and I would have been able to continue under those conditions to the end. In my opinion I did my best to act justly in all matters, by my conscience and by my sense of justice. As a result of the defeat of my country I am now being tried here as a war criminal, something which I do not fully understand because I did my best for the PWs. I believe that I have done right in the treatment of PWs and nobody could be blamed for it."

Hoshijima appealed: "I was found guilty and sentenced to suffer death by hanging by the General Court Martial of 9 Aust. Division at Labuan on 20 January 1946. This was quite beyond my expectation and I still cannot understand at all why I was found to be so. Herewith, I should like to write down after the sentence was given so that I might be favoured with more proper judgement.

"I am afraid that the court did not care to take all my efforts and endeavours made for the benefit of the PWs during the hardest times since about October 1944 into consideration. As I mentioned at the beginning of the interrogation, the majority of the Japanese people had little knowledge about PWs and had shown indifferent attitude toward them. At Sandakan, the matter was worse because Sandakan had been occupied with preparations for defence, having no time left for doing anything else. Under such a condition, I had to carry out my duty as a Commandant of the PW camp there. You can see how I had been worried about everything, especially in procuring food and medicine for them, and how I had done my best for the benefit of the PWs. It is not an exaggeration to say that everything that had been given to PWs was the result of my efforts during day and night. To my great regret all persons in the camp had not been aware of my efforts which I had made outside the camp.

"Did the Court really understand my sincerity which I concentrated for the protection of PWs? I had also established an anti-air signboard with the characters "P.O.W.", by my own suggestion for the protection of PWs from air raids, which was taken off by order of Lt. Col. Suga later on.

"Enlargement of the farm in the camp, cutting off the number of PWs for the airfield construction work, alteration of the Army order to remove Sandakan PW camp to Kemansi, and reduction of number of persons from 500 to 455, despite the strict order from the Army HQ's which insisted on removing 500 PWs to Ranau as the first party of the march. All these things show you that I had always done my best for the protection of PWs with the full hope to comply with International justice and human morality. I hope you will give impartial judgement on the abovementioned facts.

"Now confined in jail my only wish is that either Captain Cook or Captain Mills (British Army) who had known me well could be still alive. I feel in solitude the irony of my doomed destiny.

"Of these lurking facts, I am sure you had no idea at all. Moreover, I want to ask you whether you know the fact that Australian soldiers were giving each other bodily punishment for bad behaviour.

"Lastly, I earnestly hope you will calmly reconsider the real situation of beating which was done for the purpose of maintaining discipline in the Japanese Army, about which I mentioned in the court.

"It was one of my greatest regrets that I could not have a good interpreter. Since I came to Labuan in September 1945 I have met several Australian interpreters but none of them was found able to speak or understand Japanese as well as Japanese boys graduated from primary school. Especially at the time of the interrogation by Captain Brereton on 24 September 1945 the interpreter conveyed only a necessary part of the speeches without trying to make sure of them (which interrogation report has not my signature). Later, I found 15 mistakes of serious nature made on the interrogation note when I was permitted to read it.

"As an ordinary man, I must confess that I am feeling severely homesick. Soon after my graduation from a university, with flaming ambition to contribute to the community with my chemical knowledge, the war broke out. Since then I have been called out to join the military colours for these seven years. Now the war is over and peace has been restored again. But now I am sitting in the jail, my thoughts fully occupied with my home in Japan. Now my heart is about to collapse with a feeling of nostalgia. I am recollecting the day when my first son was born, just four days before my being called up to the Army on 16 September 1941. On that day, I visited my wife in hospital, accompanying my second daughter, and embraced my son just three days after the birth. This was my last moment to see my wife and embrace my son. When I think of the future fate of my wife and children I cannot help from feeling the hardest pains in my heart because I wonder how they can get along in future without my support."

During the Appeal Hoshijima endeavoured to claim his fair treatment to PWs and at times he said he did his best under the circumstances, he claimed PW officers requested certain PWs to be punished by him. Many Jap officers described him as an 'upright officer who always obeyed superior orders'.

Captain A. Moffitt, the Australian Prosecutor, said in his summing up:

"I will dispose of the question of superior orders first. The case for the Prosecution does not rest on superior orders but on a far stronger basis, for on charges 1, 2 and 4 there never has been any suggestion by the defence that the acts of brutality to the PWs and the working of sick PWs were the result of orders higher than Hoshijima, and that on charge 3 although general local shortages of food and medicines are blamed by Hoshijima the evidence proved that food and medicines issued to, or available to, Hoshijima for the PWs, were on his authority or responsibility, were withheld from the PWs as a result of which many died. Superior orders do not in any way assist Hoshijima and the crimes at Sandakan were his crimes for which he must receive the full penalty.

"On the gravity of Hoshijima's crimes I submit they were the more foul because they were part of his policy of administration. As his references state, he was intent in purpose and his purpose first was to build the aerodrome. He did so despite human life and suffering with a savagery and brutality for those 2750 defenceless PWs. For this barbarity, including the murder of the PWs who died as a result of the cage treatment, I submit the accused should suffer death.

"However, his crime is far worse, for his conduct under the third charge resulted in the deaths of about 1100 in the compound during his period of office, and vitally contributed to many of the other 1200 deaths occurring on the marches and at Sandakan shortly after he left. This was deliberate and without feeling. Hoshijima just stood by while men died at the rate of 10 and 12 a day while there was rice and medicines under his control which could have saved them. When men were dying at this terrifying rate this fiend consented to the rice being completely and officially cut. Looking at his whole conduct his motives are obvious. When the job was done he cut out the rice to PWs of his own accord — whether the policy of elimination by starvation of PWs in this invasion danger area was his idea or dictated by suggestion from higher authority we do not know, but it makes no difference to the criminality of Hoshijima. However, when the PWs were dying at an alarming rate in 1945, a rate which amounted to slaughter, and when no doubt with the end of the war in sight and the Allied talk of war criminals in the air, Hoshijima commenced a period of window dressing, a fashion then very popular in the Borneo PW Compound. After the terrible death rate of March 1945 he also commenced a subtle period of buck-passing. Firstly he outwardly made appearances of trying to get food locally — having cut off the rice which he as a chemist must have known was a vital factor — food however which went to both Japanese and PWs and of course to the latter in ineffectual quantities. He even killed his renowned horse, but that was only typical of Hoshijima. Like the PWs, the horse having finished his work, was not properly fed and kept tied up and when it was thin from starvation it was slaughtered.

"Secondly when the death rate was at its peak in March 1945 and when the war criminals of the starvation camp at Belsen were receiving the full publicity no doubt Hoshijima feared his position and wished to have the slaughter through starvation put on a basis more favourable to him. I submit his motive in consenting to the suggestion to HQ to cut out rice officially — or shall we say in himself suggesting this to HQ — for Arai in his statement significantly used the word "we suggested" — was to legalise his criminality so he could in just such an emergency as the present be able to blame higher authority. It is significant that when Col Takayama visited the camp in April 1945 Hoshijima took no steps to recitfy this order cutting out the rice. The court will have noticed Hoshijima is an intelligent man, well versed in International affairs.

"In considering the punishment it is well to pause and consider the personal pain and suffering of those splendid young men whose lives were so callously cut off in their prime, and the grief and pain now and in the years to come in thousands of Australian and British homes — and all because of the hideous crime of this man who poses as an educated, civilised member of this uncivilised Japanese Army. It is impossible to make any punishment fit this crime. Even death by the ignominy of hanging, which I submit should be the penalty, is too good for this barbarian, ironically self-termed "cultured".

The Trial of Captain Yamamoto, First March Commander, his officers and NCO's.

The first trial took place at Labuan on January 23-28, 1946. Capt. Yamamoto was in Command of the 25 Regiment stationed not far from the Sandakan PW Camp preparing defences when he was ordered to move to Tuaran and take 500 PWs with him.

Under his command were the following officers:

Capt. Iino Shigera
Lieut. Hirano Yiihikiko
Capt. Mizuta Ryuichi
Lieut. Sato Tatsuo
Lieut. Tanaka Shojiro
Lieut. Horikawa Koichi
Capt. Abe Kazuo
Warrant Officer Gotunda Kiroki
Sergeant Sato Shinichi

The charges against those:

1. Murder
2. Ill-treatment of Prisoners of War

At this trial none of the survivors was able to be present as witness. There were two survivors from the first march who reached Ranau, Keith Botterill and Bill Moxham.

On one or the other charges they were sentenced to be hanged or shot, with the exception of Tanaka who was given a life sentence. These sentences were not confirmed. The Judge Advocate General stated: "It does not appear that there is evidence to support the charge of ill-treatment by the junior officers who were in command of the separate parties and that the casualties suffered were the necessary consequences of the orders given by superior authority that the movement had to take place and were not the result of the individual actions of the officers in charge of the party. He said the real criminals are the persons who ordered the movement and I cannot see how these junior officers could have refused to carry out the orders.

"Capt. Abe, officer commanding Independent Machine Gun Unit, was in charge of the 9th and rear party. In discussing the movement with Capt. Abe, Yamamoto instructed him there would have to be a rear party and there were to be no stragglers with Japanese or prisoners and that none were to be left in the jungle. He instructed if any PW who had fallen out were too sick to be able to be brought forward and taken to Ranau they were to be shot and buried.

"The shooting of prisoners of war under the above conditions, although it may have been humane, was not lawful and the conviction for murder is legal and may be confirmed.

"The case for the prosecution has already been documented. The defence for the accused was that each of them carried out orders of superior officers. On behalf of the accused Yamamoto it was contended that the treatment of PWs prior to the march was not in any way his liability as he was immediately before the march in charge of an Infantry unit.

"He was not responsible for the provisioning of the PWs on the march, the time to be taken for the distance to be traversed or the equipment of the PWs. In fact he received his orders from the Japanese Army H.Q. and it was impossible for the accused, Yamamoto, or any of his subordinates, to refuse to carry out such orders. It was also submitted there were no individual cases of ill-treatment other than forcing sick, under-nourished men along the way as it was essential for them to reach staging points where food was available, to stop and rest on the journey would have meant the other groups on the route would also have stopped and would have increased the critical food situation."

A new trial was ordered, the prisoners were taken to Rabaul where the trial took place on 20-27 May 1946.

The sentences handed down were:

Capt. Yamamoto	— to suffer death by hanging
Capt. Abe	— to suffer death by hanging
Lt. Hirano	— sentenced to 10 years' imprisonment
Lt. Mizuta	— sentenced to 10 years' imprisonment
Lt. Sato	— sentenced to 10 years' imprisonment
Lt. Tanaka	— sentenced to 10 years' imprisonment
Lt. Sugimura	— sentenced to 10 years' imprisonment
Lt. Horikawa	— sentenced to 10 years' imprisonment
Capt. Iino	— sentenced to 10 years' imprisonment
W.O. Gotunda Kiroki	— Not Guilty
Sgt. Sato Shinichi	— Not Guilty

At the Trial Keith Botterill gave evidence that Gotunda was not guilty of any ill-treatment on the march; on the contrary, he did his best to assist PWs.

After the recent death in Japan of W.O. Gotunda Kiroki his son came to Australia to find Keith Botterill and thank him for saving his father's life.

Captain Takakuwa Takeo and Captain Watanabe Genso were jointly charged with four counts, the first charge Murder and the remaining charges for three separate massacres at Ranau on August 1, 1945.

The Prosecutor, Lieutenant Ray Balzer, set out to prove that Captain Takakuwa became C.O. of the Sandakan camp on May 17, 1945, and Captain Watanabe was his Camp Adjutant. By May 28 there were approximately 824 British and Australian PWs in the camp, including 400 stretcher cases, under their command. Takakuwa received orders to move the PWs to Ranau — because of the poor medical condition he decided to leave 288 behind and move the remaining 536 to Ranau. Of the 536 there were 439 Australians and 91 English. On Takakuwa's own estimation 112 of these were stretcher cases.

The Prosecutor's case has already described all the events which took place from May 17 till the last PWs were murdered on August 1, 1945. Lt. Balzer continues:

"Despite the fact that Takakuwa and Watanabe knew that the prisoners would die of hunger they did not provide sufficient food. They had over 50 tons of rice at Sandakan and they moved this out to the 13 Mile peg, and as the prisoners came past they gave them a total of 23/100 lb. bags only. The rest was apparently abandoned, they could have easily carried more food if it had been allowed. As it was they carried ammunition and supplies for the Japanese. Eventually the rice ration gave out altogether and the prisoners were forced to exist on roots, tapioca, scraps, snails, ferns and whatever else they could find on the way.

"I leave it to the Court to imagine just how many roots, snails, etc. there would be along this route to provide food for say 500 to 200 men accordingly as they were reduced and just how far they would suffice to keep them going on this terrible march. There were rice dumps along the way — but these were only for the Japanese.

"Large numbers of prisoners fell out and died or were killed with rifles, etc. The heroism of the victims will form an epic in the history of war and comradeship. Thc iniquities of the accused will also be long remembered. The evidence will show that each day the men who were too ill to continue or who were ordered to fall out handed over their rations and shook hands with their comrades, said goodbye, and were then taken away to be killed. Some were shot in the back, some were killed outright, others were wounded and left to die by the track. There is no evidence that they were buried and the bodies were apparently thrown into the jungle or left along the road.

"Of the 536 men who started from Sandakan only 183 arrived at Ranau on 25 June 1945. Of these, 142 were Australians. The accused were responsible for all these deaths and killings. Their orders to their subordinates were that all the sick should be killed and none left behind.

"Watanabe did the bookkeeping of the deaths with the assistance of his henchman, Fukushima. He alleges that of the 353, who did not finish the march, 6 were returned to Sandakan — 90 were killed — 203 died on the way and he could not quite account for 54, so he concluded that the latter might have escaped. In actual fact only about six escaped. All the others died on the march or were killed. It is submitted that on the evidence to be adduced by the prosecution Watanabe's figure of only 90 shot will appear to be a most conservative one, and that in fact most of the 353 killed were by shooting. These included four PWs who were already at Ranau, having arrived from Sandakan some time previously. Since 353 died on the march itself, the only reasonable inference which could be drawn is that, the remainder (less the two who escaped plus those who were shot) all died as a direct result of the deprivations suffered during the march, and these accused were responsible for all these deaths just as they are responsible for the deaths of those they actually had shot.

"By August 1st 1945 there were 33 alive and on that day Takakuwa issued orders for these remaining 33 PWs to be killed. The details of this ghastly crime have already been described.

"The accused have pleaded superior orders. The accused Takakuwa either moved these prisoners without any orders at all or if he did get any orders they were obviously unlawful and therefore are no justification or excuse. The law on this point is very clearly set out in the Manual of Military Law at page 288 and this Court is familiar with it and consequently I do not propose to quote it. The law relating to homicide is set out in the Manual of Military Law at page 128 and the accused are guilty of causing death even if they merely accelerated the actual death, and it is no excuse that the persons killed must have died very shortly from some other cause.

"The three charges of massacre need little comment. They obviously caused the 33 prisoners to be killed because they were too ill to work and were no longer useful to them.

"In all the circumstances therefore, I submit that the prosecution has proved beyond any reasonable doubt that the accused are both equally guilty of all the charges as laid. Watanabe and Takakuwa are responsible for the deaths of all those who died during the march, all those who were shot on the march and all those who later died as a result of the march. Similarly they are jointly and equally responsible for the massacres.

"Watanabe admitted that he supervised the carrying out of Takakuwa's orders for the massacre. Their infamous score in regard to this march is well over 500 and then there are the further 288 deaths who were left behind. They allege that some prisoners tried to escape, but these prisoners were in no fit condition to escape and in any case if they knew they were going to be killed and then tried to escape in order to prevent being killed, this would not constitute such an escape within the meaning of the Laws and Usages of War on Land as would justify their being shot.

"Many foul inhuman crimes have come out of this war, but I submit that this is the worst of all. Over 500 Australians were included in the 824 prisoners in Sandakan camp on 29 May last. Excepting for a very small few they are all dead now and hundreds of homes in England and Australia are empty because of the iniquities, the murders and massacres committed at the instigation of Capt. Takakuwa and Capt. Watanabe and undoubtedly this is the greatest mass murder of Australians which has ever been committed. This was not even in the guise of war for these acts violated unchallenged rules of warfare and outraged the general sentiment of humanity.

"Here there was no military necessary and no advantage to be gained by killing these prisoners. Watanabe said he knew it was a bad thing to kill the prisoners. I submit that his part in these killings went so far to make him equally guilty with Takakuwa. His party was the droving party which kept the prisoners going and the Court has seen from the evidence of Short that men were cruelly beaten to make them move faster until they fell out and were killed.

NX.45191 Cpl. Nigel Noel Brown 2/18 Bn. Died 31 March 1945. Aged 31. Somerton, N.S.W.
Pic: Cyril Brown

NX.40435 Cpl. Robert John Greenwood 2/ 18 Bn. Died 24 June 1945. Aged 27. Quirindi, N.S.W.
Pic: R. Greenwood

"Moreover, towards the end of the march, men who had not fallen out were ordered to stop and were then killed. Watanabe was no mere slave to Takakuwa's will, he took an active part and acted on his own initiative. He has no more excuse to offer than Takakuwa.

"I submit that these cold blooded murders and massacres will form one of the filthiest pages in the history of this war. Death by shooting is too good for the accused. The ignominy of their crimes deserved the greatest ignominy in punishment and I submit that death by hanging is the least punishment which these foul crimes merit."

The defending officer, Colonel Yamada, stated:

"The action of Takakuwa in this case is made clear and there is no need to mention it further. However, the action of Captain Watanabe was caused by the absolute nature of the military order of Japan for which he had no room for choice, but to obey. It is quite evident that the person who carried out the orders given by his superior has no responsibility whatsoever upon the result of the action.

"That is to say, as it is not an action due to his own initiative, it cannot be said that there is criminal intention to it. It is nothing but a lawful act for the accused Watanabe. Right or wrong of his action ought to be fairly judged by the law alone which confined him at the time when his action had taken place.

"Consequently, I firmly believe that so far as Watanabe's action is concerned, it does not form, what they call a 'War Crime'; thereby no war crime act of any kind can be applied to his action.

"May it please the Court, as I mentioned above Capt. Takakuwa's actions in these four cases were nothing but emergent actions which he was forced to take under the urgent circumstances amid the great war.

"I pray and humbly beg that the Court would take these exceptional conditions attached to his case into consideration of extenuating circumstances, and give the most generous judgement to him.

"As for Capt. Watanabe, I believe that his action does not constitute any crime. Therefore I plead that he is not guilty."

The court sentenced Captain Takakuwa to death by hanging which was carried out at Rabaul on March 16, 1946. Captain Hoshijima was hung on April 6, 1946.

Captain Watanabe was executed on April 6, 1946, at Morotai.

And so the Trials continued until the General in charge of the 37 Japanese Army in Borneo, Baba Masao, was found responsible for ordering the marches. He was hanged in Rabaul on 7 August 1947; the supervising Australian Officer was Major F.J. Duval of Narrandera, NSW.

Chapter 14

The Contact Groups and War Graves Units were approached by natives with notes from PWs indicating there were obligations outstanding. The Australian Government decided to send a representative to Borneo to investigate these claims and also assist the natives who had done so much to help the prisoners.

Major H.W.S. Jackson was chosen for this task. He had previously been to Hainan Island to investigate the report Australian prisoners of war were still held by the Chinese.

In 1946 he arrived in Borneo where he was joined by Major Dyce representing the British Army and two journalists from the ABC, Colin Simpson and William McFarlane. Major Jackson, fluent in Malay, was able to converse with all the natives in their own tongue. He arrived in the Ranau area where they had the first meeting:

"Into the hut came three normal looking Dusan men. They were dressed in either well-worn slacks or shorts, and had khaki shirts. They were Orang Tua Gunting, Barigah and Sumping, three of the men who found and harbored Short, Botterill, Moxham and Anderson and later delivered the three former into Allied hands. I told them who I was, who had sent me, what I had been sent for, and asked them to give me the full story in their own words and as complete as possible. Bill McFarlane recorded their story with my interpretation and interrogation, and I gave them some clothing and money and told them they would receive additional money through their District Officer when I had told their story to the Australian authorities and some finality had been reached regarding the total amount of reward to which they were entitled. They were obviously pleased and a little bewildered.

"Most of the people I interviewed, rewarded and thanked, were at a loss to understand why we had come so many thousands of miles to the remote part of the world where they lived just to keep faith with them and to honour notes and promises given to them during the war by sick and dying prisoners of war. They were so impressed and grateful that they couldn't express themselves in words. It wasn't so much the money, the medicines, or the clothing that we gave them, it was the fact that we had not forgotten them and had gone to so much trouble to find them. When I told them that it was the intention of the Australian and British Governments to give them 'Letters of Good Name' (Certificates of Appreciation) it increased their gratification tenfold. I think that a gift of this nature appeals to them more than actual money, they assume the proportion of family heirlooms and are handed down from father to son, they are usually kept in a small watertight bamboo container,

"After Gunting, Barigah and Sumping had gone on their way with their reward, a man named Ginasas bin Gunggas came in for interview. This was the man who found Warrant Officer Sticpewich and Dvr. Reither and later took them to the home of Dihil bin Ambilid. He could hardly walk when I first saw him, he was badly affected with oedema

Colonel H.W.S. Jackson with three of his helpers in 1986.

MINISTER FOR THE ARMY

COMMONWEALTH OF AUSTRALIA

DEPARTMENT OF THE ARMY
MELBOURNE, AUSTRALIA

No. 172 ....194..

To..............

of..............

The Minister for the Army of the Commonwealth of Australia desires to recognize your valuable assistance to Australian soldiers during the War with Japan, 1941-1945, and extends to you, on behalf of the Commonwealth and the next-of-kin, most sincere thanks for services rendered.

Cyril Chambers
MINISTER FOR THE ARMY

Issued at..............

Countersigned..............

Certificate of Appreciation

of the ankles caused through beri beri and the little boy who came with him was also crippled through ulcers of the foot. When Ginasas had told his story he was given clothing and money and told the same as was the other three natives. Major Dyce, Colin Simpson and I watched him as he painfully dragged himself atop a water buffalo and his crippled son held the beast by a bamboo cord tied to its nose. I had previously given both of them medical attention for their ailments and some medicine, etc. for additional treatment. It made our job feel worthwhile to watch Ginasas astride the buffalo, proudly clutching his bundle of clothing and money, being led by his little son painfully hobbling along on his ulcerated feet. The murmured 'terima kassi tuan' (thank you master) meant much more than that to us. We knew what they really thought about it all.

"And so the cavalcade of helpers came in. Some walked as far as 17 miles to see us. They were all sorts, old men, young lads and widows with and without children. A little eight year old girl named 'Balabiu' was the smallest and Rijan was probably the oldest. Their stories varied from surreptitious passing of food or money, to long periods of harboring under the very noses of the Japanese. Not all of the people who called came to tell a story. Some came just to pay their respects or to make a small gift of a fowl or a parcel of bananas. A spirit of friendliness and respect was everywhere, also a pleasing note of gratefulness, although actually the gratefulness was from us to them for what they did. A number of the people were visibly affected when describing the PWs during the last days that they were alive at Ranau. Tima's story was indicative of many, "They were very thin, weak and sick looking" she said. "They were without boots, some without shirts, all had long beards, long hair and walked with bowed heads that swayed from side to side. Whenever they passed they made signs with fingers to their mouths that they were hungry and wanted food." When they told stories like this they shook their heads and sucked their teeth as though it was distasteful to remember. I gathered the impression that the gallantry of our men during that awful period left an impression on their minds that will last forever. They saw our men under the worst of conditions and learned to respect their enduring valor.

"We must never forget that story, nor must our children, because the men who made it gave their lives so that we may enjoy our own way of life, and we must ensure that our way of life is worth the price that was paid for it."

Chapter 15

HONOUR ROLL

'B' FORCE				Date of Death	Age
Andrews, Stanley, Pte.	NX.42439	22 Aust.Inf.Bde.HQ	Seacliff, S.A.	05.05.45	24
Johnston, C.A., Pte.	NX.21509	22 Aust.Inf.Bde.HQ	Sydney, N.S.W.	04.06.45	29
Jackson, L.W., Pte.	NX.55844	22 Aust.Inf.Bde.HQ	Canberra, A.C.T.	16.04.45	27
Ley, Phillip, Pte.	NX.65268	22 Aust.Inf.Bde.HQ	Annandale, N.S.W.	28.04.45	42
Murray, Richard, Pte.	NX.33361	22 Aust.Inf.Bde.HQ	Hurstville, N.S.W.	20.05.45	35
McGowan, W.J., Pte.	NX.19999	22 Aust.Inf.Bde.HQ	Newtown, N.S.W.	03.04.45	43
Wynn, W.E., Cpl.	NX.32416	22 Aust.Inf.Bde.HQ	Goulburn, N.S.W.	21.03.45	27
Stockley, R.R.W., Pte.	NX.26886	22 Aust.Inf.Bde.HQ	Berrigan, N.S.W.	01.03.45	23
Pryor, D.R., Pte.	NX.37189	22 Aust.Inf.Bde.HQ	Lidcombe, N.S.W.	16.04.45	28
McIlhagga, W.J., Pte.	NX.35826	22 Aust.Inf.Bde.HQ	Mid-Calder, Mid-Lothian, Scotland	19.06.45	44
Wardale-Greenwood, Harold, Chap.	VX.38675	Aus. Army Chplns.	Stanley, Tas.	18.07.45	36
Thompson, A.H., Chap.	TX. 6093	Aus. Army Chplns.	Launceston, Tas.	19.06.45	42
Arnold, J.H., Cpl.	NX.24252	2/18 Battalion		05.04.45	44
Anderson, J.F., Pte.	NX.72705	2/18 Battalion	Sth. Grafton, N.S.W.	10.06.45	39
Allen, S.J., Pte.	NX.49447	2/18 Battalion	Wirrimah, N.S.W.	07.06.45	23
Burrows, Jack, Pte.	NX.40464	2/18 Battalion	Cullen Bullen, N.S.W.	25.04.45	42
Bryant, J. C., Pte.	NX.43424	2/18 Battalion	Lismore, N.S.W.	29.03.45	25
Bullen, E.F., Pte.	NX.32702	2/18 Battalion	Cremorne, N.S.W.	25.04.45	30
Bailey, I.S., Pte.	NX.68520	2/18 Battalion	Lidcombe, N.S.W.	04.12.44	23
Coggins, P.R.N., Sgt.	NX.59163	2/18 Battalion	Wahroonga, N.S.W.	07.06.45	27
Campbell, D.A., L/Sgt.	NX.52524	2/18 Battalion	Chatswood, N.S.W.	11.05.45	44
Crapp, H.S., L/Cpl.	NX.40492	2/18 Battalion	Manilla, N.S.W.	23.04.45	43
Cole, T.W.T., Pte.	NX.72771	2/18 Battalion	Parkes, N.S.W.	07.06.45	23
Connell, J.F., Pte.	NX.32301	2/18 Battalion		28.04.45	42
Dixon, Jonathon, W.O.I.	NX.57438	2/18 Battalion	Lane Cove, N.S.W.	09.06.45	44
Duffy, L.J., Pte.	NX. 630	2/18 Battalion	Dubbo, N.S.W.	03.04.45	34
Dixon, T.F.U., Pte.	NX.43404	2/18 Battalion	Nth. Lismore, N.S.W.	24.01.45	31
Ferguson, John, Pte.	NX.55455	2/18 Battalion	Kensington, N.S.W.	17.02.45	28
Gillespie, W.G., Pte.	NX.40763	2/18 Battalion		01.07.45	42
Green, A.A., Cpl.	NX.54528	2/18 Battalion	Bankstown, N.S.W.	13.06.45	38
Guinea, J.D., Pte.	NX.41955	2/18 Battalion	Scone, N.S.W.	09.04.45	44
Greenwood, R.J., Cpl.	NX.40435	2/18 Battalion	Quirindi, N.S.W.	24.06.45	27
Howson, H.R., Pte.	NX.40491	2/18 Battalion	Bingara, N.S.W.	18.03.45	36
Hobbs, J.S., Pte.	NX.38312	2/18 Battalion		04.03.45	25
Hogbin, C.W., Pte.	NX.40678	2/18 Battalion	Glen Innes, N.S.W.	24.03.45	40
Hickman, Cecil, Pte.	NX.40807	2/18 Battalion		20.04.45	34
Ings, J.T., Pte.	NX.58457	2/18 Battalion	Nth. Strathfield, N.S.W.	30.05.45	24
Jackes, W.K., Cpl.	NX.52112	2/18 Battalion	Sth. Armidale, N.S.W.	15.03.45	32
Jackson, L.E., Pte.	NX.71774	2/18 Battalion	Nth. Sydney, N.S.W.	08.07.45	38
Kelly, S.J., Pte.	NX.40710	2/18 Battalion	Narrabri, N.S.W.	07.06.45	37
Lane, T.H., Pte.	NX.40425	2/18 Battalion	Tamworth, N.S.W.	18.04.45	40
Lillyman, J.A., Cpl.	NX.40635	2/18 Battalion	Greenwich, N.S.W.	17.06.45	37
Le Cussan, E.W. Pte.	NX.40853	2/18 Battalion	Gunnedah, N.S.W.	08.03.45	32
Lindsay, R.L., Pte.	NX.55818	2/18 Battalion	West Maitland, N.S.W.	18.06.45	42
Lyne, Gordon, Pte.	NX.22405	2/18 Battalion	Lambton, N.S.W.	04.06.45	25
Mills, J.K., Cpl.	NX.40386	2/18 Battalion	Sydney, N.S.W.	18.05.45	35
Morris, H., Pte.	NX.58985	2/18 Battalion	Leichhardt, N.S.W.	17.01.45	23
Monaghan, H.J., Pte.	NX.40355	2/18 Battalion	Belmore, N.S.W.	29.03.45	33
Morton, H.A., Pte.	NX.49839	2/18 Battalion	Gulf Creek, N.S.W.	31.03.45	35
Maguire, H.J. Pte.	NX.40758	2/18 Battalion	Nth. Sydney, N.S.W.	07.06.45	45
McEwen, G.A., Pte.	NX.50946	2/18 Battalion		01.06.45	38
O'Keefe, H.J., Pte.	NX.40453	2/18 Battalion	Kingstown, N.S.W.	25.07.45	25
Partridge, N.E., Pte.	NX.40766	2/18 Battalion	Walcha, N.S.W.	04.07.45	32

'B' FORCE				Date of Death	Age
Priest, H.E., Sgt.	NX.60074	2/18 Battalion	Newtown, N.S.W.	06.04.45	37
Platford, Joseph, Pte.	NX.40689	2/18 Battalion	Glen Innes, N.S.W.	23.05.45	45
Plunkett, G.W., Pte.	NX.51466	2/18 Battalion	Hornsby, N.S.W.	14.06.45	26
Pepper, C.D., Pte.	NX.49425	2/18 Battalion	Petersham, N.S.W.	30.05.45	21
Robinson, G.B., Pte.	NX.30968	2/18 Battalion	Wyong, N.S.W.	08.03.45	26
Richardson, J.G., Cpl.	NX.28116	2/18 Battalion	Mosman, N.S.W.	23.05.45	32
Reading, T.A., Pte.	NX.40332	2/18 Battalion	Kogarah, N.S.W.	11.08.45	35
Rogers, J.S., Pte.	NX.31764	2/18 Battalion	Baradine, N.S.W.	17.06.45	41
Sinclair, William, Pte.	QX.22194	2/18 Battalion	Kedron, Qld.	13.04.45	31
Smith, Owen, Pte.	NX.26029	2/18 Battalion		27.06.45	25
Smith, A.W.L., Pte.	NX.56588	2/18 Battalion	Glenorie, N.S.W.	29.01.45	27
Staggs, F.L., L/Sgt.	NX.14900	2/18 Battalion	Inverell, N.S.W.	31.03.45	52
Shearman, S.G., Pte.	NX.72692	2/18 Battalion	Rukenvale, N.S.W.	31.03.45	20
Short, M.N., Pte.	NX.26580	2/18 Battalion	Epping, N.S.W.	13.07.45	25
St. Leon, Gus, Cpl.	NX.55414	2/18 Battalion	Canley Vale, N.S.W.	03.06.45	28
Sherring, Frank, L/Cpl.	NX.40730	2/18 Battalion	Sydney, N.S.W.	12.02.45	29
Whitehead, B.C., L/Sgt.	NX.54971	2/18 Battalion	Croydon, N.S.W.	13.07.45	39
Woodall, Jack, Cpl.	NX.40548	2/18 Battalion		07.06.45	34
Woolnough, A.W.J., Pte.	NX.14526	2/18 Battalion	Empire Vale, N.S.W.	15.06.45	30
Wellard, C.J., Pte.	NX.32152	2/18 Battalion	Sydney, N.S.W.	08.06.45	28
Wells, H.G., Pte.	NX.40370	2/18 Battalion	Warialda, N.S.W.	04.03.45	33
Wall, R.H., Cpl.	NX.26534	2/18 Battalion		01.03.45	28
Waller, Terence, Pte.	NX.31921	2/18 Battalion	Walcha, N.S.W.	05.06.45	21
Weissel, George, Pte.	NX. 1703	2/18 Battalion	Redfern, N.S.W.	23.05.45	35
McGrath, P.J., Cpl.	NX.29613	2/18 Battalion	Kenton, Middlesex, U.K.	25.04.45	44
McLeod, William, Pte.	NX.45826	2/18 Battalion	East Maitland, N.S.W.	28.02.45	25
Cox, G.K., Pte.	NX.13844	2/18 Battalion	Griffith, N.S.W.	05.04.45	19
Good, Gordon, Lieut.	NX.32109	2/19 Battalion	East Sydney, N.S.W.	13.07.45	35
Adams, Thomas, Pte.	NX.35315	2/19 Battalion	Tempe, N.S.W.	19.06.45	40
Beetson, G.J., Sgt.	NX.55795	2/19 Battalion	Newtown, N.S.W.	01.11.44	39
Betts, J.M., S/Sgt.	NX.59898	2/19 Battalion	Orange, N.S.W.	12.04.45	30
Burgun, Gordon, Pte.	NX.35288	2/19 Battalion	Tumbarumba, N.S.W.	06.03.45	40
Bagust, R.H., Pte.	NX.29073	2/19 Battalion	St. Mary's, N.S.W.	18.07.45	23
Boyd, J.W., Pte.	NX.49963	2/19 Battalion	Camden, N.S.W.	16.05.45	31
Bycroft, A.B., Pte.	NX.30859	2/19 Battalion	Fairfield, N.S.W.	07.03.45	23
Blunden, A.J., Pte.	NX.44576	2/19 Battalion	Barmedman, N.S.W.	06.06.45	25
Bills, Leonard, Pte.	NX.36222	2/19 Battalion	Eden, N.S.W.	14.02.45	31
Bolton, E.D., Pte.	NX.33171	2/19 Battalion	Kogarah, N.S.W.	22.06.45	23
Booth, C.L., Cpl.	NX.56154	2/19 Battalion	Leura, N.S.W.	24.11.44	26
Cavenagh, C.R., Pte.	NX.35679	2/19 Battalion	Griffith, N.S.W.	20.06.45	26
Crago, George, Pte.	NX.43552	2/19 Battalion	Smithfield, N.S.W.	29.11.44	42
Corbett, J.W.F., Pte.	NX.51622	2/19 Battalion	Sydney, N.S.W.	04.03.45	25
Capon, W.A., Pte.	NX.30166	2/19 Battalion	Portland, N.S.W.	03.03.45	22
Cousins, S.J., Pte.	QX.21876	2/19 Battalion		20.06.45	24
Dunhill, E.G., Pte.	NX.52964	2/19 Battalion	Mandurama, N.S.W.	04.06.45	24
Etheridge, J.O., Pte.	QX.18446	2/19 Battalion	Chinchilla, Qld.	19.07.45	23
Flint, A.E., Cpl.	NX.52964	2/19 Battalion	Tempe, N.S.W.	10.06.45	28
Forrester, C.H., Pte.	NX.67705	2/19 Battalion	Orange, N.S.W.	15.06.45	26
Garvin, J.T., L/Sgt.	NX.58438	2/19 Battalion	Bondi, N.S.W.	04.06.45	43
Graham, Ronald, Pte.	NX.35646	2/19 Battalion	Leeton, N.S.W.	04.06.45	26
Golding, R.S., Pte.	NX.10814	2/19 Battalion	Glebe, N.S.W.	10.03.45	25
Gentle, T.R., Pte.	NX.49469	2/19 Battalion	Paddington, N.S.W.	01.06.45	36
Hurst, R.E., Pte.	NX.35228	2/19 Battalion	Wagga Wagga, N.S.W.	02.04.45	29
Harris, C.H., Pte.	QX.22365	2/19 Battalion	Toowong, Qld.	18.06.45	27
Hargraves, J.V., Pte.	NX.35725	2/19 Battalion	Wollongong, N.S.W.	06.06.45	33

'B' FORCE

Name	Number	Unit	Home	Date of Death	Age
Hedley, G.W., Pte.	NX.39936	2/19 Battalion	Randwick, N.S.W.	28.04.45	31
Huckle, R.A., Pte.	NX.44465	2/19 Battalion	Bletchley, Bucks. U.K.	24.03.44	41
Ingham, A.E., Pte.	NX. 5754	2/19 Battalion	Sweetman's Ck. N.S.W.	29.04.45	25
Kerr, J.R., Pte.	NX.49191	2/19 Battalion	Bankstown, N.S.W.	15.02.45	23
Kline, Jack, Pte.	NX.39588	2/19 Battalion	Ashfield, N.S.W.	16.02.45	32
Moore, M.F., Pte.	NX.60225	2/19 Battalion	Dalgety, N.S.W.	13.02.45	31
Munford, F.A., Pte.	NX.47341	2/19 Battalion	Taree, N.S.W.	06.02.45	24
Menzies, H.W., Pte.	NX.42402	2/19 Battalion	Belmore, N.S.W.	28.05.45	39
Mabin, D.W., Pte.	QX.23944	2/19 Battalion	Sherwood, Qld.	14.02.45	22
Mulray, W.P., Pte.	NX.35430	2/19 Battalion	Carlton, Vic.	06.04.45	32
Platt, S.H., Pte.	NX.56047	2/19 Battalion	Bondi, N.S.W.	26.05.45	30
Power, C.G.R., Pte.	NX.50396	2/19 Battalion	Bankstown, N.S.W.	20.07.45	32
Pearce, J.S., Pte.	NX.25894	2/19 Battalion	Bankstown, N.S.W.	07.06.45	27
Rae, John, Cpl.	NX.35466	2/19 Battalion	Carlton, N.S.W.	13.07.45	33
Roebuck, J.T., Pte.	NX.56657	2/19 Battalion	Lewisham, N.S.W.	16.05.45	28
Russell, A.W., Pte.	NX.49504	2/19 Battalion	Sth. Melbourne, Vic.	23.05.45	26
Slip, E.C., Pte.	NX.49915	2/19 Battalion	Dubbo, N.S.W.	17.03.45	23
Turner, E.H., Cpl.	NX.35848	2/19 Battalion	Griffith, N.S.W.	18.06.45	27
Wallace, H.W., Pte.	NX.33806	2/19 Battalion	Rose Bay, N.S.W.	19.01.45	23
Wilson, Edward, Pte.	NX. 7123	2/19 Battalion	Newcastle-on-Tyne, U.K.	27.03.45	34
Wilson, S.C., Pte.	QX.23104	2/19 Battalion	Mt. Morgan, Qld.	16.06.45	26
Wilson, Albert, Pte.	NX.35496	2/19 Battalion	Young, N.S.W.	02.07.45	32
Winterbottom, Arthur, Pte.	QX.15818	2/19 Battalion	Redfern, N.S.W.	05.06.45	28
Temple, R.J., Pte. (Served as Moore, R.J.)	NX.30243	2/19 Battalion		03.04.45	23
Jeffrey, R.L. MO., Capt.	NX.34761	2/20 Battalion	(10 A.G.H.)	06.05.45	35
Blackie, J.W., W.O.I.	NX.65224	2/20 Battalion	Haberfield, N.S.W.	02.06.45	46
Steinbeck, W.J., W.O.II.	NX.45443	2/20 Battalion	Ocean Beach, N.S.W.	15.07.45	39
Galton, Daniel, Sgt. (Prom.Lieut. 9.2.42)	NX.50524	2/20 Battalion	Charters Towers, Qld.	12.07.45	40
Hewitt, Harry, Sgt.	NX.65365	2/20 Battalion	Manly, N.S.W.	04.06.45	42
Hutchinson, J.N., Sgt.	NX.16527	2/20 Battalion		04.02.45	35
Lawrence, A.S., Sgt.	NX.34301	2/20 Battalion	Nowra, N.S.W.	18.06.45	27
Mackenzie, Duncan, Sgt.	NX.50900	2/20 Battalion		26.02.45	40
Chapman, A.W., Cpl.	NX.27779	2/20 Battalion		09.02.45	39
Fletcher, B.A., Cpl.	NX.31591	2/20 Battalion	Zetland, N.S.W.	11.06.45	32
Ferguson, N.J., Cpl.	NX.51547	2/20 Battalion	Petersham, N.S.W.	20.06.45	27
Jackson, John, Cpl.	NX.72749	2/20 Battalion		29.04.45	29
Prendergast, J.J., L/Cpl.	NX.26818	2/20 Battalion	Forest Lodge, N.S.W.	18.06.45	23
Turner, N., L/Cpl.	NX.31793	2/20 Battalion	Tottenham, N.S.W.	23.03.45	28
Ambrose, George,, Pte.	NX.39744	2/20 Battalion	Lithgow, N.S.W.	28.04.45	24
Bayley, A.E., Pte.	NX.21899	2/20 Battalion	Enfield, N.S.W.	10.02.45	43
Bredbury, Irvine, Pte.	NX.51527	2/20 Battalion	Arncliffe, N.S.W.	23.05.45	36
Brooker, Walter, Pte.	NX.54958	2/20 Battalion	Beacon Hill, N.S.W.	27.05.45	41
Burns, Thomas, Pte.	NX.72757	2/20 Battalion		13.07.45	37
Burling, J.H., Pte.	NX.33999	2/20 Battalion	Lakemba, N.S.W.	02.04.45	30
Clarke, L.A., Pte.	NX.32502	2/20 Battalion	Redfern, N.S.W.	14.06.45	26
Cranney, R.T., Pte.	NX.31893	2/20 Battalion	Glebe, N.S.W.	21.04.45	24
Cummings, A.L., Pte.	NX.36930	2/20 Battalion	Kogarah, N.S.W.	07.06.45	27
Cooper, T.S., Pte.	NX.45522	2/20 Battalion	Whitebridge, N.S.W.	16.02.45	31
Chapman, S.H., Pte.	NX.42001	2/20 Battalion	Byron Bay, N.S.W.	03.05.45	31
Crumpton, R.F., Pte.	NX.51804	2/20 Battalion	Willoughby, N.S.W.	05.06.45	26
Campbell, Charles, Pte.	NX.45159	2/20 Battalion	Sydenham, England	19.06.45	25
Day, A.T., Pte.	NX.53571	2/20 Battalion	Lismore, N.S.W.	26.03.45	29
Davies, E.D., Pte.	NX.32677	2/20 Battalion	Austral, N.S.W.	16.06.45	25

'B' FORCE				Date of Death	Age
Fewer, J.R., Pte.	NX.56674	2/20 Battalion	Balgowlah, N.S.W.	22.03.45	27
Flanagan, W.J., Pte.	NX.68859	2/20 Battalion	Bellingen, N.S.W.	09.06.45	27
Fitzgerald, L.N., Pte.	NX.72865	2/20 Battalion	Waverley, N.S.W.	15.07.45	24
Gemmill, S.C., Pte.	NX.54810	2/20 Battalion	Omega, N.S.W.	02.06.45	29
Greenfeld, F.R., Pte.	NX.22570	2/20 Battalion	Cabramatta, N.S.W.	24.04.45	26
Hams, N.T., Pte.	NX.58754	2/20 Battalion	Arncliffe, NSW	25.03.45	24
Higham, G.E.S., Pte.	NX.53430	2/20 Battalion	Crows Nest, NSW	02.02.45	37
James, G.E., Pte.	NX.73329	2/20 Battalion	La Perouse, NSW	12.02.45	26
Jordan, W.A., Pte.	NX.52157	2/20 Battalion	Bankstown, NSW	26.05.45	29
Jones, W.N., Pte.	NX.30795	2/20 Battalion	Ryde, NSW	26.02.45	25
Lee, D.H., Pte.	NX.46082	2/20 Battalion	Sth.Murwillumbah,NSW	04.06.45	28
Mainstone, C.D., Pte.	NX. 897	2/20 Battalion	Earlwood, NSW	17.03.45	20
Moore, C.G., Pte.	NX. 1797	2/20 Battalion	Sth. Strathfield, NSW	27.05.45	24
McKenzie, W.J. Pte.	NX.73001	2/20 Battalion	Werris Creek, NSW	07.04.45	27
McLachlan, T.D., Pte.	NX.55072	2/20 Battalion	Campsie, NSW	31.05.45	29
McCormack, R.A., Pte.	NX.54292	2/20 Battalion	Ashgrove, Qld.	15.04.45	41
Mulligan, R.P., Pte.	NX.57811	2/20 Battalion	Booker Bay, NSW	21.02.45	24
McCall, K.B., Pte.	NX.45708	2/20 Battalion	Breadalbane, NSW	12.04.45	24
O'Donohue, E.J., Pte.	NX.43479	2/20 Battalion	Grafton, NSW	11.08.45	24
Ower, W.J., Pte.	NX.27807	2/20 Battalion	East Malvern, Vic.	18.07.45	44
Parker, N.L., Pte.	NX. 4668	2/20 Battalion	Weston, NSW	19.03.45	24
Pickering, J.A., Pte.	NX. 7129	2/20 Battalion	Auburn, NSW	27.03.45	43
Patterson, T.B., Pte.	NX.45411	2/20 Battalion	Hamilton, NSW	18.06.45	33
Righetti, L.J., Pte.	NX.19555	2/20 Battalion	Nth. Sydney, NSW	17.02.45	28
Robinson, Frank, Pte.	NX.72677	2/20 Battalion	Toowoomba, Qld.	10.04.45	31
Rankin, J.R., Pte.	NX.55361	2/20 Battalion	Enmore, NSW	15.03.45	33
Renaud, E.C., Pte.	NX.30168	2/20 Battalion	Nth. Bondi, NSW	14.03.45	32
Steele, A.R., Pte.	NX.55051	2/20 Battalion	Hurstville Grove, NSW	10.05.45	41
Solomon, J.H., Pte.	NX.51847	2/20 Battalion	Annandale, NSW	11.02.45	36
Scollen, T.P., Pte.	NX.57377	2/20 Battalion	Banksia, NSW	07.05.45	28
Storey, G.J., Pte.	NX.33004	2/20 Battalion	Annandale, NSW	08.04.45	29
Taylor, Ian, Pte.	NX.50899	2/20 Battalion	Fords Bridge, NSW	03.05.45	33
Trinder, L.G., Pte.	NX.73633	2/20 Battalion	Carlton, NSW	05.06.45	23
Wardman, Jack, Pte.	NX.55103	2/20 Battalion	Bathurst, NSW	10.06.44	27
Wilson, C.B., Pte.	NX.52054	2/20 Battalion	Thallon, Qld.	23.05.45	40
Young, D.G.C., Pte.	NX.60135	2/20 Battalion	Concord, NSW	21.06.45	34
Nicholls, S.T.A., Pte.	NX.49336	H.Q. 27 Bde.	Strathfield, NSW	01.02.45	24
Shields, E.J., Sgt.	QX.17829	2/26 Battalion	Fairfield, Qld.	07.06.45	43
Bancroft, E.D., Sgt.	QX. 9488	2/26 Battalion	Maroochydore, Qld.	10.06.45	25
Mann, C.N., Cpl.	QX.17181	2/26 Battalion	Coorparoo, Qld.	02.03.45	37
Hutton, A.C., W.O.II	QX.17002	2/26 Battalion	New Farm, Qld.	30.03.45	42
McLellan, A.P., L/Cpl.	QX.11487	2/26 Battalion		02.06.45	26
Allan, L.B., Pte.	NX. 7933	2/26 Battalion		21.02.45	24
Ayton, A.C.J., Pte.	TX. 5862	2/26 Battalion	Nth. Motton, Tas.	15.02.45	24
Barber, G.K., Pte.	QX.13101	2/26 Battalion	Nudgee, Qld.	08.12.44	37
Barker, D.T., Pte.	QX.18114	2/26 Battalion	Chatswood, NSW	07.06.45	25
Burgess, James, Pte.	QX.18656	2/26 Battalion	Pelican Flats, NSW	30.07.45	39
Cooke, William, Pte.	QX.18658	2/26 Battalion	Purga, Qld.	10.06.45	34
Piper, Roy, Pte.	QX.19564	2/26 Battalion	Brisbane, Qld.	21.05.45	38
Hankin, P.E., Cpl.	QX. 1606	2/26 Battalion		15.06.45	42
Roberts, Sydney, Pte.	QX.13600	2/26 Battalion	Red Hill, Qld.	21.05.45	42
White, J.A., Pte.	QX.18682	2/26 Battalion	Holme Hill, Qld.	05.06.45	30
Isbel, C.E., Pte.	QX.11408	2/26 Battalion	Prosperpine, Qld.	25.03.45	26
Charles, G.F., Pte.	QX.21352	2/26 Battalion	Lwr. Tent Hill, Qld.	07.06.45	24

'B' FORCE				Date of Death	Age
Christiansen, William, Pte.	QX.18659	2/26 Battalion	Mackay, Qld.	07.06.45	37
Clear, J.A., Pte.	TX. 5859	2/26 Battalion	Launceston, Tas.	24.05.45	36
Cook, A.J., Pte.	QX. 8463	2/26 Battalion	Gympie, Qld.	10.04.45	26
Cumming, D.A., Pte.	QX.11017	2/26 Battalion	Toowong, Qld.	21.01.45	29
Dooley, F.E.. Pte.	NX.49460	2/26 Battalion	Sth. Hurstville, NSW	30.01.45	38
Gode, Harold, Pte.	QX.14769	2/26 Battalion	Wynnum, Qld.	24.12.44	39
Griffiths, E.R., Pte.	QX.12559	2/26 Battalion	Coochin, Qld.	20.03.45	25
Hutchison, G.E., Pte.	QX.17981	2/26 Battalion	Bardon, Qld.	25.04.45	27
Iles, Clifford, Pte.	QX.19181	2/26 Battalion	Palmwoods, Qld.	21.05.45	43
Izzard, C.H.M., Pte.	QX.10462	2/26 Battalion	Crows Nest, Qld.	19.03.45	24
Jones, F.J., Pte.	QX.12915	2/26 Battalion	Gympie, Qld.	23.05.45	35
Langton, C.G., Pte.	QX.15178	2/26 Battalion	Mareeba, Qld,	25.05.45	35
Mackay, F.J., Pte.	QX.14716	2/26 Battalion	Wooloowin, Qld.	08.11.42	35
McCallum, H.D., Pte.	QX.21556	2/26 Battalion	East Brisbane, Qld.	17.04.45	34
McSweeney, J.M., Pte.	VX.62559	2/26 Battalion	East Brunswick, Vic.	29.12.44	28
Plunkett, John, Pte.	NX.33191	2/26 Battalion	Randwick, NSW	03.04.45	42
Rowe, C.H., Pte.	QX. 1826	2/26 Battalion	Prosperpine, Qld.	05.06.45	25
Rummell, V.C., Pte.	QX.11137	2/26 Battalion		18.03.45	38
Sorby, W.T., Pte.	QX.17987	2/26 Battalion	Milton, Qld.	20.01.45	34
Stirling, Christopher, Pte.	QX. 8453	2/26 Battalion		16.06.45	31
White, L.A., Pte.	QX.18691	2/26 Battalion	Home Hill, Qld.	10.06.45	27
Arnold, L.R., Pte.	VX.63028	2/29 Battalion	Richmond, Vic.	04.06.45	22
Anderson, P.A., Pte.	VX.33905	2/29 Battalion	Albert Park, Vic.	25.02.45	35
Bennett, H.C., Pte.	VX.56527	2/29 Battalion	Beechworth, Vic.	17.02.45	42
Baragwanath, Wynite, Pte.	VX.20558	2/29 Battalion	East Malvern, Vic.	19.03.45	25
Boyes, W.E., Pte.	VX.37947	2/29 Battalion	Drouin, Vic.	13.07.45	25
Boustead, M.G., Pte.	NX.38428	2/29 Battalion	Hurlstone Park, NSW	21.02.45	31
Bennett, A.D., Pte.	VX.45020	2/29 Battalion	Coleraine, Vic.	22.03.45	29
Cox, Leslie, Pte.	VX.46536	2/29 Battalion	Sth. Geelong, Vic.	20.04.45	41
Clayton, J.H.V., Pte.	VX.35863	2/29 Battalion		07.02.45	40
Chapman, B.B., Pte.	NX. 1717	2/29 Battalion	Hurstville, NSW	25.04.45	20
Crome, E.J.	NX.37694	2/29 Battalion	Woollahra, NSW	28.02.45.	20
Dobson, T.R., Pte.	TX. 8299	2/29 Battalion		10.06.45	24
Fry, V.J., Pte.	VX.36464	2/29 Battalion	Surrey, England	01.07.45	38
Foxwell, C.A., Pte.	QX.12727	2/29 Battalion	Coorparoo, Qld.	08.05.45	27
Grubb, David, Pte.	VX.39578	2/29 Battalion	Broadford, Vic.	02.04.45	40
Hancock, W.J., Sgt.	QX.15677	2/29 Battalion	Ballarat, Vic.	15.08.45	42
Holmes, R.F., Cpl.	VX.29172	2/29 Battalion	Mt. Taylor, Vic.	12.06.45	25
Hardstaff, R.A., Pte.	TX. 5821	2/29 Battalion	Burnie, Tas.	14.04.45	22
Henley, K.H., Pte.	VX.37955	2/29 Battalion	Kew, Vic.	24.04.45	26
Hollier, H.F., Pte.	VX.59783	2/29 Battalion	Malvern, Vic.	12.05.45	21
I'Anson, W.L., L/Sgt.	VX.31855	2/29 Battalion	Yackandandah, Vic.	01.05.45	44
Johnson, S.H., Pte.	NX.53458	2/29 Battalion	Vaucluse, NSW	22.06.45	27
Larkins, M.J., Pte.	VX.33942	2/29 Battalion	Pyramid Hill, Vic.	22.06.45	35
Laidlaw, A.J., Pte.	QX.23540	2/29 Battalion	Morningside, Qld.	10.04.45	30
Longley, H.B., Pte.	NX.60143	2/29 Battalion	Yass, NSW	05.07.45	22
Ghananburgh, C.M.M., Cpl. (Served as Maurice, C.M.)	NX.78033	2/29 Battalion	Erskineville, NSW	07.06.45	22
Mulvogue, R.H., Pte.	VX.43518	2/29 Battalion	Richmond, Vic.	05.03.45	31
Mercer, R.L., Pte.	VX.50413	2/29 Battalion	West Merbein, Vic.	04.05.45	25
Morgan, N.L., Pte.	VX.34894	2/29 Battalion		09.06.45	29
Murnane, W.J., Pte.	VX.22611	2/29 Battalion	Hawthorn, Vic.	26.01.43	37
Marshall, P.O., Spr.	NX.49712	2/29 Battalion	Strathfield, NSW	03.04.45	22
Milne, R.A., Pte.	NX.52194	2/29 Battalion		13.04.45	23
Moore, L.C., Pte.	VX.64236	2/29 Battalion	Richmond, Vic.	28.04.45	27
Marsh, W.R., Pte.	QX.18341	2/29 Battalion	Laidley, Qld.	16.03.45	27

'B' FORCE				Date of Death	Age
Milliken, W.E., Pte.	VX.56322	2/29 Battalion	Albert Park, Vic.	12.02.45	38
McLaughlin, R.G., Pte.	NX.74021	2/29 Battalion	Manly, NSW	31.03.45	20
McGill, Leslie, Pte.	NX.54907	2/29 Battalion	Waterloo, NSW	11.04.45	27
Nagle, M.J., Pte.	VX.44687	2/29 Battalion	Corowa, NSW	15.06.45	30
Olver, K.F., Pte.	QX.21195	2/29 Battalion	Gympie, Qld.	17.02.45	24
Pashen, J.W., Pte.	QX.21277	2/29 Battalion	Nambour, Qld.	03.02.45	34
Robertson, G.C., Pte.	VX.27643	2/29 Battalion	East Brighton, Vic.	22.03.45	28
Roberts, L.J., Pte.	VX.55846	2/29 Battalion	Fitzroy, Vic.	13.02.45	31
Rickerby, K.W., Pte.	QX.24124	2/29 Battalion	Gympie, Qld.	19.06.45	28
Smith, A.A., Pte.	NX. 643	2/29 Battalion	Ashford, NSW	25.03.45	
Simpson, H.J., Cpl.	VX.54067	2/29 Battalion	Geelong, Vic.	02.06.45	33
Sleep, Jack, Pte.	VX.60586	2/29 Battalion	Hawthorn, Vic.	06.07.45	22
Thompson, V.R., Pte.	QX.21845	2/29 Battalion	Monto, Qld.	23.05.45	26
Turner, R.E., Pte.	NX.20743	2/29 Battalion	West Ryde, NSW	25.01.45	26
Webster, A.G., Pte.	TX. 2961	2/29 Battalion	Hobart, Tas.	02.06.45	28
Woolard, A.I., L/Cpl.	VX.28818	2/29 Battalion	Chelsea, Vic.	06.03.45	41
Woods, C.J. Pte.	VX.45261	2/29 Battalion		08.02.45	36
Walters, L.E., Pte.	VX.55639	2/29 Battalion	Armadale, Vic.	04.03.45	37
Weir, S.J., Pte.	VX.63967	2/29 Battalion		15.07.45	22
Wilson, George, Pte.	VX.56240	2/29 Battalion	Belgrave Heights, Vic.	20.01.45	24
Wilson, E.W., Pte.	VX.47422	2/29 Battalion		09.02.45	33
Young, A.D., Pte.	VX.61120	2/29 Battalion	Fitzroy, Vic.	16.03.45	23
Bond, F.T., Pte.	VX.50618	2/29 Battalion	Sth. Melbourne, Vic.	07.12.43	27
Davidson, R.R., Sgt.	VX.39217	2/29 Battalion	Strathfield, NSW	06.03.45	40
Sawford, B.G., Pte.	VX.35647	2/29 Battalion	Oakleigh, Vic.	11.04.45	30
McGeary, E.D., Pte.	VX.56416	2/29 Battalion	Ballarat, Vic.	21.06.45	25
Shipsides, R.A., Pte.	VX.44447	2/29 Battalion	Reservoir, Vic.	03.04.45	32
Harstorff, D.P., Pte.	QX.22382	2/29 Battalion	Gilliat, Qld.	05.06.45	25
Louray, F.L., Pte.	VX.55995	2/29 Battalion	Coleraine, Vic.	03.06.45	43
Seeley, J.W., Cpl.	QX.22054	2/29 Battalion	New Farm, Qld.	05.01.45	25
Gillett, Keith, Pte.,	VX.50283	2/29 Battalion	Parkville, Vic.	14.03.45	25
Sankowsky, R.H., Pte.	QX.23726	2/29 Battalion	Bundaberg, Qld.	15.02.45	25
Balding, H.M., Cpl.	VX.41468	2/29 Battalion	Warrnambool, Vic.	03.04.45	45
Bice, C.J.S., Pte.	QX.18486	2/29 Battalion	Drillham, Qld.	28.01.45	31
Dixon, K.A.F., Pte.	QX.22525	2/29 Battalion	Boonah, Qld.	06.03.45	31
Jury, S.H.J., Pte.	VX.64047	2/29 Battalion	Thornbury, Vic.	15.03.45	36
Peach, J.T., Cpl.	VX.45656	2/29 Battalion	Edenhope, Vic.	16.07.45	27
Bowe, J.M., Pte. (Served as Anderson, J.M.)	NX.43983	2/30 Battalion	Wagga Wagga, NSW	12.05.45	21
Asgill, C.C., Pte.	NX.54534	2/30 Battalion	Parkes, NSW	17.07.45	25
Annear, L.J., Pte.	NX.49646	2/30 Battalion	Enmore, NSW	20.02.45	24
Beer, N.P., Pte.	NX.36657	2/30 Battalion	Wagga Wagga, NSW	09.06.45	27
Buckley, H.W., Pte.	NX.37339	2/30 Battalion	Newtown, NSW	04.08.45	28
Byrne, N.B.G., Pte.	NX. 4410	2/30 Battalion	Killara, NSW	12.01.45	36
Bollard, J.T., Pte.	NX.28142	2/30 Battalion	Coutts Crossing, NSW	27.03.45	44
Brett, N.F., Pte.	NX.42739	2/30 Battalion	Randwick, NSW	01.01.45	26
Bonis, R.T., Pte.	NX.29772	2/30 Battalion	West Maitland, NSW	03.05.45	41
Clyne, E.F., S/Sgt.	NX.53537	2/30 Battalion	Drummoyne, NSW	27.03.45	36
Cross, A.H.W., Cpl.	NX.27235	2/30 Battalion	Arncliffe, NSW	23.03.45	35
Clyne, P.J., Pte.	NX.34442	2/30 Battalion	Mayfield, NSW	10.09.45	30
Christensen, H.G., Pte.	NX.46197	2/30 Battalion	Lansdowne, NSW	28.02.45	29
Carroll, Michael, Pte.	NX.48306	2/30 Battalion	Nth. Portland, Vic.	10.05.45	42
Donohue, J.A., Pte.	NX.37419	2/30 Battalion	Wagga Wagga, NSW	30.05.45	24
Finn, J.A., Pte.	NX.37388	2/30 Battalion	Randwick, NSW	09.08.45	24
Gray, R.S., Pte.	NX.37725	2/30 Battalion	Woollahra, NSW	12.03.45	24

'B' FORCE				Date of Death	Age
Grist, N.S., Pte.	NX.36660	2/30 Battalion	Tarcutta, NSW	10.07.45	24
Hicks, V.O., Pte.	NX.72066	2/30 Battalion	Bonalbo, NSW	11.02.45	28
Hicks, H.R., Pte.	NX.47755	2/30 Battalion	Casino, NSW	01.07.45	30
Higgison, F.M.H., Pte.	NX.53504	2/30 Battalion	Marrickville, NSW	12.06.45	36
LeClerq, A.E., Pte.	NX.50287	2/30 Battalion	Bondi, NSW	04.03.45	21
Longbottom, Harold, Pte.	NX.48071	2/30 Battalion	Tyalgum, NSW	11.02.45	28
Lytton, Herbert, Pte.	QX.25599	2/30 Battalion	Milton, Qld.	15.05.45	25
Maben, R.R., Pte.	NX.36453	2/30 Battalion	Burrinjuck Dam, NSW	31.05.45	34
Marshall, Arthur, Pte.	NX.37377	2/30 Battalion	Guyra, NSW	07.06.45	34
Mackay, T., Sgt.	NX.71839	2/30 Battalion	Caithness. Scotland	02.06.45	40
Ollis, J.N., Pte.	VX.15674	2/30 Battalion	Hamilton, NSW	16.02.45	28
O'Loughlan, G.J., Pte.	NX. 2555	2/30 Battalion	Homebush, NSW	04.06.45	37
Palmer, S.J., Sgt.	NX.66171	2/30 Battalion	Inverell, NSW	19.04.45	26
Phillips, Bertram, Cpl.	NX.26183	2/30 Battalion	Dee Why, NSW	03.06.45	28
Plewes, K.A., L/Cpl.	NX. 2725	2/30 Battalion	Bronte, NSW	15.03.45	40
Richards, Evan, Pte.	NX.37675	2/30 Battalion	Willoughby, NSW	07.06.45	31
Rankin, C.W., Pte.	NX.47925	2/30 Battalion	Ellangowan, NSW	16.02.45	22
Reardon, F.W., Pte.	NX.46643	2/30 Battalion	Ballina, NSW	09.06.45	32
Rundle, C.A., Pte.	NX.31254	2/30 Battalion	Sth. Lismore, NSW	05.07.45	25
Ryan, R.T., Pte.	NX.26957	2/30 Battalion	Arncliffe, NSW	07.06.45	30
Smith, J.S., Pte.	NX.50421	2/30 Battalion		13.03.45	45
Thompson, R.J.E., Pte.	NX.72482	2/30 Battalion	Kogarah, NSW	30.03.45	33
Vollheim, E.C.N., Pte.	NX.57915	2/30 Battalion	Wollongong, NSW	12.02.45	45
Wilmott, A.J., Pte.	NX.78032	2/30 Battalion	Marrickville, NSW	10.01.45	26
West, J.S., Pte.	NX.47833	2/30 Battalion	Nimbin, NSW	20.02.45	28
Watts, D.L., Pte.	NX.37432	2/30 Battalion	Kadungle, NSW	30.07.45	23
Schmutter, W.J., Pte.	NX.57116	2/30 Battalion	Crows Nest, NSW	18.07.45	24
Quailey, A.C., Pte.	NX.41944	2/30 Battalion	Redfern, NSW	16.02.45	24
McCarthy, J.F., Pte.	QX.21245	2/30 Battalion		09.04.45	36
Hales, L.J., Pte.	NX. 2560	2/30 Battalion	Glebe, NSW	05.04.45	28
Kearney, John, Pte.	NX.37560	2/30 Battalion	Gosford, NSW	24.05.45	29
Smith, R.E., Pte.	NX.59118	2/30 Battalion	Hurlstone Park, NSW	31.03.45	36
Molde, K.C., Cpl. (Served as Dawson, L.K.)	NX.78229	2/30 Battalion	Point Piper, NSW	14.02.45	28
Hack, A.M., Pte.	WX. 8003	2/4 M.G. Battalion	Maida Vale, W.A.	04.02.45	38
Wilson, R.M., S/Sgt.	WX. 8438	2/4 M.G. Battalion	Cottesloe, W.A.	25.12.44	35
Keay, V.A., W.O.II	WX. 8431	2/4 M.G. Battalion	Highgate, W.A.,	10.05.45	39
Dunn, C.H. Cpl.	WX. 8092	2/4 M.G. Battalion	Bayswater, W.A.,	21.03.45	44
Armstrong, F. L/Cpl.	WX. 7717	2/4 M.G. Battalion	Margaret River, W.A.	30.07.42	31
Bird, C.R., Pte.	WX. 9017	2/4 M.G. Battalion	East Fremantle, W.A.	26.07.45	28
Evans, W.C., Pte.	WX. 9230	2/4 M.G. Battalion	Albany, W.A.,	14.06.45	43
Bendall, B.A., Pte.	WX.17864	2/4 M.G. Battalion	Donnybrook, W.A.	12.02.45	30
Harris, Charles, Pte.	WX. 7851	2/4 M.G. Battalion	Boyanup, W.A.	27.05.45	31
Chipperfield, R.W., Pte.	WX. 8397	2/4 M.G. Battalion		11.02.45	28
Fotheringham, T.R., Pte.	WX.10803	2/4 M.G. Battalion	West Perth, W.A.	07.06.45	24
Newling, R.W., Pte.	WX. 8865	2/4 M.G. Battalion	Leederville, W.A.	13.06.45	33
Jubelski, C.W.M., Pte. (Served as Anderson, C.W.M.)	WX. 9123	2/4 M.G. Battalion	Bonbeach, Vic.	16.06.45	31
Gibson, N.A., Pte.	WX.10994	2/4 M.G. Battalion	Sth. Perth, W.A.	24.06.45	25
Haly, S.O'G., Pte.	WX.14830	2/4 M.G. Battalion	West Perth, W.A.	15.06.45	27
Joynes, Colin, Pte.	WX. 9297	2/4 M.G. Battalion	Jitarning, W.A.	07.06.45	31
Hill, E.T., Pte.	WX. 7029	2/4 M.G. Battalion	Maylands, W.A.	28.05.45	27
Shirley, A.F., Pte.	WX. 8535	2/4 M.G. Battalion	West Northam, W.A.	10.05.45	36
Browning, J.H., Pte.	WX. 9283	2/4 M.G. Battalion	East Northam, W.A.	16.07.45	25
Osborne, S.A., Pte.	WX. 7634	2/4 M.G. Battalion	Swan View, W.A.	21.06.45	31

'B' FORCE				Date of Death	Age
Bailey, N.E., Crftsmn.	WX.10920	2/4 M.G. Battalion	Inglewood, W.A.	10.06.45	24
Attenborough, A.R., Pte.	WX. 7444	2/4 M.G. Battalion	East Perth, W.A.	12.04.45	28
Beard, W.H. Pte.	WX. 7883	2/4 M.G. Battalion	Worsley, W.A.	10.07.45	34
Burns, C.E., Pte.	WX. 7702	2/4 M.G. Battalion	Westonia, W.A.	04.02.45	28
Dorizzi, Gordon, Pte.	WX. 9274	2/4 M.G. Battalion	Mungarin, W.A.	11.02.45	28
Dorizzi, Herbert, Pte.	WX. 7997	2/4 M.G. Battalion	Mungarin, W.A.	11.02.45	26
Page, R.A., Pte.	WX. 4934	2/4 M.G. Battalion	Welshpool, W.A.	17.02.45	26
Ferguson, R.P., Pte.	WX. 7999	2/4 M.G. Battalion	Toodyay, W.A.	23.03.45	32
Spence, R.H.C., L/Cpl.	WX. 8467	2/4 M.G. Battalion	Applecross, W.A.	31.05.45	40
Taylor, G.L., Pte.	WX.14775	2/4 M.G. Battalion	Kalgoorlie, W.A.	07.06.45	25
Maconachie, R.D., Pte.	WX. 9801	2/4 M.G. Battalion	Bassendean, W.A.	05.06.45	25
Halligan, Jack, Cpl.	WX. 8819	2/4 M.G. Battalion	Kalgoorlie, W.A.	04.02.45	25
Goldie, J.McL., Pte.	WX. 7627	2/4 M.G. Battalion	Busselton, W.A.	04.06.45	26
Cook, G.R., Capt.,	NX.76185	General Base Depot	Mittagong, NSW	12.08.45	38
Osgood, Athol W.O.I.	NX.41519	General Base Depot	Kogarah, NSW	07.03.45	43
Kinder, J.W., W.O. (R.A.A.F.)	205622	General Base Depot	Ascot Vale, Vic.	10.06.45	28
Newhouse, Frank, W.O.II,	NX.41491	General Base Depot	Randwick, NSW	12.07.45	51
Waters, A.J.L., S/Sgt.	NX.54404	General Base Depot	Darling Point, NSW	09.06.45	44
Hughes, A.P., Sgt.	NX.72878	General Base Depot	Sydney, NSW	11.05.45	38
Neale, T.S., Sgt.	NX.50372	General Base Depot	Ponteland, Newcastle-on-Tyne, UK	14.09.42	43
Abbott, E.R., Pte.	NX.40023	General Base Depot	Maroubra, NSW	21.01.43	24
Bowman, H.R., Pte.	NX.43785	General Base Depot	Braidwood, NSW	27.12.44	26
Child, F.T., Pte.	NX.39994	General Base Depot	Concord, NSW	19.10.44	40
Cope, W.G., Pte.	NX.10204	General Base Depot	Bankstown, NSW	27.03.45	32
Field, S.A., Cpl.	VX.61556	General Base Depot	Nungarin, W.A.	31.01.45	47
Larcombe, C.T., Pte.	NX.10403	General Base Depot	Shepardstown, NSW	28.02.45	26
Mahoney, George, Pte.	NX.27496	General Base Depot		14.02.45	33
Radford, Clifford, Pte.	VX.56303	General Base Depot	Barmera, S.A.	26.02.45	35
Brack, D.N., Pte.	NX.51719	2/10 Fld.Ambulance	Wyoming, NSW	17.05.45	21
Bruce, R.C., Pte.	NX.46095	2/10 Fld.Ambulance	Byangum, NSW	31.03.45	36
Brown, Milton, Pte.	NX.26267	2/10 Fld.Ambulance	Goulburn, NSW	20.06.45	31
Brown, Samuel, Pte.	NX.57465	2/10 Fld.Ambulance	Sutton Forest, NSW	15.07.45	32
Bagnall, N.W., Pte.	NX.38445	2/10 Fld.Ambulance		05.05.45	23
Beasley, H.C.J., Pte.	NX.32711	2/10 Fld.Ambulance	Paddington, NSW	22.03.45	26
Ballard, G.M., Pte.	NX.38427	2/10 Fld.Ambulance	Urunga, NSW	23.03.45	22
Bolton, G.A., Pte.	NX.56960	2/10 Fld.Ambulance	Leichhardt, NSW	29.07.45	33
Burgess, Leonard, Pte.	NX.45327	2/10 Fld.Ambulance		19.09.44	34
Burridge, F.R., Pte.	NX.26720	2/10 Fld.Ambulance	Arncliffe, NSW	21.08.44	27
Copp, E.F., Cpl.	NX.65285	2/10 Fld.Ambulance	Rockdale, NSW	12.05.45	26
Coulton, G.L., Pte.	NX.45811	2/10 Fld.Ambulance	West Maitland, NSW	14.04.45	38
Chapman, Stanley, Pte.	NX.45146	2/10 Fld.Ambulance	Tighe's Hill, NSW	04.06.45	43
Coffey, M.J., Pte.	NX.71546	2/10 Fld.Ambulance	Beni, NSW	18.04.45	32
Carthew, J.A.L., Sgt.	NX.47042	2/10 Fld.Ambulance	Charlestown, NSW	12.02.45	37
Campbell, W.R.E., Sgt.	NX.53910	2/10 Fld.Ambulance	Rosebery, NSW	03.06.45	26
Crockett, E.R., Cpl.	NX.10918	2/10 Fld.Ambulance	Neutral Bay, NSW	07.06.45	32
Condon, L.J., Pte.	NX.72867	2/10 Fld.Ambulance	Petersham, NSW	16.05.45	30
Commerford, G.F., Pte.	NX.33246	2/10 Fld.Ambulance	Lwr. Lawrence, NSW	09.02.45	25
Costin, K.H., Pte.	QX.15720	2/10 Fld.Ambulance	Mareeba, Qld.	28.01.45	24
Crossman, E.R., Pte.	NX.56452	2/10 Fld.Ambulance	Katoomba, NSW	04.06.45	31
Davison, Eric, Pte.	NX.52973	2/10 Fld.Ambulance	Undercliffe, NSW	13.07.45	32
Emmett, E.V., Cpl.	NX.51899	2/10 Fld.Ambulance	Dulwich Hill, NSW	31.03.45	24
Edwards, G.E., Pte.	NX. 7934	2/10 Fld.Ambulance	Hillston, NSW	25.07.45	28
Elliott, W.G., Pte.	NX.24972	2/10 Fld.Ambulance	Cooran, Qld.	13.01.45	26

'B' FORCE				Date of Death	Age
Farrell, V.H., Sgt.	NX.47045	2/10 Fld.Ambulance	Adamstown, NSW	19.07.45	41
Fox, E.H., Pte.	NX.10841	2/10 Fld.Ambulance	Camperdown, NSW	10.02.45	27
Gardner, A.W., Pte.	NX.50579	2/10 Fld.Ambulance	Mt. Druitt, NSW	05.06.45	30
Goodear, N.F., L/Cpl.	NX.31677	2/10 Fld.Ambulance	Darlinghurst, NSW	07.06.45	30
Graham, G.A., Pte.	NX.47078	2/10 Fld.Ambulance	Lismore, NSW	21.02.45	33
Gaven, Jack, S/Sgt.	NX.57758	2/10 Fld.Ambulance	Collaroy, NSW	11.03.45	32
Gardner, C.A., L/Cpl.	NX.46000	2/10 Fld.Ambulance	Teralba, NSW	06.04.45	26
Gillies, A.J., Pte.	NX. 7351	2/10 Fld.Ambulance	Kellyville, NSW	20.06.45	37
Horder, R.J., L/Sgt.	NX.46682	2/10 Fld.Ambulance	Mosman, NSW	09.07.45	48
Hopkins, W.R., L/Cpl.	NX.35221	2/10 Fld.Ambulance	Wagga Wagga, NSW	25.07.45	31
Hodges, J.D.G., L/Cpl.	NX.45166	2/10 Fld.Ambulance	Wyee, NSW	01.07.45	44
Hallford, M.E., Pte.	NX.38424	2/10 Fld.Ambulance	Griffith, NSW	29.03.45	25
Higgs, J.A., Pte.	NX.50173	2/10 Fld.Ambulance		12.04.45	48
Hutton, J.K., Cpl.	NX.53776	2/10 Fld.Ambulance	Granville, NSW	22.04.45	30
Hayes, J.W., Pte.	NX.10303	2/10 Fld.Ambulance	Waverley, NSW	13.05.45	35
Harding, L.C., Pte.	NX.33952	2/10 Fld.Ambulance	Lismore, NSW	28.02.45	30
Ireland, G.A., Pte.	NX.69155	2/10 Fld.Ambulance	Kew, N.S.W.	15.03.45	26
Jones, H.B., Pte.	NX.58677	2/10 Fld.Ambulance	Fairfield West, NSW	05.06.45	28
Jacobs, C.J., Pte.	NX.30028	2/10 Fld.Ambulance	Bondi, NSW	22.06.45	44
Johnson, S.R., Pte.	NX.52835	2/10 Fld.Ambulance	Parramatta, NSW	28.02.45	28
Krieger, L.C., Pte.	NX.29065	2/10 Fld.Ambulance	St. George, Qld,	24.02.45	35
Kelly, F.W., L/Cpl.	NX.67911	2/10 Fld.Ambulance	Bankstown, NSW	21.06.45	28
Levey, R.E., Pte.	NX.47023	2/10 Fld.Ambulance	Hamilton, NSW	14.06.45	31
Law, A.W., Pte.	NX.57737	2/10 Fld.Ambulance	Glebe, NSW	21.03.45	25
Lowe, J.T., Pte.	NX.71562	2/10 Fld.Ambulance	Murrell, NSW	15.06.45	25
Lethbridge, T.C., Pte.	NX.45810	2/10 Fld.Ambulance		15.07.45	38
Lumby, V.A. Pte.	NX. 7344	2/10 Fld.Ambulance	Aberdeen, NSW	04.03.45	31
Mann, W.R., Sgt.	NX.58549	2/10 Fld.Ambulance	Arncliffe, NSW	06.07.45	31
Morgan, Eric, Pte.	NX.38423	2/10 Fld.Ambulance		22.03.45	25
McEwan, R.I., Cpl.	NX.52735	2/10 Fld.Ambulance	Bondi Junction, NSW	08.07.45	29
Armstrong, R.W., Pte.	NX.59184	2/10 Fld.Ambulance	Woollahra, NSW	07.05.45	26
Tickle, William, Pte.	NX.51573	2/10 Fld.Ambulance	Bankstown, NSW	24.02.45	27
Maddison, J.W., L/Cpl.	NX.26468	2/10 Fld.Ambulance	Kogarah, NSW	07.03.45	27
Munro, L.A., Pte.	NX.38435	2/10 Fld.Ambulance	Coolamon, NSW	01.06.45	23
Mortimer, H.W., Sgt.	NX.26393	2/10 Fld.Ambulance	Lakemba, NSW	17.02.45	47
Molony, S.W., Pte.	NX.32577	2/10 Fld.Ambulance	Arncliffe, NSW	13.01.45	26
MacDonald, Lachlan, Pte.	NX.47686	2/10 Fld.Ambulance	Adamstown, NSW	30.05.45	25
Ney, W.C., Pte.	NX.38425	2/10 Fld.Ambulance	Gollan, NSW	02.05.45	28
Noonan, E.G., Pte.	NX.46184	2/10 Fld.Ambulance	Kyogle, NSW	31.07.45	28
Noonan, W.A., Pte.	NX.15554	2/10 Fld.Ambulance	Kyogle, NSW	23.07.45	25
O'Brien, M.V., Pte.	NX.45791	2/10 Fld.Ambulance	East Greta, NSW	22.06.45	36
O'Hara, M.T., Pte.	NX.38895	2/10 Fld.Ambulance	Mayfield, NSW	29.05.45	34
O'Hara, R.T., Pte.	NX.19011	2/10 Fld.Ambulance	Glebe, NSW	25.05.45	24
Orr, J.S., Pte.	NX.53745	2/10 Fld.Ambulance	Epping, NSW	04.03.45	22
Pallister, Robert, Pte.	NX.45168	2/10 Fld.Ambulance	Lambton, NSW	05.06.45	42
Pearce, K.J., Pte.	NX.30613	2/10 Fld.Ambulance	Bankstown, NSW	08.06.45	43
Pride, V.H., Pte.	NX.45658	2/10 Fld.Ambulance	Talarm, NSW	27.05.45	24
Purdon, Thomas, L/Sgt.	NX.46006	2/10 Fld.Ambulance		18.03.45	44
Rankin, C.F., Pte.	NX.38426	2/10 Fld.Ambulance	Dyraaba Creek, NSW	18.04.45	23
Rankin, G.H., Pte.	NX.33210	2/10 Fld.Ambulance	Dyraaba Creek, NSW	28.04.45	25
Richards, R.M., Pte.	NX. 4415	2/10 Fld.Ambulance	Neutral Bay, NSW	11.02.45	23
Read, W.G. Pte.	NX.52402	2/10 Fld.Ambulance	Artarmon, NSW	15.07.45	25
Rooke, R.G., Cpl.	NX.36468	2/10 Fld.Ambulance	North Wagga, NSW	19.06.45	40
Richardson, John, Pte.	NX.45510	2/10 Fld.Ambulance	West Kempsey, NSW	06.04.45	32
Roberts, H.A., Pte.	NX.65983	2/10 Fld.Ambulance	Orangeville, NSW	05.03.45	21
Robinson, B.A., Pte.	NX.67605	2/10 Fld.Ambulance	Mandurama, NSW	23.05.45	23

'B' FORCE				Date of Death	Age
Rawlings, B.A., Pte.	NX.45348	2/10 Fld.Ambulance	Singleton, NSW	15.04.45	39
Lobegeiger, Jack, Pte. (Served as Randoll, Jack)	NX.32663	2/10 Fld.Ambulance	Toowoomba, Qld.	14.03.45	23
Scambrey, W.E., Cpl.	NX.29342	2/10 Fld.Ambulance	Balmain, NSW	20.03.45	37
Shepherd, G.A., L/Cpl.	NX.20560	2/10 Fld.Ambulance	New Lambton, NSW	02.08.45	25
Sinclair, I.A.D., Cpl.	NX.53074	2/10 Fld.Ambulance	Broadway, NSW	05.08.45	36
Stanley, Robert, Pte.	NX.71505	2/10 Fld.Ambulance	Neath, NSW	08.02.45	29
Smalldon, H.J., Pte.	NX.51021	2/10 Fld.Ambulance	Millers Point, NSW	04.07.45	26
Syme, A.J., Pte.	NX.20472	2/10 Fld.Ambulance	Merrylands, NSW	04.06.45	24
Stapleton, T.N., L/Sgt.	NX.53535	2/10 Fld.Ambulance	Mudgee, NSW	18.12.44	36
Sinclair, I.McD., Pte.	NX.55025	2/10 Fld.Ambulance		09.03.45	32
Skinner, E.K., Pte.	NX.41647	2/10 Fld.Ambulance	Tenterfield, NSW	16.06.45	27
Skinner, J.F., Pte.	NX.41648	2/10 Fld.Ambulance	Tenterfield, NSW	15.08.45	31
Stone, H.D., Pte.	NX. 2710	2/10 Fld.Ambulance	Carlton, NSW	12.05.45	32
Thistlethwaite, Victor, L/Cpl.	NX.67346	2/10 Fld.Ambulance	Sans Souci, NSW	15.07.45	34
Terrett, Edward, Pte.	NX.45225	2/10 Fld.Ambulance		07.08.45	25
Thomas, M.G., Pte.	NX.33263	2/10 Fld.Ambulance	Lismore, NSW	26.05.45	25
Taylor, T.C., W.O.II.	NX.47044	2/10 Fld.Ambulance	New Lambton, NSW	26.07.45	43
Thomas, A.D., Pte.	NX.57256	2/10 Fld.Ambulance	Auburn, NSW	10.08.44	25
Thomson, E.F., Pte.	NX.34321	2/10 Fld.Ambulance	Rockdale, NSW	01.04.45	33
Turner, A.J., L/Cpl.	NX.58936	2/10 Fld.Ambulance	Tattenham Cnr., Epsom, Surrey, UK	10.06.45	37
Whybird, J.A., Sgt.	NX.47046	2/10 Fld.Ambulance	West Marrickville, NSW	14.07.45	28
Westwood, Bertie, Pte.	NX.52344	2/10 Fld.Ambulance	Bankstown, NSW	01.07.45	30
Wilkes, H.R., Pte.	NX.15756	2/10 Fld.Ambulance	Lakemba, NSW	04.06.45	27
Wilkins, Kenneth, Pte.	NX.10451	2/10 Fld.Ambulance	Sydney, NSW	23.02.45	25
Wrigley, K.H., Pte.	NX.30608	2/10 Fld.Ambulance	Port Macquarie, NSW	25.07.45	25
Wye, F.R.C., Pte.	NX.38448	2/10 Fld.Ambulance	Marrickville, NSW	21.03.45	22
Webber, S.A., Pte.	NX.53777	2/10 Fld.Ambulance	Parramatta, NSW	10.08.45	28
Watson, T.N., Pte.	NX.50730	2/10 Fld.Ambulance	Parramatta, NSW	15.12.44	42
De Costa, G.F., Pte.	QX.13139	2/10 Fld.Ambulance	Eton, Qld.	04.06.45	26
Hunter, H.D., Pte.	NX.45418	2/10 Fld.Ambulance	Wallsend, NSW	04.12.44	42
Mawhinney, G.B., Cpl.	NX.46154	2/10 Fld.Ambulance	Ulmarra, NSW	20.01.45	35
Hughes, R.R., S/Sgt.	NX.47041	2/10 Fld.Ambulance	Mayfield, NSW	20.03.45	33
Burton, George, Cpl.	NX.45207	2/10 Fld.Ambulance	Morriset, NSW	07.05.45	42
French, R.F., Pte.	VX.31164	2/10 Fld.Ambulance	Burwood, Vic.	19.07.45	28
Adlington, N.C., Pte.	VX.43533	2/10 Fld.Ambulance	Mentone, Vic.	12.02.45	26
Graham, W.H., Pte.	VX.43539	2/10 Fld.Ambulance	Auburn, Vic.	09.04.45	24
Miller, S.B., Pte.	VX.57642	2/10 Fld.Ambulance	Mirboo North, Vic.	29.04.45	24
Lear, John, Pte.	NX.57920	2/10 Fld.Ambulance		17.06.45	43
Marshall, L.F., Pte.	VX.38181	2/10 Fld.Ambulance	Glenferrie, Vic.	05.11.42	27
Fogarty, M.J., Pte.	NX.55738	2/10 Fld.Ambulance	Woollahra, NSW	15.11.44	43
Kilpatrick, J., Pte.	NX.26125	2/10 Fld.Ambulance		03.04.45	40
Stanton, A.J., S/Sgt.	NX.67623	2/10 Fld.Ambulance	Concord, NSW	16.07.45	25
Wilkinson, D.L., Cpl.	NX.67842	2/10 Fld.Ambulance	Goulburn, NSW	08.08.45	25
Armstrong, J.W., Pte.	NX.67672	2/10 Fld.Ambulance	Mayfield, NSW	12.07.45	24
Belford, N.T., Pte.	NX.66964	2/10 Fld.Ambulance	Curlewis, NSW	23.05.45	35
Sproul, L.J., Cpl.	VX.12864	2/10 Fld.Ambulance	Sunshine, Vic.	03.05.45	37
Carleton, R.V., Pte.	WX.10914	2/10 Fld.Ambulance	Nedlands, W.A.	09.06.45	29
Grills, V.E., Pte.	NX.22895	2/10 Fld.Ambulance	Rous Mill, NSW	03.07.45	25
O'Connor, H.B., Cpl.	VX.47945	2/10 Fld.Ambulance	Mildura, Vic.	27.07.45	29
Leith, F.A., Pte.	VX.35607	2/10 Fld.Ambulance	Warburton, Vic.	22.05.45	25
Goldsworthy, T.W., Pte.	VX.35497	2/10 Fld.Ambulance	Maldon, Vic.	20.04.45	38
Spears, Norman, Pte.	VX.25134	2/10 Fld.Ambulance	Auburn, Vic.	13.11.42	39

'B' FORCE				Date of Death	Age
Watson, C.Y., W.O.II.	QX.17783	No.1 Coy.A.A.S.C.	Red Hill, Qld.	06.03.45	45
Murray, G.B., S/Sgt.	NX.58215	No.1 Coy.A.A.S.C.	Darling Point, NSW	21.04.45	44
Scholefield, R.B., S/Sgt.	VX.34618	No.1 Coy.A.A.S.C.	Hawthorn, Vic.	18.07.45	36
Munro, J.F., Sgt.	QX.17279	No.1 Coy.A.A.S.C.	Toowong, Qld.	28.05.45	29
Midlane, D.L., Sgt.	NX.55057	No.1 Coy.A.A.S.C.	Sydney, NSW	05.06.45	28
Bennison, R.J., Sgt.	VX.38803	No.1 Coy.A.A.S.C.	Bethanga, Vic.	14.03.45	45
Lynton, R.L.M., L/Sgt.	QX.13754	No.1 Coy.A.A.S.C.	Boronia, Vic.	06.06.45	45
Wilson, R.J., L/Sgt.	VX.45419	No.1 Coy.A.A.S.C.	Ballarat, Vic.	24.07.45	42
Nink, Laurence, Sgt.	NX.60030	No.1 Coy.A.A.S.C.	Waverley, NSW	14.07.45	32
Humfrey, P.C.C., Cpl.	NX.31680	No.1 Coy.A.A.S.C.	Parkes, NSW	23.05.45	43
Grimwood, Henry, Pte.	NX.50883	No.1 Coy.A.A.S.C.		17.07.45	33
Simpson, L.P., Cpl.	VX.37018	No.1 Coy.A.A.S.C.	Camberwell, Vic.	10.03.45	23
James, R.W., Cpl.	NX.20156	No.1 Coy.A.A.S.C.		02.04.45	44
Charlton, R.J., Cpl.	QX.14352	No.1 Coy.A.A.S.C.	Wilston, Qld.	18.07.45	42
Bourne, P.J., Cpl.	QX.14722	No.1 Coy.A.A.S.C.	Toogoolawah, Qld.	27.05.45	29
Locke, John, Cpl.	NX. 2899	No.1 Coy.A.A.S.C.	Narrabeen, NSW	20.03.45	30
Tanko, V.K., L/Cpl.	NX.34186	No.1 Coy.A.A.S.C.	Wollongong, NSW	07.02.45	32
Fahey, A.M., L/Cpl.	NX.53301	No.1 Coy.A.A.S.C.	Bowral, NSW	10.08.45	33
Martin, F.J., L/Cpl.	NX.47163	No.1 Coy.A.A.S.C.	Mayfield, NSW	04.12.44	43
Sullivan, Ronald, Cpl.	NX.33835	No.1 Coy.A.A.S.C.	Ulamambri, NSW	31.03.45	30
Juchau, R.F., L/Cpl.	NX.58711	No.1 Coy.A.A.S.C.	Randwick, NSW	23.07.45	27
Varrie, G.B., L/Cpl.	NX.27127	No.1 Coy.A.A.S.C.	Marrickville, NSW	07.06.45	31
Kemp, M.W., L/Cpl.	VX.24017	No.1 Coy.A.A.S.C.	Elsternwick, Vic.	04.04.45	48
Rochford, Francis, Dvr.	VX.55314	No.1 Coy.A.A.S.C.	Hawthorn, Vic.	30.03.45	31
Martin, J.W., Pte.	NX.25394	No.1 Coy.A.A.S.C.	Warrawee, NSW	13.02.45	27
Graf, P.F., Sgt.	NX.38327	No.1 Coy.A.A.S.C.	Tabbita, NSW	01.07.45	37
Radnedge, Gordon, Pte.	NX.57952	No.1 Coy.A.A.S.C.	Borenore, NSW	20.06.45	23
Dowling, Eric, Pte.	NX.54321	No.1 Coy.A.A.S.C.	Bowral, NSW	06.03.45	27
Molloy, James, Pte.	NX.71656	No.1 Coy.A.A.S.C.	Campsie, NSW	03.05.45	41
Gault, H.R., Pte.	NX.51227	No.1 Coy.A.A.S.C.	Trundle, NSW	27.04.45	30
Glennie, J.T., Dvr.	NX.65715	No.1 Coy.A.A.S.C.	Epping, NSW	15.03.45	34
Barnier, J.N., Pte.	NX.65700	No.1 Coy.A.A.S.C.	Grafton, NSW	12.06.45	25
Taylor, J.A., Pte.	NX.56429	No.1 Coy.A.A.S.C.	Enmore, NSW	05.02.45	27
Gloag, David, Pte.	NX.56152	No.1 Coy.A.A.S.C.	Auburn, NSW	01.03.45	30
Cooney, John, Pte.	NX.17793	No.1 Coy.A.A.S.C.	Bass Hill, NSW	15.04.45	35
Patteson, Ernest, Pte.	NX.32237	No.1 Coy.A.A.S.C.	Sydney, NSW	22.02.45	43
Robinson, Herbert, Pte.	NX.25611	No.1 Coy.A.A.S.C.	Mosman, NSW	04.06.45	27
Crawford, J.O., Pte.	NX.33062	No.1 Coy.A.A.S.C.	Carlingford, NSW	11.07.45	25
Whitelaw, J.R., Pte.	NX.54167	No.1 Coy.A.A.S.C.	Taree, NSW	26.07.45	31
Lewis, C.W.G., Pte.	NX.32213	No.1 Coy.A.A.S.C.	Bundanoon, NSW	17.01.45	39
Livet, V.L., Pte.	NX.33489	No.1 Coy.A.A.S.C.	Waverley, NSW	07.04.45	22
Phillips, W.A., Pte.	NX.58416	No.1 Coy.A.A.S.C.	North Bondi, NSW	22.01.45	43
Manks, E.F., Pte.	NX.51866	No.1 Coy.A.A.S.C.	Auburn, NSW	01.06.45	27
Johnston, C.S., Pte.	NX.65469	No.1 Coy.A.A.S.C.	Croydon, NSW	14.07.45	30
Weatherby, W.S., Pte.	NX.34401	No.1 Coy.A.A.S.C.	Yass, NSW	15.07.45	34
O'Donnell, T.E., Pte.	NX.51741	No.1 Coy.A.A.S.C.	Smithfield, NSW	28.05.45	30
Last, A.B., Pte.	NX.65726	No.1 Coy.A.A.S.C.	Lismore, NSW	10.07.45	29
Taylor, W.C., Pte.	NX.60194	No.1 Coy.A.A.S.C.	Ando, NSW	08.05.45	40
Walker, N.G., Pte.	NX.51563	No.1 Coy.A.A.S.C.	Randwick, NSW	11.02.45	23
Nixon, J.H., Dvr.	VX.42544	No.1 Coy.A.A.S.C.	South Yarra, Vic.	01.02.45	28
Chandler, M.A., Pte.	VX.23166	No.1 Coy.A.A.S.C.	Westbourne Park, S.A.	28.03.45	34
Bills, W.R., Dvr.	VX.34071	No.1 Coy.A.A.S.C.	Hawthorn, Vic.	28.02.43	27
Canning, B.C., Pte.	VX.36397	No.1 Coy.A.A.S.C.	Melbourne, Vic.	08.04.45	26
Knight, H. R., Pte.	VX.63788	No.1 Coy.A.A.S.C.		30.01.45	42
O'Rourke, T.J., Pte.	VX.27573	No.1 Coy.A.A.S.C.	Windsor, Vic.	31.05.45	26
Harrington, T.I., Pte.	VX.23670	No.1 Coy.A.A.S.C.	Whorouly, Vic.	15.12.42	30

'B' FORCE				Date of Death	Age
Hill, W., Dvr.	VX.22838	No.1 Coy.A.A.S.C.	Fitzroy, Vic.	04.04.45	27
Hastie, L.J., Pte.	VX.64472	No.1 Coy.A.A.S.C.	Kerang, Vic.	11.03.45	21
Tanner, V.G., Pte.	VX.36721	No.1 Coy.A.A.S.C.	Coburg, Vic.	21.02.45	28
Bird, J.K., Pte.	VX.36935	No.1 Coy.A.A.S.C.	Elwood, Vic.	16.04.45	30
Fitzgerald, H.R., Pte.	VX.32493	No.1 Coy.A.A.S.C.	Newport, Vic.	07.03.45	30
Swan, C.W., Pte.	VX.47244	No.1 Coy.A.A.S.C.	Ballarat, Vic.	05.03.45	33
Ridler, C.J.A., Pte.	QX.15041	No.1 Coy.A.A.S.C.	Wellington, N.Z.	05.03.45	44
Bignell, K.W., Pte.	QX.16347	No.1 Coy.A.A.S.C.	Cooroy, Qld.	11.06.45	34
Crees, R.J., Pte.	QX.14593	No.1 Coy.A.A.S.C.	Brown Hills, Qld.	08.02.45	30
Smith, E.S., Pte.	QX.14291	No.1 Coy.A.A.S.C.	Wynnum South, Qld.	14.07.45	24
Lang, J.A., Pte.	QX.14777	No.1 Coy.A.A.S.C.	Wilston, Qld.	07.02.45	36
Ainsworth, T.L., Pte.	WX.11731	No.1 Coy.A.A.S.C.	Mt. Hawthorn, W.A.,	09.06.45	24
Ortloff, F.C., Pte.	SX.10860	No.1 Coy.A.A.S.C.	Col.Light Gdns., S.A.	18.02.45	35
Ellis, K.E., Sgt.	SX. 8372	No.1 Coy.A.A.S.C.	Pt. Adelaide, S.A.,	21.01.45	42
Praetz, N.H., Pte.	SX. 8723	No.1 Coy.A.A.S.C.	Enfield, S.A.	07.06.45	36
Hardy, G.R., Pte.	TX. 5607	No.1 Coy.A.A.S.C.	Penguin, Tas.	31.05.45	27
Murray, L.W., Dvr.	QX.13269	No.1 Coy.A.A.S.C.	Kelvin Grove, Qld.	18.10.42	35
Harris, J.O., Pte.	NX.50568	No.1 Coy.A.A.S.C.	Waterloo, NSW	02.06.45	44
Stevenson, T.S., Pte.	QX.13827	No.1 Coy.A.A.S.C.		11.02.45	42
Wheeler, J.E., Cpl.	NX.54640	No.1 Coy.A.A.S.C.	Meadowbank, NSW	28.06.45	40
Willmott, K.W.A., L/Cpl.	VX.50836	No.1 Coy.A.A.S.C.	Windsor, Vic.	15.05.45	33
Gladwin, F.J., Pte.	QX. 9932	No.1 Coy.A.A.S.C.	Kangaroo Pt., Qld.	22.01.45	43
Joseland, K.A., S/Sgt.	NX.56353	No.2 Coy.A.A.S.C.	Potts Point, NSW	01.11.44	44
Doyle, L.H, Sgt.	NX.66892	No.2 Coy.A.A.S.C.	Yoogali, NSW	02.08.45	37
Parkinson, D.S., Sgt.	QX.13579	No.2 Coy.A.A.S.C.	Greenslopes, Qld.	19.02.45	34
Peterson, J.W., Sgt.	QX.14032	No.2 Coy.A.A.S.C.	Greenslopes, Qld.	08.07.45	26
Taylor, H.T., Sgt.	QX.11174	No.2 Coy.A.A.S.C.		05.06.45	38
Waddington, Gilbert, Sgt.	NX.58387	No.2 Coy.A.A.S.C.	Abbotsford, NSW	10.06.44	42
Whereat, M.C., Sgt.	NX.27558	No.2 Coy.A.A.S.C.	Croydon, NSW	22.03.45	40
Witt, K.C., Sgt.	NX.58548	No.2 Coy.A.A.S.C.	Wollstonecraft, NSW	20.04.45	27
Bailey, E.G. Cpl.	NX.45627	No.2 Coy.A.A.S.C.	Bellington, NSW	05.06.45	32
Crane, A.B.E., Cpl.	NX.52023	No.2 Coy.A.A.S.C.	Lane Cove, NSW	09.06.45	44
Kingsley, C.M., Cpl.	VX.23352	No.2 Coy.A.A.S.C.	St. Kilda, Vic.	02.06.45	39
Lancaster, W.J., Cpl.	VX.22839	No.2 Coy.A.A.S.C.	Glen Iris, Vic.	07.06.45	46
MacDonald, R.H., Cpl.	QX.18514	No.2 Coy.A.A.S.C.	Mackay, Qld.	21.02.45	39
Wapling, J.H., Cpl.	VX.48817	No.2 Coy.A.A.S.C.	Essendon, Vic.	22.05.45	25
Connor, H.F., L/Cpl.	VX.25521	No.2 Coy.A.A.S.C.	Rosebud, Vic.	15.03.45	30
Coy, F.T., L/Cpl.	NX.72666	No.2 Coy.A.A.S.C.	Concord, NSW	20.06.45	27
Harper, B.G., L/Cpl.	NX.27910	No.2 Coy.A.A.S.C.	Moulamein, NSW	30.03.45	41
Kealey, J.V., L/Cpl.	QX.17149	No.2 Coy.A.A.S.C.	Bexhill, NSW	30.07.45	35
Meagher, G.F., L/Cpl.	QX.16241	No.2 Coy.A.A.S.C.	Toowoomba, Qld.	29.05.45	32
Prosser, W.R., L/Cpl.	VX.36516	No.2 Coy.A.A.S.C.	Chelsea, Vic.	15.02.45	24
Woodley, E.G., L/Cpl.	NX.59574	No.2 Coy.A.A.S.C.	Canterbury, NSW	05.08.45	26
Allingham, M.A.G., Pte.	VX.48847	No.2 Coy.A.A.S.C.	Northcote, Vic.	08.04.45	31
Addison, P.R., Pte.	NX.31849	No.2 Coy.A.A.S.C.	Inverell, NSW	15.05.45	26
Bell, R.M., Pte.	NX.27215	No.2 Coy.A.A.S.C.	Guildford, NSW	29.04.45	43
Bexton, Thomas, Pte.	NX.69495	No.2 Coy.A.A.S.C.	Willoughby, NSW	25.07.45	25
Bexton, S.O., Pte.	NX.52685	No.2 Coy.A.A.S.C.	Willoughby, NSW	14.06.45	24
Bloom, Eric, Pte.	VX.30185	No.2 Coy.A.A.S.C.	Chiltern, Vic.	08.02.45	42
Bobbin, R.J., Pte.	NX.26258	No.2 Coy.A.A.S.C.	Yass, NSW	27.07.45	29
Carr, Burdett, Pte.	NX.67398	No.2 Coy.A.A.S.C.	Byron Bay, NSW	06.06.45	32
Clark, R.P., Pte.	VX.31077	No.2 Coy.A.A.S.C.	Shepparton, Vic.	24.02.45	42
Cochrane, E.A., Pte.	QX.17043	No.2 Coy.A.A.S.C.	Brisbane, Qld.	06.10.44	40
Collins, S.G., Pte.	QX.16223	No.2 Coy.A.A.S.C.		13.02.45	40
Connor, J.C., Pte.	VX.25598	No.2 Coy.A.A.S.C.	Windsor, Vic.	25.02.45	32
Code, L.J., Dvr.	QX. 2363	No.2 Coy.A.A.S.C.	Longreach, Qld.	02.02.45	25

'B' FORCE				Date of Death	Age
Davison, Jack, Pte.	QX.12904	No.2 Coy.A.A.S.C.	Manly, Qld.	30.03.45	39
DeFaye, C.L., Pte.	VX.39938	No.2 Coy.A.A.S.C.		04.02.45	25
DeFaye, John, Pte.	VX.35490	No.2 Coy.A.A.S.C.		03.01.45	28
Dickie, G.O., Pte.	QX.17153	No.2 Coy.A.A.S.C.	Bexhill, NSW	12.04.45	28
Docwra, G.A., Pte.	NX.53893	No.2 Coy.A.A.S.C.	Waverley, NSW	26.02.45	33
Douglas, W.E., Pte.	QX. 2431	No.2 Coy.A.A.S.C.	Pyrmont, NSW	20.06.45	32
Doyle, A.G., Dvr.	NX.53898	No.2 Coy.A.A.S.C.	Bexley, NSW	09.08.45	27
Dyer, Wally, Pte.	NX.57510	No.2 Coy.A.A.S.C.	Neutral Bay, NSW	24.06.45	26
Earle, L.H., Pte.	QX.16326	No.2 Coy.A.A.S.C.	Nobby, Qld.	12.06.45	44
Folkard, S.B., Dvr.	NX.67404	No.2 Coy.A.A.S.C.	Sherwood, NSW	10.06.45	27
Garrard, J.H., Pte.	NX.40892	No.2 Coy.A.A.S.C.	Gunnedah, NSW	07.06.45	30
Gower, E.H., Pte.	QX.17462	No.2 Coy.A.A.S.C.		15.09.42	41
Evans, O.R., Dvr.	NX.35953	No.2 Coy.A.A.S.C.	Wyalong, NSW	12.08.45	24
Harris, R.C., Pte.	NX.19931	No.2 Coy.A.A.S.C.	Ashfield, NSW	19.06.45	44
Headford, F.W., Pte.	NX.56981	No.2 Coy.A.A.S.C.	Narrabeen Nth., NSW	10.04.45	34
Hodges, R.E.C., Pte.	QX.10822	No.2 Coy.A.A.S.C.	Blackbutt, Qld.	09.06.45	26
Humphreys, P.G., Pte.	NX.37031	No.2 Coy.A.A.S.C.	Currumbin Bch., Qld.	26.05.45	41
Hutchison, C.E., Pte.	QX.17837	No.2 Coy.A.A.S.C.	Albion, Qld.	19.04.45	36
Jarrett, Peter, Dvr.	VX.35059	No.2 Coy.A.A.S.C.	Brighton, Vic.	20.04.45	28
Jenyns, N.W., Pte.	QX.12594	No.2 Coy.A.A.S.C.	Ipswich, Qld.	12.06.45	27
Macadam, S.J.A., Pte.	NX.29481	No.2 Coy.A.A.S.C.	Annandale, NSW	03.04.45	44
Maskey, L.W., Pte.	NX.27883	No.2 Coy.A.A.S.C.	Burwood, NSW	09.08.45	27
Matchett, H.D., Pte.	NX.67279	No.2 Coy.A.A.S.C.	Kogarah, NSW	22.07.45	43
Mildenhall, J.S., Pte.	NX.46432	No.2 Coy.A.A.S.C.	Byron Bay, NSW	09.06.45	36
Molan, D.T., Pte.	NX.59377	No.2 Coy.A.A.S.C.	Auburn, NSW	20.05.45	37
MacKenzie, D.H., Pte.	QX.17465	No.2 Coy.A.A.S.C.	New Farm, Qld.	22.06.45	44
Neal, K.T., Pte.	QX.11352	No.2 Coy.A.A.S.C.	Brisbane, Qld.	14.04.45	25
O'Brien, W.M., Pte.	QX.18009	No.2 Coy.A.A.S.C.	Warwick, Qld.	01.04.45	35
Patterson, H.A., Pte.	QX.17074	No.2 Coy.A.A.S.C.	Shorncliffe, Qld.	21.06.45	28
Phelps, R.L., Dvr.	NX.31101	No.2 Coy.A.A.S.C.	Hornsby, NSW	12.04.45	41
Pringle, F.W., Pte.	QX.13560	No.2 Coy.A.A.S.C.	Brisbane, Qld.	14.02.45	42
Rolls, W.F., Pte.	NX.59717	No.2 Coy.A.A.S.C.	Wellington, NSW	09.04.45	27
Shields, Ralph, Pte.	NX.57251	No.2 Coy.A.A.S.C.	Concord, NSW	21.11.44	52
Steen, W.S., Dvr.	QX.17743	No.2 Coy.A.A.S.C.	Brisbane, Qld.	15.07.45	35
Stewart, S.K., Dvr.	VX.26211	No.2 Coy.A.A.S.C.	Lwr.Ferntree Gully, Vic.	25.12.44	36
Taylor, G.J., Pte.	NX.32613	No.2 Coy.A.A.S.C.	Bankstown, NSW	12.04.45	27
Tierney, M.J., Pte.	QX.20219	No.2 Coy.A.A.S.C.	Aramac, Qld.	02.06.45	34
Tully, N.McK., Pte.	VX.42847	No.2 Coy.A.A.S.C.	Geelong, Vic.	01.07.45	50
Warren, J.McK., Pte.	QX.13888	No.2 Coy.A.A.S.C.	Red Hill, Qld.	14.06.45	39
White, S.H., Pte.	VX.32185	No.2 Coy.A.A.S.C.	Toorak, Vic.	06.02.45	25
Wilson, A.E., Pte.	VX.24065	No.2 Coy.A.A.S.C.	Yarraville, Vic.	29.11.44	44
Wolfe, E.J., Pte.	QX.17500	No.2 Coy.A.A.S.C.	Goodna, Qld.	02.07.45	26
Phillips, Roy, Pte.	VX.32718	No.2 Coy.A.A.S.C.	Chelsea, Vic.	26.07.45	27
Crouch, A.G., L/Cpl.	VX.31614	No.2 Coy.A.A.S.C.	Pt. Melbourne, Vic.	24.04.45	27
McNaughton, Donald, Pte.	NX.45306	H.Q. A.A.S.C.	Charlestown, NSW	28.06.45	43
Reid, R.D., Sgt.	VX.39843	4th Res. M.T.	St. Kilda, Vic.	27.02.45	44
Brown, E.G., Sgt.	VX.39881	4th Res. M.T.	Sth. Yarra, Vic.	04.02.45	47
Coker, R.H., Cpl.	SX.11479	4th Res. M.T.	Maroubra Junct., NSW	07.05.45	45
McDonald, Alfred, Cpl.	SX. 4982	4th Res. M.T.	Dudley Park, S.A.	05.02.43	40
McCarthy, J.F., Cpl.	SX. 9726	4th Res. M.T.	Mitcham, S.A.	01.06.45	42
Davis, H.R.W.P. Cpl.	SX.11608	4th Res. M.T.	Nth. Glenelg, S.A.	23.02.45	40
Barkla, E.A., L/Cpl.	SX.11627	4th Res. M.T.	Edwardstown, S.A.	07.06.45	44
Gould, R.G., Cpl.	WX.10929	4th Res. M.T.	Perth, W.A.	03.03.45	39
Rudd, W.T., L/Cpl.	VX.43384	4th Res. M.T.	Windsor, Vic.	13.07.45	40

'B' FORCE				Date of Death	Age
Speake, C.R., Pte.	SX.11576	4th Res. M.T.	Queenstown, S.A.	25.05.45	41
Jankte, R.J., Pte.	SX.11625	4th Res. M.T.	Woodville, S.A.	21.03.45	42
Rea, E.H., Dvr.	VX.29870	4th Res. M.T.	Fitzroy, Vic.	01.06.45	35
Phillips, E.J., Pte.	VX.32621	4th Res. M.T.		27.04.45	40
Ryan, J.J., Dvr.	VX.36941	4th Res. M.T.	Kerang, Vic.	05.04.45	25
Morland, R.G., Pte.	VX.37720	4th Res. M.T.	Dreeite, Vic.	20.03.45	28
McKelvie, Michael, Pte.	VX.39937	4th Res. M.T.	Coburg, Vic.	24.04.45	48
Carter, G.C.D., Dvr.	VX.51056	4th Res. M.T.	West Melbourne, Vic.	13.04.45	23
Carlson, R.D., Pte.	VX.46761	4th Res. M.T.	Chelsea, Vic.	22.06.45	43
Telford, G.F., Pte.	VX.56970	4th Res. M.T.	Mowbray, Tas.	12.12.44	21
Candlish, G.A., Pte.	QX.12954	4th Res. M.T.	Clayfield, Qld.	04.12.42	44
Gould, A.R., Pte.	QX.15254	4th Res. M.T.	Brighton-le-Sands, NSW	16.03.45	38
Percival, E.J., Dvr.	QX.16818	4th Res. M.T.	Goondiwindi, Qld.	25.02.45	39
Hood, R.J., Pte.	QX.20737	4th Res. M.T.		05.12.44	39
Gooud, Leslie, Pte.	NX.45653	4th Res. M.T.	Auburn, NSW	18.06.45	42
O'Neale, J.T., Pte.	NX.57057	4th Res. M.T.	Leichhardt, NSW	03.06.45	28
Stevens, J.J., Pte.	NX.68616	4th Res. M.T.	Nth. Sydney, NSW	19.04.45	44
McCardle, P.E.J., Pte.	NX.68663	4th Res. M.T.	Mascot, NSW	20.04.45	43
McClintock, W.A., Pte.	NX.69507	4th Res. M.T.	Rose Bay, NSW	22.03.45	36
Smith, F.A.O., Pte.	NX.72016	4th Res. M.T.	Sth. Gundagai, NSW	07.06.45	36
Jacobson, Alexis, Pte.	WX.10171	4th Res. M.T.	Tallinn, Estonia, USSR	24.12.44	40
Porteous, A.A., Dvr.	WX. 9414	4th Res. M.T.		03.11.44	39
Willmott, A.C., Pte.	WX.10178	4th Res. M.T.	Wiluna, W.A.	29.06.45	40
Crilly, R.J., Dvr.	WX.10413	4th Res. M.T.	Como, W.A.	06.04.45	44
McConnell, Alexander, Pte.	WX.10523	4th Res. M.T.	West Lothian, Scotland	09.06.45	42
Dalton-Goodwin, C.R., Dvr.	WX.10610	4th Res. M.T.		01.05.43	40
Thomas, Evan, Pte.	WX.10966	4th Res. M.T.	Perth, W.A.	21.03.45	38
Burke, F.J., Pte.	SX. 4577	4th Res. M.T. Coy.	Maitland,S.A.	07.06.45	34
Cundy, M.H., Pte.	SX. 6178	4th Res. M.T. Coy.	Greenock, S.A.	04.10.42	27
Watters, L.L., Pte.	SX. 7894	4th Res. M.T. Coy.	Kenton Valley, S.A.	22.12.44	38
Player, G.C., Pte.	SX. 8903	4th Res. M.T. Coy.	Warooka, S.A.	07.06.45	35
Toombs, R.E., L/Cpl.	SX. 9105	4th Res. M.T. Coy.	Mile End, S.A.	23.05.45	51
McClounan, R.L., Pte.	SX. 9155	4th Res. M.T. Coy.	Wilkawatt, S.A.	09.06.45	25
Barker, G.J., Pte.	SX. 9269	4th Res. M.T. Coy.	Tea Tree Gully, S.A.	03.03.45	29
Lester, John, Pte.	SX.10704	4th Res. M.T. Coy.	Mt. Gambier, S.A.	30.03.45	38
Fergusson, N.W., Pte.	SX.10846	4th Res. M.T. Coy.	Hilton,S.A.	14.06.45	31
Hunt, R.P., Pte.	SX.11096	4th Res. M.T. Coy.	Melbourne, Vic.	13.02.45	42
Parham, A.G., Pte.	SX.11464	4th Res. M.T. Coy.	Beulah Park, S.A.	29.06.45	27
Coombe, R.J., Pte.	SX.11545	4th Res. M.T. Coy.	Croydon, S.A.	16.03.45	44
Comber, C.O., Pte. (Served as Dempsey, Patrick)	SX.11546	4th Res. M.T. Coy.	Dubbo, NSW	28.03.45	39
Gauld, G.T., Pte.	SX.11588	4th Res. M.T. Coy.	Adelaide, S.A.	10.02.45	43
Gillen, P.P.M., Pte.	SX.11641	4th Res. M.T. Coy.	Clare, S.A.	08.01.45	47
Robbins, T.H., Pte.	SX.11693	4th Res. M.T. Coy.	Heidelberg, Vic.	04.06.45	43
Sandercock, H.A., Pte.	SX.11728	4th Res. M.T. Coy.	Col. Light Gdns., S.A.	03.04.45	40
Priester, Frederick, Pte.	SX.11733	4th Res. M.T. Coy.	Renmark, S.A.	22.03.45	44
Cooling, M.W., Pte.	SX.11762	4th Res. M.T. Coy.	Mt. Gambier, S.A.	08.06.45	40
Scott, Charles, Pte.	QX. 9423	4th Res. M.T. Coy.	Sth. Brisbane, Qld.	14.04.45	43
Ross, Walter, Dvr.	VX.35081	4th Res. M.T. Coy.	Moonee Ponds, Vic.	12.02.45	44
Smith, M.H., Pte.	VX.35176	4th Res. M.T. Coy.	Richmond, Vic.	01.12.44	43
Obee, A.L., Dvr.	VX.35455	4th Res. M.T. Coy.	Chelsfield, Kent, UK	23.04.45	37
Smith, F.S., Dvr.	VX.36035	4th Res. M.T. Coy.	Beeac, Vic.	17.05.45	40
Skews, R.McL., Pte.	VX.39890	4th Res. M.T. Coy.	West Brunswick, Vic.	07.06.45	42
Pearce, W.H., Pte.	VX.39976	4th Res. M.T. Coy.	Richmond, Vic.	01.04.45	30
Evans, W.R., Dvr.	VX.40253	4th Res. M.T. Coy.	Camberwell, Vic.	28.08.42	42
Cornish, Frank, Pte.	VX.40553	4th Res. M.T. Coy.		21.05.45	42

'B' FORCE				Date of Death	Age
Hotchin, D.P., Pte.	VX.43981	4th Res. M.T. Coy.	Auburn, Vic.	07.03.45	53
Fitzpatrick F.J., Dvr.	VX.45352	4th Res. M.T. Coy.	Pascoe Vale, Vic.	05.08.45	45
Pursell, A.L., Pte.	VX.46340	4th Res. M.T. Coy.	Blackburn, Vic.	06.04.45	38
Cook, L.C., Pte.	VX.47694	4th Res. M.T. Coy.	Mumbannar, Vic.	22.03.45	38
Reither, Herman, Dvr.	VX.48478	4th Res. M.T. Coy.	Ballarat, Vic.	08.08.45	38
Winter, S.C., Pte.	VX.50002	4th Res. M.T. Coy.	Mordialloc, Vic.	02.03.45	31
Morris, R.W., Pte.	VX.50005	4th Res. M.T. Coy.	Fairfield, Vic.	23.06.45	24
Thonder, W.C., Pte.	VX.50079	4th Res. M.T. Coy.	West Brunswick, Vic.	19.06.45	27
Hunt, N.F., Dvr.	VX.51527	4th Res. M.T. Coy.	Croydon, Vic.	29.05.45	40
Dickson, L.H., L/Cpl.	VX.53442	4th Res. M.T. Coy.	East Coburg, Vic.	26.05.45	32
Stirling. G.McB., Dvr.	VX.50941	4th Res. M.T. Coy.	Pt. Melbourne, Vic.	23.05.45	24
Bott, J.E., Pte.	VX.55436	4th Res. M.T. Coy.	Corowa, NSW	02.07.45	25
Campbell, D.S., Sgt.	VX.30277	2/2 M.A.C.	Glen Iris, Vic.	23.03.45	41
Potter, Nelson, Dvr.	VX.19685	2/2 M.A.C.	Mid. Brighton, Vic.	25.03.45	44
Richmiller, K.J., Pte.	VX.11491	2/2 M.A.C.	Yarraville, Vic.	30.04.45	27
Fullgrabe, A.C., Dvr.	SX. 7962	2/2 M.A.C.	Sandwell, S.A.	20.04.45	25
Frost, H.T., Cpl.	VX.39422	1st Field Bakery	Stawell, Vic.	24.07.45	25
Frost, E.I., Dvr.	VX.50469	1st Field Bakery	Stawell, Vic.	02.08.45	28
Delahant, C.W., Pte.	VX.39508	1st Field Bakery	Geelong, Vic.	21.04.45	28
Moore, S.L., Sgt.	NX.68415	2/3 M.A.C.	Bondi, NSW	03.01.45	46
Murray, D.A., Sgt.	NX.69389	2/3 M.A.C.	Roseville, NSW	25.03.45	40
Haddon, Thomas, Sgt.	NX.69230	2/3 M.A.C.	Moore Park, NSW	13.07.45	38
Trevillien, R.G., Cpl.	NX.68731	2/3 M.A.C.	Haberfield, NSW	25.01.45	47
Allen, J.M.E., Cpl.	NX.33148	2/3 M.A.C.		23.07.45	44
Halls, R.S., Cpl.	NX.71392	2/3 M.A.C.		14.10.43	37
Young, T.O., Cpl.	NX.69196	2/3 M.A.C.	Padstow, NSW	10.06.45	35
Ludbey, R.B., L/Cpl.	TX. 4457	2/3 M.A.C.	East Melbourne, Vic.	05.11.44	48
Mathew, A.W., Pte.	NX.71825	2/3 M.A.C.	Katoomba, NSW	02.06.45	36
Keating, Michael, Pte.	NX.68380	2/3 M.A.C.	Kilkenny, Irish Rep.	05.02.45	49
Hannan, M.E., Pte.	NX.65864	2/3 M.A.C.	Kyogle, NSW	05.02.45	36
Lysaght, H.W., Cpl.	NX.69225	2/3 M.A.C.	Neutral Bay, NSW	04.07.45	36
Board, W.E., Dvr.	NX.68405	2/3 M.A.C.	Ashfield, NSW	11.09.42	44
Grave, R.L., Cpl.	NX.68391	2/3 M.A.C.	Potts Point, NSW	07.06.45	40
Anderson, Albert, Pte.	NX.69261	2/3 M.A.C.	Glebe Point, NSW	11.05.45	39
Barrie, John, Pte.	NX.68426	2/3 M.A.C.	Reid, Canberra, ACT	15.06.45	56
Black, John, Pte.	NX.68428	2/3 M.A.C.	Strathfield, NSW	24.03.45	46
Coghlan, R.V., Pte.	NX.69286	2/3 M.A.C.	Cremorne, NSW	03.04.45	41
Chapman, W.P., Dvr.	TX. 4471	2/3 M.A.C.	Kingston Bch., Tas.	10.02.45	40
Clair, T.E., L/Cpl.	NX.27483	2/3 M.A.C.	Glebe, NSW	01.06.45	39
Caterson, K.R., L/Cpl.	NX.29443	2/3 M.A.C.	Guildford, NSW	13.05.45	38
Crowther, G.G., Pte.	NX.69199	2/3 M.A.C.		08.03.45	44
Davis, J.T., Pte.	NX.59722	2/3 M.A.C.	Croydon Park, NSW	05.01.45	41
Ferris, G.R., Dvr.	TX. 4456	2/3 M.A.C.	Neutral Bay, NSW	22.03.45	48
Forster, W.C.O., Dvr.	NX.68430	2/3 M.A.C.	St. Peters, NSW	08.03.45	44
Fisher, P.L., Dvr.	NX.68388	2/3 M.A.C.	Auburn, NSW	10.04.45	48
Grant, F.M., Dvr.	NX.67898	2/3 M.A.C.	Matraville, NSW	14.02.45	38
Harcourt, R.B., Dvr.	NX.68400	2/3 M.A.C.		03.05.45	48
Hardy, L.E., Pte.	NX.68861	2/3 M.A.C.	Taree, NSW	19.05.45	41
Halden, W.J., Pte.	NX.69644	2/3 M.A.C.	Ashbridge, NSW	23.06.45	39
Hansell, H.N., Pte.	NX.55773	2/3 M.A.C.	Parkes, NSW	27.02.45	43
Johnson, H.L., Pte.	NX.68865	2/3 M.A.C.	Bondi Junction, NSW	14.03.45	47
Jones, A.F., Dvr.	NX.69187	2/3 M.A.C.	Sydney, NSW	02.06.45	41
Ezzy, A.J.C., Dvr.	NX.68928	2/3 M.A.C.	Richmond, NSW	05.03.45	38

'B' FORCE				Date of Death	Age
Midgley, J.J., Pte.	NX.25816	2/3 M.A.C.	Croydon, NSW	16.03.45	44
Macklin, K.G., Pte.	NX.49406	2/3 M.A.C.	Marrickville, NSW	17.05.45	22
McCarthy, Leo, Dvr.	NX.68904	2/3 M.A.C.	Five Dock, NSW	02.03.45	44
Noakes, A.H., Pte.	NX.57746	2/3 M.A.C.	Meadows Flat, NSW	13.02.45	32
Pawson, Charles, Dvr.	NX.68432	2/3 M.A.C.	Rozelle, NSW	19.04.45	56
Parsons, J.W., Dvr.	NX.73060	2/3 M.A.C.	Broadmeadow, NSW	12.07.45	49
Rodgers, E.A., Pte.	NX.57816	2/3 M.A.C.	Maroubra, NSW	07.06.45	41
Reynolds, Charles, Dvr.	NX.69272	2/3 M.A.C.	Hove, Sussex, UK	05.06.45	42
Toms, Harry, Pte.	NX.68403	2/3 M.A.C.	Berowra, NSW	02.04.45	48
Wells, G.D.W., Pte.	NX.68850	2/3 M.A.C.	Potts Point, NSW	05.07.45	43
Logan, R.W.B., Dvr.	NX.68763	2/3 M.A.C.	Burwood, NSW	26.03.45	41
Wolfe, George, Pte.	NX.69248	2/3 M.A.C.	Patonga, NSW	07.06.45	45
Brown, A.A., L/Cpl.	QX.16937	2/3 M.A.C.	Mitchell, Qld.	02.06.45	21
Perrott, C.E., Dvr.	NX.69153	2/3 M.A.C.	Tumbarumba, NSW	15.02.45	33
O'Brien, Francis, Sgt.	NX.26088	2/3 M.A.C.	Nth. Sydney, NSW	23.05.45	34
Anderson, E.R., Crftsmn.	VX.67161	2/10 Ordnce.Wkshps.	Coburg, Vic.	09.02.45	25
Abfalter, P.J., Pte.	VX.66960	2/10 Ordnce.Wkshps.	Malvern, Vic.	26.03.45	26
Albress, A.S., Pte.	QX.24479	2/10 Ordnce.Wkshps.	Home Hill, Qld.	19.06.45	41
Burchnall, F.R., Cpl.	VX.64477	2/10 Ordnce.Wkshps.	Bendigo, Vic.	19.05.43	52
Burchnall, F.A., Cpl.	VX.58285	2/10 Ordnce.Wkshps.	Bendigo, Vic.	04.06.45	23
Bateson, D.F., Pte. (Served as Chandler, R.W.)	VX.53556	2/10 Ordnce.Wkshps.	St. Kilda, Vic.	26.12.44	23
Cordy, Frank, Crftsmn.	VX.65567	2/10 Ordnce.Wkshps.	Essendon, Vic.	15.03.45	23
Crawford, V.O., Pte.	TX. 5206	2/10 Ordnce.Wkshps.	Invermay, Tas.	07.06.45	32
Downes, I.G., Pte.	VX.64357	2/10 Ordnce.Wkshps.	Reservoir, Vic.	12.04.45	22
Duddington, Harold, Pte.	WX. 9893	2/10 Ordnce.Wkshps.	Suffolk, UK	28.03.45	37
Duncan, J.W.H., Pte.	VX.59476	2/10 Ordnce.Wkshps.	Hampton, Vic.	15.03.45	25
Ewing, Herbert, Pte.	VX.54326	2/10 Ordnce.Wkshps.	Avoca, Vic.	11.02.45	38
Feldbauer, T.A., Sgt.	VX.51733	2/10 Ordnce.Wkshps.	Research, Vic.	27.03.45	35
Foote, P.N., Pte.	VX.57114	2/10 Ordnce.Wkshps.		05.02.45	40
Gaynor, B.G., Crftsmn.	VX.67018	2/10 Ordnce.Wkshps.	Perth, W.A.	09.03.45	25
Hankinson, R.F., Pte.	VX.59423	2/10 Ordnce.Wkshps.	Harcourt, Vic.	07.06.45	41
Irving, R.F., Pte.	VX.64385	2/10 Ordnce.Wkshps.	Colac, Vic.	02.06.45	41
Knight, Victor, Pte.	VX.63596	2/10 Ordnce.Wkshps.	Ballarat, Vic.	16.02.45	45
Lowe, A.J. Crftsmn.	VX.62006	2/10 Ordnce.Wkshps.	Ascot Vale, Vic.	17.03.45	31
Monro, William, Pte.	VX.26269	2/10 Ordnce.Wkshps.	Ferny Creek, Vic.	27.05.45	42
Oakley, J.H., Pte.	VX.63247	2/10 Ordnce.Wkshps.	East Malvern, Vic.	23.05.45	33
O'Malley, G.F., Pte.	VX.60918	2/10 Ordnce.Wkshps.	East Malvern, Vic.	17.02.45	25
Powell, K.N., Crftsmn.	VX.66324	2/10 Ordnce.Wkshps.	Ringwood, Vic.	17.06.45	22
Prior, Leslie, Cfn.	WX. 9135	2/10 Ordnce.Wkshps.	Mt. Hawthorn, W.A.,	18.04.45	40
Reitze, Harry, Crftsmn.	VX.61196	2/10 Ordnce.Wkshps.		30.05.45	27
Rodriquez, J.F., Pte.	VX.66152	2/10 Ordnce.Wkshps.	Black Rock, Vic.	04.02.45	34
Sampson, H.R., Pte.	VX.62741	2/10 Ordnce.Wkshps.	Brunswick, Vic.	23.03.45	24
Shepherd, W.P., Pte.	VX.66586	2/10 Ordnce.Wkshps.	Bendigo, Vic.	05.06.45	29
Sligar, G.W., Pte.	QX.19768	2/10 Ordnce.Wkshps.	New Farm, Qld.	05.02.45	43
Starkie, J.D.F., Pte.	VX.64061	2/10 Ordnce.Wkshps.	Sunbury, Vic.	10.05.45	24
Stewart, H.J., Crftsmn.	VX.66054	2/10 Ordnce.Wkshps.	Sth. Caulfield, Vic.	25.05.45	42
Swan, W.A., Cpl.	WX.11665	2/10 Ordnce.Wkshps.	Victoria Park, W.A.	01.02.45	42
Whyte, R.J.R., Pte.	VX.64181	2/10 Ordnce.Wkshps.		05.06.45	28
Woods, F.H., Pte.	NX.47215	2/10 Ordnce.Wkshps.	Glendon Brook, NSW	06.07.45	32
Fosbury, B.J.A., Pte.	VX.67624	2/10 Ordnce.Wkshps.	Surrey, UK	14.02.45	25
Bartils, G.H., Crftsmn.	VX.54880	2/10 Ordnce.Wkshps.	West Footscray, Vic.	21.06.45	31
Barnes, R.G., Crftsmn.	VX.38074	22 Bde. Workshops	Essendon, Vic.	07.03.45	26
Butherway, J.H. Crftsmn.	VX.37645	22 Bde. Workshops	Eltham, Vic.	08.07.45	26

'B' FORCE				Date of Death	Age
Durand, G.P., Pte.	VX.39481	22 Bde. Workshops	Hawthorn, Vic.	04.02.45	24
Essex, R.F., L/Cpl.	VX.36782	22 Bde. Workshops	Macleod, Vic.	14.03.45	43
Gordon, Thomas, Pte.	VX.40999	22 Bde. Workshops	Ballarat, Vic.	15.07.45	34
Loader, K.M., Sgt.	SX.10163	22 Bde. Workshops	Kensington Park, S.A.	13.05.45	33
McCulloch, C.R., Crfstmn.	VX.52700	22 Bde. Workshops	Nth. Richmond, Vic.	01.03.45	20
McMahon, John, Pte.	VX.20512	22 Bde. Workshops	Nth. Brighton, Vic.	10.07.45	26
Morgan, L.G., Pte.	VX.64581	22 Bde. Workshops	Moonee Ponds, Vic.	05.04.45	22
May, D.J., Crftsmn.	VX.30008	22 Bde. Workshops		03.08.45	28
Merritt, R.L., Pte.	VX.64633	22 Bde. Workshops	Caulfield, Vic.	07.06.45	32
O'Meara, J.J., Pte.	VX.61791	22 Bde. Workshops	Watchem, Vic.	09.06.45	25
Perry, W.G., Crftsmn.	VX.61709	22 Bde. Workshops	Richmond, Vic.	05.06.45	24
Pontin, R.W., Crftsmn.	VX.62247	22 Bde. Workshops	Balaclava, Vic.	26.06.45	23
Ralph, W.D., Crftsmn.	VX.34708	22 Bde. Workshops	Coburg, Vic.	12.01.45	33
Roberts, W.F., Crftsmn.	VX.60640	22 Bde. Workshops	Northcote, Vic.	30.03.45	31
Ralph, B.D., Crftsmn.	VX.34719	22 Bde. Workshops	Footscray, Vic.	18.02.45	35
Sewell, A.E., Pte.	VX.36971	22 Bde. Workshops	West Melbourne, Vic.	05.03.45	41
Schutt, L.V., Pte.	VX.36899	22 Bde. Workshops	Yarraville, Vic.	02.04.45	26
Broughton, W.E., Crftsmn.	VX.47483	27 Bde. Workshops	Euroa, Vic.	03.12.44	28
Boyley, W.A., Pte.	SX.11770	27 Bde. Workshops	Adelaide, S.A.	17.06.45	34
Capper, G.H., Pte.	VX.65245	27 Bde. Workshops		21.03.45	22
Cooper, J.A., Pte.	NX.72963	27 Bde. Workshops	Dora Creek, NSW	05.04.45	23
Dawes, L.A., Cpl.	SX.11602	27 Bde. Workshops	Glenunga, S.A.	13.01.45	28
Duckworth, Sam, Crftsmn.	SX.11290	27 Bde. Workshops		10.03.45	46
Fraser, T.W., Crftsmn.	VX.54178	27 Bde. Workshops	Albert Park, Vic.	25.02.45	39
Morgan, L.C., Cpl.	SX.10794	27 Bde. Workshops	Adelaide, S.A.	21.02.45	34
Schiphorst, Albert, Cfn.	SX.12031	27 Bde. Workshops	Semaphore, S.A.,	17.03.45	41
Stewart, Walter, Pte.	VX.61176	27 Bde. Workshops	Grimsby, Lincs., UK	14.05.45	29
Strang, P.McK., Sgt.	SX. 7870	27 Bde. Workshops	Toorak Gardens, S.A.	20.02.45	41
Trodd, R.J., Pte.	VX.58054	27 Bde. Workshops	Essendon, Vic.	22.10.44	41
Walker, E.T., Pte.	SX.12151	27 Bde. Workshops	Burnside, S.A.	09.06.45	43
Ward, S.W., Pte.	VX.64440	27 Bde. Workshops	West Footscray, Vic.	02.04.45	22
Pederson, P.M., S/Sgt.	SX.10764	27 Bde. Workshops	Norwood, S.A.,	21.01.45	47
Ward, Roy, Pte.	VX.64876	27 Bde. Workshops	Geelong, Vic.	22.04.45	42
Dunne, J.J. Pte.	VX.57393	22 Bde. Ord.Wkshops		16.04.45	35
Parnell, R.J. Crftsmn.	VX.39199	22 Bde. Ord.Wkshops		29.05.45	28
Smith, A.J. Crftsmn.	VX.20596	22 Bde. Ord.Wkshops	Albert Park, Vic.	14.04.45	26
Allnutt, S.G., Cpl.	VX.57809	2/10 Ord.Fld.Park	Hampton, Vic.	20.05.45	40
Brown, Frederick, Pte.	NX.31685	2/10 Ord.Fld.Park		10.03.45	44
Craig, A.C., Pte.	VX.63272	2/10 Ord.Fld.Park	West Brunswick, Vic.	26.03.45	39
Dawson, A.B.G., Spr.	NX.66500	2/10 Ord.Fld.Park	West Footscray, Vic.	04.12.44	39
Dawson, Thomas, Pte.	VX.62668	2/10 Ord.Fld.Park	West Brunswick, Vic.	29.04.45	39
Graham, J.L., Pte.	VX.62306	2/10 Ord.Fld.Park	Rainbow, Vic.	24.04.45	33
Veal, R.J., Pte.	VX.62776	2/10 Ord.Fld.Park	Ascot Vale, Vic.	08.03.45	23
Watson, F.W., Cpl.	VX.37884	2/10 Ord.Fld.Park	Yarrawalla, Vic.	04.07.45	33
Hay, C.G., Sgt.	SX.13254	2/10 Ord.Fld.Park	Millswood Estate, S.A.	18.02.45	38
Hill, C.S., Pte.	VX.63829	2/10 Ord.Fld.Park	Elwood, Vic.	02.06.45	36
King, Edward, Pte.	VX.61904	2/10 Ord.Fld.Park	Albert Park, Vic.	10.06.45	48
Main, C.D., Pte.	VX.66942	2/10 Ord.Fld.Park	Queenscliff, Vic.	05.06.45	22
Ramsay, G.A., Pte.	VX.37752	2/10 Ord.Fld.Park	Turiff, Vic.	21.07.45	28
Gay, A.P.R.L., Cpl.	VX.58690	22 Bde.Ord.Fld.Park	Preston, Vic.	14.06.45	41
Jacks, R.J., Pte.	VX.62747	22 Bde.Ord.Fld.Park	Richmond, Vic.	11.04.45	36
Learmonth, R.G., Pte.	VX.58602	22 Bde.Ord.Fld.Park	Minyip, Vic.	06.03.45	26
Lewis, John, Pte.	VX.58062	22 Bde.Ord.Fld.Park		19.04.45	33
Macaulay, W.A., Pte.	VX.56999	22 Bde.Ord.Fld.Park	Myrtleford, Vic.	29.04.45	45

'B' FORCE				Date of Death	Age
Maizey, C.W., Cpl.	VX.63699	22 Bde.Ord.Fld.Park	West Brunswick, Vic.	18.07.45	26
Maunsell, J.F., Pte.	VX.60972	22 Bde.Ord.Fld.Park	Murrumbeena, Vic.	19.03.45	20
Phelan, M.J., Pte.	VX.50588	22 Bde.Ord.Fld.Park	Oakleigh, Vic.	27.06.45	36
Kroschel, E.M., Pte.	VX.63470	27 Bde.Ord.Fld.Park	East Brighton, Vic.	18.01.45	24
Thorneycroft, C.H., Pte.	VX.60926	27 Bde.Ord.Fld.Park	Preston, Vic.	30.10.44	32
Wraight, D.C.C., Pte.	VX.60012	27 Bde.Ord.Fld.Park	Caulfield, Vic.	11.02.45	43
Eastwood, G.E., L/Cpl.	QX. 5157	69 Group L.A.D.	Surrey, UK	21.02.45	33
Jones, D.H. Crftsmn.	NX.65363	73 L.A.D.	Woy Woy, N.SW	13.07.45	42
Hodder, W.J., Cpl.	NX.50879	74 L.A.D.	Cowra, NSW	31.01.45	52
Neal, C.S., Pte.	NX.30273	74 L.A.D.	Greenethorpe, NSW	02.10.44	37
Neaves, G.M., Cpl.	NX.40286	74 L.A.D.	Barraba, NSW	07.06.45	39
Hazelgrove, M.B.F., Crftsmn.	NX. 7357	84 L.A.D.	Alexandria, NSW	27.01.45	25
Launder, F.A., Crftsmn.	NX.65845	84 L.A.D.	Campsie, NSW	24.05.45	41
Wastnidge, Richard, Cpl.	VX.35374	84 L.A.D.	Sheffield, Yorks. UK	13.02.45	44
Connell, Frederick, Cpl.	VX.40871	86 L.A.D.	Windsor, Vic.	08.04.45	32
McKenna, C.R., Crftsmn.	WX. 8566	86 L.A.D.	Victoria Park, W.A.	01.02.45	34
Thorley, I.E., Sgt.	WX. 9562	86 L.A.D.	Nth. Perth, W.A.	04.03.45	43
Baxter, M.P., Sgt.	NX.68141	87 L.A.D.	Marrickville, NSW	08.06.45	34
Bird, J.E., Pte.	NX.67878	87 L.A.D.		10.10.42	41
Henley, J.B., Sgt.	VX.45368	8 Div.Mobile Bath	Colac, Vic.	06.06.45	42
Benson, G.E., Pte.	QX.23738	2/3 Ordnce. Store	Kingaroy, Qld.	09.04.45	24
Binstead, A.H., Pte.	QX.22033	2/3 Ordnce. Store	Nth. Tamborine, Qld.	28.05.45	23
Cameron, C.M., Pte.	QX.22902	2/3 Ordnce. Store	Strathfield, NSW	31.01.45	33
Chapman, J.J., W.O.II.	QX.17585	2/3 Ordnce. Store	Tweed Heads, NSW	05.07.45	38
Christie, N.McN., Cpl.	QX. 8389	2/3 Ordnce. Store	Milton, Qld.	05.06.45	40
Conley, H.S., Pte.	TX. 4960	2/3 Ordnce. Store	Hobart, Tas.	06.04.45	39
Davis, J.A., Cpl.	QX.17869	2/3 Ordnce. Store	Coolangatta, Qld.	09.08.45	34
Gregory, G.E.H., Pte.	QX.23284	2/3 Ordnce. Store	Woody Point, Qld.	06.05.45	37
Griffin, T.M., Pte.	VX.62750	2/3 Ordnce. Store	Coburg, Vic.	06.02.45	39
Hasted, J.J., Cpl.	QX.17867	2/3 Ordnce. Store	Roma, Qld.	29.01.45	37
King, P.C., Pte.	QX.20002	2/3 Ordnce. Store	Southport, Qld.	17.06.45	36
Kyte, H.G., Pte.	QX.22246	2/3 Ordnce. Store		18.06.45	25
Grinter, C.A., Pte.	VX.55109	2/3 Ordnce. Store	Nathalia, Vic.	28.03.45	42
Jeffrey, V.A., Pte.	TX. 8114	2/3 Ordnce. Store	Melbourne, Vic.	13.02.45	25
McLeod, C.J., Cpl.	VX.47591	2/3 Ordnce. Store	Lake Boga, Vic.	14.05.45	30
Ruscoe, George, L/Cpl.	QX.21729	2/3 Ordnce. Store	Monto, Qld.	02.06.45	34
Simpson, S.A., Pte.	QX.19741	2/3 Ordnce. Store	Cardwell, Qld.	24.03.45	25
Stewart, A.B., Pte.	QX.19998	2/3 Ordnce. Store	Valley, Qld.	04.02.45	31
Tanzer, H.J., Cpl.	QX.17872	2/3 Ordnce. Store	Milton, Qld.	02.06.45	32
Tyrrell, R.C., Pte.	QX.23747	2/3 Ordnce. Store	Canberra, ACT	07.02.45	22
Wilson, R.S., Pte.	QX.21634	2/3 Ordnce. Store	Sandgate, Qld.	13.05.45	29
Hyett, R.G., Pte.	QX.12044	2/3 Ordnce. Store	Sandgate, Qld.	10.04.45	40
Egel, R.C., Pte.	SX. 7706	8 Div.Salvage Unit	Mannum, S.A.	06.02.45	25
Hales, R.A., Pte.	SX. 4713	8 Div.Salvage Unit	Summertown, S.A.	04.12.44	44
Knapp, W.G., Pte.	SX. 9006	8 Div.Salvage Unit	Mile End, S.A.	15.06.45	30
Larner, V.G., Sgt.	SX.10531	8 Div.Salvage Unit	Royston Park, S.A.	03.03.45	31

'B' FORCE

				Date of Death	Age
McKinnon, V.H., Pte.	SX.10091	8 Div.Salvage Unit	Gawler, S.A.	14.04.45	29
Richards, E.M., Pte.	SX. 9634	8 Div.Salvage Unit	Somerton, S.A.	18.03.45	44
Robertson, E.E., Pte.	SX. 4394	8 Div.Salvage Unit	Pt. Wakefield, S.A.	23.05.45	44
Rouse, M.H., Cpl.	SX. 9709	8 Div.Salvage Unit	Medindie, S.A.	17.03.45	32
Yates, Garth, Pte.	SX. 9909	8 Div.Salvage Unit	Angaston, S.A.	09.03.45	31
Evans, L.M., Cpl.	SX. 6923	8 Div.Salvage Unit	Wallaroo, S.A.	14.02.45	39
Picone, D.G., Capt. (A.A.M.C. Attach.)	QX. 6380	2/10 Fld. Regiment		06.08.45	36
Heaslop, J.E. Capt.	QX. 6413	2/10 Fld. Regiment	Cremorne, NSW	19.07.45	30
Crewdson, A.J., Sgt.	QX.14413	2/10 Fld. Regiment	Coorparoo, Qld.	27.04.45	26
Pegnall, C.W. Sgt.	QX. 1872	2/10 Fld. Regiment	Townsville, Qld.	02.05.45	27
Down, T.H. Sgt.	QX.14727	2/10 Fld. Regiment	Taringa, Qld.	05.01.45	27
Campbell, John. L/Sgt.	QX.14645	2/10 Fld. Regiment	Gaythorne, Qld.	08.06.45	26
Hayes, W.C. L/Sgt.	QX.17098	2/10 Fld. Regiment	New Farm, Qld.	12.05.45	25
Paulett, Laurence. Sgt.	QX.13170	2/10 Fld. Regiment	Mackay, Qld.	29.07.45	33
Powell, L.V. L/Sgt.	QX.14902	2/10 Fld. Regiment	Cloncurry, Qld.	29.07.45	25
Salter, P.J. L/Sgt.	QX.14873	2/10 Fld. Regiment	Buranda, Qld.	14.02.45	32
Barnes, R.G. Bdr.	QX. 9965	2/10 Fld. Regiment	Bulimba, Qld.	14.02.45	25
Commins, J.S.H. Bdr.	QX. 5989	2/10 Fld. Regiment	Whangarei, Auck.NZ	08.05.45	33
Jeavons, J.A. Bdr.	QX. 8433	2/10 Fld. Regiment	East Brisbane, Qld.	14.07.45	37
Jukes, C.G.H. Bdr.	QX.10433	2/10 Fld. Regiment	Annerley, Qld.	23.07.45	39
Treseder, H.A. L/Bdr.	QX.17430	2/10 Fld. Regiment	Highgate Hill, Qld.	12.05.45	48
Arthur, R.G. Gnr.	QX.14374	2/10 Fld. Regiment	Windsor, Qld.	05.06.45	28
Arthur, H.A. Gnr.	QX.16912	2/10 Fld. Regiment	Holland Park, Qld.	11.06.45	28
Barnard, L.G. Gnr.	QX. 9260	2/10 Fld. Regiment		18.03.45	24
Balgue, D.N. Gnr.	QX.13672	2/10 Fld. Regiment	Wynnum Central, Qld.	04.06.45	24
Boyd, Robert. Gnr.	QX. 8386	2/10 Fld. Regiment		23.05.45	44
Bock, H.J. Gnr.	QX. 9908	2/10 Fld. Regiment	5th. Bundaberg, Qld.	07.03.45	25
Brown, Charles. Gnr.	QX. 8356	2/10 Fld. Regiment		03.01.45	52
Barker, J.H. Gnr.	QX.10572	2/10 Fld. Regiment	Maryborough, Qld.	15.02.45	28
Carter, P.W.F. Gnr.	QX.21002	2/10 Fld. Regiment	Belmont, Qld.	02.03.45	26
Cameron, Finlay. Gnr.	QX. 8427	2/10 Fld. Regiment	Mackay, Qld.	07.06.45	42
Chisholm, R.S. Gnr.	QX.12066	2/10 Fld. Regiment		07.06 45	44
Copelin, H.V. Gnr.	QX. 9698	2/10 Fld. Regiment	Coorparoo, Qld.	27.05 45	29
Collins, H.W. Gnr.	QX.14618	2/10 Fld. Regiment	5th. Brisbane, Qld.	15.02.45	30
Cribb, T.B. Gnr.	QX.21392	2/10 Fld. Regiment	Corinda, Qld.	19.02.45	23
Cunningham, J.M. L/Bdr.	QX.16443	2/10 Fld. Regiment	Sandgate, Qld.	22.02.45	32
Farrow, Harold. Gnr.	QX.17027	2/10 Fld. Regiment	Kangaroo Pt., Qld.	30.05.45	34
Greenup, C.R. Gnr.	QX. 923	2/10 Fld. Regiment	Brisbane, Qld.	12.03.43	32
Honor, Basil. Gnr.	QX.14854	2/10 Fld. Regiment	West Bundaberg, Qld.	08.04.45	36
Hogan, Douglas. Gnr.	QX. 1905	2/10 Fld. Regiment	Ipswich, Qld.	17.10.42	21
Humbler, B.P. Gnr.	QX.15450	2/10 Fld. Regiment		05.12.44	32
Johnson, C.G. Gnr.	QX.14844	2/10 Fld. Regiment	Toowoomba, Qld.	11.02.45	32
Leinster, V.P. L/Bdr.	QX.15180	2/10 Fld. Regiment	Atherton, Nth.Qld.	22.02.45	26
Mitchell, W.G. Gnr.	QX.10092	2/10 Fld. Regiment	5th. Brisbane, Qld.	05.02.45	43
Mahony, K.P. Gnr.	QX.17433	2/10 Fld. Regiment	Charleville, Qld.	24.01.45	34
Newlands, T.S. Gnr.	QX. 8486	2/10 Fld. Regiment	Glasgow, Scotland	05.03.45	44
Ogilvie, D.J. Gnr.	QX.19014	2/10 Fld. Regiment	Cremorne, NSW	30.06.45	32
Peters, C.J. Gnr.	QX.14815	2/10 Fld. Regiment	Alderley, Qld.	07.06.45	42
Purtill, J.F. Gnr.	QX.12091	2/10 Fld. Regiment	Ravensbourne, Qld.	20.04.45	28
Purvis, R.C. Gnr.	QX.21043	2/10 Fld. Regiment	Alexandria, NSW	04.06.45	31

'B' FORCE				Date of Death	Age
Robins, C.W., Gnr.	QX.14209	2/10 Fld. Regiment	Wynnum Heights, Qld.	09.02.45	36
Rush, M.J., Gnr.	QX.16930	2/10 Fld. Regiment	Toowoomba, Qld.	08.02.45	24
Reid, D.A., Gnr.	QX. 9270	2/10 Fld. Regiment	Ashgrove, Qld.	29.06.45	41
Shaw, D.R., Gnr.	QX.15018	2/10 Fld. Regiment	Gympie, Qld.	17.03.45	31
Slatter, A.J., Gnr.	QX.12552	2/10 Fld. Regiment	Old Naroon, Qld.	23.03.45	24
Strachan, George, Gnr.	QX.16280	2/10 Fld. Regiment	Gillingham, Kent, UK	06.04.45	45
Walter, R.W., Gnr.	QX.17516	2/10 Fld. Regiment	Albion, Qld.	24.06.45	30
Wolter, G.J., Gnr.	QX.20996	2/10 Fld. Regiment	Southport, Qld.	03.02.45	32
Watson, Clarence, Gnr.	QX.11283	2/10 Fld. Regiment		14.03.45	30
Wehl, F.G., Gnr.	QX.16680	2/10 Fld. Regiment	Roma, Qld.	02.08.45	39
Williams, G.E., Gnr.	QX. 9184	2/10 Fld. Regiment	Corina, Qld.	15.02.45	35
Winks, A.K., Gnr.	QX. 9284	2/10 Fld. Regiment	Wynnum, Qld.	07.07.45	41
Wright, F.P., Gnr.	QX.15144	2/10 Fld. Regiment	Babinda, Qld.	12.06.45	25
Ovens, Hugh, Gnr.	QX.14719	2/10 Fld. Regiment	Paddington, Qld.	05.06.45	26
Sinnamon, Francis, Gnr.	QX.10094	2/10 Fld. Regiment	Toowoomba, Qld.	07.06.45	28
Walters, A.F., Gnr.	QX.13638	2/10 Fld. Regiment	Spring Hill, Qld.	18.02.45	28
Winning, Harry, Gnr.	QX. 9669	2/10 Fld. Regiment	Bowen Hills, Qld.	07.02.45	31
Hanson, K.D., Gnr.	QX. 9390	2/10 Fld. Regiment	New Farm, Qld.	15.02.45	27
Corney, L.C., Gnr.	QX. 8244	2/10 Fld. Regiment	Mackay, Qld.	25.02.45	24
Costello, John, Gnr.	QX.21581	2/10 Fld. Regiment	Strathfield, NSW	21.06.45	32
McIver, C.A., Gnr.	QX. 8863	2/10 Fld. Regiment	Wooloowin, Qld.	19.08.44	39
O'Connor, Gerald, Gnr.	QX. 8487	2/10 Fld. Regiment	Albert Park, Vic.	07.03.45	27
Sykes, R.W., W.O.II.	NX.67296	2/15 Fld. Regiment	West Wallsend, NSW	11.07.45	34
Turner, K.M., W.O.II.	NX.68217	2/15 Fld. Regiment	Kings Cross, NSW	15.07.45	25
Brown, R.G., S/Sgt.	NX.39190	2/15 Fld. Regiment	Hamilton, NSW	11.07.45	31
Coughlin, C.J., S/Sgt.	NX.39189	2/15 Fld. Regiment	Merewether, NSW	16.04.45	30
Symons, G.H., Sgt.	NX.26317	2/15 Fld. Regiment	Tumut, NSW	10.04.45	26
Shackell, J.H., Bdr.	NX.32260	2/15 Fld. Regiment	Randwick, NSW	14.04.45	30
Glover, C.R., Bdr.	NX.27110	2/15 Fld. Regiment	Mosman, NSW	24.05.45	27
Brownlee, G.F., Bdr.	NX.46612	2/15 Fld. Regiment	Bellingen, NSW	11.07.45	33
Cross. J.R., L/Bdr.	NX.30581	2/15 Fld. Regiment	Coffs Harbour, NSW	12.06.45	28
Ebzery, Thomas, Bdr.	NX.33024	2/15 Fld. Regiment	Narooma, NSW	05.06.45	40
Knight, H.E., Gnr.	NX.10946	2/15 Fld. Regiment	Ashbury, NSW	01.05.45	39
Palmer, Athol, L/Bdr.	NX.27967	2/15 Fld. Regiment		11.06.45	44
Stevens, C.C.H., Bdr.	NX.27035	2/15 Fld. Regiment	Naremburn, NSW	18.04.45	30
Scott, J.M., L/Bdr.	NX.26119	2/15 Fld. Regiment	Wellington, NSW	28.02.45	33
Dunkinson, J.L., L/Bdr.	NX.27640	2/15 Fld. Regiment	Belmore, NSW	12.06.45	36
Bluford, E.H., Pte.	NX.23730	2/15 Fld. Regiment	Aberdeen, NSW	02.06.45	37
Fuller, E.J., Gnr.	NX.34384	2/15 Fld. Regiment	Branxton, NSW	14.02.45	26
Francis, F.C., Gnr.	NX.46716	2/15 Fld. Regiment	Ryde, NSW	24.04.45	29
Findlay, J.G., Gnr.	NX.56338	2/15 Fld. Regiment	Riverstone, NSW	12.06.45	24
Gardner, I.L.G., L/Bdr.	NX.28552	2/15 Fld. Regiment	Aberdeen, NSW	28.03.43	27
Godson, C.H., Gnr.	NX.18641	2/15 Fld. Regiment	Maidenhead, Berks. UK	06.06.45	38
Grimwood, J.R., Gnr.	NX.25502	2/15 Fld. Regiment	Newcastle, NSW	02.07.45	28
Hotston, Leslie, Gnr.	NX.10746	2/15 Fld. Regiment	Punchbowl, NSW	06.06.45	27
Jackson, F.P., Gnr.	NX.70110	2/15 Fld. Regiment	New Lambton, NSW	02.07.45	27
Miller, A.M., Gnr.	NX.10554	2/15 Fld. Regiment	West Ryde, NSW	26.03.45	24
Perry-Circuitt, E.F., Gnr.	NX.53349	2/15 Fld. Regiment	Moss Vale, NSW	17.04.45	40
Sullivan, R.H., Gnr.	NX.28000	2/15 Fld. Regiment	Kingsford, NSW	17.06.45	26
Shaw, A.D., Gnr.	NX.10472	2/15 Fld. Regiment	Kensington, NSW	10.06.45	25
Travis, J.H., Gnr.	NX.29662	2/15 Fld. Regiment	Richmond, NSW	07.06.45	29
Richardson, J.L., Gnr.	NX.45217	2/15 Fld. Regiment	Bellbird, NSW	04.06.45	25
Stewart, B.P., Gnr. (Served as MacNab, R.)	NX. 5655	2/15 Fld. Regiment	West Maitland, NSW	29.01.45	21
Mongan, Daniel, Gnr.	NX.37342	2/15 Fld. Regiment	Hornsby, NSW	30.10.44	43

'B' FORCE				Date of Death	Age
Moule-Probert, John, Gnr.	NX.10894	2/15 Fld. Regiment	Griffith, NSW	10.05.45	48
McIlroy, K.A., Gnr.	NX. 7338	2/15 Fld. Regiment	Greenwich, NSW	05.07.45	25
McGlinn, A.J., Gnr.	NX. 6627	2/15 Fld. Regiment	Denistone, NSW	09.07.45	41
Bray, E.W., Gnr.	NX.31286	2/15 Fld. Regiment	Sutherland, NSW	02.06.45	27
Glover, F.M., Gnr.	NX.55670	2/15 Fld. Regiment	Mosman, NSW	18.06.45	27
Dale, Albert, Gnr.	QX.21994	2/15 Fld. Regiment	Coorparoo, Qld.	14.02.45	38
Brown, J.E., Gnr.	NX.29736	2/15 Fld. Regiment	Lambton, NSW	07.02.45	24
Beer, W.H., Gnr.	NX.19307	2/15 Fld. Regiment	Hornsby, NSW	21.03.45	41
Bovey, A.R., Gnr.	QX.18776	2/15 Fld. Regiment	Mackay, Qld.	24.04.45	23
Cleary, A.N., Gnr.	VX.52128	2/15 Fld. Regiment	East Geelong, Vic.	20.03.45	22
Coughlan, Thomas, Gnr.	NX. 7347	2/15 Fld. Regiment	Morundah, NSW	14.02.45	31
Deshon, F.H., Gnr.	QX.19556	2/15 Fld. Regiment	Dirranbandi, Qld.	24.04.45	38
Finch, W.H., Gnr.	NX.23555	2/15 Fld. Regiment	Petersham, NSW	07.06.45	25
Hodges, Douglas, Gnr.	NX.27704	2/15 Fld. Regiment		07.06.45	24
Holland, John, Gnr.	NX.46821	2/15 Fld. Regiment	Milsons Point, NSW	02.05.45	29
Herd, Bruce, Gnr.	NX.42238	2/15 Fld. Regiment	Kyogle, NSW	12.07.45	23
Knowles, John, Gnr.	NX.26019	2/15 Fld. Regiment	Dunoon, NSW	20.02.45	49
Leadbeatter, W.C., Gnr.	NX.46793	2/15 Fld. Regiment	Ballina, NSW	15.05.45	24
Mackie, A.G., Gnr.	NX.41929	2/15 Fld. Regiment	Willoughby, NSW	13.05.45	26
Mortimer, C.H., Gnr.	QX.22187	2/15 Fld. Regiment	Manly, Qld.	23.05.45	33
Rooke, D.R., Gnr.	NX.30325	2/15 Fld. Regiment	Eastwood, NSW	06.04.45	27
Small, R.D., Gnr.	NX.29863	2/15 Fld. Regiment	Bowral, NSW	23.06.45	27
Quintal, E.A., Gnr.	NX.53125	2/15 Fld. Regiment		02.02.45	42
Hewitt, N.L., Gnr.	VX.32910	2/15 Fld. Regiment	East Brunswick, Vic.	05.03.45	26
Grosvenor, R.J., Gnr.	NX.28295	2/15 Fld. Regiment	Dulwich Hill, NSW	30.04.45	27
Crease, Wally, Gnr.	NX.38584	2/15 Fld. Regiment		20.08.44	24
Grosvenor, L.L., Gnr.	NX.27856	2/15 Fld. Regiment	Marrickville, NSW	06.03.45	24
Heyworth, William, Gnr.	NX.10694	2/15 Fld. Regiment	Waikato, N.Z.	19.04.45	36
Motley, Leslie, Gnr.	NX.24065	2/15 Fld. Regiment	Randwick, NSW	05.06.45	35
Adair, James, Gnr.	NX. 4733	2/15 Fld. Regiment		22.02.45	24
Maddock, N.L., W.O.II.	VX.40573	4th A/T. Regiment	Toorak, Vic.	24.07.45	25
Macmeikan, D.J.G., Sgt.	VX.39078	4th A/T. Regiment	Malvern, Vic.	18.07.45	30
Ferguson, A.J., Sgt.	VX.43593	4th A/T. Regiment	Geelong West, Vic.	30.07.45	38
McManus, S.J.A., L/Sgt.	VX.32003	4th A/T. Regiment	Toorak, Vic.	27.03.45	28
Jones, J.W.MacP., L/Sgt.	VX.40648	4th A/T. Regiment	Bentleigh, Vic.	18.03.45	35
Robinson, F.G.B., Bdr.	VX.24791	4th A/T. Regiment	Uppr. Hawthorn, Vic.	14.02.45	25
Howard, E., Bdr.	VX.32425	4th A/T. Regiment	Sunderland, Co. Durham, UK	18.11.44	35
Hamilton, Jack, L/Bdr. (Served as Colville, J.H.)	VX.22992	4th A/T. Regiment		30.03.45	40
McDonald, G.A., L/Bdr.	VX.19389	4th A/T. Regiment	East Malvern, Vic.	26.12.44	57
Dennehy, A.C., Gnr.	VX.31652	4th A/T. Regiment	Bentleigh, Vic.	24.04.45	28
Kilpatrick, C.H., Gnr.	VX.26569	4th A/T. Regiment		22.03.45	43
Taylor, G.C., Gnr.	VX.50676	4th A/T. Regiment	Brunswick Vic.	14.04.45	29
Smith, R.J.V., Gnr.	VX.27460	4th A/T. Regiment	Coburg, Vic.	10.11.42	50
Johnston, S.G., Gnr.	VX.37083	4th A/T. Regiment	Burnley, Vic.	21.04.45	21
Brien, D.H., Gnr.	VX.15008	4th A/T. Regiment	Elwood, Vic.	24.02.45	26
Tyres, K.H., Gnr.	VX.35140	4th A/T. Regiment	Numurkah, Vic.	05.02.45	27
McLeod, J.R., Gnr.	VX.35983	4th A/T. Regiment	Dunkeld, Vic.	09.03.45	24
McCracken, W.E., Gnr.	VX.37108	4th A/T. Regiment	Kaneghy, Nthn.Ireland	04.08.45	35
Alberts, Wallace, Gnr.	VX.38057	4th A/T. Regiment	Lake Condah, Vic.	31.03.45	26
Barlow, W.J., Gnr.	VX.35674	4th A/T. Regiment	Moonee Ponds, Vic.	07.06.45	28
Marr, Stuart, Gnr.	VX.32760	4th A/T. Regiment	Nth. Melbourne, Vic.	28.03.45	40
Clarkson, J.M., Gnr.	VX.11741	4th A/T. Regiment	South Yarra, Vic.	14.02.45	24
White, Bernard, Gnr.	VX.32051	4th A/T. Regiment	Prahran, Vic.	06.04.45	32

'B' FORCE				Date of Death	Age
Blackwood, L.C., Crftsmn.	VX.33897	4th A/T. Regiment	South Yarra, Vic.	07.06.45	42
Chamberlain, J.P., Gnr.	VX.27808	4th A/T. Regiment	Evington, Leics., UK	08.10.44	43
Doherty, L.L., Gnr.	VX.18536	4th A/T. Regiment	Springvale, Vic.	13.04.45	44
Barratt, R.H., Gnr.	VX.43489	4th A/T. Regiment	Rosslyn Park, S.A.,	10.12.44	35
Skinner, G.T., Gnr.	VX.43478	4th A/T. Regiment	St. Leonards-on-Sea, Sussex, UK	17.01.45	44
Reed, E.A., Gnr.	VX.27470	4th A/T. Regiment	West Ballarat, Vic.	19.09.43	33
Elliott, S.W., Gnr.	VX.57559	4th A/T. Regiment	Upper Lurg, Vic.	15.06.45	27
Sheedy, R.H., Gnr.	VX.40106	4th A/T. Regiment	Hamilton, Vic.	27.03.45	31
Duggan, S.J., Gnr.	VX.42638	4th A/T. Regiment	Pt. Melbourne, Vic.	26.03.45	27
Etchell, A.E., Gnr.	VX.59787	4th A/T. Regiment	East St. Kilda, Vic.	16.02.45	23
Hagston, George, S/Sgt.	VX.27442	2/10 Fld.Coy. RAE	Warrnambool, Vic.	30.06.45	26
Bray, John, Sgt.	VX.37753	2/10 Fld.Coy. RAE	Sandringham, Vic.	07.06.45	43
Burnell, A.D., Cpl.	VX.31566	2/10 Fld.Coy. RAE	Thornbury, Vic.	17.07.45	30
Connolly, T.W.J., Cpl.	NX.51283	2/10 Fld.Coy. RAE	Randwick, NSW	09.08.45	36
Kelly, B.H., Cpl.	VX.37767	2/10 Fld.Coy. RAE	Toorak, Vic.	08.05.45	27
Palmer, Donald, Cpl.	VX.32200	2/10 Fld.Coy. RAE	Brighton, Vic.	13.02.45	38
Peck, Francis, L/Cpl.	VX.29567	2/10 Fld.Coy. RAE	Tungamah, Vic.	16.03.45	35
Ashby, F.R., Spr.	VX.18668	2/10 Fld.Coy. RAE	Glenferrie, Vic.	15.03.45	38
Bacon, S.T., Spr.	VX.38059	2/10 Fld.Coy. RAE	Elsternwick, Vic.	20.06.45	31
Barnes, K.G., Spr.	VX.44182	2/10 Fld.Coy. RAE	Geelong, Vic.	01.05.45	37
Bryant, F.L. Spr.	VX.46208	2/10 Fld.Coy. RAE	Dennis, Vic.	08.06.45	36
Cameron, J.K., Spr.	VX.41921	2/10 Fld.Coy. RAE	Warracknabeal, Vic.	13.05.45	23
Harrison, W.R., Spr.	VX.38354	2/10 Fld.Coy. RAE	Ultima, Vic.	16.03.45	24
Horne, G.D., Spr.	TX. 8103	2/10 Fld.Coy. RAE	Echuca, Vic.	05.11.44	22
Leedham, C.A., Spr.	SX. 8097	2/10 Fld.Coy. RAE	Enmore, NSW	18.02.45	43
Lock, B.C., Spr.	VX.38249	2/10 Fld.Coy. RAE	Rochester, Vic.	18.02.45	26
Morgan, H.A., Spr.	VX.46194	2/10 Fld.Coy. RAE	Thornbury, Vic.	26.03.45	31
McKean, Ivor, Spr.	VX.40456	2/10 Fld.Coy. RAE	Elsternwick, Vic.	14.06.45	30
Panton, O.W., Spr.	TX. 5183	2/10 Fld.Coy. RAE	Penguin, Tas.	20.06.45	24
Peoples, D.J., Spr.	VX.38917	2/10 Fld.Coy. RAE	Preston, Vic.	09.02.45	28
Reid, William, Spr.	VX.27811	2/10 Fld.Coy. RAE	Seaford, Vic.	27.12.44	39
Short, E.R., Spr.	VX.42365	2/10 Fld.Coy. RAE	Benalla, Vic.	26.04.45	32
Tait, Robert, Spr.	VX.46094	2/10 Fld.Coy. RAE	Williamstown, Vic.	16.03.45	42
Tolliday, A.S., Spr.	VX.32359	2/10 Fld.Coy. RAE	North Kew, Vic.	18.02.45	37
Walsh, F.V., Spr.	VX.20752	2/10 Fld.Coy. RAE	Geelong West, Vic.	04.03.45	34
Warren, H.J., Spr.	VX.18324	2/10 Fld.Coy. RAE	Warrnambool, Vic.	22.03.45	42
Woodley, F.E., Cpl.	VX.24588	2/10 Fld.Coy. RAE	Phillip Island, Vic.	06.02.45	39
Whyman, H.A., Spr.	TX. 4455	2/10 Fld.Coy. RAE	Burnie, Tas.	24.03.45	25
O'Connell, James, Spr.	VX.61050	2/10 Fld.Coy. RAE	Springvale, Vic.	14.01.45	37
Doran, P.M., Sgt.	NX.50343	2/12 Fld.Coy. RAE	Annandale, NSW	13.02.45	40
Adams, Henry, Spr.	NX. 4526	2/12 Fld.Coy. RAE		14.06.45	43
Beaumont, F.J., Spr.	NX.66388	2/12 Fld.Coy. RAE		10.03.45	37
Carley, F.A., Spr.	NX.20419	2/12 Fld.Coy. RAE	Punchbowl, NSW	13.06.45	28
Coleman, W.J., Spr.	NX.31433	2/12 Fld.Coy. RAE		02.03.45	35
Clark, G.W., Spr.	NX.54786	2/12 Fld.Coy. RAE	Punchbowl NSW	08.06.45	29
Fletcher, F.G.W., Spr.	NX.53515	2/12 Fld.Coy. RAE	Mascot, NSW	11.10.42	37
Grono, P.R., Spr.	NX.54517	2/12 Fld.Coy. RAE	Fairfield, NSW	01.05.45	25
Gullidge, H.E., Spr.	NX.44236	2/12 Fld.Coy. RAE	Balgowlah, NSW	28.05.45	26
Hancock, M.J., Spr.	NX.27802	2/12 Fld.Coy. RAE	Cooks Hill, NSW	23.04.45	47
Hinchcliff, W.H.W., Spr.	NX.57905	2/12 Fld.Coy. RAE	Corrimal, NSW	10.04.45	27
Hurley, E.T., Spr.	NX.44098	2/12 Fld.Coy. RAE	Kensington, NSW	10.12.44	24
Meredith, D.H., Spr.	NX.43299	2/12 Fld.Coy. RAE	Coniston, NSW	15.04.45	23
Neal, F.W., Spr.	NX.68381	2/12 Fld.Coy. RAE	Sans Souci, NSW	05.06.45	42

'B' FORCE				Date of Death	Age
Neilson, R.R., Spr.	NX.45309	2/12 Fld.Coy. RAE	Newcastle, NSW	18.11.44	31
Pope, J.G., Spr.	NX. 5763	2/12 Fld.Coy. RAE		02.03.45	37
Patten, C.E., Spr.	NX.44566	2/12 Fld.Coy. RAE	Ganmain, NSW	04.03.45	22
Redman, W.H., Spr.	NX.38351	2/12 Fld.Coy. RAE	Gloucester, NSW	12.08.42	31
Richardson, L.W., Spr.	NX.37146	2/12 Fld.Coy. RAE	Mudgee, NSW	18.06.45	25
Ring, Ronald, Spr.	NX.72976	2/12 Fld.Coy. RAE		29.06.45	40
Smith, W.H., Spr.	NX.54922	2/12 Fld.Coy. RAE		05.03.45	42
Thomson, Alexander, Spr.	NX.67444	2/12 Fld.Coy. RAE		13.01.45	36
Twiss, R.T., Spr.	NX.67030	2/12 Fld.Coy. RAE	Birchgrove, NSW	15.10.44	23
Walsh, L.J., Spr.	NX.52354	2/12 Fld.Coy. RAE	Kirribilli, NSW	22.01.45	42
White, C.H., Spr.	NX.72848	2/12 Fld.Coy. RAE	Roseville, NSW	06.04.45	38
Wilkins, G.H., Spr.	NX.25058	2/12 Fld.Coy. RAE	Potts Point, NSW	09.04.45	54
Williams, H.P., Spr.	NX.32469	2/12 Fld.Coy. RAE	Bellevue Hill, NSW	14.04.45	26
Drinkwater, J.R., Spr.	NX.68039	2/12 Fld.Coy. RAE	Dobies Bight, NSW	10.06.45	29
Elsley, G.L.E., Spr.	NX.58773	2/12 Fld.Coy. RAE	Crows Nest, NSW	01.04.45	42
Spurling, Thomas, W.O.II.	WX. 8488	2/6 Fld.Pk.Coy.RAE	Fremantle, W.A.	11.03.45	42
Stuchbury, Ian, S/Sgt.	WX. 8548	2/6 Fld.Pk.Coy.RAE	Victoria Park, W.A.	17.11.44	42
Lynch, J.J., Cpl.	WX. 6317	2/6 Fld.Pk.Coy.RAE	Kells, Ireland	20.06.45	44
Blewett, C.B., L/Sgt.	WX. 8159	2/6 Fld.Pk.Coy.RAE	Greenbushes, W.A.	23.03.45	43
Hooper, W.R., L/Cpl.	WX. 7685	2/6 Fld.Pk.Coy.RAE	Perth, W.A.	21.05.45	41
Beazley, J.D., Spr.	WX. 6222	2/6 Fld.Pk.Coy.RAE	Boulder, W.A.	07.07.45	31
Burley, K.B., Spr.	WX. 8780	2/6 Fld.Pk.Coy.RAE	Bridgetown, W.A.	18.05.45	40
Boxhorn, Kenneth, Spr.	WX.12478	2/6 Fld.Pk.Coy.RAE	Perth, W.A.	17.05.45	35
Cadwgan, A.D., Spr.	WX. 7472	2/6 Fld.Pk.Coy.RAE	Sth. Perth, W.A.	02.06.45	43
Davey, C.W., Spr.	WX.14710	2/6 Fld.Pk.Coy.RAE	Sth. Perth, W.A.	04.03.45	34
Davies, D.T., Spr.	WX.12011	2/6 Fld.Pk.Coy.RAE	Yorkrakine, W.A.	04.01.45	37
Evans, B.H., Spr.	WX. 7339	2/6 Fld.Pk.Coy.RAE	Victoria Park, W.A.	20.06.45	29
Evans, W.G., Spr.	WX. 9668	2/6 Fld.Pk.Coy.RAE	Victoria Park, W.A.	06.11.42	24
Field, G.L.C., Spr.	WX. 7360	2/6 Fld.Pk.Coy.RAE	Albany, W.A.	01.06.45	41
Fitzpatrick, D.A., Pte.	NX.43446	2/6 Fld.Pk.Coy.RAE	Croydon Park, NSW	10.06.45	28
Foster, Dawson, Spr.	WX. 7104	2/6 Fld.Pk.Coy.RAE	Palmyra, W.A.	07.06.45	40
Gardner, E.J., Spr.	WX. 6998	2/6 Fld.Pk.Coy.RAE	Nth. Perth, W.A.	09.07.45	41
Glover, Sydney, Spr.	WX. 8683	2/6 Fld.Pk.Coy.RAE	Norseman, W.A.	05.06.45	36
Goldfinch, S.C., Spr.	WX. 7054	2/6 Fld.Pk.Coy.RAE	Innahoo, W.A.	13.07.45	44
Grigson, A.G., Spr.	WX. 7134	2/6 Fld.Pk.Coy.RAE	Beverley, W.A.	09.06.45	28
Harvey, G.E.O., Spr.	WX.13183	2/6 Fld.Pk.Coy.RAE	Cottesloe, W.A.	08.03.45	43
Hasluck, L.N., Spr.	WX. 8090	2/6 Fld.Pk.Coy.RAE	Herne Hill, W.A.	06.04.44	42
Haye, L.J., Spr.	WX. 7247	2/6 Fld.Pk.Coy.RAE		08.02.45	39
Howell, D.W., Spr.	WX. 8053	2/6 Fld.Pk.Coy.RAE	Victoria Park, W.A.	11.06.45	28
Hustler, F.E., Spr.	WX. 8714	2/6 Fld.Pk.Coy.RAE	Clydesdale, Vic.	05.06.45	36
Jones, Victor, Spr.	WX.15404	2/6 Fld.Pk.Coy.RAE	Chidlow, W.A.	05.04.45	43
Kilminster, E.G., Spr.	WX. 8633	2/6 Fld.Pk.Coy.RAE	Perth, W.A.	04.12.44	32
King, J.S., Spr.	WX. 8564	2/6 Fld.Pk.Coy.RAE	Bayswater, W.A.	13.06.45	35
Marsh, H.A., Spr.	WX. 8794	2/6 Fld.Pk.Coy.RAE		08.06.45	40
Milne, G.W.H., Spr.	WX. 8461	2/6 Fld.Pk.Coy.RAE	Cottesloe, W.A.	14.02.45	41
Moore, A.W., L/Cpl.	WX. 8412	2/6 Fld.Pk.Coy.RAE	Mosman Park, W.A.	29.03.45	40
McDonough, J.B., Spr.	WX.10877	2/6 Fld.Pk.Coy.RAE	Yarloop, W.A.	15.03.45	41
McFarlane, John, Spr.	WX. 7227	2/6 Fld.Pk.Coy.RAE	Leederville, W.A.	20.06.45	37
Passmore, E.W., Spr.	WX. 8220	2/6 Fld.Pk.Coy.RAE		13.02.45	41
Rowley, Bernard, Spr.	WX. 5339	2/6 Fld.Pk.Coy.RAE	Wickepin, W.A.	16.03.45	43
Scott, James, Spr.	WX. 8224	2/6 Fld.Pk.Coy.RAE	Sth. Perth, W.A.	19.01.45	43
Small, R.P., Spr.	WX. 8420	2/6 Fld.Pk.Coy.RAE	Fremantle, W.A.	08.04.45	43
Smith, G.J.H., Spr.	WX. 9888	2/6 Fld.Pk.Coy.RAE	Belmont, W.A.	04.06.45	40
Smith, Ernest, Spr.	WX.11588	2/6 Fld.Pk.Coy.RAE	Perth, W.A.	08.03.43	34
Thurston, H.W., Spr.	WX. 8008	2/6 Fld.Pk.Coy.RAE	Bencubbin, W.A.	11.03.45	37

'B' FORCE				Date of Death	Age
Wood, R.B., Spr.	WX. 3118	2/6 Fld.Pk.Coy.RAE		02.11.44	32
Young, J.S., Spr.	WX. 8152	2/6 Fld.Pk.Coy.RAE	Yarra Junction, Vic.	04.04.45	37
Palmer, H.W., Spr.	NX.56225	2/6 Fld.Pk.Coy.RAE	Balgowlah, NSW	27.03.45	25
McAppion, H.E., Spr.	WX. 7015	2/6 Fld.Pk.Coy.RAE	Nth. Fremantle, W.A.	04.06.45	26
Peacock, C.K., Sgt.	VX.19246	H.Q. RAE.	Brighton, Vic.	15.03.45	28
Bird, A.W., Spr.	NX.67306	H.Q. RAE	Stanmore, NSW	09.07.45	28
McHenery, L.G., Spr.	NX.57143	H.Q. RAE	Newtown, NSW	07.05.45	41
Hutchinson, Valentine, L/Sgt.	NX.53080	8 Div. Signals	East Brighton, Vic.	02.06.45	39
Moore E.J., Sigmn.	VX.38000	8 Div. Signals	Carnegie, Vic.	01.07.45	32
Ratcliff, R.B., Sigmn.	NX.31069	8 Div. Signals	Watsons Bay, NSW	08.05.45	39
Johnson, A.E., Sigmn.	VX.64262	8 Div. Signals		16.02.45	43
Argo, D.M., Sigmn.	VX.28139	8 Div. Signals	Richmond, Vic.	25.05.45	24
Evans, R.B., Sigmn.	VX.58804	8 Div. Signals	Bunyip, Vic.	14.03.45	43
Ayres, C.H., Sigmn.	NX.44536	8 Div. Signals	Bellbird, NSW	10.04.45	31
Vogele, G.L., Sigmn.	VX.63607	8 Div. Signals	Preston, Vic.	14.02.45	26
Ball, C.G., Sigmn.	QX. 9300	8 Div. Signals	Southport, Qld.	04.06.45	24
Sefton, B.L., Sigmn.	NX.53102	8 Div. Signals	Colac, Vic.	01.03.45	44
Fogarty, J.M.H., Sigmn.	NX.26313	8 Div. Signals	Killara, NSW	03.03.45	43
Dengate, A.J., Sigmn.	NX.42967	8 Div. Signals	St. Marys, NSW	17.06.45	23
Franklin, F.G., Sigmn.	NX.36659	8 Div. Signals	Wagga Wagga, NSW	14.02.45	38
Livingstone, H.H., Sigmn.	QX. 3482	8 Div. Signals	Burnett Heads, Qld.	28.03.45	32
Doyle, P.J., Sigmn.	NX.43426	8 Div. Signals	West Tamworth, NSW	12.06.45	25
Bougoure, O.W., Sigmn.	QX.10026	8 Div. Signals	Dalby, Qld.	21.05.45	43
Power, R.G., Sigmn.	QX. 7461	8 Div. Signals	Brisbane, Qld.	08.05.45	29
Mackay, T.R.B, Sigmn. (Served as Mackenzie, D.S.)	QX.15656	8 Div. Signals	Pt. Piper, NSW	11.05.43	32
Scully, J.S., L/Cpl.	NX.40088	8 Div. Signals	Cassilis, NSW	20.03.45	26
King, C.H., Sig.	VX.63472	8 Div. Signals	Bendigo, Vic.	18.07.45	41
Kent, E.J., Sig.	NX.72857	8 Div. Signals	Sydney, NSW	24.04.45	27
McMartin, Jack, Sig.	VX.59467	8 Div. Signals	Thornton, Vic.	07.08.45	23
Kerris, J.L., Sig.	VX.35766	8 Div. Signals	Seymour, Vic.	26.06.45	30
Garde, H.G., Sig.	NX.41804	8 Div. Signals	Ryde, NSW	12.03.45	24
Stolarski, C.D., Pte.	VX.52764	8 Div. Signals		24.03.45	25
Gow, A.W., Sig.	NX.65359	8 Div. Signals	Merewether, NSW	25.06.45	40
Fingher, R.E.A., Sig.	VX.58301	8 Div. Signals	Moonee Ponds, Vic.	21.03.45	24
Lister, A.W., Sig.	NX.49847	8 Div. Signals	Burwood, NSW	15.06.45	23
Harvey, H.F., Sig.	NX.49419	8 Div. Signals	Townsville, Qld.	11.05.43	21
MacKenzie, Colin, Sig.	VX.50215	8 Div. Signals	Ellerslie, Vic.	20.04.45	21
Lewis, F.A., Sig.	NX.41922	8 Div. Signals	Canberra, ACT	24.03.45	23
Downward, N.L., Sig.	VX.35804	8 Div. Signals	East Brunswick, Vic.	23.05.45	28
Constable, W.A.J., Sig.	VX.34179	8 Div. Signals	Kyneton, Vic.	18.05.45	29
Warrington, C.W., W.O.II.	NX.31091	H.Q. 8 Div.	Coogee, NSW	14.05.45	32
Bundey, G.W., Sgt.	NX.65429	H.Q. 8 Div.	Toorak Gdns., S.A.	29.04.45	28
Badgery, B.L., Sgt.	NX.65880	H.Q. 8 Div.	Mosman, NSW	30.03.45	30
Hensby, Henry Pte.	NX.55145	H.Q. 8 Div.	Cremorne, NSW	27.03.45	30
Patterson, R.A., Pte.	NX. 1719	H.Q. 8 Div.	Taree, NSW	29.05.45	30
Finn, A.H., Pte.	NX.65601	H.Q. 8 Div.	Coonabarabran, NSW	20.07.45	36
Rowan, H.J., Sigmn.	NX.19365	H.Q. 8 Div.	Glebe, NSW	24.05.45	24
Welch, W.A., Pte.	NX.10264	H.Q. 8 Div.	Newtown, NSW	09.06.45	44
Searle, L.E., Sgt.	VX.30130	2nd Echelon	Sth. Yarra, Vic.	07.06.45	49
Fitzgerald, J.D., Cpl.	NX.53667	2nd Echelon	St. Leonards, NSW	02.03.45	37

'B' FORCE				Date of Death	Age
Codlin, J.M., Sgt.	NX.68401	Command Pay Office	Coogee, NSW	06.08.45	36
Lloyd, H.G., Cpl.	NX. 5694	Command Pay Office		05.06.45	42
Clark, J.C., Cpl.	NX.72293	Command Pay Office	Rockdale, NSW	15.04.45	43
Green, E.A., Cpl.	QX.19255	Command Pay Office	Buranda, Bris., Qld.	12.04.45	30
Sadler, R.E.H., W.O.I.	NX.68161	Audit Sectn. AAPC	Kogarah, NSW	01.06.45	26
O'Neill, C.F., Cpl.	QX. 1907	Audit Sectn. AAPC	New Farm, Qld.	19.03.45	41
Cripps, W.G., Pte.	VX.27627	Audit Sectn. AAPC	Burnley, Vic.	04.07.45	34
Betts, Jack, Cpl.	NX.55556	8 Div.Postal Unit		15.02.45	30
Daughters, J.S., L/Cpl.	VX.60633	8 Div.Postal Unit	Sth. Caulfield, Vic.	11.02.45	42
Greenway, A.C., Pte.	NX.44684	8 Div.Postal Unit	Craigie, Vic.	05.06.45	39
Hogg, Walter, Cpl.	VX.64151	8 Div.Postal Unit	Cranbourne, Vic.	03.03.45	39
Keating, W.M., Pte.	NX. 5829	8 Div.Postal Unit	Annandale, NSW	03.02.45	36
Tipping, N.A., Pte.	NX.44279	8 Div.Postal Unit	Crows Nest, NSW	04.07.45	22
Woods, M.P., Pte.	VX.61816	8 Div.Postal Unit	Carisbrook, Vic.	10.03.45	34
Lake, W.T., Cpl.	NX.56820	8 Div.Postal Unit	Mosman, NSW	25.05.45	34
Dunhill, M.R., Cpl.	SX.10070	8 Div.Postal Unit	Ovingham, S.A.	22.03.45	41
Ewers, C.E., L./Cpl.	QX.18800	8 Div.Postal Unit	Mackay, Qld,	17.05.45	22
Kinnon, V.R., Pte.	QX.18786	8 Div.Postal Unit	Mackay, Qld.	07.06.45	28
Porritt, N.A., Pte.	VX.63691	8 Div.Postal Unit	Glen Iris, Vic.	20.05.45	27
McDonald, F.R.A., Pte.	NX.42341	8 Div.Postal Unit	Earlwood, NSW	30.03.45	24
Cowley, M.C., Pte.	QX.18815	8 Div.Postal Unit	Mackay, Qld.	17.05.45	27
Wilson, G.E., Pte.	VX.62417	8 Div.Postal Unit	West Portland, Vic.	13.05.45	24
Hunter, A.C.A., S/Sgt.	NX.24461	8 Div.Provost Coy.	Ashbury, NSW	12.07.45	23
Mitchell, W.E., Sgt.	NX.51926	8 Div.Provost Coy.	Enfield, NSW	10.05.45	45
Bousie, George, Cpl.	NX.35472	8 Div.Provost Coy.	Fitzroy, Vic.	26.01.45	38
Colyer, G.W., Cpl.	NX.25213	8 Div.Provost Coy.	Nowra, NSW	12.02.45	31
Cassidy, L.A., Cpl.	NX.57540	8 Div.Provost Coy.	Gladesville, NSW	26.04.45	24
Clement, A.W.M., Pte.	NX.33343	8 Div.Provost Coy.	Canterbury, NSW	09.03.45	23
Gibson, J.B., Pte.	NX. 5710	8 Div.Provost Coy.	Stockport, Cheshire, UK	28.02.45	24
Hargrave, C.H., Cpl.	NX.40244	8 Div.Provost Coy.	Walcha, NSW	03.03.45	38
Henwood, E.J., Cpl.	NX. 5671	8 Div.Provost Coy.	Punchbowl, NSW	20.03.45	37
Mitchell, E.E.J., Cpl.	NX.57520	8 Div.Provost Coy.	Canterbury, NSW	28.03.45	39
Moore, E.G., Cpl.	NX.33566	8 Div.Provost Coy.	Sydney, NSW	04.06.45	24
Stone, R.D., Pte.	NX.23033	8 Div.Provost Coy.	Ballina, NSW	17.02.45	24
Smith, C.T., Pte.	NX. 1647	8 Div.Provost Coy.	Nth. Sydney, NSW	24.03.45	30
Smith, E.I., Pte.	QX.22622	8 Div.Provost Coy.	Nth. Sydney, NSW	15.03.45	25
Wilson, D.G., Cpl.	NX.55798	8 Div.Provost Coy.	Quaama, NSW	21.03.45	24

'E' FORCE				Date of Death	Age
Smyth, C.G. S/Sgt.	NX.67741	10 AGH	Clyde, NSW	07.05.45	36
Garland, A.W., Cpl. Acting Chaplain	VX.32307	2/9 Fd.Amb.	Glenelg, SA	18.03.45	40
Canterbury, L.C., Pte.	VX.57641	10 AGH	Kingsville, Vic.	07.05.45	25
Falco, Jack, Pte.	VX.58565	13 AGH	Richmond, Vic.	26.02.45	26
Columbine, R.E. Pte. (Served as Aylett, Roy)	VX.57176	13 AGH	Williamstown, Vic.	07.02.45	20
Bowe, W.J., Pte.	VX.22115	2/9 Fd.Amb.	Sth. Preston, Vic.	26.07.45	28
Day, Garth, Pte.	VX.33620	2/9 Fd.Amb.	Cheltenham, Vic.	08.07.45	25
Keays, D.C., Pte.	VX.21158	2/9 Fd.Amb.	Nth. Fitzroy, Vic.	19.03.45	22
Oakeshott, J.B., Capt.	NX.76223	10 AGH	Lismore, NSW	01.08.45	44

'E' FORCE				Date of Death	Age
Bedford, K.D.E, Sgt.	NX.59155	2/18 Battalion	Lindfield, NSW	10.06.45	26
Clack, J.P., Sgt.	NX.53688	2/18 Battalion	Killara, NSW	01.06.45	28
McDonald, W.B., S/Sgt.	NX.25571	2/18 Battalion	Armidale, NSW	13.08.45	44
Stacy, R.L., Sgt.	NX.26451	2/18 Battalion	Singleton, NSW	25.07.45	27
Smith, W.J., Sgt.	NX.24152	2/18 Battalion	Balmain, NSW	14.04.45	34
Bastin, J.C., Cpl.	NX.52944	2/18 Battalion	Bondi, NSW	17.03.45	37
Butler, T.L., Cpl.	NX.40445	2/18 Battalion	Tamworth, NSW	17.04.45	29
Brown, N.N., Cpl.	NX.45191	2/18 Battalion	Somerton, NSW	31.03.45	29
Duffy, S.D., Cpl.	NX.72698	2/18 Battalion	Kyogle, NSW	19.03.45	28
Mitchell, J.W., L/Cpl.	NX.40893	2/18 Battalion	Armidale, NSW	20.02.45	31
Taylor, N.H., L/Cpl.	NX.26026	2/18 Battalion	Kingswood, NSW	05.06.45	32
Annand, David, L/Cpl.	NX.50181	2/18 Battalion	Campsie, NSW	14.04.45	35
MacGregor, J.A. L/Cpl.	NX.41005	2/18 Battalion	Warialda, NSW	03.05.45	36
Armstrong, T.E., Pte.	NX.25086	2/18 Battalion		13.05.45	23
Alexander, E.C., Pte.	NX.32241	2/18 Battalion		07.04.45	26
Allie, N.R., L/Cpl.	NX.48419	2/18 Battalion	Battery Point, Tas.	12.06.45	26
Bowerman, H.F., Pte.	NX.26368	2/18 Battalion	Harris Park, NSW	17.06.45	25
Brown, S.W., Pte.	NX.24736	2/18 Battalion	Stuart Town, NSW	15.07.45	26
Broomham, C.F., Pte.	NX.56176	2/18 Battalion	Corrimal, NSW	27.05.45	26
Bracken, C.N., Pte.	NX.73099	2/18 Battalion	Coonabarabran, NSW	13.04.45	23
Boyce, A.R., Pte.	NX.31417	2/18 Battalion	Paddington, NSW	06.03.45	24
Blair, W.F. Pte.	NX.40262	2/18 Battalion	Paddington, NSW	14.05.45	40
Collins, C.R., Pte.	NX.40769	2/18 Battalion	Tia, NSW	08.06.45	36
Clydsdale, T.J., Pte.	NX.32345	2/18 Battalion	Singleton, NSW	28.03.45	26
Carveth, A.J., Pte.	NX. 23210	2/18 Battalion	Narellan, NSW	05.06.45	31
Clifford, E.T., Pte.	NX.30050	2/18 Battalion	Bonnyrigg, NSW	08.02.45	31
Clissold, J.J., Pte.	NX.24769	2/18 Battalion	Wentworthville, NSW	14.07.45	35
Crighton, R.S., Pte.	NX.31044	2/18 Battalion	Brighton-le-Sands, NSW	20.05.45	32
Chenhall, N.G., Pte.	NX.19852	2/18 Battalion	Northcote, Vic.	07.04.45	27
Clark, W.B., Pte.	NX.40455	2/18 Battalion	Lwr. Quipolly, NSW	02.08.45	25
Demas, H.J., Pte.	NX.48079	2/18 Battalion	Bathurst, NSW	28.04.45	34
Darragh, L.A., Pte.	NX.69767	2/18 Battalion	Ghin Ghi, NSW	20.06.45	26
Dempster, Cyril, Pte.	NX.33899	2/18 Battalion	Dunbulbalane, Vic.	06.02.45	32
Dundas, R.C., Pte.	NX.73066	2/18 Battalion	Sth. Coast, NSW	21.04.45	28
Dezius, F.C., Pte.	NX.40910	2/18 Battalion	Bundarra, NSW	29.05.45	27
Evans, E.C., Pte.	NX.32229	2/18 Battalion		11.06.45	24
Frame, C.W., Pte.	NX.40365	2/18 Battalion	Muswellbrook, NSW	19.05.45	35
Farrell, A.R., Pte.	NX.28667	2/18 Battalion		26.01.45	44
Grant, J.J., Pte.	NX.71313	2/18 Battalion	Lakemba, NSW	07.06.45	20
Gagan, L.A., Pte.	NX. 1710	2/18 Battalion	Petersham, NSW	30.07.45	24
Gillham, A.J.C., Pte.	NX.42846	2/18 Battalion	Crows Nest, NSW	13.03.45	25
Gaskin, John, Pte.	NX.65605	2/18 Battalion	Waverley, NSW	20.07.45	35
Graham, R.J., Pte.	NX.71570	2/18 Battalion	Hurstville, NSW	05.06.45	26
Grant, E.T., Pte.	NX.48267	2/18 Battalion	Gateshead, NSW	21.06.45	23
Holland, L.U., Pte.	NX.26562	2/18 Battalion	Chatswood, NSW	06.07.45	26
Hall, T.B., Pte.	NX.71751	2/18 Battalion	Crows Nest, NSW	12.04.45	40
Hewitt, Howard, Pte.	VX.19059	2/18 Battalion	Sth. Yarra, Vic.	28.07.45	26
Holden, N.N., Pte.	NX.17183	2/18 Battalion		21.03.45	40
Harris, L.A., Pte.	NX.66085	2/18 Battalion	Ashfield, NSW	04.06.45	25
Harris, C.M., Pte.	NX.56235	2/18 Battalion	Mosman, NSW	20.04.45	37
Ince, J.W.J., Pte.	NX.18955	2/18 Battalion	Randwick, NSW	04.06.45	26
Kane, G.F., Pte.	NX.13718	2/18 Battalion	Lismore, NSW	12.01.45	25
Lever, A.L. Pte.	NX.32255	2/18 Battalion	Murwillumbah, NSW	02.06.45	26
Loveridge, A.A., Pte.	NX.43489	2/18 Battalion	Junee, NSW	09.01.45	42
Moore, J.E., Pte.	NX.40209	2/18 Battalion	Guyra, NSW	20.03.45	29
Moore, A.C., Pte.	NX.39905	2/18 Battalion	Pennant Hills, NSW	10.04.45	43

'E' FORCE				Date of Death	Age
McLachlan, K.J., Pte.	NX.52739	2/18 Battalion	Elizabeth Bay, NSW	20.06.45	30
McLeenan, L.A. Pte.	NX.24743	2/18 Battalion	Crows Nest, NSW	22.05.45	21
Noakes, A.W., Pte.	NX.40875	2/18 Battalion	Gladesville, NSW	27.03.45	30
Nunn, J.O., Pte.	NX.52256	2/18 Battalion	Orange, NSW	09.02.45	32
Pogson, C.R., Pte.	NX.32904	2/18 Battalion	Thornleigh, NSW	15.06.45	40
Roberts, Stanley, Pte.	NX.40215	2/18 Battalion	Tamworth, NSW	19.06.45	28
Sharp, William, Pte.	NX.33739	2/18 Battalion	Earlwood, Nsw	01.04.45	22
Stanley, J.R., Pte.	NX.56325	2/18 Battalion	Glebe Point, NSW	25.05.45	31
Stevens, Charles, Pte.	NX.13738	2/18 Battalion	Sth. Lismore, NSW	13.12.44	24
Symes, A.V.J. Pte.	NX.50445	2/18 Battalion	Chatswood, NSW	11.04.45	25
Stanton, Edward, Pte.	NX. 1080	2/18 Battalion	Nth. Sydney, NSW	18.03.45	28
Sherwood, Sidney, Pte.	NX.30197	2/18 Battalion		22.04.45	25
Stace, R.A., Pte.	NX.40828	2/18 Battalion	Uralla, NSW	07.06.45	26
Standring, H.C. Pte.	NX.40154	2/18 Battalion	Tamworth, NSW	08.04.45	25
Sullivan, Darryl, Pte.	NX.34234	2/18 Battalion	Edgecliffe, NSW	18.01.45	32
Smith, H.V.G., Pte.	NX.34377	2/18 Battalion	Eastwood, NSW	01.06.45	29
Hackland, E.C.C., Pte. (Served as Toohey, C.J.)	NX.49347	2/18 Battalion	Sydney, NSW	27.01.45	38
Tyrrell, R.C., Pte.	NX.71702	2/18 Battalion	West Ryde, NSW	23.07.45	25
Thompson, Frederick, Pte.	NX.66614	2/18 Battalion	Warren, NSW	10.06.45	25
Tapper, S.G., Pte.	NX. 1231	2/18 Battalion	Sth. Grafton, NSW	06.03.45	24
Waterhouse, Albert, Pte.	NX.42335	2/18 Battalion	Naremburn, NSW	30.01.45	27
Williamson, L.R., Pte.	NX.40836	2/18 Battalion	Kentucky Sth., NSW	04.06.45	25
Ruane, R.M., Pte.	NX. 1655	2/18 Battalion	Lismore, NSW	25.06.45	24
Harper, H.C., Pte.	NX.27476	2/18 Battalion	Nth. Sydney, NSW	13.05.45	41
Harwood, Frank, Pte.	NX.33883	2/18 Battalion	Darwen, Lancs. UK	31.03.45	24
Sotheron, B.E., Pte.	NX.44894	2/18 Battalion		03.04.45	35
Watts, E.R., Pte.	NX.32277	2/18 Battalion	Ashford, NSW	17.06.45	24
Watson, W.J.H., Pte.	NX.40976	2/18 Battalion	Ebor, NSW	23.03.45	33
Holdaway, L.J., Sgt.	NX.72964	2/19 Battalion	Randwick, NSW	01.04.44	41
Dickman, F.H., Cpl.	NX.70002	2/19 Battalion	Bowral, NSW	21.05.45	31
Knox, J.W., Cpl.,	NX.35900	2/19 Battalion	Paddington, NSW	22.03.45	31
Archard, Clyde, Pte.	NX.44381	2/19 Battalion	Nelsons Bay, NSW	14.07.45	24
Bennett, W.D., Pte.	NX. 7061	2/19 Battalion	Lane Cove, NSW	14.07.45	22
Biggs, Frank, Pte.	NX.44154	2/19 Battalion	Granville, NSW	23.03.45	29
Bow, W.N., Pte.	NX.39772	2/19 Battalion	Balmain, NSW	13.06.45	31
Boyd, R.T., Pte.	NX.27788	2/19 Battalion	Leichhardt, NSW	22.03.45	26
Boyle, C.R., Pte.	NX.35254	2/19 Battalion	Cheltenham, NSW	07.02.45	28
Burke, J.E., L/Cpl.	QX.15847	2/19 Battalion	Millaa Milla, Qld.	31.07.45	38
Byrne, Brian, L/Cpl.	NX.48361	2/19 Battalion	Rozelle, NSW	09.03.45	35
Buckley, J.J., L/Cpl.	NX.48677	2/19 Battalion	Everton Park, Qld.	08.06.45	23
Cameron, D.T., L/Cpl.	NX.52540	2/19 Battalion	Surry Hills, NSW	11.04.45	29
Core, S.R., L/Cpl.	NX.48471	2/19 Battalion	Cowra, NSW	20.06.45	19
Corcoran, F.L., L/Cpl.	NX.60171	2/19 Battalion	Bondi, NSW	10.07.45	33
Cull, Arthur, L/Cpl.	NX.41895	2/19 Battalion	Woy Woy, NSW	17.06.45	38
Davis, R.J., L/Cpl.	NX.49304	2/19 Battalion	Lismore Sth., NSW	13.07.45	22
Doyle, E.A., L/Cpl.	NX.35361	2/19 Battalion	Camperdown, NSW	15.02.45	27
Ferguson, K.D., Cpl.	NX.50271	2/19 Battalion	Fairfield, NSW	14.07.45	20
Flemming, A.C., Pte.	NX.19386	2/19 Battalion	Baradine, NSW	17.03.45	28
Gallard, R.F., Pte.	NX.49255	2/19 Battalion	Eastwood, NSW	30.05.45	25
Easton, Harold, Pte.	NX.48715	2/19 Battalion	Marrickville, NSW	20.04.45	22
Hamilton, Hector, Pte.	NX.49269	2/19 Battalion	Lidcombe, NSW	29.05.45	36
Hubbard, E.A.F., Pte.	NX.59839	2/19 Battalion	Fairfield, NSW	24.06.45	42
Hine, V.M., Pte.	NX.49288	2/19 Battalion	Newcastle, NSW	10.02.45	24
Hopkins, A.G., Pte.	NX.60231	2/19 Battalion	Queanbeyan, NSW	10.04.45	33

'E' FORCE				Date of Death	Age
Horne, Norman, Pte.	NX.25306	2/19 Battalion	Cumberforth, Yorks.UK	01.04.45	25
Hughes, K.G., Pte.	NX.49648	2/19 Battalion	Boolaroo, NSW	15.07.45	24
Humphries, David, Pte.	NX.58270	2/19 Battalion	Auburn, NSW	13.02.45	27
Ings, E.H., Pte.	NX.60355	2/19 Battalion		24.02.45	41
Erwin, L.R., Pte. (Served as Irwin, L.G.)	NX. 2140	2/19 Battalion	Ashfield, NSW	02.06.45	35
James, J.R., Pte.	NX.10826	2/19 Battalion		06.07.45	25
Johnston, A.B., Pte.	NX.50852	2/19 Battalion	Kew, Vic.	10.05.45	38
Justice, A.J., Pte.	NX.50257	2/19 Battalion	Arncliffe, NSW	21.03.45	26
Ledgwidge, F.B., Pte.	NX.36469	2/19 Battalion	Merriwagga, NSW	12.03.45	43
Lennon, V.J., Pte.	NX.41863	2/19 Battalion	Hawthorn, Vic.	07.02.45	26
Love, W.H., Gnr.	VX.34801	2/19 Battalion	West Geelong, Vic.	18.11.44	44
Madden, Walter, Pte.	NX.35726	2/19 Battalion	Narrandera, NSW	13.07.45	34
Makim, G.J., Pte.	NX.42217	2/19 Battalion	Gum Flat, NSW	17.06.45	23
McGuire, A.D., Pte.	NX.35602	2/19 Battalion	Junee, Nsw	14.07.45	34
Marsh, C.K., Pte.	NX.44954	2/19 Battalion	Wollongong, NSW	08.11.44	29
Martin, J.T., Pte.	NX.41305	2/19 Battalion	Hillgrove, NSW	18.03.45	25
Moran, Patrick, Pte.	Nx.49559	2/19 Battalion		07.04.45	27
Neale, D.M., Pte.	NX.56129	2/19 Battalion	Penrith, NSW	09.03.45	26
O'Connor, A.H., Pte.	NX. 7991	2/19 Battalion	Lismore, NSW	26.02.45	25
O'Connor, R.M., Pte.	NX. 7941	2/19 Battalion	Lismore, NSW	15.06.45	22
Parfrey, T.H., Pte.	NX.36013	2/19 Battalion	Morundah, NSW	10.06.45	36
Perry, J.C., Pte.	NX. 6578	2/19 Battalion	Redfern, NSW	28.05.45	28
Powell, C.A., Pte.	NX.44671	2/19 Battalion	Bilpin, NSW	03.09.45	34
Purcell, J.S., Pte.	NX.73463	2/19 Battalion	Goulburn, NSW	17.06.45	24
Raphael, H.N., Pte.	NX.55284	2/19 Battalion		02.06.45	23
Roberts, H.E., Pte.	NX. 6638	2/19 Battalion	Marrickville, NSW	26.03.45	25
Robertson, R.J., Pte.	NX.35896	2/19 Battalion	Griffith, NSW	02.06.45	39
Roberts, Fred, L/Cpl.	NX.23624	2/19 Battalion	Leichhardt, NSW	23.06.45	35
Robertson, F.H. Cpl.	NX.40024	2/19 Battalion	Nth. Mackay, Qld.	11.07.45	26
Rouse, J.F., Cpl.	NX.43021	2/19 Battalion	Paddington, Qld.	02.06.45	36
Shaw, Gilbert, Cpl.	NX.52285	2/19 Battalion	Waverton, NSW	19.04.45	33
Shaw, Ruben, Cpl.	NX.48206	2/19 Battalion	Milthorpe, NSW	19.07.44	36
Smith, G.A., Cpl.	NX.26819	2/19 Battalion	Cronulla, NSW	08.03.45	43
Smith, W.S.C., Cpl.	NX.23002	2/19 Battalion	Ballina, NSW	07.06.45	33
Spencer, H.F., Cpl.	NX.35656	2/19 Battalion	Grong Grong, NSW	27.03.45	34
Taylor, A.A., Cpl.	NX.73715	2/19 Battalion	Wickham, NSW	13.03.45	36
Thorpe, Harry, Cpl.	NX.52646	2/19 Battalion	Harbord, NSW	08.04.45	28
Walton, D.R., Sgt.	NX.49860	2/19 Battalion		07.06.45	38
Whitehead, William, Cpl.	NX.43543	2/19 Battalion	Schofields, NSW	15.02.45	21
Woodcroft, K.R., Cpl.	NX.51640	2/19 Battalion	Concord, NSW	10.12.44	23
Wright, C.L., Cpl.	NX.35877	2/19 Battalion		08.06.45	39
Wright, T.J., Cpl.	NX.52261	2/19 Battalion	Glebe Point, NSW	16.01.45	23
Ward, J.A. Cpl.	NX.41867	2/19 Battalion	Elizabeth Bay, NSW	10.06.45	23
Wilson, Harry, Cpl.	QX.22943	2/19 Battalion	Brisbane, Qld.	16.03.45	30
Brady, W.P., Cpl.	NX.56147	2/19 Battalion	Alexandria, NSW	08.02.45	24
Davidson, F.G., Cpl.	NX.73453	2/19 Battalion	Young, NSW	04.07.45	24
Burnes, F.C., Cpl.	NX.26234	2/20 Battalion	Taree, NSW	23.05.45	37
Smith, J.B.I., Sgt.	NX.20593	2/20 Battalion	Wonga Park, Vic.	13.02.45	25
Tinning, R.J., L/Cpl.	NX.45945	2/20 Battalion	Rockdale, NSW	23.05.45	36
Harpley, J.C., Cpl.	NX.52259	2/20 Battalion	Parkes, NSW	10.07.45	28
Meek, D.R., Cpl.	NX.56172	2/20 Battalion	Hobbys Yards, NSW	18.03.45	26
Meek, E.L., Cpl.	NX.46083	2/20 Battalion	Nth. Bondi, NSW	14.07.45	40
Pepper, G.D., Cpl.	NX.54537	2/20 Battalion	Paddington, NSW	10.03.45	30
Spurway, R.S., Cpl.	NX.59479	2/20 Battalion	Cremorne, NSW	21.04.45	23

'E' FORCE

Name	Number	Unit	Home	Date of Death	Age
Brinkman, J.H. L/Cpl.	NX.32936	2/20 Battalion	Epping, NSW	07.03.45	27
Levis, Hugh. Cpl.	NX.59144	2/20 Battalion	Peakhurst, NSW	16.06.45	43
Stewart, H.T.H. Cpl.	NX.32012	2/20 Battalion	Penrith, NSW	21.06.45	24
Adam, J.C. Pte.	NX.30008	2/20 Battalion	Cremorne, NSW	26.05.45	28
Auld, R.J. Pte.	NX.31973	2/20 Battalion	Manly, NSW	05.06.45	30
Bates, A.E.R. Pte.	NX.68983	2/20 Battalion	Mayfield, NSW	26.03.45	24
Burns, S.A.N. Pte.	NX.45310	2/20 Battalion	Wallsend, NSW	31.01.45	20
Baccus, A.A. Pte.	NX.32443	2/20 Battalion	Newcastle, NSW	23.05.45	28
Brabham, V.G. Pte.	NX.56861	2/20 Battalion	Guildford, NSW	26.05.45	39
Buckley, L.F. Pte.	NX.30123	2/20 Battalion	Bankstown, NSW	11.02.45	32
Bell, M.C. Pte.	NX.34074	2/20 Battalion	Lithgow, NSW	05.06.45	25
Brown, William. Pte.	NX.56832	2/20 Battalion	Bexley, NSW	19.03.45	38
Clarke, D.S. Pte.	NX.33782	2/20 Battalion	Kinross-Shire, Scot.	29.12.44	42
Cook, J.T. Pte.	NX.57478	2/20 Battalion	Concord, NSW	19.04.45	24
Chapman, C.K. Pte.	NX.72773	2/20 Battalion	Glenmore, NSW	28.07.45	30
Chisholm, H.F. Pte.	NX.34092	2/20 Battalion	Campsie, NSW	09.02.45	25
Cox, A.H. Pte.	NX.56097	2/20 Battalion	Lithgow, NSW	07.05.45	25
Dalton, W.J. Pte.	NX.72893	2/20 Battalion	Wallerawang, NSW	16.11.44	35
Davis, R.V. Pte.	NX.34224	2/20 Battalion	Balmain, NSW	07.06.45	26
Elderton, W.J. Pte.	NX.33360	2/20 Battalion	Marrickville, NSW	25.03.45	38
Emmett, Gordon. Pte.	NX.33583	2/20 Battalion	Nth. Bondi, NSW	31.03.45	42
Fisher, R.J. Pte.	NX.72889	2/20 Battalion	Gulgong, NSW	16.04.45	23
Griffen, K.C. Pte.	NX.56161	2/20 Battalion	Hurstville, NSW	07.06.45	30
Gilligan, C.A. Pte.	NX.52439	2/20 Battalion	Coonamble, NSW	22.05.45	34
Helliwell, K.J. Pte.	NX.31559	2/20 Battalion	Tenterfield, NSW	19.05.45	30
Jewiss, A.C. Cpl.	NX.31807	2/20 Battalion	Glebe, NSW	13.07.45	27
Loan, J.B. Pte.	NX.53259	2/20 Battalion	Glasgow, Scotland	19.01.45	38
McLaughlin, B.L. Pte.	NX.46221	2/20 Battalion	Manning River, NSW	18.03.45	28
Hodges, Pte. (Served as McIntosh, G.H.)	NX. 1212	2/20 Battalion	Aberdeen, NSW	11.02.45	
Mitchell, A.L. Pte.	NX.32273	2/20 Battalion	Lwr. Towamba, NSW	22.06.45	43
Myers, C.D. Pte.	NX.45482	2/20 Battalion	Bondi, NSW	29.04.45	32
McConville, J.H. Pte.	NX.60504	2/20 Battalion	Queanbeyan, NSW	16.04.45	35
Nicholson, E.C. Pte.	NX.45544	2/20 Battalion	Marrickville, NSW	11.06.45	44
Olive, E.R.J. Pte.	NX.54657	2/20 Battalion	Bonnyrigg, NSW	18.05.45	30
Rennie, G.B.D. Pte.	NX.41679	2/20 Battalion	Mark's Point, NSW	07.06.45	28
Rendall, David. Pte.	NX.31844	2/20 Battalion	Orkney, Scotland	09.06.45	36
Raison, V.R. Pte.	NX.53184	2/20 Battalion	Murwillumbah, NSW	02.06.45	29
Reilly, V.A. Pte.	NX.72761	2/20 Battalion	Coonabarabran, NSW	02.06.45	30
Steel, J.A. Pte.	NX.55165	2/20 Battalion	Botany, NSW	25.06.45	31
Simpson, H.J. L/Cpl.	NX.54679	2/20 Battalion	Orange, NSW	10.02.45	32
Schibeci, Donald. Pte.	NX.42215	2/20 Battalion	Woollahra, NSW	13.06.45	28
Thoroughgood, H.J. Pte.	NX.45885	2/20 Battalion	Newcastle, NSW	10.02.45	26
Worland, N.C. Pte.	NX.67081	2/20 Battalion	St. Peters, NSW	15.02.45	29
Whiting, W.G. Pte.	NX.10940	2/20 Battalion	Turramurra, NSW	17.07.45	25
Weston, W.E. Pte.	NX. 620	2/20 Battalion	Newtown, NSW	14.03.45	27
Williams, A.T. Pte.	NX.52089	2/20 Battalion	Campsie, NSW	05.07.45	39
Ryan, W.A. Gnr.	QX. 1866	Royal Aust. Arty.	Newnes Junction, NSW	04.06.45	27
Hamalainen, F.F. Gnr.	QX.14424	Royal Aust. Arty.	Norman Park, Qld.	17.03.45	43
Cox, R.C. L/Sgt.	NX.32585	Royal Aust. Arty.	Shellharbour, NSW	13.04.45	35
Dell, W.C. Bdr.	VX.31902	Royal Aust. Arty.	Pt. Melbourne, Vic.	04.03.45	30
Walker, J.S. Bdr.	NX.32966	Royal Aust. Arty.	Ashfield, NSW	19.02.45	24
Gannon, W.J. L/Bdr.	QX.17342	Royal Aust. Arty.	Nundah, Qld.	17.06.45	26
Brown, V.M.W. Gnr.	QX.20993	Royal Aust. Arty.	Moorooka, Qld.	21.05.45	28
Campbell, Ronald. Gnr.	VX.41962	Royal Aust. Arty.	Westgarth, Vic.	05.07.45	23

'E' FORCE				Date of Death	Age
Clements, Thomas, Gnr.	QX. 8428	Royal Aust. Arty.	Mackay, Qld.	16.04.45	44
Edwards, H.J., Gnr.	VX.37804	Royal Aust. Arty.	Mathoura, NSW	27.04.45	36
Hibbert, S.E., Gnr.	VX.43092	Royal Aust. Arty.		21.11.44	42
Macleod, N.P., Gnr.	VX.38709	Royal Aust. Arty.	Sth. Yarra, Vic.	13.02.45	32
Murray, R.J., Gnr.	VX.32221	Royal Aust. Arty.	Moonee Ponds, Vic.	10.03.45	26
Robinson, J.F., Gnr.	VX.45743	Royal Aust. Arty.	Avoca, Vic.	29.06.45	24
Woodford, C.A., Gnr.	VX.47230	Royal Aust. Arty.	Canterbury, Vic.	30.05.45	23
Bruce, F.W., Gnr.	VX.38066	Royal Aust. Arty.	West Brunswick, Vic.	14.02.45	32
Tennyson, B.G., Gnr.	VX.37653	Royal Aust. Arty.	Preston, Vic.	07.05.45	22
Ross, J.H.N., Gnr.	VX.41746	Royal Aust. Arty.	Preston, Vic.	10.02.45	29
Warner, B.J., Gnr.	VX.44989	Royal Aust. Arty.	Winchelsea, Vic.	15.06.44	34
Swift, D.S., Gnr.	NX.33555	Royal Aust. Arty.	Coogee, NSW	30.06.45	31
Chapman, E.F., Bdr.	NX.66710	Royal Aust. Arty.	Sydney, NSW	29.03.45	28
McCorley, Kevin, Bdr.	QX.10144	Royal Aust. Arty.	Taroom, Qld.	22.07.45	33
Hardy, A.A., Bdr.	NX.25495	Royal Aust. Arty.	Mayfield, NSW	18.04.45	32
Taylor, David, Bdr.	NX.52096	Royal Aust. Arty.	Abbotsford, NSW	01.04.45	23
McCrum, Alfred, Gnr.	NX.29117	Royal Aust. Arty.		25.03.45	43
Ingram, C.E., Pte.	NX.67727	Royal Aust. Arty.	Fifield, NSW	05.06.45	31
Kirby,E.A.N.H., Gnr.	NX.33792	Royal Aust. Arty.	Matraville, NSW	19.04.45	32
McKinnon, D.C., Gnr.	NX.20300	Royal Aust. Arty.	Nth. Sydney, NSW	01.07.45	29
Nicholson, J.F.D., Gnr.	NX.10233	Royal Aust. Arty.	West Ryde, NSW	15.02.45	25
Nicholson, Gerard, Gnr.	NX. 7113	Royal Aust. Arty.	West Ryde, NSW	26.01.45	26
Ryan, J.G., Gnr.	NX.53067	Royal Aust. Arty.	Redfern, NSW	18.04.45	29
Sefton, I.G., Gnr.	NX.32151	Royal Aust. Arty.	Boggabri, NSW	04.04.45	42
Tuckerman, J.H., Gnr.	NX.34112	Royal Aust. Arty.	Scarborough, NSW	18.06.45	27
Lea, Reginald, Gnr.	NX.28385	Royal Aust. Arty.	Waverley, NSW	22.03.45	34
Perry, K.G., Gnr.	NX.65780	Royal Aust. Arty.	Kensington, S.A.	18.02.45	25
Blatch, W.G., Gnr.	NX.10791	Royal Aust. Arty.	Strathfield, NSW	01.06.45	25
Thompson, William, Gnr.	NX.28362	Royal Aust. Arty.	Woollahra, NSW	04.03.45	24
Dyson, R.R., Bdr.	NX.72868	Royal Aust. Arty.	Burwood, NSW	19.03.45	31
McGee, W.A., Bdr.	NX.28980	Royal Aust. Arty.	Willoughby, NSW	14.04.45	28
King, R.A., Gnr.	NX.29720	Royal Aust. Arty.	Cardiff, NSW	12.05.45	40
Sheard, W.A., Gnr.	QX.14497	Royal Aust. Arty.	Mosman, NSW	15.03.45	36
Monley, F.J., L/Sgt.	QX.17015	Royal Aust. Arty.	Annerley, Qld.	22.02.45	26
Carlson, A.R., L/Sgt.	QX. 9899	Royal Aust. Arty.	Kalinga, Qld.	23.05.45	27
Victorsen, L.M. Bdr.	QX.14230	Royal Aust. Arty.	Cooparoo, Qld.	18.03.45	23
Tierney, J.E., L/Bdr.	QX.12221	Royal Aust. Arty.	Aramac, Qld.	17.06.45	24
Malin, W.M., Gnr.	QX.17089	Royal Aust. Arty.	Cooparoo, Qld.	07.06.45	29
Colls, L.W., Gnr.	QX.13176	Royal Aust. Arty.	Emu Park, Qld.	16.04.45	27
Ernst, J.A., Gnr.	QX. 7811	Royal Aust. Arty.	Innisfail, Qld.	08.01.45	43
Lupton, S.J., Gnr.	QX.16924	Royal Aust. Arty.	Brisbane, Qld.	05.06.45	31
Oliver, James, Gnr.	QX.13185	Royal Aust. Arty.	Finch Hatton, Qld.	16.03.45	30
Payne, H.J., Gnr.	QX.13772	Royal Aust. Arty.	Tewantin, Qld.	04.06.45	25
Sutton, J.E., Gnr.	QX.10150	Royal Aust. Arty.	Texas, Qld.	23.03.45	28
Wiseman, E.W., Gnr.	QX. 9629	Royal Aust. Arty.	Ipswich, Qld.	10.06.45	24
Boese, R.J., Pte.	QX.23326	Royal Aust. Arty.		29.03.45	26
Bunch, N.H., Gnr.	QX.11039	Royal Aust. Arty.	Brisbane, Qld.	17.06.45	27
Currey, W.J., Gnr.	QX.10200	Royal Aust. Arty.	Injune, Qld.	04.07.45	25
Currey, J.E., Gnr.	QX.18216	Royal Aust. Arty.	Injune, Qld.	18.12.44	27
Jillett, R.E., Gnr.	QX.17167	Royal Aust. Arty.	Clayfield, Qld.	05.06.45	25
Raymond, K.M., Gnr.	QX.21329	Royal Aust. Arty.	Chelmer, Qld.	10.02.45	24
Behrendorff, C.S., Gnr.	QX.21027	Royal Aust. Arty.	Biloela, Qld.	17.05.45	27
Light, J.W., Gnr.	QX. 9563	Royal Aust. Arty.	Brisbane, Qld.	15.02.45	24
Smith, George, Cpl.	WX.4891	2/4 MG Battalion	Como W.A.	07.6.45	42
Stanwell, O.M., Cpl.	WX. 7798	2/4 MG Battalion	Bayswater, W.A.	12.03.45	39

'E' FORCE				Date of Death	Age
Taylor, G. W., Cpl.	WX. 8867	2/4 MG Battalion	Subiaco, W.A.	02.03.45	43
Beer, W.J., Pte.	WX. 7636	2/4 MG Battalion	Bunbury, W.A.	14.06.45	28
Bennett, H.P., Pte.	WX. 9340	2/4 MG Battalion	Gnowangerup, W.A.	15.02.45	30
Burton, E.G., Pte.	WX. 7007	2/4 MG Battalion	Midland Jnctn., W.A.	21.02.45	24
Chilvers, H.A.T., Pte.	WX. 8123	2/4 MG Battalion	Byford, W.A.	31.03.45	33
Cole, E.H., Crftmn.	SX.11457	2/4 MG Battalion	Perth, W.A.	18.05.45	35
Dorizzi, T.H., Crftmn.	WX.12884	2/4 MG Battalion	Toodyay, W.A.	11.03.45	31
Earnshaw, W.H., Crftmn.	WX. 6262	2/4 MG Battalion	Kalgoorlie, W.A.	15.03.45	25
Edwards, G.H., Crftmn.	WX. 7266	2/4 MG Battalion		20.03.45	34
Floyed, A.E., Crftmn.	WX.12663	2/4 MG Battalion	Narrogin, W.A.	12.03.45	26
Gibbs, S.H., Crftmn.	WX. 9255	2/4 MG Battalion	Woodville, S.A.	24.02.45	41
Holme, Charles, Crftmn.	WX.16416	2/4 MG Battalion	Worsley, W.A.	07.06.45	22
Holst, E.J., Crftmn.	WX. 8678	2/4 MG Battalion	Maylands, W.A.	20.03.45	31
Holland, H. W., Crftmn.	WX.17636	2/4 MG Battalion	Sth. Belmont, W.A.	15.06.45	30
Lane, D.R., Crftmn.	WX.16439	2/4 MG Battalion	Boulder, W.A.	16.01.45	24
Lake, George, Crftmn.	WX.17582	2/4 MG Battalion	Collie Burn, W.A.	08.04.45	23
Lear, H.B., Crftmn.	WX. 7043	2/4 MG Battalion	Bassendean, W.A.	17.03.45	25
Moran, R.K., Crftmn.	WX.15386	2/4 MG Battalion	Subiaco, W.A.	28.06.45	21
Nash, C.O., Crftmn.	WX.17363	2/4 MG Battalion	Subiaco, W.A.	23.03.45	26
Negri, P.J., L/Cpl.	WX.12985	2/4 MG Battalion	Greenbushes, W.A.	21.01.45	25
Noble, F.R., Pte.	WX. 9413	2/4 MG Battalion	Perth, W.A.	26.05.45	25
Nazzari, Frank, Cpl.	WX. 8707	2/4 MG Battalion	Perth, W.A.	24.04.45	29
O'Neil, Leslie, Pte.	WX. 5222	2/4 MG Battalion	Mundaring, W.A.	16.12.44	36
Ross, Donald, Pte.	WX. 9253	2/4 MG Battalion	Albany, W.A.	23.05.45	32
Shelvock, C.B., Pte.	WX. 5018	2/4 MG Battalion	Leederville, W.A.	17.04.45	38
Sevier, Joseph, Pte.	WX. 8544	2/4 MG Battalion	Glenelg, S.A.	07.06.45	38
Smith, T.E., Pte.	WX. 8731	2/4 MG Battalion	Grass Patch, W.A.	18.12.44	32
Turner, H.R., Pte.	WX.17593	2/4 MG Battalion	Perth, W.A.	08.05.45	25
Thorns, A.S., Pte.	WX.10289	2/4 MG Battalion	Kalgoorlie, W.A.	08.08.45	27
Trigwell, A.G., Pte.	WX.17882	2/4 MG Battalion	Donnybrook, W.A.	04.05.45	23
Wilkie, James, Pte.	WX. 8706	2/4 MG Battalion	Perthshire, Scotland	17.05.45	36
Currow, R.W., Cpl.	NX.39085	Royal Aust. Engrs.	Mosman, N.S.W.	28.03.45	23
Deagan, Michael, Spr.	NX.22693	Royal Aust. Engrs.	Brunswick, Vic.	27.05.45	41
Jesperson, T.F., Spr.	NX.24827	Royal Aust. Engrs.	Auburn, N.S.W.	01.03.45	28
Clarke, Alan, Spr.	WX. 6201	Royal Aust. Engrs.	Cottesloe, W.A.	04.06.45	27
Luton, H.W., Spr. (Served as McCormick,H.W.)	NX. 1654	Royal Aust. Engrs.	Pt. Kembla, N.S.W.	04.07.45	22
Souter, G.A.J., Spr.,	NX. 7272	Royal Aust. Engrs.	Ashfield, N.S.W.	02.06.45	30
Farrey, L.W., Spr.	NX.30219	Royal Aust. Engrs.	Kogarah, N.S.W.	20.06.45	27
Elliott, S., Spr.	NX.67323	Royal Aust. Engrs.	Bega, N.S.W.	21.02.45	33
Clark, F.H., Spr.	NX. 6558	Royal Aust. Engrs.	Granville, N.S.W.	05.03.45	26
Archibald, G.R., L/Cpl.	NX.27554	Royal Aust. Engrs.	Bankstown, N.S.W.	31.03.45	37
Worby, R.P., Pte.	SX. 8947	8 Div. Sal. Unit	Pt. Pirie, S.A.	19.06.45	26
Walker, R.G., Pte.	QX.10891	L Coy. A.A.S.C.	Toowoomba, Qld.	02.07.45	28
Young, David, Pte.	VX.65242	27 I.B.G.O. W/S	Northcote, Vic.	26.05.45	25
Ely, T.H., Pte.	VX.65080	27 I.B.G.O. W/S	Dandenong, Vic.,	13.02.45	22
Kohler, L.G., Pte.	SX.13927	27 I.B.G.O. W/S		27.03.45	34
Avice, Stanley, Pte.	NX.10640	8 Div. Mob. Lay.	Ultimo, N.S.W.	21.01.45	25
Elliott, T.A., Cpl.	NX.67894	H.Q. A.I.F.	Ashfield, N.S.W.	08.03.45	31
Palmer, N.W., Pte.	NX.72752	2/10 Ord. Fld. W/S.	Taree, N.S.W.	07.06.45	32
Wrigley, K.G., Pte.	QX.21789	2/10 Ord. Fld. W/S.	Murgon, Qld.	26.02.45	24
Frazier, J.W., W.O.II	VX.39246	2/10 Ord. Fld. W/S.	Malvern, Vic.	03.06.45	25
Gellatly, R.A., L/Sgt.	NX.30883	2/10 Ord. Fld. W/S.	Canberra, A.C.T.	09.07.45	25
McGregor, Robert, Sgt.	NX.58166	2/10 Ord. Fld. W/S.	Bankstown, N.S.W.	05.04.45	25
Munro, E.L., Sgt.	VX.55381	2/10 Ord. Fld. W/S.	Traralgon, Vic.	03.08.45	34
Bird, B.S., Cpl.	VX.61527	2/10 Ord. Fld. W/S.	Shepparton, Vic.	22.06.45	25

'E' FORCE				Date of Death	Age
Brown, W.F., Pte.	VX.65389	2/10 Ord. Fld. W/S.	Portsea, Vic.	15.05.45	26
Strout, E.A., Cpl.	QX.14241	2/10 Ord. Fld. W/S.	Indooroopilly, Qld.	28.03.45	35
Collins, A.C., Pte.	VX.58560	2/10 Ord. Fld. W/S.	Sydney, N.S.W.	12.06.45	21
Harris, W.L., Pte.	VX.62895	2/10 Ord. Fld. W/S.	Altona, Vic.	26.02.45	23
Jacobs, F.W., Pte.	VX.67873	2/10 Ord. Fld. W/S.	Nth. Richmond, Vic.	06.07.45	22
Johnson, H.V., Pte.	NX.51975	2/10 Ord. Fld. W/S.	Mile End, S.A.	29.06.45	31
Marshall, J.L., Pte.	VX.64312	2/10 Ord. Fld. W/S.	Tottenham, Vic.	02.06.45	26
Raleigh, John, Pte.	VX.66445	2/10 Ord. Fld. W/S.	East Brunswick, Vic.	23.07.45	24
Smith, J.D., Pte.	NX.36868	2/10 Ord. Fld. W/S.		16.03.45	38
Garner, G.C. Crfstm.	VX.61991	2/10 Ord. Fld. Park	Parkdale, Vic.	05.04.45	27
Gill, H.M., Pte.	VX.62613	2/10 Ord. Fld. Park	Bendigo, Vic.	23.02.45	37
Neal, Ronald, Pte.	VX.64831	2/10 Ord. Fld. Park	Armadale, Vic.	25.05.45	23
Pile, E.N., Pte.	QX.20451	2/10 Ord. Fld. Park	Rockhampton, Qld.	13.06.45	23
Burke, W.J., Pte.	VX.39200	22 I.B.G.O. W/S	Williamford, Tas.	12.06.45	30
Fletcher, J.S., Pte.	VX.47892	22 I.B.G.O. W/S	Frankston, Vic.	10.06.45	28
Kopanica, J.F., Pte.	VX.39252	22 I.B.G.O. W/S	Seymour, Vic.	05.08.45	25
Otter, L.T., Pte.	VX.64659	22 I.B.G.O. W/S	Nth. Melbourne, Vic.	02.04.45	23
Watts, T.J., Pte.	VX.37741	22 I.B.G.O. W/S	Kilsyth, Vic.	15.03.45	32
Burns, R.N.B., Pte.	VX.54832	22 I.B.G.O. W/S	Box Hill, Vic.	05.06.45	25
Jones, Keith, Pte.	VX.30350	22 I.B.G.O. W/S	Bendigo, Vic.	17.05.45	27
Evans, G.J., L/Cpl.	SX. 8384	22 I.B.G.O. W/S	Torrensville, S.A.	21.07.45	29
Morgan, H.C.B. Crftsm.	SX.11064	22 I.B.G.O. W/S	Welland, S.A.	10.04.45	27
Wiseman, R.H. Pte.	VX.39259	27 I.B.G.O. W/S	Oakleigh, Vic.	30.07.45	25
Boyd, J.W. Pte.	VX.39859	27 I.B.G.O. W/S	Pomborneit, Vic.	23.06.45	26
Callander, H.W., Crftsm.	VX.56512	27 I.B.G.O. W/S	Richmond, Vic.	05.06.45	30
Costello, Kevin, Pte.	VX.59912	27 I.B.G.O. W/S	Ensay, Vic.	01.07.45	28
Bushell, R.F., Pte.	SX.10450	8 Div. Sal. Unit	Adelaide, S.A.	07.06.45	24
Craze, Richard, Pte.	VX.66955	B.O.D. A.A.O.C.	Henty, N.S.W.	02.04.45	25
Coulter, W.J.R., Sgt.	SX.10824	8 Div.Amm.Sub.Park	Seacliff, S.A.	03.06.45	27
Reid, F.C.D., L/Sgt.	SX. 9600	8 Div.Amm.Sub.Park	Murrumbeena, Vic.	20.06.45	27
Martin, M.F.J., Cpl.	SX. 6216	8 Div.Amm.Sub.Park	Evandale, S.A.	04.10.43	29
Mumme, L.W., L/Cpl.	SX. 9839	8 Div.Amm.Sub.Park	Toorak Gardens, S.A.	02.03.45	26
Wachner, E.C., L/Cpl.	SX. 9933	8 Div.Amm.Sub.Park	Henley Beach, S.A.	24.03.45	26
Engelhart, Neil, Pte.	SX. 9407	8 Div.Amm.Sub.Park	Mt. Benson, S.A.	02.06.45	25
Campbell, M.L. Dvr.	SX. 3655	8 Div.Amm.Sub.Park	Unley, S.A.	03.06.45	29
Brody, Leonard, Pte.	SX.14640	8 Div.Amm.Sub.Park	Naracoorte, S.A.	04.06.45	23
Burzacott, Murray, Pte.	SX.10648	8 Div.Amm.Sub.Park	Victor Harbour, S.A.	03.05.45	34
Davey, B.A., Pte.	SX.10183	8 Div.Amm.Sub.Park	Underdale, S.A.	09.02.45	38
Finn, W.M.G., Pte	SX. 8421	8 Div.Amm.Sub.Park	Adelaide, S.A.	06.04.45	40
How, V.K., Pte.	SX. 9426	8 Div.Amm.Sub.Park	Peake, S.A.	03.06.45	28
Kavanagh, L.M., Pte.	SX. 9198	8 Div.Amm.Sub.Park	New Hindmarsh, S.A.	15.02.45	42
Lindqvist, L.R. Pte.	SX.11609	8 Div.Amm.Sub.Park	Parkside, S.A.	29.05.45	32
Mitchell, R.J., Pte.	SX. 9673	8 Div.Amm.Sub.Park	St. Peters, S.A.	22.06.45	29
Manton, L.C. Pte.	SX.10635	8 Div.Amm.Sub.Park	Wolseley, S.A.	22.07.45	27
Nolan, George, L/Cpl.	SX. 9314	8 Div.Amm.Sub.Park		18.06.45	26
Orr, E.J.K., Pte.	SX.14343	8 Div.Amm.Sub.Park	Bordertown, S.A.	20.03.45	23
Paterson, Stewart, Pte.	SX. 9419	8 Div.Amm.Sub.Park	Adelaide, S.A.	16.03.45	25
Sherman, M.O., Pte.	SX. 4977	8 Div.Amm.Sub.Park	Glenelg, S.A.	16.03.45	26
Skinner, T.R., Pte.	SX.10637	8 Div.Amm.Sub.Park	Bordertown, S.A.	17.04.45	31
Turner, H.R., Pte.	SX. 9619	8 Div.Amm.Sub.Park	Mt. Gambier, S.A.	18.02.45	25
Wright, C.L., Pte.	SX. 9592	8 Div.Amm.Sub.Park	Glenelg, S.A.	13.06.45	30
Wilson, L.A., Pte.	SX.12793	8 Div.Amm.Sub.Park	Semaphore, S.A.	30.12.44	33
Cummings, N.G., Sgt.	VX.35037	8 Div. Signals	East Malvern, Vic.	24.06.45	29
Vaughan, W.J., Sgt.	VX.47920	8 Div. Signals	St. Kilda, Vic.	30.07.45	26
Wren, C.R., Sig.	VX.38422	8 Div. Signals	Irymple, Vic.	13.05.45	23
Harris, S.N. Cpl.	VX.63884	8 Div. Signals	Middle Park, Vic.	05.06.45	24

'E' FORCE				Date of Death	Age
Wilson, C.W., Sig.	NX. 613	8 Div. Signals	Boorowa, N.S.W.	23.05.45	43
Clucas, J.B., Sig.	SX.10201	8 Div. Signals	Malvern, S.A.	19.05.45	26
Digby, G.H., Sig.	NX.26263	8 Div. Signals	Burwood, N.S.W.	30.03.45	29
Duncalf, V.A., Sig.	NX.56270	8 Div. Signals	Mosman, N.S.W.	20.01.45	26
Jackaman, G.E., Sig.	QX.15242	8 Div. Signals	Innisfail, Qld.	02.06.45	24
Reay, S.V.J., Sig.	NX.56694	8 Div. Signals	Eastlakes, N.S.W.	08.02.45	23
Stirling, D.H., Sig. (Served as Matson, Donald)	VX.54364	8 Div. Signals	Blackburn, Vic.	15.07.45	19
Craig, R.F., Sig.	VX.64347	8 Div. Signals	Glen-Huntly, Vic.	08.06.45	20
Conquit, G.D., Sig.	NX.36653	8 Div. Signals	Wagga Wagga, N.S.W.	02.06.45	24
Weeks, F.N., Sig.	VX.53225	8 Div. Signals		04.02.45	34
Savage, Ernest, Sig.	WX. 6479	8 Div. Signals	Perth, W.A.	10.06.45	34
Savage, Tom, Sig.	WX. 5447	8 Div. Signals	Whitebridge, W.A.	30.01.45	40
Hughes, Robert, Sig.	WX. 6725	8 Div. Signals	Moonta, S.A.	04.06.45	38
Hawkins, C.A., Sig.	VX.30686	8 Div. Signals		04.06.45	42
McKerrow, E.A., Sig.	QX. 5230	8 Div. Signals	Annerley, Qld.	28.06.45	26
Beves, E.N., Sig.	NX.39634	8 Div. Signals	Earlwood, N.S.W.	13.07.45	21
LeBeau, W.H., Sig.	NX.69320	8 Div. Signals	Surry Hills, N.S.W.	24.01.45	22
Hall, R.W., Sgt.	NX. 1123	8 Div. Signals	Parkdale, Vic.	10.07.45	34
Anderson, F.D., Gnr.	QX. 6866	Royal Aust. Artry.	Kelvin Grove, Qld.	29.07.45	25
Clarke, L.B:, Gnr.	QX. 9364	Royal Aust. Artry.	Valley, Qld.	05.06.45	24
Starky, C.B., L/Bdr.	QX.17071	Royal Aust. Artry.	Cunnamulla, Qld.	17.01.45	38
McIver, G.D., Gnr.	QX.19914	Royal Aust. Artry.	Newmarket, Qld.	26.02.45	31
Collins, R. B., Gnr.	QX.21956	Royal Aust. Artry.	Kyogle, N.S.W.	26.04.45	26
Smeeton, B.L.J., Gnr.	NGX. 143	Royal Aust. Artry.	Hobart, Tas.	15.02.45	27
Ellis, A.G., Gnr.	NX.20431	Royal Aust. Artry.	Campsie, N.S.W.	15.02.45	38
Filewood, Alexander, Gnr.	NX.30862	Royal Aust. Artry.	Newtown, N.S.W.	01.08.45	26
McLennan, L.H., Gnr.	VX.56410	Royal Aust. Artry.	Nullawil, Vic.	22.05.45	34
Tomkyns, E.A., Gnr.	NX.41261	Royal Aust. Artry.	Chester Hill, N.S.W.	25.06.45	31
Flavell, R.R., Gnr.	NX. 4745	Royal Aust. Artry.	Dapto, N.S.W.	17.02.45	28
MacPherson, S.D., Gnr.	NX.72219	Royal Aust. Artry.	Randwick, N.S.W.	19.03.45	23
McGee, H.A., Pte.	NX.71856	Royal Aust. Artry.	Willoughby, N.S.W.	25.02.45	24
Carson, W.J., Pte.	VX.65027	2/10 Ord. Fd. W/S	Geelong, Vic.	28.02.45	22
Burnett, E.R., Pte.	QX.12664	2/10 Ord. Fd. W/S	Clermont, Qld.	30.03.45	29
Gale, P.R. Pte.	VX.67597	2/10 Ord. Fld. Park	Murchison, Vic.	16.04.45	25
Neale, S.E., Pte.	WX. 9260	88 L.A.D.	Maylands, W.A.	28.02.45	30
Newman, C.W., Pte.	NX.73279	88 L.A.D.	Scone, N.S.W.	11.03.45	24
Downey, H.A., L/Cpl.	NX.31046	74 L.A.D.	Marrickville, N.S.W.	08.02.45	37
Newson, J.A., Pte.	NX.69587	8 Mob.Ldry./Fd.Dec.	Bexley, N.S.W.	06.06.45	29
Noon, J.T., Pte.	NX.44005	8 Mob.Ldry./Fd.Dec.	Lidcombe, N.S.W.	15.03.45	25
Thomas, J.O., Dvr.	SX. 6889	2/2 Res. M.T.	Kangaroo Is., S.A.	15.05.45	26
Chandler, R.K., Pte.	SX. 9730	2/2 Res. M.T.	Stansbury, S.A.	20.03.45	26
Peters, K.A., Cpl.	NX.68410	2/3 Res. M.T.	Ettalong Bch., N.S.W.	07.06.45	40
Chant, J.R.A., Pte.	NX.69600	2/3 Res. M.T.	Randwick, N.S.W.	02.06.45	34
Davidson, G.L.H., Cpl.	VX.44190	2/4 Res. M.T.	Hawthorn, Vic.	10.06.45	30
Fuss, C.R. L/Cpl.	SX. 9391	2/4 Res. M.T.	Lameroo, S.A.	17.03.45	44
Ohlson, F.J. Pte.	VX.39999	2/4 Res. M.T.	West Richmond, Vic.	02.02.45	25
Dwyer, John, Dvr.	VX.60454	2/4 Res. M.T.	Wodonga, Vic.	17.04.45	26
Harrington, R.E., Pte.	VX.47493	2/4 Res. M.T.		29.05.45	43
Knox, E.G., Pte.	VX.50845	2/4 Res. M.T.	West Brunswick, Vic.	19.04.45	39
Paxman, Charles, Pte.	VX.24438	2/4 Res. M.T.	Frankston, Vic.	10.06.45	42
Carnie, R.M., Pte.	VX.39896	2/4 Res. M.T.	Sth. Yarra, Vic.	17.03.45	24
Taylor, H.B., Pte.	NX.33383	2/4 Res. M.T.	Henty, N.S.W.	14.06.45	27
Fitzgerald, G.S., Cpl.	NX.53140	2/3 M.A.C.	Croydon, N.S.W.	02.06.45	37
Flood, L.A., Spr.	NX. 5659	Royal Aust. Engrs.	Narrabri, N.S.W.	03.07.45	32

EX JAVA - MIDDLE EAST and SINGAPORE

Adams, A.M. Pte.	*NX.39989	G.B.D.	Homebush, NSW	26.01.45	22
(Served as White, A.M.)					
Anderson, W.O. Dvr.	NX.41097	3 M.T.	Bingara, NSW	25.12.44	23
Brady, Charles. Pte.	VX.19215	2/2 Pnr.Bn.	Shepparton, Vic.	22.01.45	35
Cain, C.J. Dvr.	NX.70018	3 Res.MT.AASC	Shepparton, Vic.	17.05.45	39
Dyson, F.A. Pte.	VX.42614	2/2 Pnr.Bn.	Yallourn, V.ic.	09.04.45	27
Evans, J.W. Dvr.	NX.68531	3 Res.MT.AASC	Manly, NSW	16.06.45	28
Ford, W.D. Pte.	*VX.61084	2/29 Bn.	Arncliffe, NSW	03.12.44	23
Geelan, W. Pte.	*NX.67801	2/19 Bn.	Honoured Singapore		
Green, T.W. Pte.	WX. 8540	2/4 MG. Bn.	Perth, W.A.	22.01.45	24
Hitchens, J.R. Dvr.	VX.20253	1 Corps.Pet.Pk.AASC	Albert Park, Vic.	19.04.45	37
Jacobs, G.W. Spr.	*NX.29198	2/6 Fd.Coy.RAE	Nth. Dubbo, NSW	09.04.45	38
Kelly, H.A. Bd.	19235	HMAS PERTH	Maroubra, NSW	20.01.45	
Kemp, H.A.J. Pte.	NX.36810	3 Res.MT.Coy.AASC		05.04.45	43
Lambert, George. Pte.	VX.57889	2/2 Pnr.Bn.	Windsor, Vic.	08.03.45	42
LeFevre, Robert.Pte.	NX.72037	3 Res.MT.Coy.AASC	Hay, NSW	06.05.45	34
Lupton, Leslie.Pte.	NX.37324	2/2 Pnr.Bn.		08.04.45	30
McCullough, William. Cpl.	WX.12209	105 Gnl.Tpt.Coy.	Nth.Perth, W.A.	20.04.45	40
McDonald, C.H. Pte.	NX.49756	2/18 Bn.		03.06.45	32
Moore, T.A. L/Cpl.	VX.19532	2/2 Pnr.Bn.	Wodonga, Vic.	31.03.45	24
Morris, G.B. A.B.	23670	HMAS PERTH	Frankston, Vic.	09.05.45	
O'Connor, J.H. Pte.	VX.20159	2/2 Pnr.Bn.	Meatian, Vic.	11.04.45	40
Radcliffe, K.E. Pte.	*VX.20450	2/2 Pnr.Bn.	Prahran, Vic.	28.09.44	25
Sligo, N.K. Lieut.		R.N.V.R. Attach.A.I.F.			
Sommerville, A.C. Pte.	VX.41337	2/2 Pnr.Bn.	Boronia, Vic.	14.04.45	44
Tyrrell, Albert. Cpl.	WX.11900	2/2 Pnr.Bn.	Nedlands, W.A.	24.06.45	40
Zinn, A.C. Spr.	*NX.19562	2/6 Fd.Coy.RAE	Cape Town,Sth.Africa	20.11.44	37

*Died Labuan - Volunteered to go on English party of 200 from Kuching.

KUCHING CAMP

Campbell,G.N.S.Major.E.D.	NX.70836	2/3 Mtr.Amb.Co.AASC	Armadale, Vic.	02.09.45	49
Flett, F.J. Lieut.	VX.39047	4 A/Tk.Regt.RAA	Williamstown, Vic.	18.08.45	29
Harrington, T.I. Pte.	*VX.23670	8 Div.Pet.Co.AASC	Whorouly, Vic.	15.12.42	30
Keating, E.J. L/Cpl.	*WX. 8818	2/6 Fd.Pk.Co.AASC	Bayswater, W.A.	11.02.44	36
Matthews,L.C.Capt.G.C.,M.C.	*VX.24597	8 Div. Sigs.	Marryatville, S.A.	02.03.44	31
Pascoe-Pearce, Bradford.Lt.	NX.71989	4 A/Tk.Regt.RAA	Woollahra, NSW	15.08.45	36
Picken, James. Pte. -	**NX.65767	2/18 Bn.	Greta, NSW	03.04.43	23
Stewart, Peter. Lt.	QX. 9864	2/26 Bn.	Coorparoo, Qld.	08.07.45	30
Young, C.F. Capt.	VX.62921	8Div.Ord.Fd.Pk.AASC	Sth.Yarra, Vic.	27.07.45	27

*Capt. Matthews – G.C. – George Cross – M.C. Military Cross.
*Ex Sandakan **Electrocuted

NOTE: (A) The Units shown are those which the personnel were allocated to for draft to Borneo and not necessarily their regular Unit. They are shown in order of allocation

(B) The Regimental Numbers and Names have been taken from the War Graves Register and correspond with 'B' and 'E' Force Rolls.

(C) The location of origin shown is taken from the War Graves Register and not necessarily the place of Enlistment.

(D) The dates of death are taken from the Japanese translated records and are reasonably reliable up to January 1945. Those signed by Tsuji Yamamoto, the Medical Officer at Kuching, are suspect and many falsified to cover those massacred. (A.W.M. Ref.127 Item 70).

(E) The Labuan War Graves Memorial Register honours those Australians lost in the South China Sea after the sinking of the "Rakuyu Maru". These men were from BurmaThailand and were being transported to Japan. There are also names of those recorded in the Cemetery Register who died in Japan - their ashes were buried at Labuan.

Chapter 16

At the time of the Japanese surrender the 9 Australian Division was restricted to the Miri area. On August 15 the area of responsibility was extended to the whole of British North Borneo, Brunei and Sarawak.

Ten POW Contact and Investigation Groups were sent to localities where POWs and Internees were known to have been. The initial investigations took place between August 15 and November 27, 1945. Particular attention was focussed on Sandakan, Ranau, Jesselton (Kota Kinabalu), Brunei, Kuala Belait, Miri, Labuan and Kuching. Their task was to identify all Allied prisoners of war and internees – this included British, Australian, Dutch, Javanese, Chinese and a few Americans. Most of these were located at Kuching, the principal POW and Internee Compound which was under the command of Colonel Suga of the Prisoner of War Information Bureau in Tokyo.

Up to the Surrender the 9 Division had captured sensitive Japanese documents relating to prisoners of war – the S.R.D. (cover name for Special Operations) parties were well informed on the locality and the approximate number of POWs. A cable sent by L.H.Q. Melbourne to Mountbatten's South East Asia Command (SEAC) described the plight of the POWs in June. This cable was located in London and confirmed the Australian Government was well informed of the prisoners' plight.

The contact groups interrogated Japanese in custody and the survivors rescued by Special Forces. It was not until the War Crimes Investigations completed their task of collecting evidence did the full account become known of the Sandakan tragedy.

It appears Murozumi would have recorded the dates of death and passed them on to Kuching where Dr. Yamamoto recognised the evidence of massacre: many of these dates were altered to imply the prisoners progressively died of illness over a period up till August 15, 1945.

The following information extracted from the Recovery Reports lists the items found after thorough searching as the Japanese destroyed most of the Records and Paybooks by fire.

Pte. William Matthew Keating. NX.5829. 8 Div.Postal Unit. Annandale, NSW. Sandakan February 3, 1945. Age 36.
Pic: Jack Keating

Cpl. Albert Tyrrell. WX.II900. 2/2 Pnr.Bn. 7 Division. Nedlands, W.A. 24 June 1945. Age 40. Sent to Sandakan with the British party from Java.
Pic: Vic Tyrrell

Sgt. Harry Hewitt. NX.65365 2/20 Bn. Manly, NSW. Age 42. Hewitt was assistant to Capt. George Cook in Administration. During Hoshijima's trial he mentioned Cook and Hewitt fully understood the difficulties he had in obtaining food.

Pic: Ian Hewitt

Driver James Allan Charles Ezzy. NX.68928.2/3 M.A.C. A.A.S.C. Richmond, NSW. 5 March 1945. Age 38. Pack found at Snadakan.
Pic: Mrs. N. Woods

IDENTIFICATIONS FROM PAYBOOKS RECOVERED AT NO.2 COMPOUND – SANDAKAN 18-19 OCTOBER 1945

*AUTHOR'S INTERPRETATION

			Pay/Bk. No.			
VX.46208	Spr.	Bryant, Frank Leslie	D.3228	Dennis, Vic.	08.06.45	36
WX.10914	Pte.	Carleton, Ronald Victor		Nedlands, WA	09.06.45	29
QX.21352	Pte.	Charles, Guy Fraser	169310	Lwr.Tent Hill,Qld.	07.06.45	24
WX. 6201	Spr.	Clarke, Alan	139055	Cottesloe, WA	04.06.45	27
NX.24769	Pte.	Clissold, John Joseph		Wentworthville,NSW	14.07.45	35
NX.60171	Pte.	Corcoran, Francis Leslie	91321	Bondi, NSW	10.07.45	33
TX. 5206	Pte.	Crawford, Valmont Oswald	146886	Invermay, Tas.	07.06.45	32
NX.51804	Pte.	Crumpton, Ronald Frederick	86211	Willoughby, NSW	05.06.45	26
WX. 7360	Spr.	Field, Gilbert Lawrence Cottle	141375	Albany, WA	01.06.45	41
NX.31591	Cpl.	Fletcher, Barney Alan		Zetland, NSW	11.06.45	32
NX.50579	Pte.	Gardner, Archibald William	83348	Mt.Druitt, NSW	05.06.45	30
NX.28552	L/Bdr.	Gardner, Irwin Lane Gunstone	71943	Aberdeen, NSW	28.03.43	27
NX.65605	Pte.	Gaskin, John		Waverley, NSW	20.07.45	35
VX.58690	Cpl.	Gay, Arthur Peter Robert Leslie	266116?	Preston, Vic.	14.06.45	41
NX.18641	Gnr.	Godson, Colin Henry		Maidenhead, ,Berks., UK	06.06.45	38
VX.27442	S/Sgt.	Hagston, George	112952	Warrnambool, Vic.	30.06.45	26
NX.50568	Pte.	Harris, John Oscar	83397	Waterloo, NSW	02.06.45	44
SX. 9426	Pte.	How, Vernon Kingsley		Peake, S.A.	03.06.45	28
NX.53458	Pte.	Johnson, Stanley Henry	91163	Vaucluse, NSW	22.06.45	27
SX.10704	Pte.	Lester, John	283731	Mt.Gambier, SA	30.03.45	38
SX.11609	Pte.	Lindqvist, Leonard Roy	285136	Parkside, SA	29.05.45	32
QX.16924	Gnr.	Lupton, Stanley Joseph		East Brisbane, Qld.	05.06.45	31
(VX. 3708?		McCrane, Edward	96207			
(VX.37108	Gnr.	McCracken, William Edward	96207	Kaneghy, Nthn.Ireland	04.08.45	35
NX.45306	Pte.	McNaughton, Donald	81167	Charlestown, NSW	28.06.45	43
WX.15386	Pte.	Moran, Ronald Keith	319365	Subiaco, WA	28.06.45	21
				Note: Aged 16 on Enlistment.		
NX.68381Spr.		Neal, Frederick William	191094	Sans Souci, NSW	05.06.45	42
NX.45544	Pte.	Nicholson, Ernest Charles		Marrickville, NSW	11.06.45	44
WX.7634	Pte.	Osborne, Sydney Albert		Swan View, WA	21.06.45	31
NX.27967	L/Bdr.	Palmer, Athol			11.06.45	44
NX. 1719	Pte.	Patterson, Ronald Alton		Taree, NSW	29.05.45	30
VX.24438	Pte.	Paxman, Charles	11144	Frankston, Vic.	10.06.45	42
VX.50588	Pte.	Phelan, Michael John	240790	Oakleigh, Vic.	27.06.45	36
NX.44671	Pte.	Powell, Charles Allen	215937	Bilpin, NSW	03.09.44	34
SX. 8723	L/Sgt.	Praetz, Norman Harry	286458	Enfield, SA	07.06.45	36
NX.73463	Pte.	Purcell, John Stanislaus	45344	Goulburn, NSW	17.06.45	24
NX.23624	L/Cpl.	Roberts, Fred		Leichhardt, NSW	23.06.45	35
	Known as "Nutsey", gave Bible to Chaplain Rogers.					
VX.43384	L/Cpl.	Rudd, William Thomas		Windsor, Vic.	13.07.45	40
NX.72016	Pte.	Smith, Francis Albert Oliver		Sth.Gundagai, NSW	07.06.45	36
	Only name and next of kin details found.					
WX. 8867	Cpl.	Taylor, George William		Subiaco, WA	02.04.45	43
NX.10264	Pte.	Welch, William Albert		Newtown, NSW	09.06.45	44
NX.54640	Cpl.	Wheeler, James Edward	180130	Meadowbank, NSW	28.06.45	40
QX.9629	Gnr.	Wiseman, Edward William	55696	Ipswich Nth., Qld.	10.06.45	24

Driver Herman Reither. VX.48478.
4 Res.M.T. Coy. Age 38. Ballarat, Vic.
Escaped from Ranau with W.O. Sticpewich
on July 28, 1945 and died August 8, 1945.
Pic: Allan Clissold

Pte. Victor Robert Raison. NX.53184.
2/20 Bn. Age 29. Murwillumbah, NSW.
Pic: Fay Payne

Pte. Kenneth Gabriel Macklin. NX.49406.
2/3 M.A.C. A.A.S.C. Marrickville, NSW. 17
May 1945. Age 22.
Pic: Sisters May Jobling
and Veronica Nelson

Gnr. David Alan Reid. QX.9270. 2/10 Fd.
Regt. R.A.A. Ashgrove, Qld. 29 June 1945.
Age 41. *Pic: Peggy Finlayson*

NX.36294	Pte.	Wood, Frederick Allen	77915			

The records marked this entry with a "X", indicating he was not a member of 'B' or 'E' Force. The regimental number indicated he enlisted from Wagga Wagga, suggesting 2/19 Bn. This Unit History confirmed he died 25.04.42 Malaya. Further research found the entry in Taiping War Graves Register having died at Pudu Gaol. Jack DeLoas said, "I was with Freddie Wood when he died." Of the seventyone 2/19 personnel at Pudu who were sent to Changi Gaol, four were allocated on 'E' Force in April 1943. Of those on the 2/19 Bn. draft three came from the Griffith area of New South Wales where Fred's father was a wellknown Hairdresser.

Two 2/19 'E' Force men, NX.35896 R.J. Robertson and NX.36469 Frank Ledwidge, died at Sandakan. 02.05.45 and 12.03.45 respectively. It is probable one of the above men was given the paybook to take home.

NX.47215	Pte.	Woods, Frederick Henry	94269	Glendon Brook, NSW	06.07.45	32
SX.12151	Pte.	Walker, Ernest Thomas		Burnside, SA	09.06.45	43

MISCELLANEOUS ITEMS LOCATED

Kitbag marked – VX.41946 Spr. V. Wilson

*This kitbag was not brought to Sandakan by Wilson. Spr. Wilson left Changi before kitbags were distributed in June 1942 just prior to 'B' Force embarking for Borneo. In 1944 Spr. Wilson sailed on the RAKUYO MARU and was drowned 12.09.44.

Kitbag marked: "J.H. Humphreys 2357584" also "31705(?8)"			
*Royal Corps Sigs. Husband of Alice Marjorie.	East Finchley, Middlesex, UK	30.06.45	38
Kitbag marked – "LAC 1121082 Baguley"			
*R.A.F. Husband of Ada Maude Baguley.	Sherwood, Nottingham, UK		
Kitbag marked – "VX.33897 Blackwood, L.C. 4 A/Tk"			
*VX.33897 Crftsmn. Leslie Clarence Blackwood.	Sth.Yarra, Vic.	07.06.45	42
Kitbag marked – "NX.40689 J Platford"			
*NX.40689 Pte. Joseph Platford.	Glen Innes, NSW	23.05.45	45
Paybook Ranau 110 1/4 Mile peg.			
Kitbag marked – "VX.... G Day"			
*VX.33620 Pte. Garth Day.	Cheltenham, Vic.	08.07.45	25
Kitbag marked – "NX.66981 End..."			
Kitbag re-marked – "T. Commins 2/10 RAA"			
*QX.5989 Bdr. John Seymour Handley Commins.	Whangarei, NZ	08.05.45	33
Kitbag marked – "TX.1188"			
Kitbag marked – "NX.32416 W E W"			
*NX.32416 Cpl. Wallace Ellis Wynn.	Goulburn, NSW	21.03.45	27
Kitbag marked – "QX.17500 E J Wolfe AASC"			
*QX.17500 Pte. Ernest John Wolfe.	Goodna, Qld.	02.07.45	26
Letter from Oddfellows mentioning B. Henley			
*VX.45368 Sgt. John Benson Henley.	Colac, Vic.	06.06.45	42
Dixie lid marked – "NX.53458 S Johnson"			
*NX.53458 Pte. Stanley Henry Johnson.	Vaucluse, NSW	22.06.45	27
1941 Diary marked – "1130962 LAC Jack Hobbs RAF"			
*1190962 Cpl. Frederick William Hobbs, RAF	Luton, Bedfordshire, UK		

Pewter mug – "London Division RAMC Seaford 1936"

Mess tin, Hairbrush and Money Pouch marked: Humphries 1059747"

Pte. Edward Stanton. NX.1080. 2/19 Bn. North Sydney. Sandakan. 18 March 1945. Age 28. *Pic: Margaret Fisher*

Pte. George William Plunkett. NX.51466. 2/18 Bn. Hornsby, NSW. Sandakan 14 June 1945. Age 26. *Pic: Toni Trotter*

Pte. Frank Maurice Harold Higgison. NX.53504. 2/30 Bn. Marrickville, NSW. Sandakan 12 June 1945. Age 36. *Pic: Lillian Wells*

Cpl. Edward Godfrey Bailey. NX.45627. 27 Bde.Coy. A.A.S.C. Bellingen, NSW. Age 32. *Pic: Mrs. E.G. Rowley*

Two Mess tins marked – "Paxman" and "(1859) Dvr. C. Paxman VX.24438 2/4 MT.Coy.AIF"			
*VX.24438 Pte. Charles Paxman.	Frankston, Vic.	01.06.45	41
Mess tin marked – "NX.29342"			
Web pack marked – "NX.49847 A W L Signals"			
*NX.49847 Sigmn. Anthony Walter Lister.	Burwood, NSW	15.06.45	23
Web pack marked – "NX.1183 Holden 2/18 Bn"			
*NX.17183 Pte. Neville Noel Holden.		21.03.45	40
Web pack marked – "11052176 LAC Jones RAF"			
Web pack marked – "QX.6584 R W...."			
Haversack marked – "WX.?7634"			
Haversack marked – "NX.40244 Cpl C Hargreave"			
*NX.40244 Cpl. Claude Hope Hargrave.	Walcha, NSW	03.03.45	38
Haversack marked – "Rolfe"			
*NX.72410 Pte. Sydney Bernard Rolfe. (Drowned RAKUYO MARU)	Lidcombe, NSW	12.09.44	32
Haversack marked – "NX.29073 Skeeler?			
Haversack marked – "H A Sandercock" (Two haversacks found)			
*SX.11728 Pte. Henry Alan Sandercock	Colonel Light Gardens, SA	03.04.45	40
Haversack marked – "642298 Kitchingham"			
Haversack marked – "WX 10567 J H James"			
Haversack Respirator marked – "NX 25816 J Midgley"			
*NX.25816 Pte. James Johnston Midgley.	Croydon, NSW	16.03.45	44
Haversack Respirator marked – "VX 30578 D Grubb"			
*VX.39578 Pte. David Grubb.	Broadford, Vic.	02.04.45	40
Web belt marked – "VX 46193(8) R Spain" or "R Spring"			
Web belt RAAF or RAF marked – "A 1127314"			
(Identity discs inscribed: "1817403 Gnr Holder G"			
(*Gnr. Charles James Holder.	Walthamston, Essex, U.K.	14.06.45	27
(Also Metal disc inscribed: "W B C			
(WARDENS			
(Other side: "C J Holder"			
Identity discs inscribed: "VX 64585 Irving R F "			
*VX.64385 Pte. Ray Francis Irving.	Colac, Vic.	02.06.45	41
Identity discs inscribed: "?X 63609? Mazey"			
*VX.63699 Cpl. Charles William Maizey.	West Brunswick, Vic.	18.07.45	26
Identity discs inscribed: "1059715 Smith G B "			
Identity discs inscribed: "643028 Dyer"			
Identity discs inscribed: "14780001 E Woods"			
*Bdr. Edward Arthur Woods. R.A.	Ipswich, Suffolk U.K.	18.06.43	22
Identity discs inscribed: "QX 17430 H A Treseder"			
*QX.17430 L/Bdr. Harry Ayrshire Treseder, MM. (Graves at 14 Mile – note by Graves Officer)	Highgate Hill, Qld.	12.05.45	48
Identity discs inscribed: "1106684 F J Jordan RAF"			
*1106684 AC.2 Frederick John Jordan RAF(VR) (Graves at 14 Mile – note by Graves Officer)	Liverpool, UK	12.06.45	31
Identity discs inscribed: "NX 50568 (Name obliterated)			
Identity discs inscribed: "NX 69621 2/3 MAC Glebe NSW – metal disc, not Issue.			
*NX.69261 Pte. Albert Anderson.	Glebe Point, NSW	11.05.45	39
Identity discs marked: "VX 57753 J Bray"			
*VX.37753 Sgt. John Bray.	Sandringham, Vic.	07.06.45	43
Identity discs inscribed: "WX.8694 Marsh H A"			
*WX.8794 Spr. Henry Arthur Marsh.		08.06.45	40

Pte. Raymond David Carlson. VX.46761. 4 Res.M.T.Coy, Chelsea, Vic. 22 June 1945. Age 43. Father of 11 children. He wrote "Don't worry about me I'll be in the Cookhouse". Loved gambling, when he had a good win he sent 11 presents home for the children. *Pic: Joy Farnham*

Pte. Cecil Henry Rowe. QX.1826. 2/26 Bn. Proserpine, Qld. 5 June 1945. Age 25.
Pic: Jean Rosanoff

Spr. William Henry Smith. NX.54922. 2/12 Fld.Coy.R.A.E. 5 March 1945. Age 42. Known as "Gunboat". Served in Royal Navy. Had large battleship tattoed on his back. He displayed his fighting skills in the ring at Sandakan. *Pic: Bob Lloyd*

Gnr. Percival William Frederick Carter. QX.21002 2/10 Fd.Regt.R.A.A. Belmont, Qld. 2 March 1945. Age 26. First March. His name was written in pencil on back of picture found by S.R.D. member Kulang and handed to Lieut. Hollingsworth.
Pic: Jack Carter – youngest in group see Page 206

Identity discs inscribed: "NX 33555 Swift S D"

*NX.33555 Gnr. Dean Samuel Swift. Coogee, NSW 30.06.45 31

Identity discs inscribed: "QX 21876 Cousins S J"

*QX.21876 Pte. Stanley Joseph Cousins. 20.06.45 24

Identity discs inscribed: "NX 30243 R J Moore"

*NX.30243 Pte. Reginald James Temple. 03.04.45 23
(Served As Moore, Pte. Reginald James)

Identity discs inscribed – "1826753 Watson P"

*1826753 R.A. Watson Glasgow, Scot. 17.06.42 29

Identity discs inscribed – "E T Walker C E..—-151"

*SX.12151 Pte. Ernest Thomas Walker Burnside, S.A. 09.06.45 43

Identity discs inscribed – "SX.11609 L R Lindqvist Meth"

*SX.11609 Pte. Leonard Roy Lindqvist. Parkside, S.A. 29.05.45 32

Identity discs inscribed – "VX.63967 S J Weir CofE"

*VX.63967 Pte. Samuel James Weir. 15.07.45 22

Identity discs inscribed – "NX.60171 Pte Corcoran F L A3 2/19"

*NX.60171 Pte. Francis Leslie Corcoran. Bondi, NSW 10.07.45 33

Identity discs inscribed – "1624305? F W Barnes CofE"

*1624395 Frederick William Barnes. R.A. 25.03.45 35

Identity discs inscribed – "1710408 Tunkinson J S RC"

Aluminium plate inscribed – "W A Swan POW Changi Singapore 1502042"

*WX.11665 Cpl. William Andrew Swan. Victoria Park, WA 01.02.45 42

Heart-shaped disc inscribed – "NX 35498 A Wilson"

*NX.35496 Pte. Albert Wilson. Young, NSW 02.07.45 32

Piece of aluminium inscribed – "NX.41648 J Skinner" and
QX.16680 F Wehl 4-6-45", also Fork marked: "QX.16680 F Wehl"

*NX.41648 Pte. John Frederick Skinner. Tenterfield, NSW 15.08.45 31
*QX.16680 Gnr. Frederick George Wehl. Roma, Qld. 02.08.45 39
*The dates of the deaths of Skinner and Wehl appear false.
It is likely these two were buried together 4 June 1945.

Piece of aluminium inscribed – "WX.11015 E McAppion RAE 1942-3-4"

*WX.7015 Spr. Henry Edward McAppion. Nth.Fremantle, WA 04.06.45 26

Piece of metal inscribed – "2357584 (31705) J H Humphreys"

*2357584 L/Cpl. John Harry Humphreys. East Finchley,Middlesex, UK 20.06.45 38

Piece of metal inscribed – "NX.45166 Pte J D Hodges 2/10 Fd Amb.
Home Address Bungaree St. Wyee NSW"

*NX.45166 L/Cpl. James Douglas Gordon Hodges. Wyee, NSW 01.07.45 44
*Note: Up to 29 May 1945 survivor Dick Braithwaite was engraving identity metal tags to be placed on graves.It seems likely after he left someone else continued the practice.

Wrist Identity tag inscribed – "1184669 C E Cossey"

Gold ring inscribed – "W G N Gollan", Gold ring marked: "H G"

Cigarette lighter inscribed – " G S"

Cigarette case inscribed – "From Staff of S Richards & Co" and "S W R" or "L W R"

Cigarette case inscribed – "T J C"? Scroll Initials"

Cigarette case inscribed – "NX.58457 J Ings"

*NX.58457 Pte. John Thomas Ings Nth.Strathfield, NSW 30.05.45 24

Cigarette case inscribed – " E C"

Matchbox holder inscribed – "C E Maguire 21 Baroona Rd Northbridge"

Matchbox holder inscribed – "SX.8097 C A Leedham"

*SX.8097 Spr. Clarence Albert Leedham Enmore, NSW 18.02.45 43

Matchbox holder inscribed – "NX.71825 A W M AIF POW Camp Changi 15-2-42"

*NX.71825 Pte. Arthur William Mathew. Katoomba, NSW 02.06.45 36

Cpl. Thomas Alexander Elliott. NX.67894. H.Q. A.A.S.C. 8 Div. Ashfield, NSW. 8 March 1945. Age 31. *Pic: Brian Elliott*

L/Bdr. George Alexander McDonald. VX.19389. 4 A/Tk. R.A.A. East Malvern, Vic. 26 December 1944. Age 57. Sandakan. *Pic: Daughters Helen Norman and Jeannie*

Pte. Jack Sidney Orr. NX.53745. 2/10 Fd.Ambulance. Epping, NSW. 4 March 1945. Age 22. Shot by Japanese – see story Page 83. *Pic: Elizabeth Moore*

Gnr. Wally Crease. NX.38584. 2/15 Fd.Regt.R.A.A. Age 24. Shot by the Japanese while escaping early July 1945 – Japanese records state 20 August 1944! See story Page 79. *Pic: Alan Gardner*

Watch inscribed – "VX.46194 H A Morgan"
*VX.46194 Spr. Harry Arthur Morgan | Thornbury, Vic. | 26.03.45 | 31
Watch inscribed – "QX.14769"
*QX.14769 Pte. Harold Gode. | Wynnum, Qld. | 24.12.44 | 39
Watch inscribed – "A 1143 F C Ortloff Renmark S A"
*SX.10860 Pte. Frederick Charles Ortloff. | Colonel Light Gardens, S.A. | 18.02.45 | 35
Watch inscribed – "22 Nov 43"
Wallet inscribed – "VX.3383 H B Taylor"
*VX.33383 Pte. Horace Bryce Taylor. | Henty, NSW | 14.06.45 | 27
Photo wallet inscribed – "VX.63788 Knight H R No 1 Postal Coy AASC (P)?"
*VX.63788 Pte. Herbert Richard Knight. | | 30.01.45 | 42
Waterproof wallet inscribed – "2314668 W J Teasdale RCOS"
*2314668 W J Teasdale | Mitcham, Surrey,UK | 21.02.45 | 41
Jack-knife inscribed – "NX.35726"
*NX.35725 Pte. John Vivian Hargraves. | Wollongong, NSW | 06.06.45 | 33
Fork F S inscribed – "S Bacon"
*VX.38059 Spr. Stanley Thomas Bacon. | Elsternwick, Vic. | 20.06.45 | 31
Two Forks F S inscribed – NX.18071 and S O L and Spoon inscribed – S O L
Fork F S inscribed – "QX.10200 J Currey"
*QX.10200 Gnr. William John Currey. | Injune, Qld. | 04.07.45 | 25
Spoon F S inscribed – "VX.50413 R L M"
*VX.50413 Pte. Roy Leslie Mercer. | West Merbein, Vic. | 04.05.45 | 25
Hold-all marked – NX.1814? M T Bax...?
*NX.68141 Sgt. Michael Paul Baxter. | West Marrickville, NSW | 08.06.45 | 34
*A watch belonging to Sgt. Baxter was confiscated by Capt. Ripley ('Z' Special, the leader of the party which picked up Moxham's party) from a Japanese – Sergeant's chevrons were also found at Ranau.
RSL Badge 1914-18 War – "200..." and "N 1895"
St.Johns Ambulance Assn. Badge 367857 Charles E. Ellerington.
Plate from raft on PW ship "YUBAU MARU" "SX.11693"
*SX.11693 Pte. Thomas Henry Robbins. | Heidelberg, Vic. | 04.06.45 | 43
*The ship YUBAU MARU took 'B' Force to Borneo.
Leave Pass marked – "NX.7357 Pte B F Hazelgrove Mulo"
*NX.7357 Crftsmn. Mitchell Bronte Farrell Hazelgrove. | Alexandria, NSW | 27.01.45 | 25
Paybook marked – "VX.33383 Taylor Horace Bryce, Pte."
*VX.33383 Pte. Horace Bryce Taylor. | Henty, NSW | 14.06.45 | 27
Paybook marked – "QX.16241 Meagher Gordon Francis"
*QX.16241 L/Cpl. Gordon Francis Meagher. | Toowoomba, Qld. | 19.05.45 | 32
Tin mug inscribed – "VX.56735 L K Bird"
*VX.36935 Pte. John Kingston Bird. | Elwood, Vic. | 16.04.45 | 30
Tin mug inscribed – "WX.7634 S Osborne"
*WX.8634 Pte. Sydney Albert Osborne. | Swan View, W.A. | 21.06.45 | 31
Pair shorts marked – "SX.11478"
Jacket (British) marked – "2356248 J Allen"
Cloth wallet marked – "VX.25251 Cpl. – – Johnston"?
Ground sheet marked – "?X.41962 Gnr Ron Campbell"
*VX.41962 Gnr. Ronald Campbell. | Westgarth, Vic. | 05.07.45 | 23
Jacket WD marked – "Davies E D"
*NX.32677 Pte. Evan David Davies. | Austral, NSW | 16.06.45 | 25
Jacket KL marked – "NX.30897 A G Kennedy"
Jacket WD marked – "NX.43(5)78 Braithwaite"

Gnr. Harry Albert McGee. NX.71856. H.Q. 8 Div. Willoughby, NSW. 25 February 1945. Age 24. *Pic: John McGee*

Bdr. William Andrew McGee. NX.28980. 2/15 Fd.Regt. R.A.A. Willoughby, NSW. 14 April 1945. Age 28. His identity discs were found. *Pic: John McGee*

Pte. William Alfred Jordan. NX.52157. 2/20 Bn. Bankstown, NSW. 26 May 1945. Age 29. *Pic: Bill Jordan*

L/Cpl. Frederick William Kelly. NX.67911. 2/10 Fd.Amb. Bankstown, NSW. 21 June 1945. Age 28. *Pic: Joan Kelly*

Battledress (British) marked – "218604"			
Australian felt hat marked – "VX.32213"			
Australian felt hat marked – "R F H"			
*VX.29172 Cpl. Robert Francis Holmes.	Mt.Taylor, Vic.	12.06.45	25
Australian felt hat marked – "Tyrr..."?			
Cloth gaiter marked – "19816 G D McIver"			
*QX.19914 Gnr. Gordon David McIver	Newmarket, Qld.	26.02.45	31
Paybook marked – "1415018 H J Fitzgerald"			
*1445018 L/Sgt. Harry James Fitzgerald. Royal Artillery.	Newport, Monmouthshire, U.K.	17.01.45	33
Boot-polish Satchel marked – "NX.26551"			
Amn. Pouch marked – "QX.4245 R I Marshall"			
Amn. Pouch marked – "NX.40429 Simmonds"			
Shirt marked – "G. Good"			
*NX.32108 Lt. Gordon Good.	East Sydney, NSW	13.07.45	35
Khaki shorts marked – "SX.11479 R Coker"			
*SX.11479 Cpl. Raymond Horace Coker.	Maroubra Jnctn.NSW	07.05.45	45
Piece of khaki material marked – "NX.17183 N Holden"			
*NX.17183 Pte. Neville Noel Holden.		21.03.45	40
Wooden bucket with initials "C H" carved on it.			
NX.40807 Pte. Cecil Hickman.		20.04.45	34

FOUND BESIDE TWO ISOLATED GRAVES 111 MILE PEG

Sam Browne belt – marked but indecipherable.
One shirt KD with holes for epaulettes to fit badges of rank for Captain. Thermometer found in pocket.
Three British Army pattern web belts.
Two expended.25 Jap cartridge cases found 5 ft. from grave.
One RAF Officer's cap and badge found alongside grave.

*See Pages 108.

*The only RAF Officer was Flt.Lt. Burgess.

VX.34179 Sigmn. W.A.J. Constable. 8 Div.Sigs. Died 18 May 1945. Age 29. Castlemaine, Vic.
Photo: Mrs. M. Clark

NX.69155 Pte. G.A. Ireland. 2/10 Fd.Amb. Died 15 March 1945 Age 26. Kew, N.S.W.
Photo: Mrs. B. Bonser

Sgt. Henry William Mortimer. NX.26393. 2/10 Fd.Amb.,A.M.C. 17 February 1945. Age 47. Known as "Harry". A former Ambulance Officer with a distinguished career when he enlisted. Father of six. *Pic: Joan Kelly*

ITEMS FOUND AT NO.2 POW CAMP RANAU

Part of paybook: NX.67030 Robert? Twiss
*NX.67030 Spr. Robert Trevor Twiss. Birchgrove, NSW 15.10.44 23
Date of death 15.10.44 would not be correct if book found at Ranau.
Paybook photo insert: QX.14593
*QX.14593 Pte. Randle John Crees. Brown Hills, Qld. 08.02.45 30
Identity disc: VX.38249 9? C Lock A2 CofE
*VX.38249 Spr. Basil Clyde Lock. Rochester, Vic. 18.02.45 26

ITEMS FOUND NO.2 POW CAMP RANAU (Outside enclosure near suspect Grave area).

Ground Sheet: NX.33246 G. Comerford
*NX.33246 Pte. Gerald Francis Commerford. Lower Lawrence, NSW 09.02.45 25
Sweat band of beret: 1484235(?) A(?) Eaden ?
*Sgt. Ronald Stuart Eaden. 21 Lt.A.A. Regt. Royal Arty. U.K.
Nondescript garment: VX.58436 G. Hill ?
Kitbag: Stirling
*There were two Stirlings – one served as Matson, Sgnmn. Donald
*VX.54364. Blackburn, Vic. 15.07.45. 19
(Aged 16 on Enlistment)
*QX.8453 Pte. Christopher Stirling 16.06.45 31
Identity Disc: NX.27640 J.L. Dunkinson A2 RC
*NX.27640 L/Bdr. John Leslie Dunkinson. Belmore, NSW 12.06.45 36

ITEMS FOUND AT NO.1 POW CAMP RANAU

Identity disc: QX.17783 C. Watson. W0.2 1 Coy.AASC C? 04 Brisbane Qld (Local pattern)
*QX.17783 W.O.II Charles Young Watson. Red Hill, Qld. 06.03.45 45
Identity discs (2): NX.28980 W.A. McGee A2
*NX.28980 Bdr. William Andrew McGee. Willoughby, NSW 14.04.45 28
Identity disc: NX.46793? Leadbeater B3 CofE
*NX.46793 Gnr. William Charles Leadbeatter. Ballina, NSW 15.05.45 24
Identity disc: SX.10637 T.R. Skinner? 04 CofE
*SX.10637 Pte. Thomas Roy Skinner. Bordertown, S.A. 17.04.45 31
Identity disc: WX.7997 S. Dorizzi 04 RC
*WX.7997 Pte. Herbert Dorizzi. Mungarin, W.A. 11.02.45 26
Identity disc (Local pattern): NX.24152 W J Smith 04 Bap
*NX.24152 Sgt. William James Smith. Balmain, NSW 14.04.45 34
Identity disc (Local pattern): WX.7444 A R Attenborough Cof E
*WX.7444 Pte. Arthur Richard Attenborough East Perth, W.A. 12.04.45 28
Souvenir (metal plate): NX.31849 P R Addison, Pte PW Changi
*NX.31849 Pte. Percy Romer Addison. Inverell, NSW 15.05.45 26
(See picture Page 53)
Souvenir (metal plate): WX.15404 V Jones
*WX.15404 Spr. Victor Jones. Chidlow, W.A. 05.04.45 43

ITEMS FOUND AT 110½ MILE PEG

Greatcoat: NX.40689 J Platford
*NX.40689 Pte. Joseph Platford. Glen Innes, NSW 23.05.45 45

Hat: NX.40244 C Hargreave
*NX.40244 Cpl. Claude Hope Hargrave. Walcha, NSW 03.03.45 38
Towel: NX.35868 G E Bromfield
Haversack: NX 66892
Haversack:..37031 Humphries
*NX.37031 Pte. Percy George Humphreys. Currumbin Beach, Qld. 26.05.45 41
Towel: TX.4314 G Cook
Kitbag: NX.72293
Housewife: NX.73050 J W Parsons 2/3 MAC
*NX.73060 Dvr. John William Parsons. Broadmeadow, NSW 12.07.45 49
Hatband: NX 50127 H D
Identity disc: QX.15047 J E Bourke 2/19 Aust.Inf.Bn. Millaa Millaa Qld., and Spoon.
*QX.15847 L/Cpl. John Edward Burke. Millaa Millaa, Qld. 31.07.45 38
Clothing:..?.2200 ? Palmer
*VX.32200 Cpl. Donald Palmer. Brighton, Vic. 13.02.45 38
Metal tag: NX 7934
Housewife: QX 14693
Identity disc (local pattern): VX.39422 H T Frost 1 Fd.Bakery 04 Stawell Vic
*VX.39422 Cpl. Henry Thomas Frost. Stawell, Vic. 24.07.45 25
Paybook: J A Finn
*NX.37388 Pte. James Allen Finn 09.08.45? 24
Identity disc (local pattern): QX.17516 R W Walter 2/10 Fd.Regt. Brisbane Qld.
*QX.17516 Gnr. Roy Williams Walter. Albion, Qld. 24.06.45 30
Groundsheet: NX 69225 H W Lysaght
*NX.69225 Cpl. Henry William Lysaght. Neutral Bay, NSW 04.07.45 36
Identity disc (local pattern): NX 40286 G.M. Neaves 2/18 Inf.Bn. A2 RC
Return to G M Neaves, PO, Barraba
*NX.40286 Cpl. Gordon Montague Neaves. Barraba, NSW 07.06.45 39
Identity disc (local pattern): NX.58549 W R Mann 2/10 Fd Amb 04 Meth
89 Edward St Arncliffe NSW
*NX.58549 Sgt. Wesley Richard Mann. Arncliffe, NSW 06.07.45 31
Paybook cover: VX.33620 Garth Day 2/9 Fd.Amb.
*VX.33620 Pte. Garth Day. Cheltenham, Vic. 08.07.45 25
Paybook: NX. Robert George Brown. Gnr. Age on Enlistment – 28 yrs. ALSO
Souvenir shield metal disc: NX.39190 R.G. Brown 2/15 Fd.Reg.
*NX.39190 S/Sgt. Robert George Brown. Hamilton, NSW 11.07.45 31
(Picture in "Abandoned ?")
Will: QX.22064 John William Seeley
*QX.22054 Cpl. John William Seeley. New Farm, Qld. 05.01.45 25
Paybook: Last – Allottee Wife: Patricia Evelyn Mary Last, Summer Hill.
*NX.65726 Pte. Arthur Blandford Last. Lismore, NSW 10.07.45 29
Part of leather wallet?: NX.30123?5
Paybook: Ernest Henry Turner
*NX.35848 Cpl. Ernest Henry Turner. Griffith, NSW 18.06.45 27
Part of Draft Roll: Dissection would reveal Names and Numbers
*Have copies.
Identity disc: NX.42?184 E.G. Noonan A2 RC
*NX.46184 Pte. Edmund George Noonan. Kyogle, NSW 31.07.45 28
Identity disc: NX.66892 L H Doyle 04 CofE
*NX.66892 Sgt. Leonard Harold Doyle. Yoogali, NSW 02.08.45 37
Identity disc: NX.47044 C Taylor 04
*NX.47044 W.O.II Thomas Clarence Taylor. New Lambton, NSW 26.07.45 43

CLOTHING AND GEAR BROUGHT IN BY LOCAL INHABITANTS – RANAU AREA

Mark *: Author's Note & Comments

Shorts – ... 69199 Crowther.			
*NX.69199 Pte. George Gladstone Crowther.		08.03.45	44
Pack – QX. 10572 Barker J.H.			
*QX.10572 Gnr. John Henry Barker.	Maryborough, Qld.	15.02.45	28
Towel – NX. 82702 Brown			
Working Jacket – ... 69201 Robertson			
Kitbag – Gleeson, M.			
Pack – NX. 54517			
*NX.54517 Spr. Percy Raymond Grono.	Fairfield, NSW	01.05.45	21
Working Jacket – NX. 72726 Prior, F.W.			
Working Jacket – SX. 11623 Greenwood, J. S.			
Pack – Jackson, J.P. 2/15 Fd.Regt.			
*NX.70110 Gnr. Fred Percy Jackson.	New Lambton, NSW	02.07.45	27
See picture Page 104.			
Towel – NX. 7 3060			
Working Jacket – NX. 28046 Mc ? ?nton, D.			
Pack – NX.68410 Peters, K.A.			
*NX.68410 Cpl. Keith Anderson Peters.	Ettalong Beach, NSW	07.06.45	40
Pack – QX. 3482 Livingston, H.H. 8 Div. Sigs.			
*QX. 3482 Sigmn. Hugh Hilary Livingstone	Burnett Heads, Qld.	28.03.45	32
Working Jacket – Chapman, S. H.			
*NX. 42001 Pte. Stanley Howard Chapman.	Byron Bay, NSW	03. 05.45	31
Pack – NX. 68928 Ezzy, A.J.C. 2/3 MAC			
*NX. 68928 Dvr. Allan James Charles Ezzy.	Richmond, NSW	05. 03. 45	38
Working Jacket – Manton L..			
*SX.10635 Pte. Lindsay Clive Manton.	Wolseley, S.A.	22.07.45	27
Working Jacket – NX. 72650 Mulligan D J			
Haversack – McCarthy L. 2/3 MAC			
*NX. 68904 Dvr. Leo McCarthy.	Five Dock, NSW	02. 03. 45	44
Coat – SX.10846 Dwyer, T. A.Coy.			
*SX.10846 Pte. Neil Wilfred Dwyer.	Hilton, S.A.	14.06.45	31
Pack – NX.53301 Tony Fahey			
*NX.53301 L/Cpl. Anthony Milton Fahey.	Bowral, NSW	10.08.45	33
Working Jacket – Leinster			
*QX.15180 L/Bdr. Victor Pascoe Leinster.	Atherton, Nth.Qld.	22.02.45	26
Working Jacket – Ellis, A.			
*NX.20431 Gnr. Arthur George Ellis.	Campsie, NSW	15.02.45	38
Haversack and Officers hat – NX.32109 Good, G. B H Q			
*NX.32109 Lt. Gordon Good.	East Sydney, NSW	13.07.45	35
Shorts – NX.57195 Crattn S C			
Pack – MX.21899			
*NX.21899 Pte. Arthur Ernest Bayley.	Enfield, NSW	10.02.45	43
? NX.72726 Prior E W			
Working Jacket – Jeavis			
*QX.8433 Bdr. James Albert Jeavons.	East Brisbane, Qld.	14.07.45	37
Working Jacket – WX.9815 E J H			
Working Jacket – Bunch N			
*QX.11039 Gnr. Norman Henry Bunch.	Sth.Brisbane, Qld.	17.06.45	27

Dixie – NX.30883 Gellatly AAOC
*NX.30883 L/Sgt. Richard Alder Gellatly. Canberra, ACT 09.07.45 25
Dixie – NX.28667 Farrell, A R 2/18 Bn.
*NX.28667 Pte. Arthur Richard Farrell. 26.01.45 44
Blanket – G Taylor
There were four "G. Taylor".
Jap Haversack – Walker J No.4
*NX.32966 Bdr. James Scott Walker. Ashfield, NSW 19.02.45 24
British Army Jacket – Roeduck.
*NX.56657 Pte. John Thomas Roebuck. Lewisham, NSW 16.05.45 28
Jacket, working, superimposed on "Forrest" NX.71897 McAllister, R.
Shorts – WX.8090 Hazluck
*WX.8090 Spr. Lewis Norman Hasluck. Herne Hill, W.A. 06.04.44 42
Buried Sandakan.
Pack – NX.53646 J M J
Wallet with photo woman and child – NX Buckley, L.F.
*NX.30123 Pte. Lawless Fenton Buckley. Bankstown, NSW 11.02.45 32
2/20 Bn. Known as "Leo" in 2/20 Bn.

MISCELLANEOUS ITEMS – AS REPORTED

Mark *: Author's Note & Comments

Badges – Northamptonshire Gordons, Singapore Royal Engineers, RAMC
Royal Corps of Sigs, RASC, RE, Malay States Volunteer Rifles
Letter addressed to – WX.7360 Spr. G.L. Field 2/6 Fd.Pk.Coy. AIF.
*Spr. Gilbert Lawrence Cottle Field. Albany, WA. 01.06.45 41
Canteen Order to – NX.32... Pte.(?) Lever, L.
*NX.32255 Pte. Alfred Lyal Lever. Murwillumbah, NSW 02.06.45 26
Piece of paper with Address – Mr. (K?) Neal 266 Brae St. Rockhampton, Qld.
*QX.11352 Pte. Keith Thomas Neal. Brisbane, Qld. 14.04.45 25
Slip of paper signed: G. William Bundey
*NX.65429 Sgt. George William Bundey. Toorak Gardens, S.A. 29.04.45 28
Unidentified Paybook – Soldier's signature R.D. Small – NOK Father, NSW
*NX.29863 Gnr. Robert Darcy Small. Bowral, NSW 23.06.45 27
Unidentified Paybook – 97009 NOK Father. Ernest Albert Garvin. Penkivil Street. Bondi NSW
*NX.58438 Sgt. Jack Thomas Garvin. Bondi, NSW 04.06.45 43
Unidentified Paybook – NOK Mrs. Alice Shirley, 8 Jackson Street, North Fremantle, W.A.
*WX.8535 Pte. Arthur Francis Shirley. West Northam, W.A. 10.05.45 36
Unidentified Paybook – ?6076 Ham(?n)kin Percival E... NOK Friend K.W. Phillips Cnr. Nash St. & Bald Hills Rd., Sandgate Brisbane Qld. (Entry cancelled)
*QX.1606 Cpl. Percival Edmund Hankin. 15.06.45 42
Unidentified Paybook – (Might be Gordon Andrew James Son— or Smith)
*NX.7272 Spr. Gordon Andrew James Soutar. Ashfield, NSW 02.06.45 30
Returned Soldier's Badge (RSL) N.1895
Two Masonic Club Badges found: Nos. NSW MC No.885 and NSW MC No.275 Honorary Members.
*Masonic Club Records not available
Web Equipment marked – "NX.69195 – Young T"
*NX.69196 Cpl. Thomas Oswald Young. Padstow, NSW 10.06.45 35
Web Equipment marked – NX.52416
*NX.32416 Cpl. Wallace Ellis Wynn. Goulburn, NSW 21.03.45 27
Web Equipment marked – "VX.4338? Rudd W.T." ?
*VX.43384 L/Cpl. William Thomas Rudd. Windsor, Vic. 13.07.45 40

Web Equipment marked – "VX.41946 Wilson V"

*VX.41946 Cpl. Vivian Wilson. Moe, Vic. 12.09.44 25

Cpl. Wilson died on the RAKUYO MARU and not in Borneo where this equipment was found.

Web Equipment marked – "NX.40763 Gillespie W G Embarkation No.374(344)"

*NX.40763 Pte. William George Gillespie. 01.07.45 42

Web Equipment marked – "WX.7(67)34 S A D"

Web Equipment marked: "VX.29567 F Peck"

*VX.29567 L/Cpl. Francis Peck. Tungamah, Vic. 16.03.45 35

Web Equipment marked – "NX.40244 Cpl. C. Hargreave"

*NX.40244 Cpl. Claude Hope Hargrave. Walcha, NSW 03.03.45 38

Web Equipment marked – "Lt.Rolfe R.A." (May be Royal Artillery or initials)

Name engraved on floor of hut – "P. Gale"

*VX.67597 Pte. Peter Ripley Gale. Murchison, Vic. 16.04.45 25

Identification Tags or Discs of following personnel:

QX.8427 Cameron,F. 2/20 Fd.Regt. P, B3. Home Address: 51 Bridge Rd., Mackay, Qld.

*QX.8427 Gnr. Finlay Cameron. Mackay, Qld. 07.06.45 42

NX.69261 Anderson A. 2/3 MAC Home Address: Glebe NSW

*NX.69261 Pte. Albert Anderson. Glebe Point, NSW 11.05.45 39

WX.9297 Joynes, C. 2/4 MG Bn. Home Address: Kulin WA

*WX.9297 Pte. Colin Joynes. Jitarning, W.A. 07.06.45 31

NX.32255 Lever, A.L. (two discs)

*NX.32255 Pte. Alfred Lyal Lever. Murwillumbah, NSW 02.06.45 26

WX.8794 Marsh, H.A. (two discs)

*WX.8794 Spr. Henry Arthur Marsh. 08.06.45 40

NX.50568 (H)arris

*NX.50568 Pte. John Oscar Harris. Waterloo, NSW 02.06.45 44

QX.9390 Hanson, K.D. 2/10 Fd.Regt.

*QX.9390 Gnr. Kenneth David Hanson. New Farm Qld. 15.02.45 27

VX.37753 Bray, J. 2/10

*VX.37753 Sgt. John Bray. Sandringham, Vic. 07.06.45 43

SX.11479 Coker, R.H. C E

*'SX.11479 Cpl. Raymond Horace Coker Maroubra Jnctn., NSW 08.05.45 45

NX.40678 Hog.in C W M A2

*NX.40678 Pte. Charles William Hogbin. Glen Innes, NSW 24.03.45 40

NX.50445 Symes (Sig.) A V J C E

*NX.50445 Pte. Arthur Victor John Symes. Chatswood, NSW 11.04.45 25

NX.72889 (Disc broken) No name

*NX.72889 Pte. Robert John Fisher. Gulgong, NSW 16.04.45 23

2/20 Bn. AIF

1717709 Venton C C E

*1717709 Gnr. Charles Leslie Venton. Truro, Cornwall, UK 06.02.45

242 Bty., 48 Lt. A.A. Regt. Royal Artillery

PW Red Cross envelope addressed to – NX.5694 Cpl. H.G. Lloyd, HQ 8 Div.

*NX.5694 Cpl. Hector George Lloyd 05.06.45 42

Cover of notebook marked – H. Richardson RHQ – A/T Regt. Ingleburn. NX.30962

Sgt.'s chevron armlet marked -M.P. Baxter NX.68141

*NX.68141 Sgt. Michael Paul Baxter West Marrickville, NSW 08.06.45 34

Army Driving Licence G.11 No.92713 VX.63485 Pte. Laving, R.F.

Cigarette lighter engraved: NX.40758 (Initials J.H.M.)

*NX.40758 Pte. Harold John Maguire. Nth.Sydney, NSW 07.06.45 45

All preceding information AWM. Reference No. AWM.54. Written Records Item 779/1/2. Report on Investigations Australian Allied Prisoners of War 9 Div. Area Aug./Nov. 1945

SANDAKAN — RANAU REVISITED

In 1981 Keith Botterill visited Sandakan and Ranau with Bruce Ruxton's party; located the camp at Sandakan and pointed out the place where Gnr. Cleary was chained to a stake at Ranau. Botterill said "Ruxton immediately responded by saying 'We'll put a plaque there.'"

In 1986 Bruce Ruxton arranged for a group of Australians including many relatives of those lost at Sandakan to visit Ranau for the occasion of the Chief Minister of Sabah, Datuk Joseph Pairin Kitingan, unveiling the Memorial.

Chief Minister, Datuk Joseph Pairin Kitingan and Bruce Ruxton, O.B.E., at the unveiling ceremony.

Sandakan Memorial Wagga Wagga Dedication 1995 Minister for Veterans Affairs Mr. Con Sciacca talking to Keith Botterill, one of the survivors. Author talking to Frank Coughlan showing where his brother Tom died on the death march. *Photo: Wagga Advertiser*

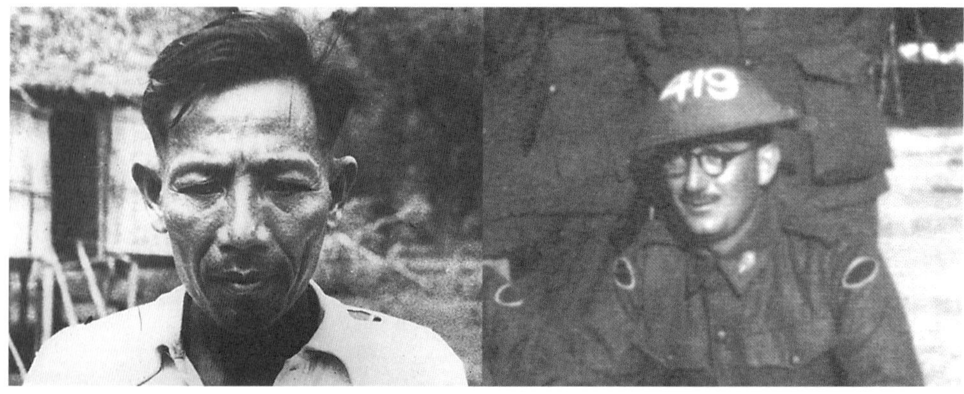

O.T. Kulang. A member of Services Reconnaissance under Lieut. Harmer. He later assisted Australian War Graves in locating victims.
Photo: A.W.M. No.042512.

NX.6627 Gnr. A.J. McGlinn. 2/15 Fd.Regt. R.A.A. Died 9 July 1945. Age 41. Denistone, N.S.W.
Photo: Mrs. E. McGrath

Soh Tuen Kam, whose late husband, Ng Ho Kong, was sentenced to 10 years imprisonment for his part in the Sandakan Underground, attended the Memorial Service August 1, 1992. With her is her son Frank Ng of Melbourne and daughter Irene Ng of Sydney. Four of her six children are Australian citizens.
Pic: Don Wall

Sgt. Ernest Leslie Munro. VX.55381. 2/10 Ord.Wk.Shps. Traralgon, Vic. Date of death given by Japanese as 3 August 1945.? Died Sandakan.
Pic: Graham, Fred and Peggy Munro

Chapter 17

LABUAN PARTY UNDER CAPTAIN NAGAI

As the tide of war was moving against the Japanese in all theatres Japanese Command decided that Brunei Bay could be important to them if further losses occurred in the Philippines region. In May 1944 they commenced construction of an airstrip on Labuan Island.

Captain Nagai was appointed to command the PWs work force to be used in its construction, at this time he was second in command to Hoshijima at Sandakan. He left there with 100 British PWs by ship and arrived at Labuan on 16 June, 1944.

Colonel Suga was instructed to send a further 200 British PWs from Kuching, these were despatched on August 15, 1944, to complete the work force of 300 required for the task. At this time the Kuching PW working force comprised several hundred British who had come from Java-Sumatra and a few Australians from Java and Singapore, and several others who had been returned from Sandakan.

Conditions at the OR's camp at Kuching were grim, the PWs were employed on aerodrome construction and ship building in the Kuching River. Deaths were occurring daily and when volunteers were called for a new working party many felt any camp could not be as bad as conditions in the Kuching working camp. There were several Australians included in this group, they were taken to Labuan by ship.

The camp was located in the grounds of the Victoria Golf Club, later, when Allied air raids over the waterfront area became more frequent, they were moved to a new compound north of the harbour. Here they remainded until they departed for Brunei on 7 March 1945.

As in all areas, following the 'No Rice' order in October 1944, health of the PWs deteriorated and conditions became harsher. Deaths occurred almost daily. There were to be no survivors from this force of 300 men, the only source of information was gained by interrogating the Japanese, of course they concocted their own version in the hope their own lives would be saved. One aspect is certain, the orders and directives issued by Hirohito's Imperial General H.Q. were carried out to the letter and were consistent with atrocities committed in all other occupied countries.

On 23 January 1945, Capt. Nagai was transferred to Ranau and his place was taken by Sgt. Major Sugino. In the meantime 143 PWs died. The story is best told by Sugino — the 9 Division Contact Group who carried out the investigation of PWs relied on the death certificates prepared by the Japanese and issued by them and at NO time did they record any shootings. Their cover for the shooting was always the PWs were going to escape. This order was taken from one of the directives sent out to all Commands.

Sgt. Major Sugino Tsuruo: "I took charge of 157 European PWs at Labuan with orders from Lt. Col. Suga to take them from Labuan to Kuching. They were all fit but some had malaria. Between 23 January and 7 March forty-five of these died of malaria and beri beri in Labuan. I left Labuan on 7 March with 112 PWs and 15 Formosan Civilian Guards. We reached Brunei on 8 March 1945 and remained there until 2 or 3 May 1945, and during that time 30 PWs died of malaria and beri beri. There was no doctor there, but I often issued medicine for malaria and beri beri to the medical orderlies who in turn issued it to the sick PWs. One of the PWs tried to escape here and I know that the Kempe Tai took him and I did not see him again. On about 2 or 3 May with 82 PWs I left Brunei for Kuala Belait and arrived the next day. On arriving at Kuala Belait I reported to 1/Lt. Kamimura and a W.O. in command of Kempe Tai. While I was in Kaula Belait the PWs camped in the old picture theatre, where we remained until 26 or 27 May 1945. While in Kuala Belait 37 PWs died of malaria and beri beri. During this time I received seven Indian PWs from Lt. Kamimura, one of whom was an officer, but I do not remember his name. We left Kuala Belait on 27 May 1945 and arrived in Miri on the following day. On arriving in Miri I reported to Lt. Nishimura, who was OC of 20 Aerial Supply Coy. He ordered me to go to Cape Lobang and the PWs were camped in a house inside a barbed wire compound. The PWs house was made of bush timber and roofed with coconut leaves and was built ready for us when we arrived there. The PWs remained here until 8 June 1945. During this time they were employed growing vegetables in the vicinity of the PW compound, except for two days they worked in Miri township unloading rice from boats and loading trucks.

"On arrival at Cape Lobang I reported to Capt. Hasegawa but after that I had nothing whatever to do with him. While the PWs were at Cape Lobang four of them died of malaria and beri beri. There were two English doctors among the PWs (previously there had been none) and they examined the dead men and signed the death certificates stating the cause of death to be malaria and beri beri. Copies of these certificates were forwarded to Kuching. The PWs were buried in four graves near the compound. Most of the sick PWs were sick with malaria, beri beri, sores and ulcers. While at Cape Lobang the PWs diet consisted of meat, rice, sugar, tea, vegetables and tobacco. Those PWs who were not sick were fat and well.

"At 1500 hours June 1945 Sgt. Major Hasegawa Tai told me that an English fleet was approaching Borneo. I became anxious for the safety of the PWs and decided to move to a safer place. I then ordered the PWs to make small bundles of their personal gear to take with them. We left the Compound at 2000 hours and went via a jungle track over the hill to Riam road and reached the 3½ Mile Riam road at midnight. The whole party remained here until 0400 hours 9 June 1945 when a party of 15 fit PWs and 5 guards returned to Cape Lobang to pick up stores consisting of rice, salt, officer stores and medicine. There were at this time 20 fit men but only 15 went back, and of the remaining 28 sick ones, 5 were unable to walk and had to be carried by the fit men. The carrying party of fit men returned about 1000 hours. At about this time one of the PWs died of malaria and beri beri. In this move down the Riam road I was responsible to no one and in complete charge of the PWs.

"At 0400 hours on 9 June when the 15 fit PWs returned to Cape Lobang I sent a written message by one of the guards to Nishimura telling him that I was going down the Riam road. At 1800 hours that night I received a written message from Nishimura telling me to take plenty of food and go to the mountains. At 1300 hours 9 June 15 PWs left 3½ Mile and again returned to Cape Lobang with 5 guards. They returned at 1800 hours carrying similar stores to the last trip. All the PWs had a meal at 1800 hours and then at 2000 hours the whole party left and went to 5½ Mile Riam road, arriving at 2200 hours. The whole party made camp in a deserted house and went to sleep.

"At 0600 hours 10 June 1945, the PWs arose, breakfasted, and then were allowed to rest throughout the morning. The PWs had a midday meal and at 1500 hours the same healthy PWs and four guards returned to 3½ Mile Riam road to bring back stores.

"At midday I burnt some old PW documents and letters. The only documents I kept were those relating to the living PWs and pay matters. Documents concerning PWs who died at Brunei and Kuala Belait had already been forwarded to Kuching. While I was burning the documents about 100 metres from the house I saw Capt. Chambers going into the house acting in what I thought was a suspicious manner as he was looking to all sides as he walked. Capt. Chambers was among the party who went back and I told Nago, the civilian guard in charge, that he would probably try to escape in which case he was to be killed.

"At 1900 hours five or six men, led by Sgt. Ackland, jumped up from where they were sitting outside the house and started to run away. I called out to the guard to open fire on the escaping PWs. In the confusion some of the bullets went in the house and caused the PWs to come out. As they came out of the house they were shot or bayonetted by the guards. The sick PWs tried to crawl away and they were shot or bayonetted coming out of the house or outside the house, I did not give any orders to cease fire in order to save the sick because I was so excited that I did not know what was happening. Those PWs who were not killed outright were put out of their agony by shooting or bayonetting. When this was over there were thirty-two bodies.

"I then ordered three or four of the guards to bury the PWs. I then heard a burst of firing coming from about 1000 metres back along the Riam road. I called out about six guards and ran in the direction of the firing. When I arrived there I found that the PWs were then dead and were being carried to one place for burial by the guards. In addition to the guards I saw eight men belonging to the Nishimura Tai. Several men were digging two graves that were about one foot deep when I arrived. When the graves were dug the PWs were buried and the whole work was completed by about 2030 hours. I asked Nago what had happened and he told me that the PWs had been shot trying to escape and eight men of Nishimura Tai had helped to kill them, I did not ask any further questions because I understood that the PWs had not been trying to escape when they were killed. Although I gave orders before they left to kill the PWs if they attempted to escape I knew myself that they would be killed in any case. After the PWs were buried at the road I returned to the house to supervise the burial of the others, which finished at midnight. Some personal belongings were buried with the PWs and the remainder were burnt.

"After saluting the dead all the guards went to sleep."

Following his first statement, Sgt. Maj. Sugino Tsuruo was interrogated again, so some weeks later he said: "I now admit the statement I made on 11 October 1945 was not completely true. I will now tell the complete truth — the information I gave concerning the killing of the 32 PWs at the 5½ Mile Riam road is all true. After the killing of the 32 PWs I, together with six or seven Formosan guards, immediately went to the 5½ Mile and waited until the arrival of Nago and three other Formosan guards escorting 15 PWs, who rested on a small track leading off the road and opposite us. Shortly afterwards, L/Cpl. Kaneko and eight members of the Nishimura Tai also arrived from the 5½ Mile.

"I thought at the time that as food was getting short some of the PWs might try to escape, so I decided that it would be better that we kill them. After the PWs had been resting about ten minutes, one of the European PWs tried to escape by running into the grass. I then gave the order to shoot the whole fifteen PWs. All the Nishimura Tai and five or six Formosan guards took part in the shooting.

"After the shooting, some of the PWs were not dead so I ordered that they be shot and bayonetted as they lay on the ground. The man who had previously run into the grass was also shot. We then buried the bodies in two graves and I sent the members of the Nishimura Tai straight back to the 7 Mile and together with my own men I returned to 5½ Mile to complete the burial of the PWs killed there. I later went to the 7 Mile where I spent the night."

NX.67346 L/Cpl. Victor Thistlethwaite, Sans Souci, N.S.W. Died 15.7.45.

Photo: Mrs. B. Betteridge.

NX.68861 Pte. Leslie Earl Hardy, Taree, N.S.W. Died. 19.5.45.

Photo: Earl Hardy.

This photograph was obtained by O.T. Kulang in the Maunad area at the time of the first march. He witnessed the Japanese killing of Pte. Hayes, WX. 7247 (see story page 65) and later wrote his name on the back of this photograph. Later he handed it to SRD Commando, Lt. Hollingsworth, and it found its way through the system and the original is now with the Australian Archives.

On the back of the photograph is written "Dear Perce — All here except Dad — will get one of him for next letter — Love Mum" and some faint pencil writing.

In order to identify Perce, all first and second names of Percival—Percy—were extracted and their numbers compared with the faint marking on the picture. With aids, the number QX.21002 Gunner P.W.F. Carter can be read. Gunner Carter's death was recorded by the Japanese as 2.3.45 at Ranau.

It is unlikely that such a treasured possession would have been disposed of willingly. It is more likely Gnr. Carter died in the Maunad area. The picture was not water damaged.

NX.10791 Gnr. Wallace Gordon Blatch, Yeoval, N.S.W.
The Japanese gave his date of death as June 1st, 1945. This could not be the correct date as he was known to be alive and in good shape at the time of Braithwaite's escape in the Sapi River area. The death certificate states he died at Tawinto, believed to be in the Boto area. (Story page 97.) *Photo: By Lois Job.*

NX.41261 Gnr. Eric Tomkyns, Warialda, N.S.W..
Photo: H.E. Tomkyns.

NX.30581 L/Bdr. James Reginald Cross, Coffs Harbour, N.S.W.. Died 12.6.45 Sandakan.
Photo: E. Cross.

NX.33024 Bdr. Tom Ebzery, Narooma, N.S.W.. Died 5.6.45, 46 Mile Second March.
Photo: Annette Burke.

NX.46682 Sgt. Robert James Horder, Mosman, N.S.W..
Died 9.7.45, Age 48. Served World War I. Put his age back to serve in World War II. (See story page 106.)
Photo: Shirley George.

QX.17167 Gnr. Robert Edward Jillett, Clayfield, Qld. Died 5.6.45, Sandakan.
Photo; Mrs. E. Jillett.

NX.41804 Sig. H.G. Garde, Ryde, N.S.W.. Died 12.3.45.
Photo: Bob Garde and Sister Joyce.

NX.53777 Pte. Sidney Arthur Webber, Parramatta, N.S.W.
Died 18.6.45. Japs stated 10.8.45. (See story page 92.)
Photo: June Fowler-Smith.

NX.67404 Driver Stanley Barden Folkard, Sherwood, N.S.W. Died 10.6.45.

Photo: H. Quintal.

NX.73633 Pte. Leslie George Trinder, Carlton, N.S.W. Died 5.6.45, Sandakan.

Photo: Mrs. Hirtes

NX.45443 W.O.II William John Steinbeck. Died 15.7.45, Ranau.

Photo: Robin Meywes

NX. 36468 Cpl. Richard George Rooke, Wagga Wagga, N.S.W. Died 19.6.45, Sandakan.

Photo: Barney Rooke.

VX.41337 Pte. Andrew Carnegie Sommerville, 2/2 Pioneer Bn. Member of 7 Div. Born in Liverpool, U.K. Landed Java 1942. Became friendly with British Medical Officer, volunteered to go with him to Borneo. Known to have joined the Australian camp in 1944. Died 14.4.45.

Photo: Mrs. A. Sommerville.

VX.58301, Sig. Robert Edward Archibald Fingher, Moonee Ponds, Vic. Enlisted aged 15 years 5 months — was 16 years when taken prisoner. Died 12.6.45 aged 19 years.

Photo: R.J. Fingher, Doncaster, Vic.

This group of reinforcements for the 2/10 Fld. Ambulance left Sydney December 1941.
Second from Left: NX.10841 Pte. Edward Horace Fox, Camperdown, N.S.W. Died 10.2.45.
Seventh from Left: NX.10303 Pte. John William Hayes, Waverley, N.S.W. Died 13.5.45.
Eighth from Left: NX.72867 Pte. Leonard James Condon, Petersham, N.S.W. Died 16.5.45.

Photo: Mrs. Pat Hunt.

WX.8707 Cpl. Frank Nazzari, West Perth, W.A. 2/4 M.G. Died 29.4.45.
The 2/4 M.G. Unit arrived Singapore late January 1942 and distinguished itself during the fighting on Singapore Island.

Photo: P. Roberts, Geraldton, W.A.

WX.14710 Spr. Cyril William Davey, South Perth, W.A. Died 4.3.45.

Photo: Maureen Aitken.

VX.51733 Sgt. Theordore Albert Feldbauer, Research, Vic. Died 27.3.45.

Photo: June Snell, Doncaster, Vic.

NX.72219 Gnr. Stanley Douglas Macpherson, Randwick, N.S.W. Died 19.3.45 on first march.

Photo: W. Cook

Index

	PAGE
Abin, Cpl.	35,39,43
Abe, Lt.	59,62
Abing Bin Luma	98
Abe, Capt. Kazuo	142,143
Adzcona, Felix	39,43
Akashi, Major General	85
Allen	10
Ali Asa	122
Ambiau	94
Amit	98
Anderson, (J.M. Bowe)	6,17,53,105, 111,113,146
Annear, Pte.	53
Andong Ajak, O.T.	113
Apostal, Lamberto	35,38,39,40
Austin, Pte.	91,92
Awabe, Sgt.	107
Baba, Lt. Gen. Masao	55,116,125, 126,145
Balzer, Lt. Ray	143
Balabiu	147
Bancroft, A., H.M.A.S. Perth	51,53
Barber, Pte.	54
Barnier, Pte. J.	4
Barigah	110,111,113, 115,146
Bastin, Cpl. J.	82
Bathgate, Capt. A.	18
Beale, Major	37
Beardshaw, L.A.C., (U.K.)	70
Beppu, Sgt.	77,78,108,110
Bexton, Pte. T.	5,130
Bexton, Pte. S.O.	5,130
Bird, Spr. A.W.	79,100
Blatch, Gnr. W.	97
Blanksby, Major	132
Blamey, General	57,58,137
Blain, Sgt. W.	56
Blackie, W/O. J.W.	4
Blow, Lt. R.	32,33,57,58, 120
Botterill, Pte. K.	53,62,66,72, 75,79,81,101, 105,110,111, 113,115,142, 143,146
Bowe, Pte. J.M. (S/A Anderson)	6,17,53
Braithwaite, Bdr. R.	97,98
Brereton, Capt.	138,140
Brinkman, Pte. J.	28
Britz, Capt.	19
Buang	98
Burchnall, Cpl. F.	4
Burgess, Flt./Lt. (R.A.F.)	88,108
Burnett, Pte. E.R.	29
Burns, Pte. S.	28,130
Butler, Pte.	33
Campbell, Major G.N.	15,17,132
Campbell, Gnr. O.	84,91,92,93, 94,96,97
Carr, Pte. M.	10
Carter, Pte. G.C.	65,66
Carter, Major	132
Chan Ping (Ah Ping)	15,21,39
Chenhall, Pte. N.	82
Chin Chee Kong	35
Chin Min Choi	90
Chopping, Lt. (U.K.)	88,108
Clement, Pte.	54
Cleary, Gnr. A.	79
Codlin, Sgt. J.M.	108
Connolly, Cpl.	108
Connor, Pte. H.	5,130
Connor, Pte. J.	5,130
Cook, Capt. G.	17,24,38,41, 43,83,85,88, 101,107,108, 140
Cooper, Pte. A.	2
Cooper, Flt./Lt. (R.A.A.F.)	116
Core, Pte. S.R.	128
Coughlan, Gnr. T.	5
Crease, Gnr. W.	79
Crome, Pte. J.	17,130
Crozier, Capt.	34
Cull, Pte.	82
Cummings, Sgt./Maj.	32
Damodaran	39
Daniels, Capt. (R.A.M.C.)	88,108,110
Darling, Capt. L.G.	126,128
Darlington, Pte. J.	14,23
Davis, Pte. E.J.	6,17,24
Davis, Pte. S.G.	37
Davidson, Pte.	38
Davis, Spr. R.	40
Dawson, Pte.	70
DeFaye, Pte.	130
DeFaye, Pte.	130
Dixon, W/O.	88,91

Dihil Bin Ambilid 107,146
Dixon, Lt. R. 128
Dorrizzi, Pte. G. 130
Dorrizzi, Pte. H. 130
Dorrizzi, Pte. T. 130
Doyle, Pte. A.G. 108
Doyle, Sgt. L.H. 108
Duval, Major, F.J. 145
Dyce, Major 146,147

Eddy, Major, H. 28
Edwards, S/Sgt. (U.K.) 108
Emmett, Cpl. 91,92
Esler, Lt. 44
Evans, Dvr. 105
Ewin, Lt. R. 15,44,133

Fairey, Cpl. 10
Fairley, Major, J. 27,28,29,31, 132
Ferguson, Sgt. 108
Filmer, Capt. 38
Fitzgerald, Cpl. 40,105
Fleming, Major, E.A. 17,21,24,25, 26,33,132
Flight 200 115
Foo Seng Chow 10,11,39
Ford, Pte. W. 17
Forster, Major 115
Forrester, Pte. C. 48
Fraser, Major 17,132
Frost, Pte. (U.K.) 79,105
Frost, Pte. E. 130
Frost, Pte. H. 130
Fujita, Sgt./Maj. 87,91,106,108
Fukushima 144
Fuller, Gnr. 70
Funk, Alex 38,39,43
Funk, Johnny 39,40
Funk, Paddy 35,39
Fusataro Teshima, Lt. Gen. 137

Galleghan, Lt. Col 27,31,32
Galunting 93,94,96
Galenty, Sgt. 107
Garland, Lt. D. 13
Garland, Act./Padre 41,74,82,88
Gaven, Capt. F. 29,32,33
Gaven, S/Sgt. J. 33
Gettens, Lt. 126
Gilenki, O.T. 113
Gilham, Sgt. L. 115
Gillegan, Pte. C.A. 28
Gillon, Lt. M. 33
Gimbahan 113
Girgaas Bin Gangass 107,146,147
Goh Teck Seng 10,39
Good, Lt. G. 41,57,88
Gore, Sgt. E.G. 115
Gotanda Kiroku, W/O 61,65,67,98, 99,142,143
Graham, Cpl. T. 37
Greenwood, Padre H. Wardale 49,88
Grinham, Cpl. 116
Grinter, Pte. C. 14
Grist, Pte. N. 79
Gunting, O.T. 111,113,146
Gurlaman, Insp. N.B.A.C. 39

Hamilton, Capt. T. 3
Haneda 79
Hardie, Sqd./Ldr. G. (R.A.F.) 25,26
Harlem, Capt. 96
Harrington, Pte. 10
Harvey, Sig. 25
Hashimoto Masao 108
Haye, Spr. 65
Hearl, Sgt. W. 51
Heaslop, Capt. 18,41,88
Heath, General 13
Heng Joo Ming 18,25,35,39, 43
Henthorne, Padre (Civ.) 44
Hewitt, Pte. H. (The Turk) 28
Hewitt, Sgt. H. 41
Hinchcliffe, Spr. 52
Hinata Genzo 83,118
Hirano Yukikiko, Lt. 61,142,143
Hirohito, Emperor 1,3,49,51,84, 107,122,124, 125,134
Hodges, Sgt. J.A. 115
Holly, Sgt. 37
Hollingsworth, Lt. 'Jock' 96
Horder, S/Sgt. 106
Horikawa Koichi, Lt. 142,143
Hoshijima, Lt. 1,10,13,16,17, 21,22,23,24, 25,26,27,32, 33,34,37,38, 40,41,42,43, 44,54,56,57, 58,59,60,82, 83,84,85,101, 126,138,139, 140,141.
Hosotani, Sgt. 90
Hussin 70
Hutchinson, Sgt. J. 14,15
Hywood, Sgt. 115

Ichikawa Takagorah, Sgt. 19,40,57,87, 108
Iino Shiguro, Capt. 60,66,142,143
Ince, Pte. J.W. 130
Ishii Fujio 77,78

Ito Takeo, S/Maj. 62
Iwabe, Sgt. 79
Iwashita, Lt. 119

Jacka, Pte. 10
Jackson, Major H.W.S. 146
Jackson, Pte. J. 4,82
James, Lt. (U.S.N) 98
Jeffrey, Capt. R. 18,41,60,74, 77,79
Jenson, Spr. 40
Johns, W/O. A.E. (U.K.) 62,64
Johnstone, Major 44
Johnstone, Flt./Lt. C.J. 25

Kalingal 115
Kantong 111
Katayama, Cpl. 89,90
Kawakami 79
Kealey, L/Cpl. J.V. 108
Keating, Spr. 40,44
Keith, Mr. Harry 40
Kennedy, Pte. 33
Kinder, W/O. J.N. 62,71,74
Koponica, Pte. J.F. 108
Koram, L/Cpl. N.B.A.C. 25,32,33,35, 37
Kulang, O.T. 55,64,65,93, 94,96
Kumabe Tanuki, (Jap. Governor of N.B.) 21

Ladooma 111
Lagan, Ernesto 11,35,36,37, 39,41,42,43
Lander, Sgt. C. 37,44
Lap 93,94
Lawler, Major 132
Limbuang 107
Lo, Jack 33,34,35
Loxton, Lt. A. 23

Madden, Colonel 3
Madden, Bdr. W. 28
Maddock, W/O. L. 41,82
Magador 111
Maguire, Bugler, H.J. (Paddy) 11,24
Mainstone, Pte. C.D. 130
Mangulong 98
Martin, Sgt. F. 18,24
Marshall, Spr. 40
Maskey, Cpl. L.W. 108,110
Matusup Bin Gungau 33,34,43
Matthews, Capt. L. 14,15,18,19, 33,34,35,36, 38,39,40,41, 43,44,45
Mavor, Mr. 15,21,39,43,44
Maxwell, Capt. G. 24,25
MacArthur, Gen. 58,125
McDonagh, Sgt. 19
McDonald, S/Sgt. W.B. 108
McFarlane, W. 146
McKay, Sig. (S/A. McKenzie) 25
McLaren, Pte. 29,33,57,58
McManus, A.B. H. 128
McNeale, Sgt. 115
Mentod, P.C. N.B.A.C. 115
Mills, Cpl. C.C. 19,38
Mills, Capt. (U.K.) 43,140
Mills, Capt. F. 133
Mizuto, Capt. Ryuchi 62,142,143
Mohamed Zamen 11
Moffitt, Capt. A. 140
Moo Sing 40
Morikawa, Lt. 62
Moricka Teickichi 110
Moritake, Lt. 26,38,40,82, 85,87,118,119, 120
Morozumi, Sgt./Maj. 87,118,122
Mosher, Capt. K. 17,18,26
Mountbatten, Lord Louis 101
Moxham, Gnr. T. 51
Moxham, Gnr. H. 51
Moxham, Bdr. W. 51,62,73,79, 105,111,113, 115,142,146
Murray, Pte. R. 79
Myers, Pte. C. (Bluey) 28

Nagai, Capt. Hirawa 25,26,27,71, 72,77,78,101, 108,110
Naguri, Takeshi, L/Cpl. 25
Neil, Sgt. 122
Nekarta, Lt. 132,133
Ng Ho Kong 21
Nicolls, Capt. 115
Nishikawa, Moriji 110
Nishikawa, Yoshinori 118,119

Oakeshott, Capt. J.B. 28,41,88,99, 106,107,108
O'Donohue, Pte. E.J. 4,108,110
Ojaga Singh 43
Okahara, Lt. 10,15,16,40
Okada, Toshimaru, Sgt. 77,78,108,110
Omar 98
Orr, Pte. J. 83,118
Osawa San 24,38,44,87, 91
Otsuka, Colonel 52,85
Owen, Capt. 132

Padua 98

Percival, Gen. 13
Phillips, Mr. 39
Picken, Pte. J. 29
Pickford, Capt. C. 2,17,21,132
Pickering, Pte. 38
Picone, Capt. D. 15,23,24,40, 41,81,88,106, 107,108
Porter, Brig. 101

Ramsay, Lt. Col. G. 2,3
Rankin, Pte. J. (Lofty) 6
Rayson, Major 14
Reither, Dvr. H. 37,107,113, 146
Rice-Oxley, Major 14
Richards, Cpl. 19,38
Richards, Pte. 69
Richardson, Capt. R.J.D. 31,32
Rijan 147
Ripley, Capt. 107,113,115, 116
Roberts, Pte. F. (Nutsy) 32,
Roberts, Gnr. B. (U.K.) 70
Rooker, S/Sgt. (U.K.) 108
Rowell, Capt. 10,19,38,44
Rumble, Pte. T.H. 37

Sagan 98
Salim 98
Saliam, O.T. 94
Sapan 98
Sato, Tatsuo Lt. 60,62,64,142, 143
Sato, Hideo, S./Maj. 62
Sato, Shinichi Sgt. 142,143
Saurez, Colonel 33
Scrivener, Capt. J.D.H. 15,16,17,132
Sentences — List of 47,48
Sexton, Padre 49
Shelley, Pte. 10
Sheppard, Lt. Col. E.M. 17,132,133
Short, Pte. N. 31,82,87,90, 99,105,111, 113,115,146
Simpson, Cpl. H. (Gunboat) 89
Simpson, Colin 146,147
Skinner, Pte. E.K. 91,92
Slater, Pte. S. 28
Sligo, Lt. Cdr. (R.A.N.R.) 4,10,15
Small, Cpl. A.L. 19,38
Smith, Governor 14,15
Smith, ('Happy Harry') 43
Smyth, Sgt. C. 29,60,101
Spurway, Cpl. R. 28,52
St. John, Capt. 26
Stacy, Sgt. 75,79,100
Staggs, Sgt. F. 5
Staggs, Pte. F. 5
Stanley, Pte. J. 82
Steele, Capt. R. 29,31,32,33, 56
Stevens, Sgt. A. 15,38,39
Stewart, B. (S/A McNab) 5
Sticpewich, W/O. W.H. 10,14,38,54, 56,71,88,91, 100,101,106, 107,108,113, 146
Stone, C.P.O. (U.S.N.) 128
Stookes, Dr. (Civ.) 11
Storey, Pte. G. 6
Suga, Colonel 11,17,24,31, 40,44,84,85, 106,126,128, 132,133,134, 140
Sugamura, Lt. 62,65,143
Sumping 111,146
Sutcliffe, Major 96
Suzuki, 2/Lt. 77,78,79,105
Suzuki, Lt. 87,106

Takeda Kazuhiro, W/O. 61
Takahara 78,106,107
Takakuwa Takuo, Capt. 84,85,87,88, 106,107,108, 110,122,143, 144,145
Takata 79
Takayama, Colonel 141
Tanaka, Lt. Shojiro 62,69,71,141, 143
Taylor, Dr. 15,25,35,36, 39,41,43,45
Taylor, Brig. 4
Thorne, Pte. A.S. 108
Tinning, Pte. R. 28
Tima 147
Toyo, W/O. 62
Toyada 79
Toyohara, Lt. 61,65
Toyuoka Eijiiro 110
Trackson, Pte. H. 10,15
Tsuji, Sgt. 87,89,90,108, 110

Varley, Brig. A. 3,51
Vaughan, Sgt. W.J. 108

Waddle, Capt. 38
Wagner, Lt. C. 29,33
Wallace, Sgt. 24,25,33,35, 56
Wallace, Sgt. N.A. 115
Wallace, Flt./Lt. J. 115

Walsh, Lt. Col. A.W. 4,10,16,17,44, 126,132,133
Wands, Dr. 35
Washington, Lt. F. 6,37,132
Watanabe Yoshio, Major 68,71,72,78, 108
Watanabe Genzo, Capt. 87,88,90,107, 108,143,144, 145
Watanabe, Lt. 110
Watson, W/O. 60
Watts, Pte. E. 90,128
Webber, Cpl. S. 91,92
Weeks, Pte. 54
Weir, F/O. 115
Weston, L/Sgt. A. 37,44,126
Wells, Lt. R. 15,21,37,38, 43
Weynton, Lt. 19,34,38
Whimster, Col. 27,29
White, Pte. 52
Wilson, Mr. 17,132
Wilson, Colonel 126
Windeyer, Brig. 101
Wiseman, Pte. 108
Wong, Mr. and Family 13
Wong Mu Sing 35,43
Wong Hiong 54,118,119, 120,122
Wong Yun Siow (Pop) 38, 39
Wootten, General G. 126
Workman, Major 16,17,132

Yamada, Colonel 145
Yamaguchi, Sgt. 62
Yamamoto Katsuji, Lt. (Doctor) 14,128,130, 133
Yamamoto Shoici, Capt. 58,59,60,61, 66,67,68,72, 85,142,143
Yamashita General 1
Yaten, N.B.A.C. 90
Young, Pte. 52
Yusup, Sgt. N.B.A.C. 45

Prime Minister Paul Keating speaking with the Chairman of the Sandakan Memorial Foundation, Mr. J. Milner, and the author at the unveiling of the Burwood Sandakan Memorial 1993.

Members of the R.S.L. Tour

Bruce Ruxton
June Healy
Harry Secomb
Fred Holdsworth
Ken Bilney
Phyl Bilney
Ron Hatch
Len Rowan
Alice Peckman
Gwen Markwell
Ces Stewart
Howard Perkins
Eric Marks
Ellen Marks
Jack O'Rourke
Thelma O'Rourke
Ken Baker
June Baker
Geoff Golden
Les Kennedy
Olive Clarke
Richard Hunter
Dick Morris
Judith Morris
Hugh Browne
Ruth Browne
Maurie Robinson
Fred Stebbings
Margaret Stebbings
Ron Talbot
Chris Yeoman
G. Pritchard
Monica Bourke
Eve Shepherd
Frank Murray
Bill Young
Kevin Ward
Faye Corbett
Val Glennon
Marguerite Knight
Phil Knight
Roni Hodges
Lofty Hodges
Leslye Ollis
Judy Hunter
Sep Prosser
Helena Prosser
Tony Wilkins
Col Bailey
Maureen Devereaux
Ron Quadroy
Bev Lynn
Bill Lynn
Lily Whybird
Allan Whybird
Allan Gibb
Colin Wagener
Joy Farnham
Colin Nicholson
Nigel Nicholson
Len & Dorothy Tadman
Alan Schmidt
Harold Chivers
Myrtle Chivers
Danny Pennisi
Bessie Pennisi
Barbara Evans
Fred Wright
Sandi Wright
Ada Wright
Jack Donovan
Shirley Donovan
Blue Conn
Gerald Moore
Murray Moore
Mae McKenzie
Rod Jully
Jenniver Jolly
May Donovan
Danny O'Connor
Frank O'Connor
Russell Davis
Vic Wilson
Mr. B. Bracht
Mrs. B. Bracht

THE SANDAKAN MEMORIAL FOUNDATION TOUR MEMBERS WHO ATTENDED SERVICES AT SANDAKAN, RANAU ON AUGUST 1ST AND LABUAN WAR CEMETERY.

BEV & DES CARTER 35 KOOKABURRA AVE BENDIGO VIC 3550 054-433653.

JAN FARRINGTON 6 COLLINS CRT EAGLEHAWK VIC 3556 054 469398

ALAN & JENNY DIETRICH - 34 THE LINKS ALICE SPRINGS 0870 N.T.

Jock & Josie Matheson 16/3-7 Park St. Sutherland NSW 2232

Sue & Trevor Tough - 36 HARMAN Rd. BROOME. W.A 6725
P.O. Box 599, BROOME, W.A 6725.

KAYE & BARRY GRAHAM 16 SUNDALE ROAD WARRNAMBOOL VIC 3280

KEN & BARBARA TUNKS - KATOOMBA NSW

Kevin Marcina May 29 Werina Pde Blue Bay NSW 2261

LORRAINE SCOTT - LISMORE - NSW

PATRICIA PRACY - ROSEBAY NSW

Sister Margaret Prendergast - NOWRA, NSW

PATRICIA TURNER 56 WIMBLEDON GROVE KOTARA NEWCASTLE 2289

GWENDA BOUTON RMB442 OURA RD. WAGGA WAGGA 2650

MARGARET BEGENT P.O. BOX 24 SOMERVILLE VIC 3912

Sadie Brown (WIDOW) 5 Ranch Close St Geo Basin 2540 NSW 044434396

Molly Cumming } Terrigal NSW 2260
Myra Davies }

NORMA COX (SISTER IN LAW) 14 JOYCE ST PUNCHBOWL 2196.

Ken Ireland. Box 370 Port Macquarie

Ernest Kirby 10/47 Chamberlain Rd. PADSTOW 2211

MARIE STEELE 22 WARATAH ST. BEXLEY. N.S.W 2207.

Judy Tomkyns, Mosman, N.S.W. 2088.

Jim, Jean Milner Wahroonga NSW 2110

TOM CONNOLLY FORESTVILLE N.S.W 2087